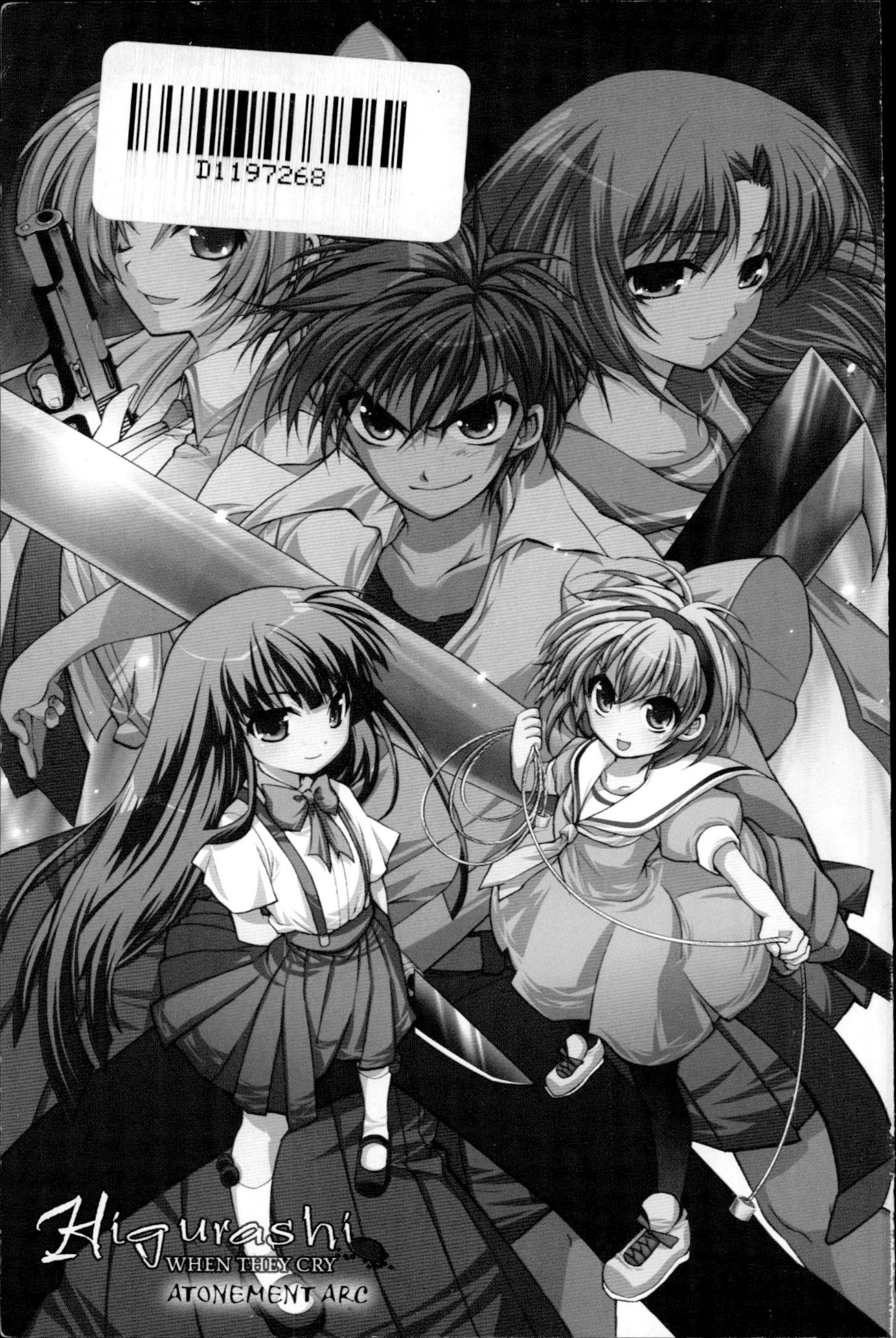
Higurashi
WHEN THEY CRY
ATONEMENT ARC

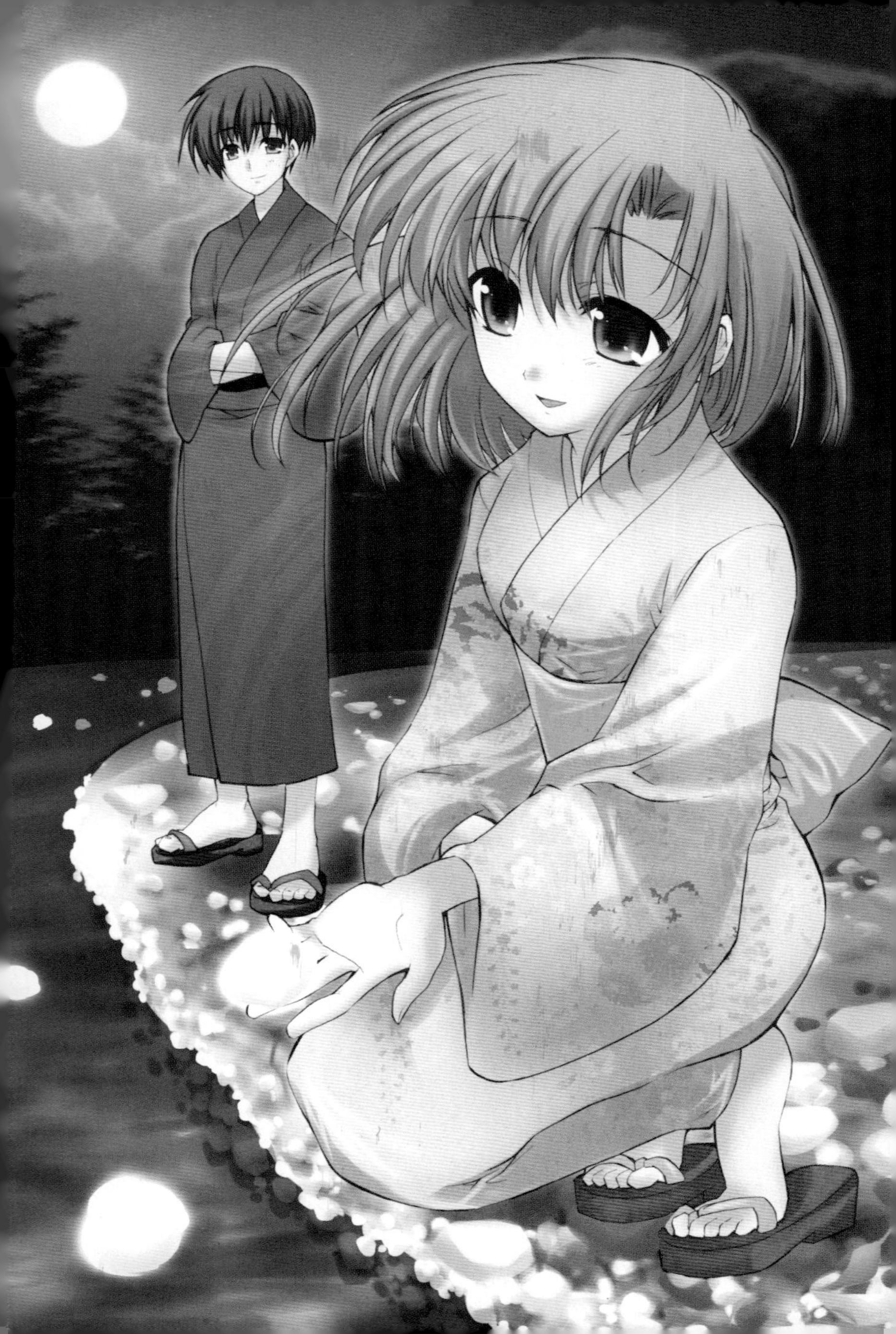

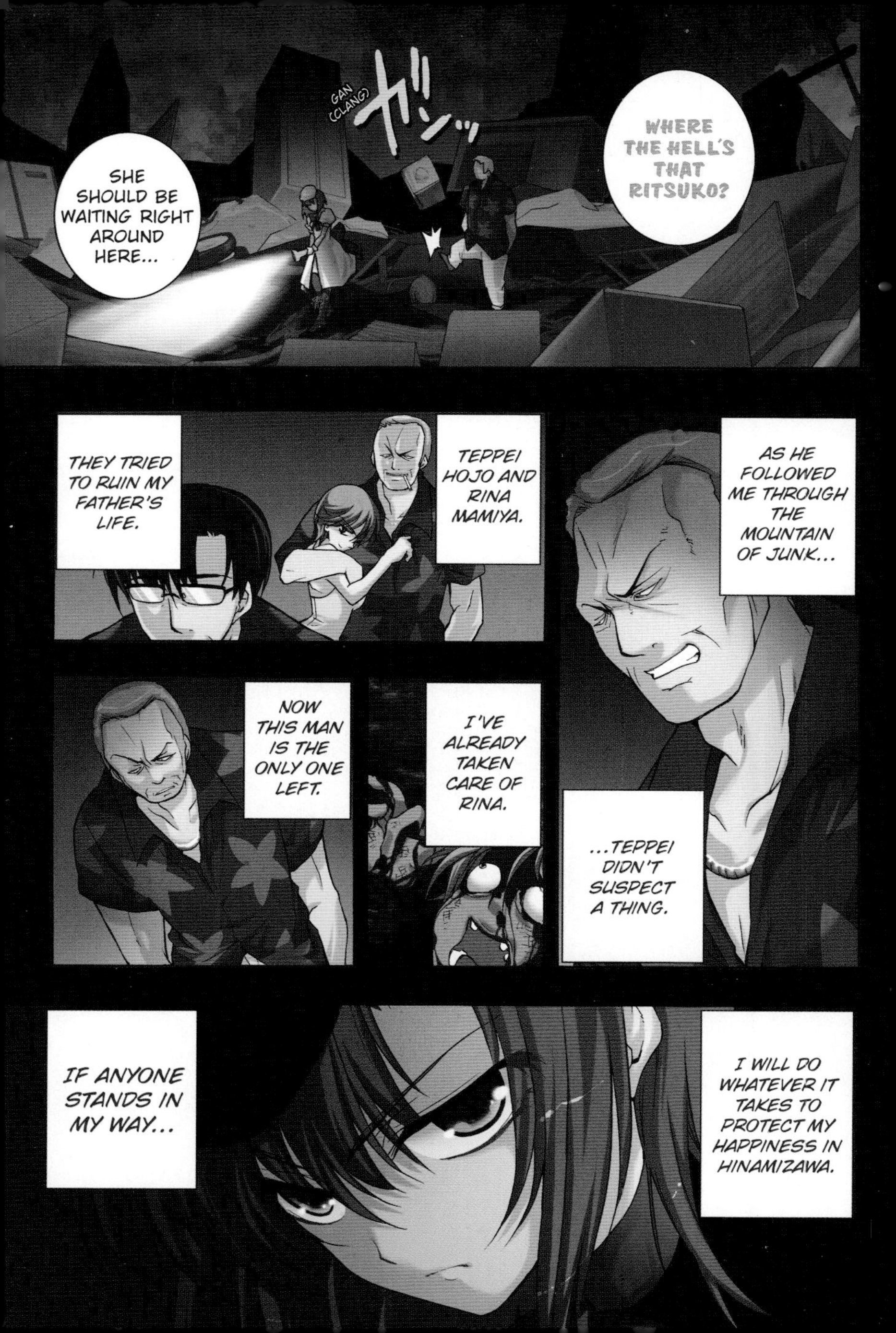
WHERE THE HELL'S THAT RITSUKO?
GAN (CLANG)
SHE SHOULD BE WAITING RIGHT AROUND HERE...
AS HE FOLLOWED ME THROUGH THE MOUNTAIN OF JUNK...
...TEPPEI DIDN'T SUSPECT A THING.
TEPPEI HOJO AND RINA MAMIYA.
THEY TRIED TO RUIN MY FATHER'S LIFE.
I'VE ALREADY TAKEN CARE OF RINA.
NOW THIS MAN IS THE ONLY ONE LEFT.
I WILL DO WHATEVER IT TAKES TO PROTECT MY HAPPINESS IN HINAMIZAWA.
IF ANYONE STANDS IN MY WAY...

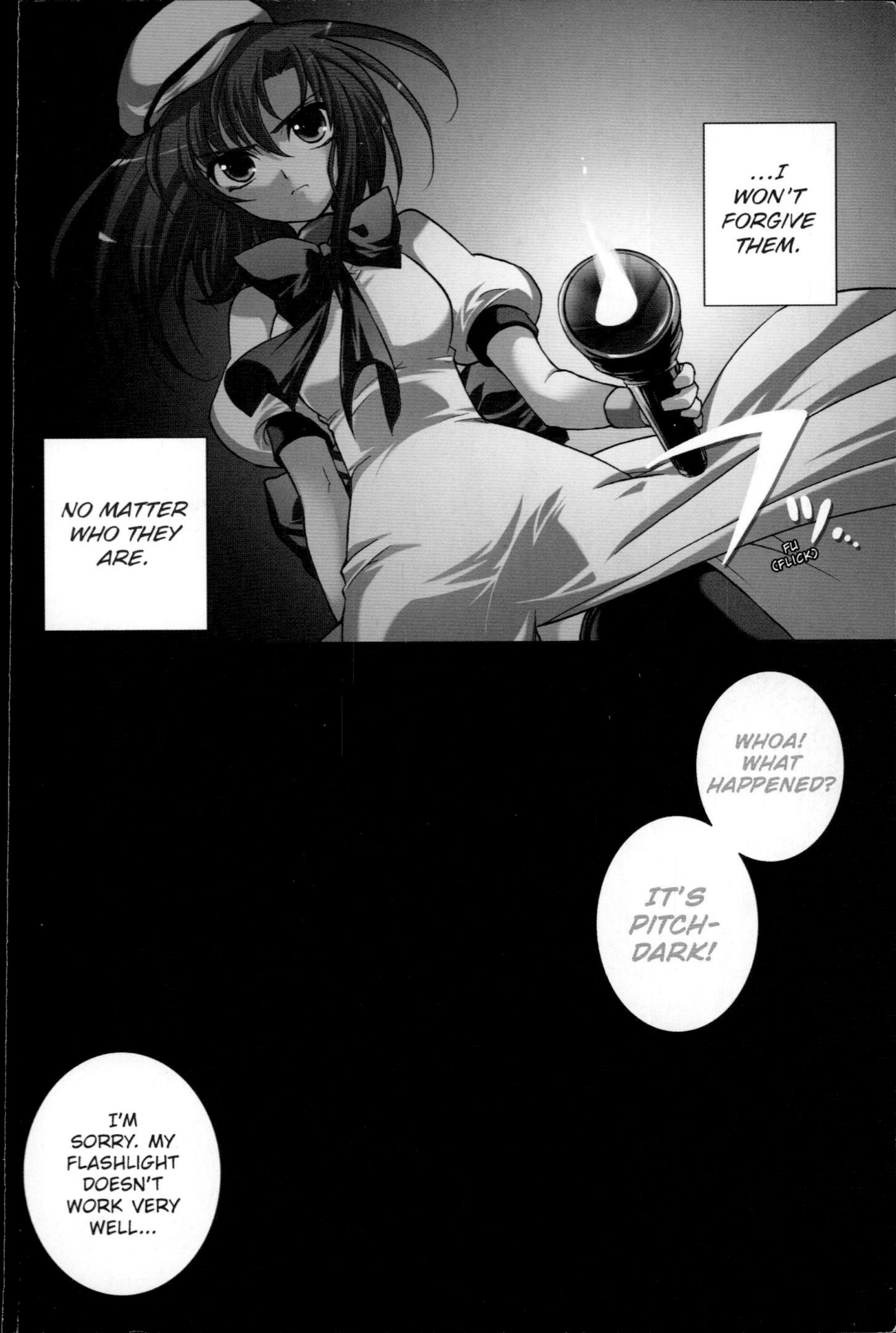
...I WON'T FORGIVE THEM.
NO MATTER WHO THEY ARE.
FU (FLICK)
WHOA! WHAT HAPPENED?
IT'S PITCH-DARK!
I'M SORRY. MY FLASHLIGHT DOESN'T WORK VERY WELL...

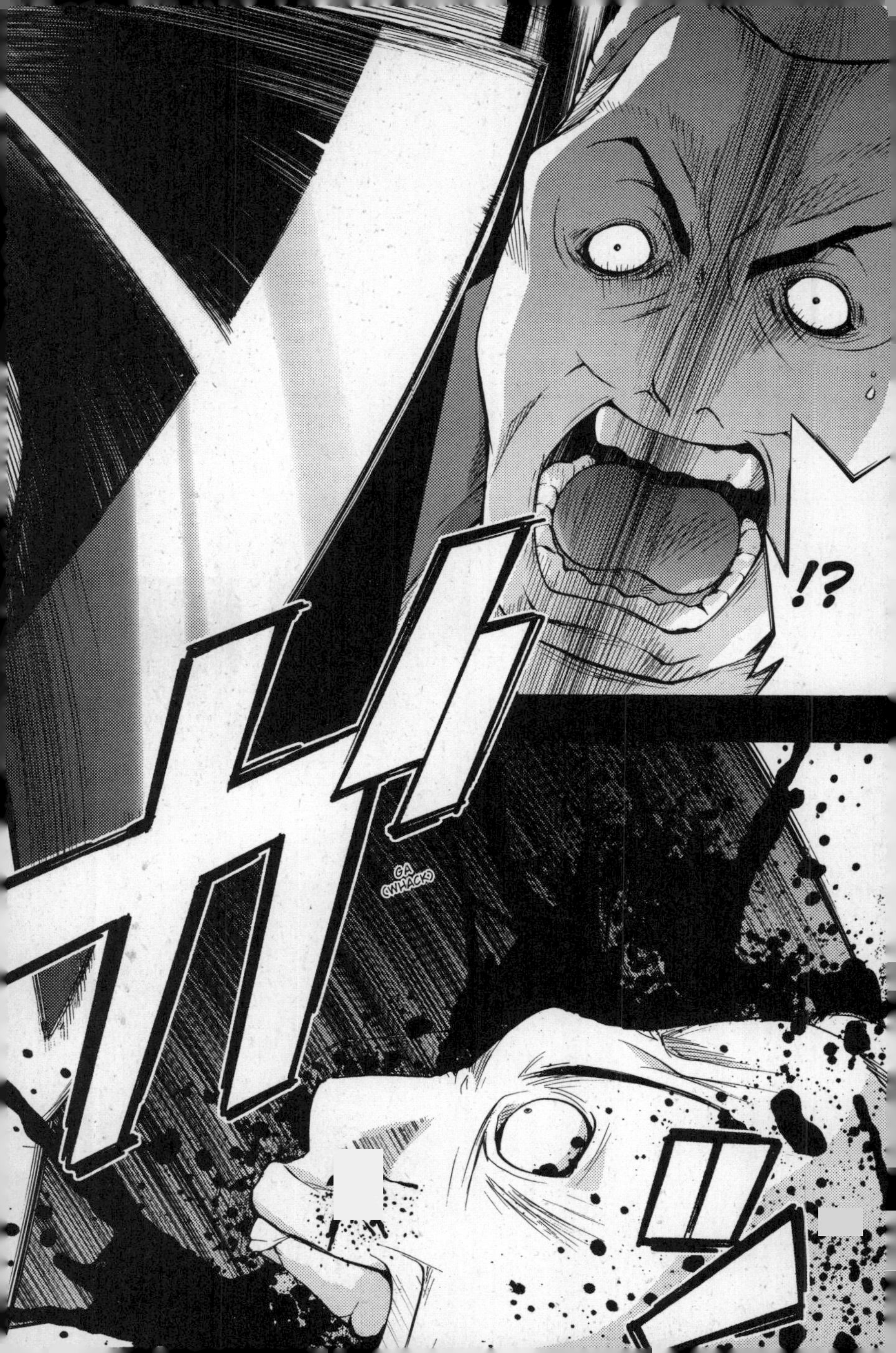
!?
GA
(WHACK)

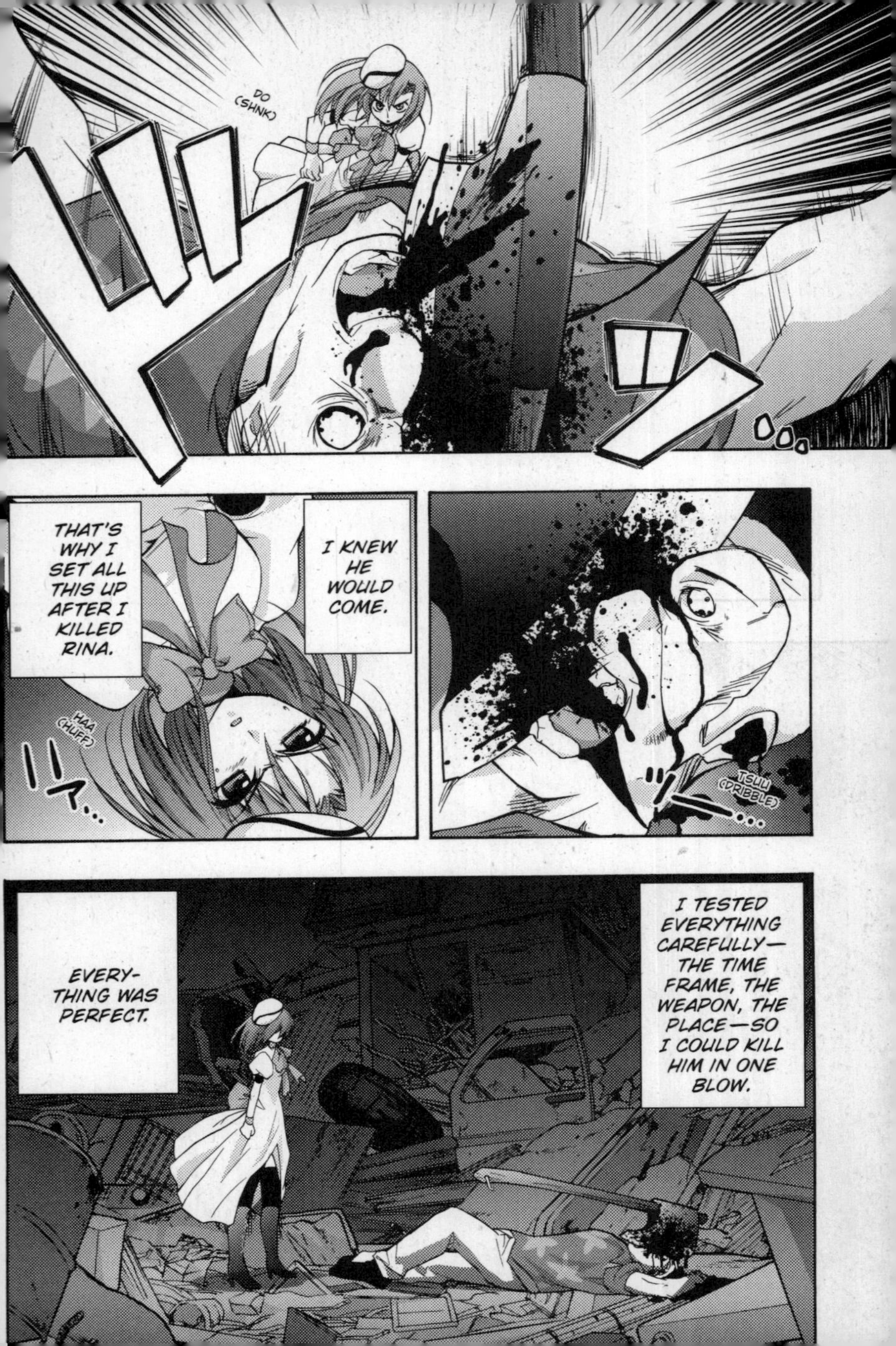
DO (SHNK)
TSUU (DRIBBLE)
I KNEW HE WOULD COME.
THAT'S WHY I SET ALL THIS UP AFTER I KILLED RINA.
HAA (HUFF)
I TESTED EVERYTHING CAREFULLY—THE TIME FRAME, THE WEAPON, THE PLACE—SO I COULD KILL HIM IN ONE BLOW.
EVERY-THING WAS PERFECT.

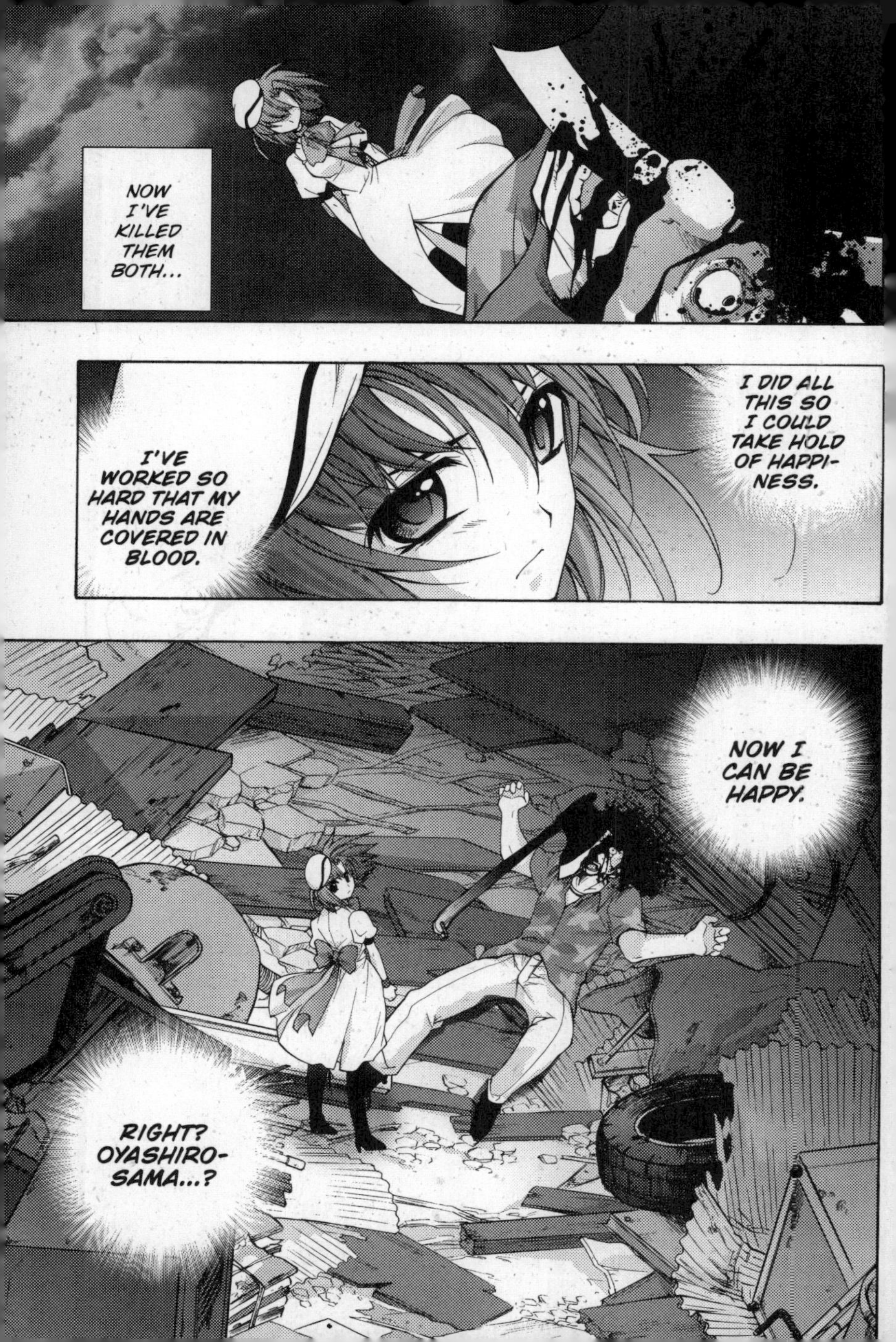
NOW I'VE KILLED THEM BOTH...
I DID ALL THIS SO I COULD TAKE HOLD OF HAPPI-NESS.
I'VE WORKED SO HARD THAT MY HANDS ARE COVERED IN BLOOD.
NOW I CAN BE HAPPY.
RIGHT? OYASHIRO-SAMA...?

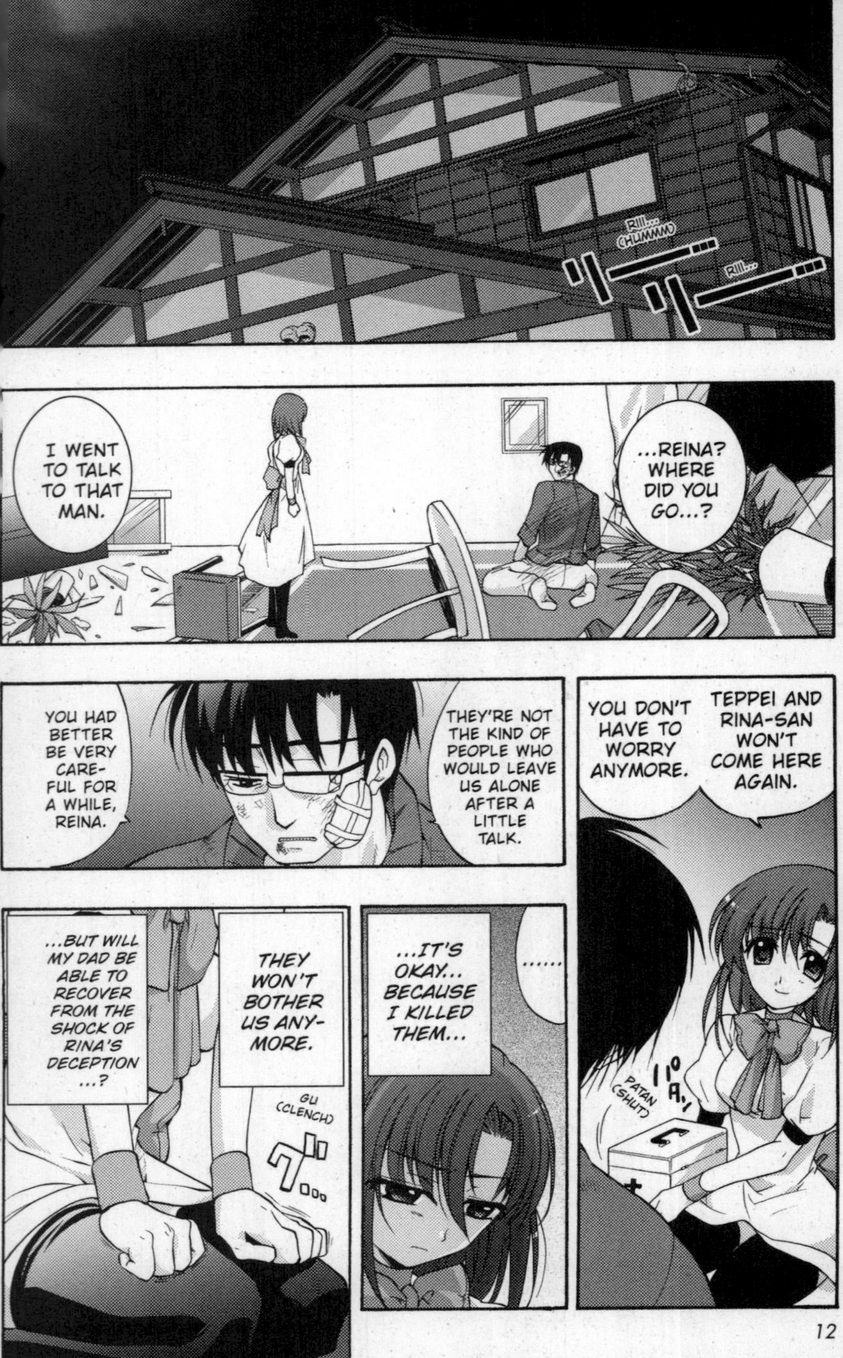
RIII... (HUMMM)
RIII...
...REINA? WHERE DID YOU GO...?
I WENT TO TALK TO THAT MAN.
TEPPEI AND RINA-SAN WON'T COME HERE AGAIN.
YOU DON'T HAVE TO WORRY ANYMORE.
THEY'RE NOT THE KIND OF PEOPLE WHO WOULD LEAVE US ALONE AFTER A LITTLE TALK.
YOU HAD BETTER BE VERY CAREFUL FOR A WHILE, REINA.
......
PATAN (SHUT)
...IT'S OKAY... BECAUSE I KILLED THEM...
THEY WON'T BOTHER US ANYMORE.
...BUT WILL MY DAD BE ABLE TO RECOVER FROM THE SHOCK OF RINA'S DECEPTION...?
GU (CLENCH)

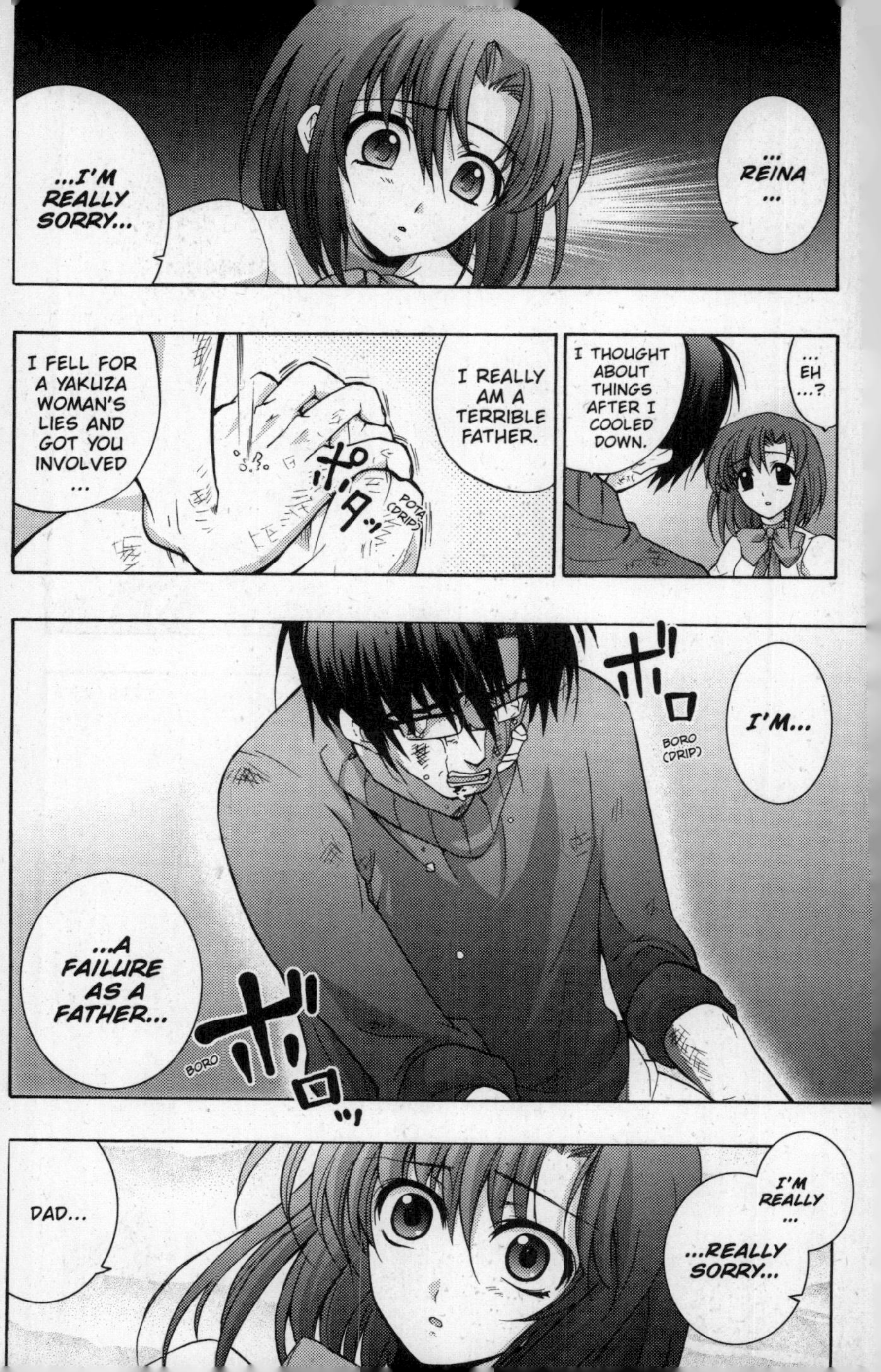
...REINA...
...I'M REALLY SORRY...
...EH...?
I THOUGHT ABOUT THINGS AFTER I COOLED DOWN.
I REALLY AM A TERRIBLE FATHER.
ポタッ
POTA (DRIP)
I FELL FOR A YAKUZA WOMAN'S LIES AND GOT YOU INVOLVED...
ボロ
BORO (DRIP)
I'M...
...A FAILURE AS A FATHER...
ボロッ
BORO
I'M REALLY... ...REALLY SORRY...
DAD...

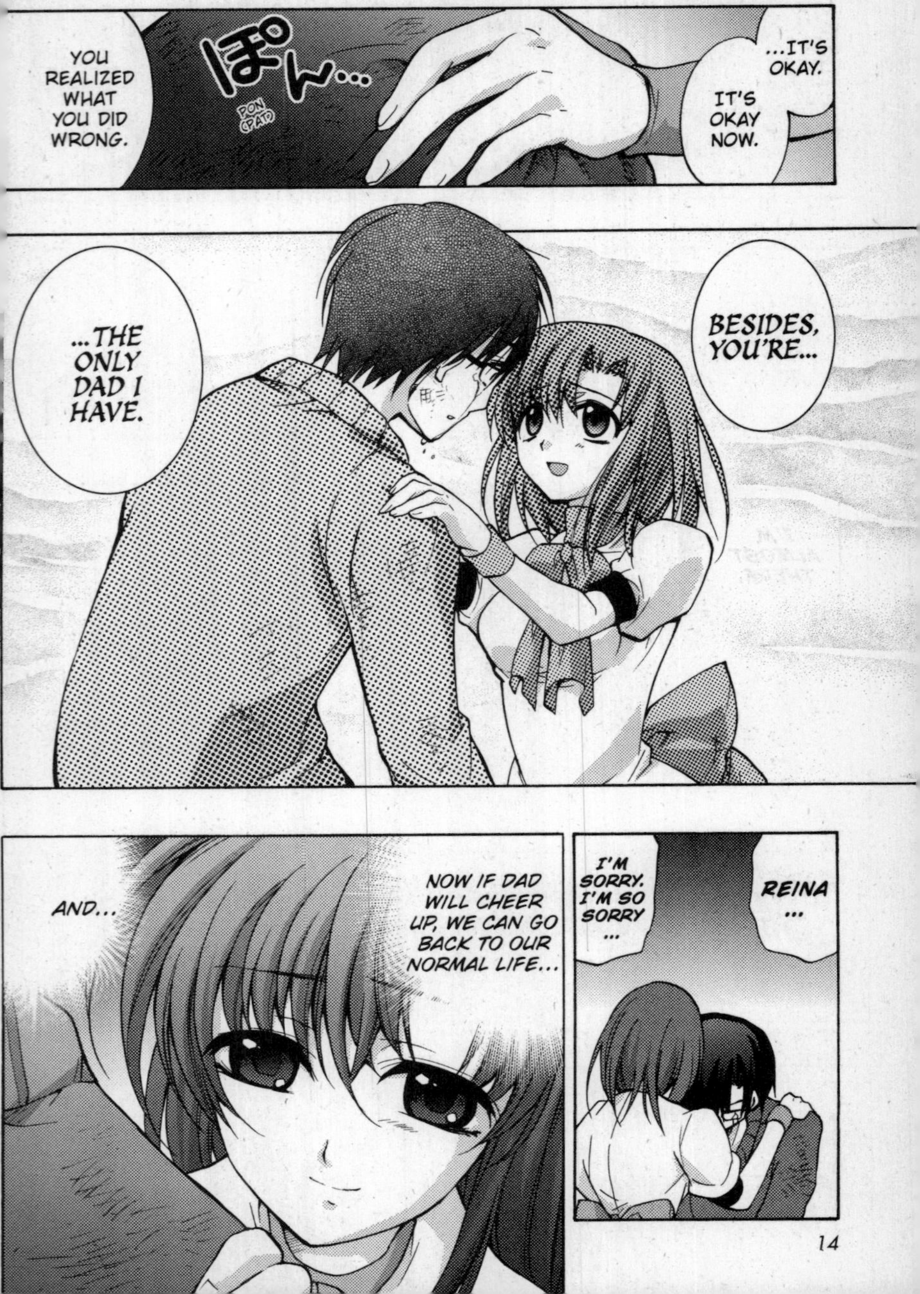
...IT'S OKAY.
IT'S OKAY NOW.
ぽん...
PON (PAT)
YOU REALIZED WHAT YOU DID WRONG.
BESIDES, YOU'RE...
...THE ONLY DAD I HAVE.
REINA ...
I'M SORRY. I'M SO SORRY ...
NOW IF DAD WILL CHEER UP, WE CAN GO BACK TO OUR NORMAL LIFE...
AND...

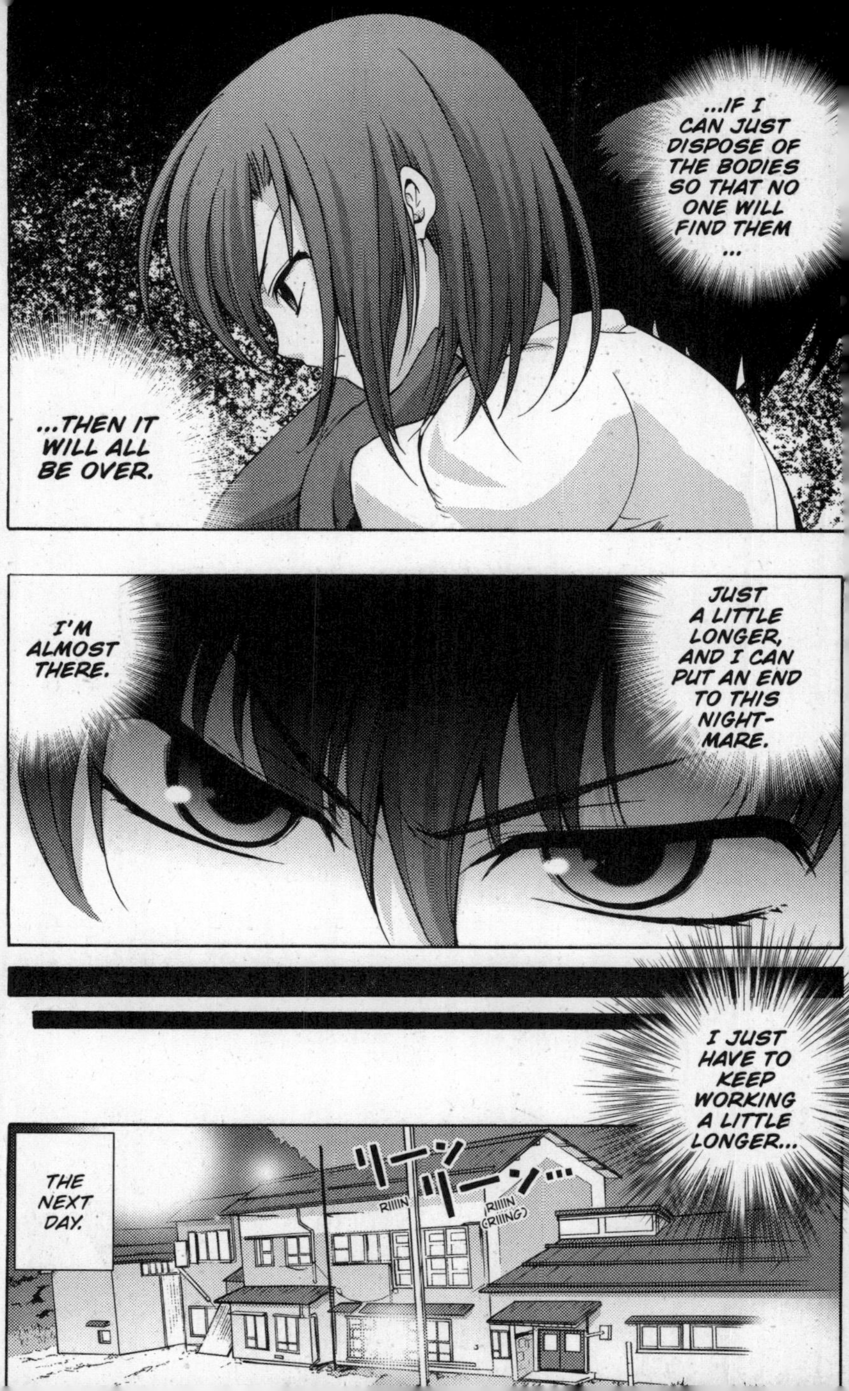
...IF I CAN JUST DISPOSE OF THE BODIES SO THAT NO ONE WILL FIND THEM ...
...THEN IT WILL ALL BE OVER.
JUST A LITTLE LONGER, AND I CAN PUT AN END TO THIS NIGHT-MARE.
I'M ALMOST THERE.
I JUST HAVE TO KEEP WORKING A LITTLE LONGER...
リーン
リーン…
RIIIN
RIIIN (RIIING)
THE NEXT DAY.

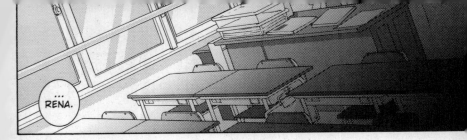

... RENA.

RENA?

... RENA.

GOSU
(KONK)

WAKE UP.

CLASS IS OVER.

UH...

OHH?

I FELL ASLEEP ...?

OHH.

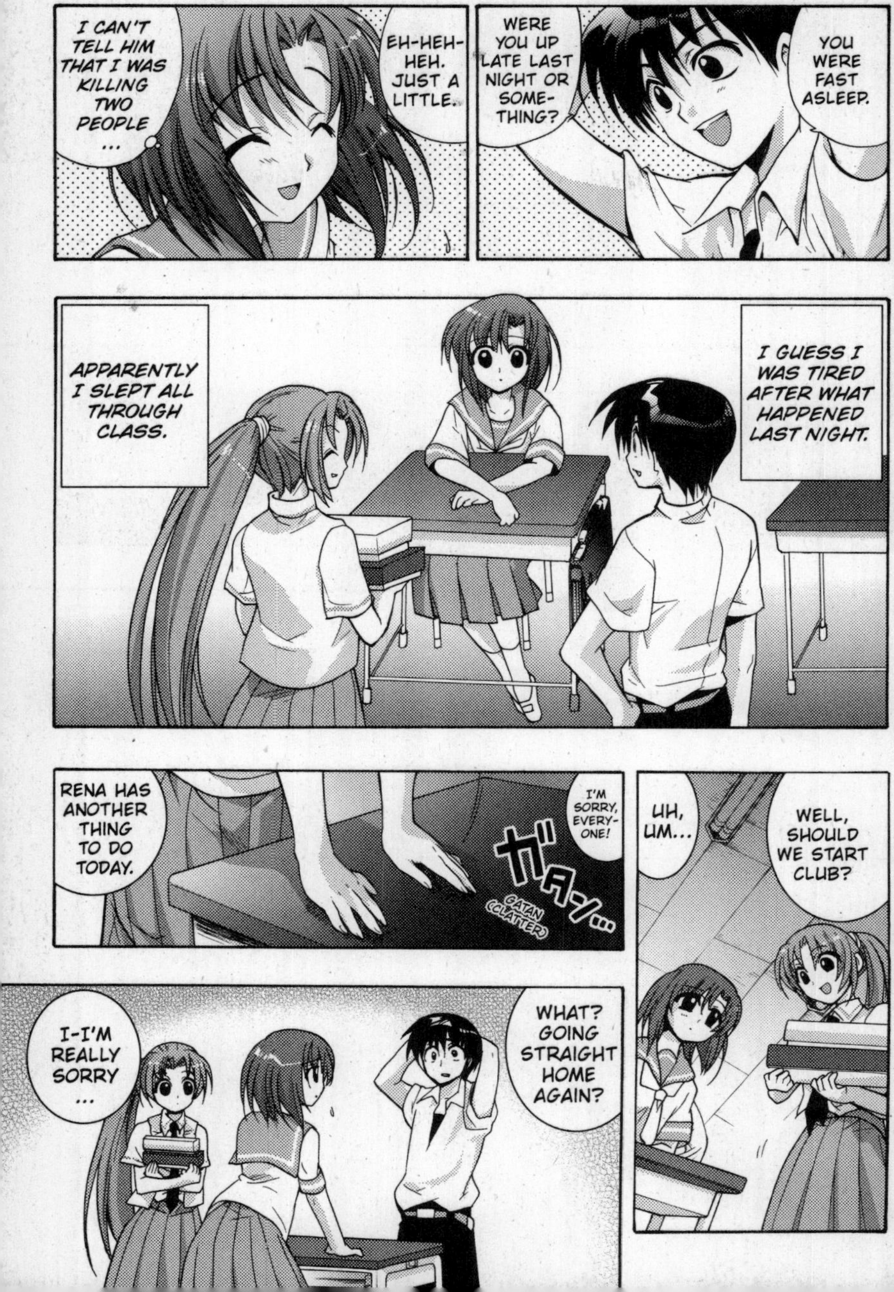
YOU WERE FAST ASLEEP.
WERE YOU UP LATE LAST NIGHT OR SOME-THING?
EH-HEH-HEH. JUST A LITTLE.
I CAN'T TELL HIM THAT I WAS KILLING TWO PEOPLE ...
I GUESS I WAS TIRED AFTER WHAT HAPPENED LAST NIGHT.
APPARENTLY I SLEPT ALL THROUGH CLASS.
WELL, SHOULD WE START CLUB?
UH, UM...
I'M SORRY, EVERY-ONE!
ガタン…
GATAN (CLATTER)
RENA HAS ANOTHER THING TO DO TODAY.
WHAT? GOING STRAIGHT HOME AGAIN?
I-I'M REALLY SORRY ...

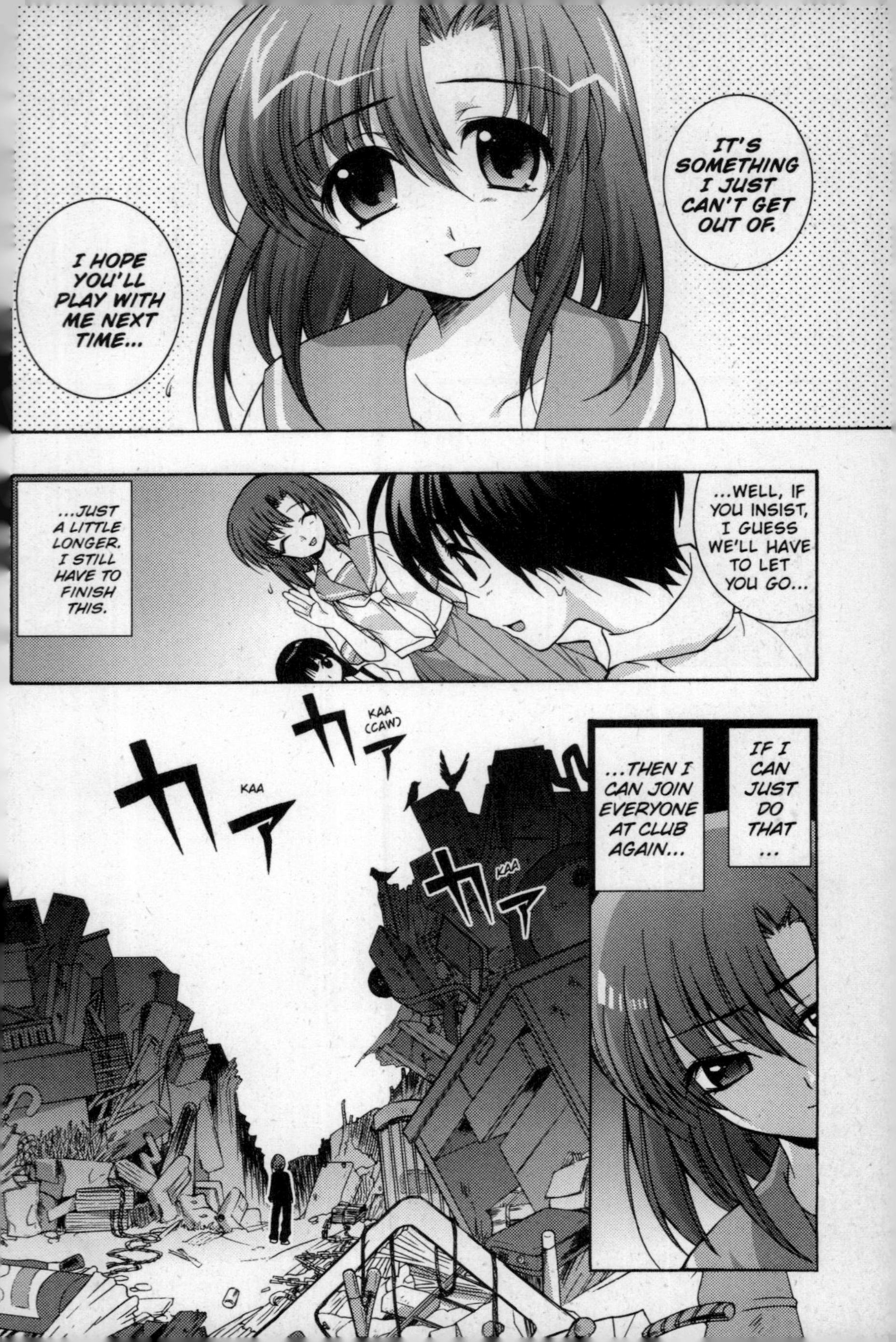
IT'S SOMETHING I JUST CAN'T GET OUT OF.
I HOPE YOU'LL PLAY WITH ME NEXT TIME...
...WELL, IF YOU INSIST, I GUESS WE'LL HAVE TO LET YOU GO...
...JUST A LITTLE LONGER. I STILL HAVE TO FINISH THIS.
IF I CAN JUST DO THAT...
...THEN I CAN JOIN EVERYONE AT CLUB AGAIN...
カァ
KAA (CAW)
カァ
KAA
カァ
KAA

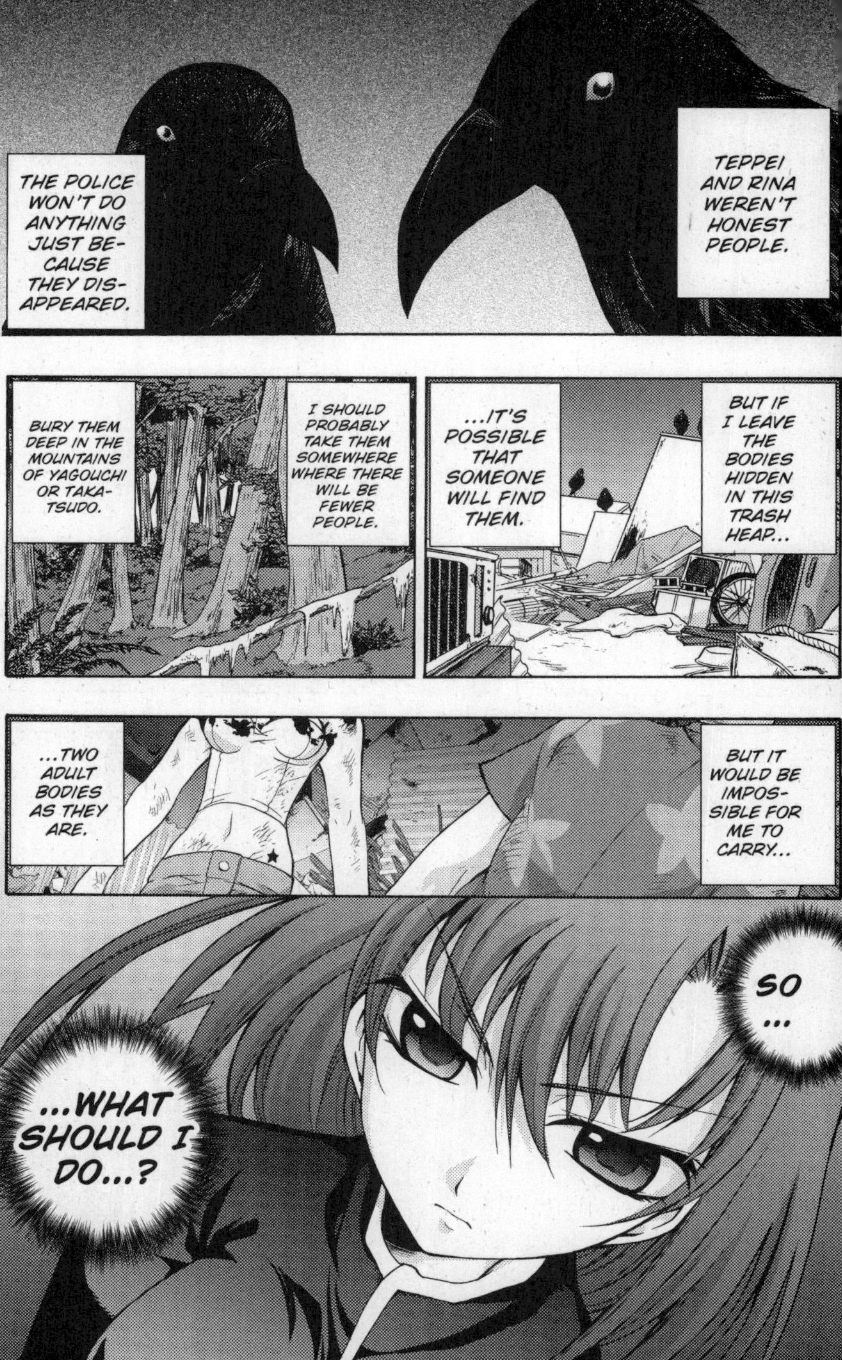
TEPPEI AND RINA WEREN'T HONEST PEOPLE.
THE POLICE WON'T DO ANYTHING JUST BE-CAUSE THEY DIS-APPEARED.
BUT IF I LEAVE THE BODIES HIDDEN IN THIS TRASH HEAP...
...IT'S POSSIBLE THAT SOMEONE WILL FIND THEM.
I SHOULD PROBABLY TAKE THEM SOMEWHERE WHERE THERE WILL BE FEWER PEOPLE.
BURY THEM DEEP IN THE MOUNTAINS OF YAGOUCHI OR TAKA-TSUDO.
BUT IT WOULD BE IMPOS-SIBLE FOR ME TO CARRY...
...TWO ADULT BODIES AS THEY ARE.
SO ...
...WHAT SHOULD I DO...?

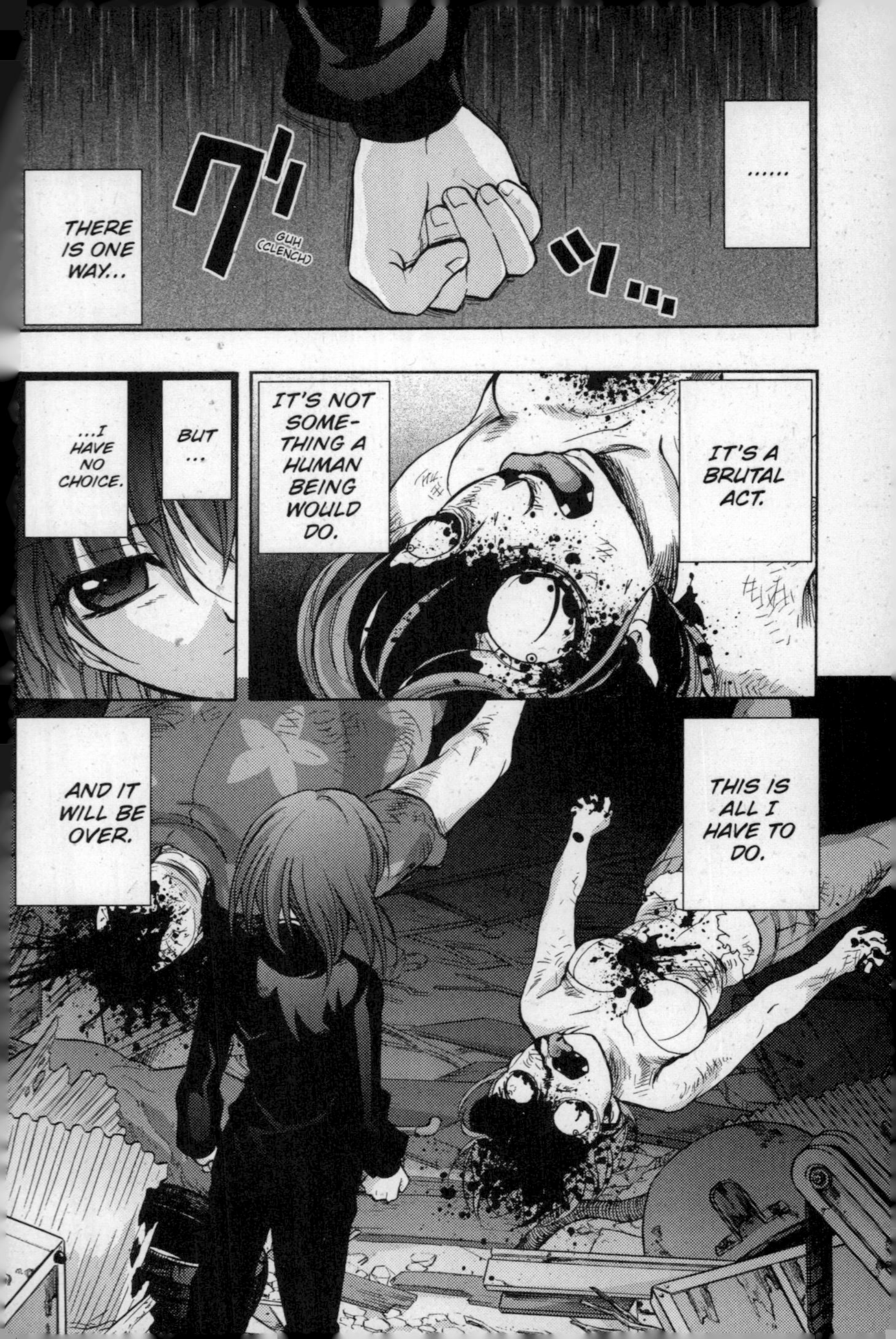
......
グッ...
GUH (CLENCH)
THERE IS ONE WAY...
IT'S A BRUTAL ACT.
IT'S NOT SOME-THING A HUMAN BEING WOULD DO.
BUT ...
...I HAVE NO CHOICE.
THIS IS ALL I HAVE TO DO.
AND IT WILL BE OVER.

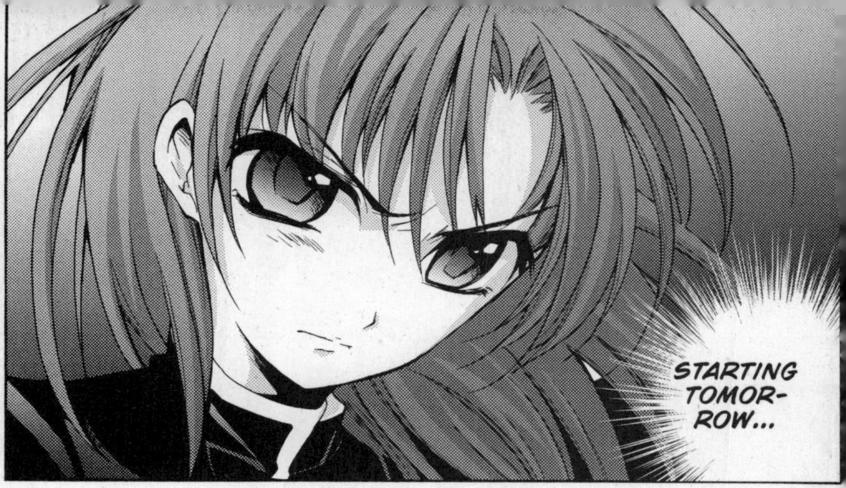
STARTING TOMORROW...

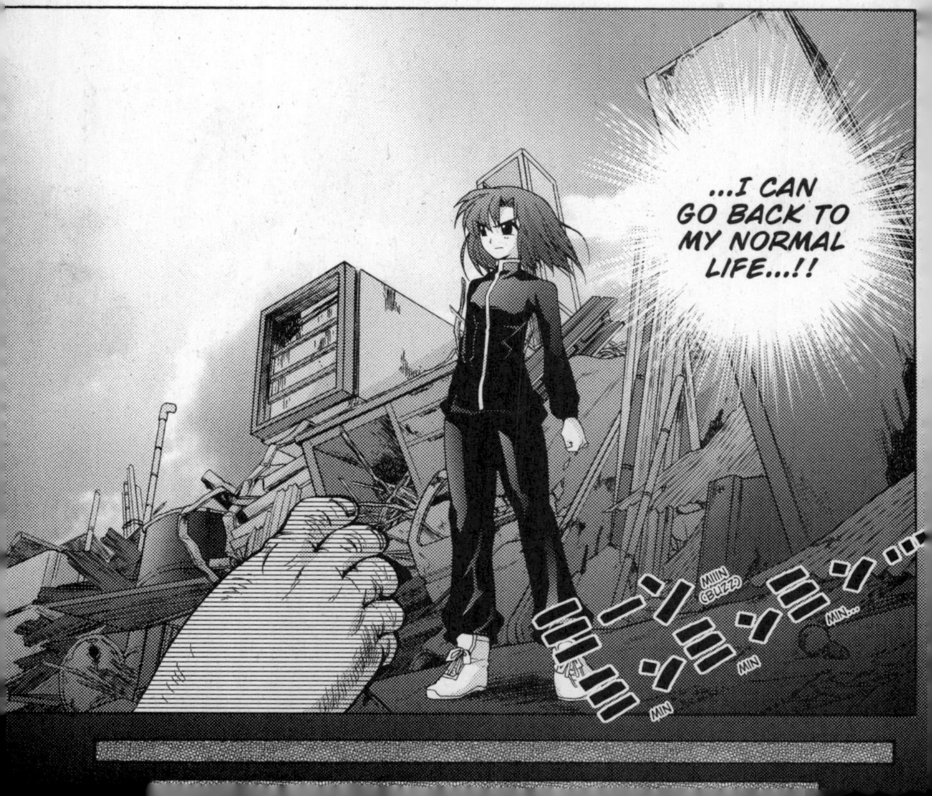
...I CAN GO BACK TO MY NORMAL LIFE...!!
MIIIN (BUZZ)
MIN
MIN
MIN...

MEANWHILE...

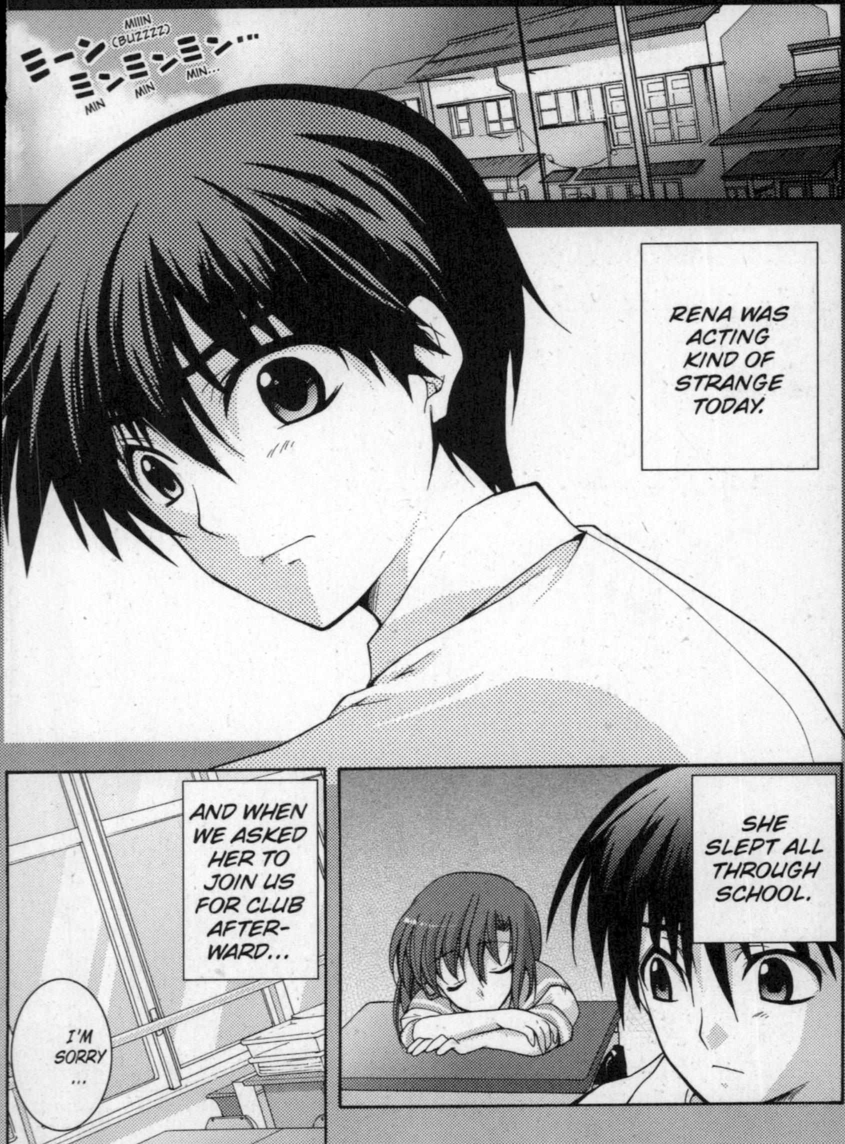
ミーン ミンミンミン…
MIIIN (BUZZZZ) MIN MIN MIN...
RENA WAS ACTING KIND OF STRANGE TODAY.
SHE SLEPT ALL THROUGH SCHOOL.
AND WHEN WE ASKED HER TO JOIN US FOR CLUB AFTER-WARD...
I'M SORRY...

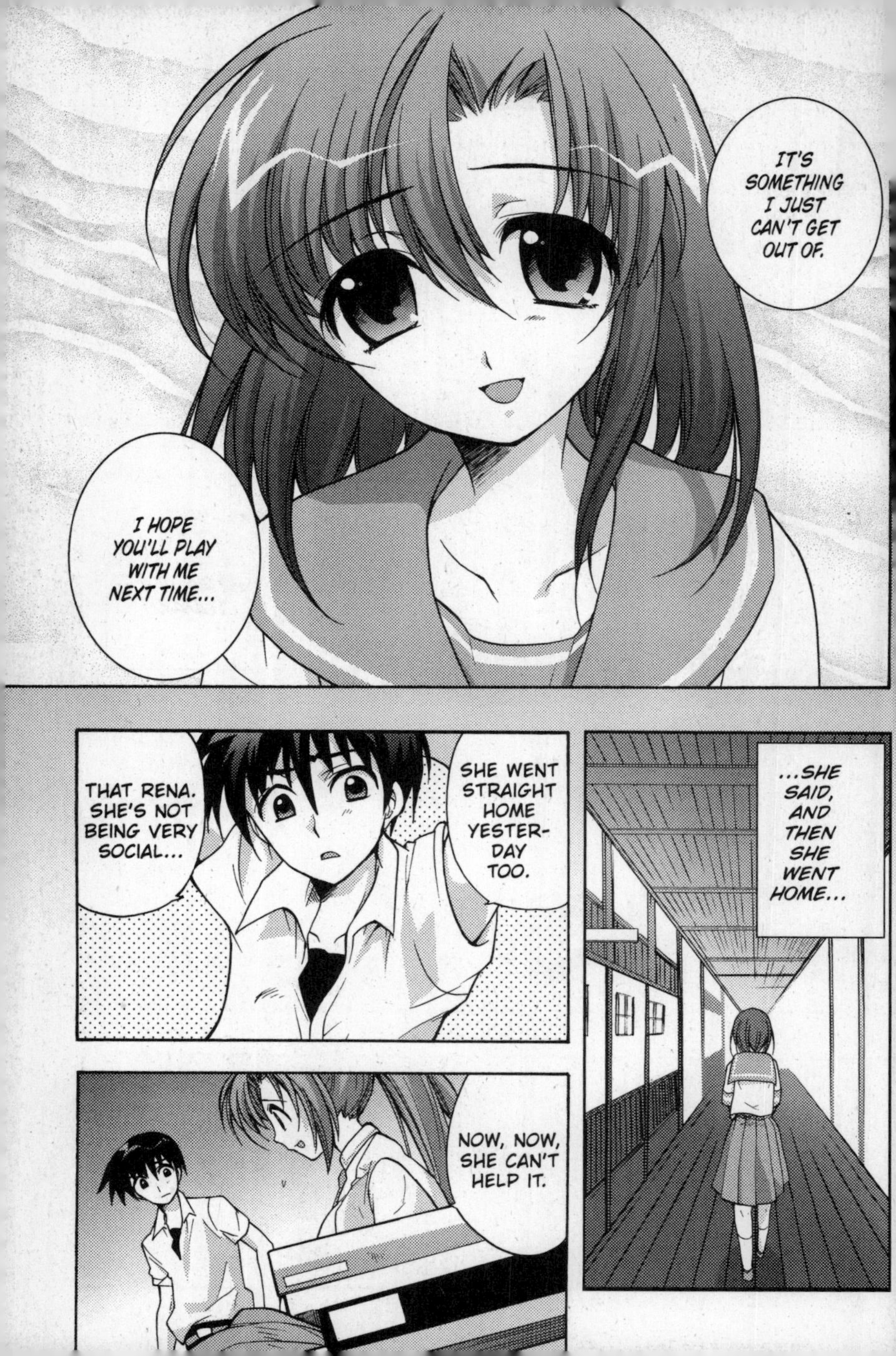
IT'S SOMETHING I JUST CAN'T GET OUT OF.
I HOPE YOU'LL PLAY WITH ME NEXT TIME...
...SHE SAID, AND THEN SHE WENT HOME...
SHE WENT STRAIGHT HOME YESTER-DAY TOO.
THAT RENA. SHE'S NOT BEING VERY SOCIAL...
NOW, NOW, SHE CAN'T HELP IT.

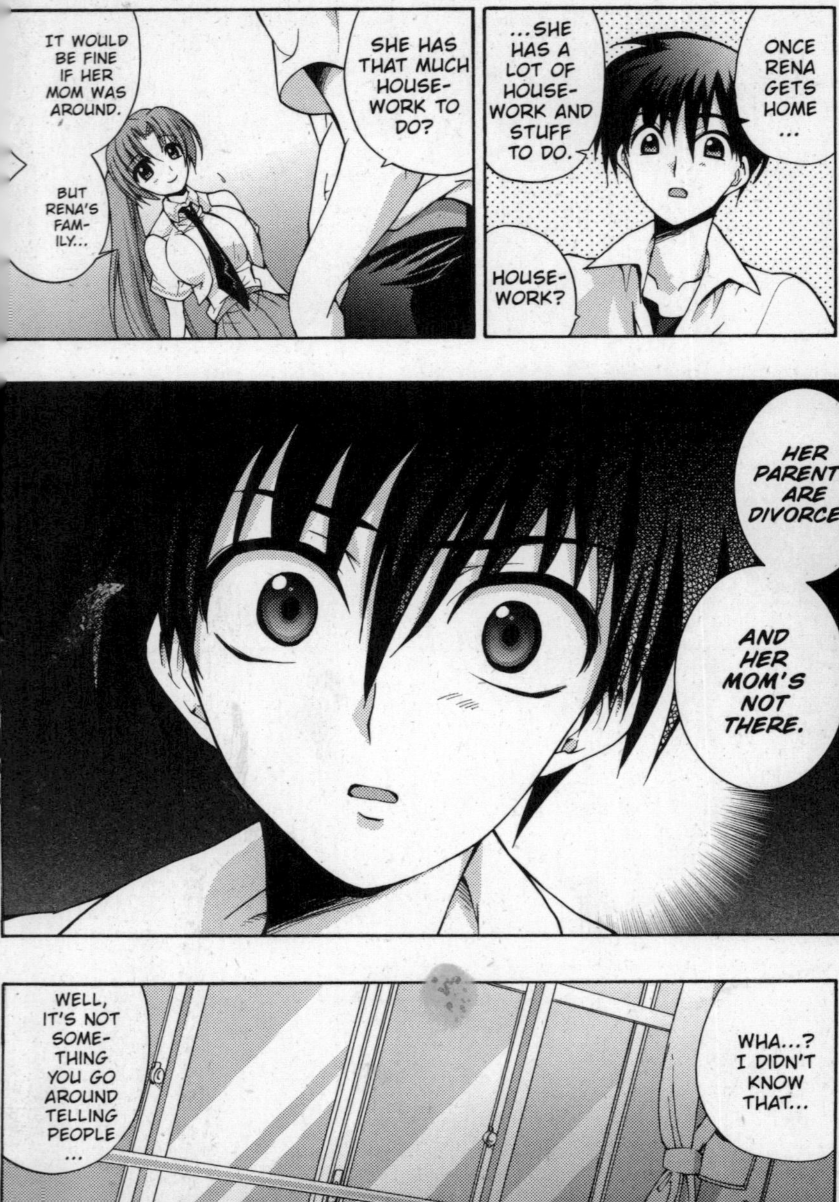
ONCE RENA GETS HOME ...
...SHE HAS A LOT OF HOUSE-WORK AND STUFF TO DO.
HOUSE-WORK?
SHE HAS THAT MUCH HOUSE-WORK TO DO?
IT WOULD BE FINE IF HER MOM WAS AROUND.
BUT RENA'S FAM-ILY...
HER PARENTS ARE DIVORCED.
AND HER MOM'S NOT THERE.
WHA...? I DIDN'T KNOW THAT...
WELL, IT'S NOT SOME-THING YOU GO AROUND TELLING PEOPLE ...

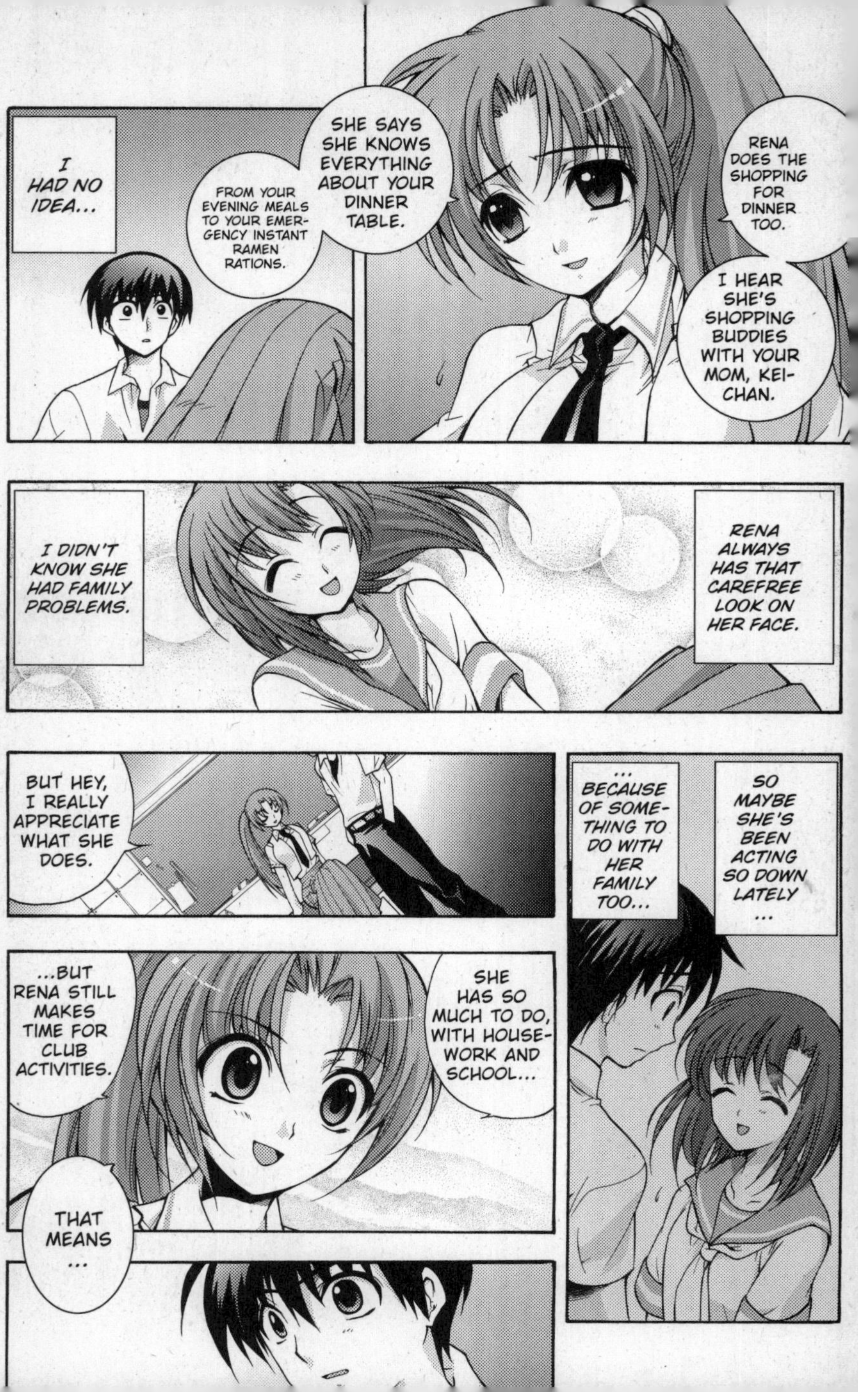
RENA DOES THE SHOPPING FOR DINNER TOO.
I HEAR SHE'S SHOPPING BUDDIES WITH YOUR MOM, KEI-CHAN.
SHE SAYS SHE KNOWS EVERYTHING ABOUT YOUR DINNER TABLE.
FROM YOUR EVENING MEALS TO YOUR EMERGENCY INSTANT RAMEN RATIONS.
I HAD NO IDEA...
RENA ALWAYS HAS THAT CAREFREE LOOK ON HER FACE.
I DIDN'T KNOW SHE HAD FAMILY PROBLEMS.
SO MAYBE SHE'S BEEN ACTING SO DOWN LATELY...
...BECAUSE OF SOMETHING TO DO WITH HER FAMILY TOO...
BUT HEY, I REALLY APPRECIATE WHAT SHE DOES.
SHE HAS SO MUCH TO DO, WITH HOUSEWORK AND SCHOOL...
...BUT RENA STILL MAKES TIME FOR CLUB ACTIVITIES.
THAT MEANS...

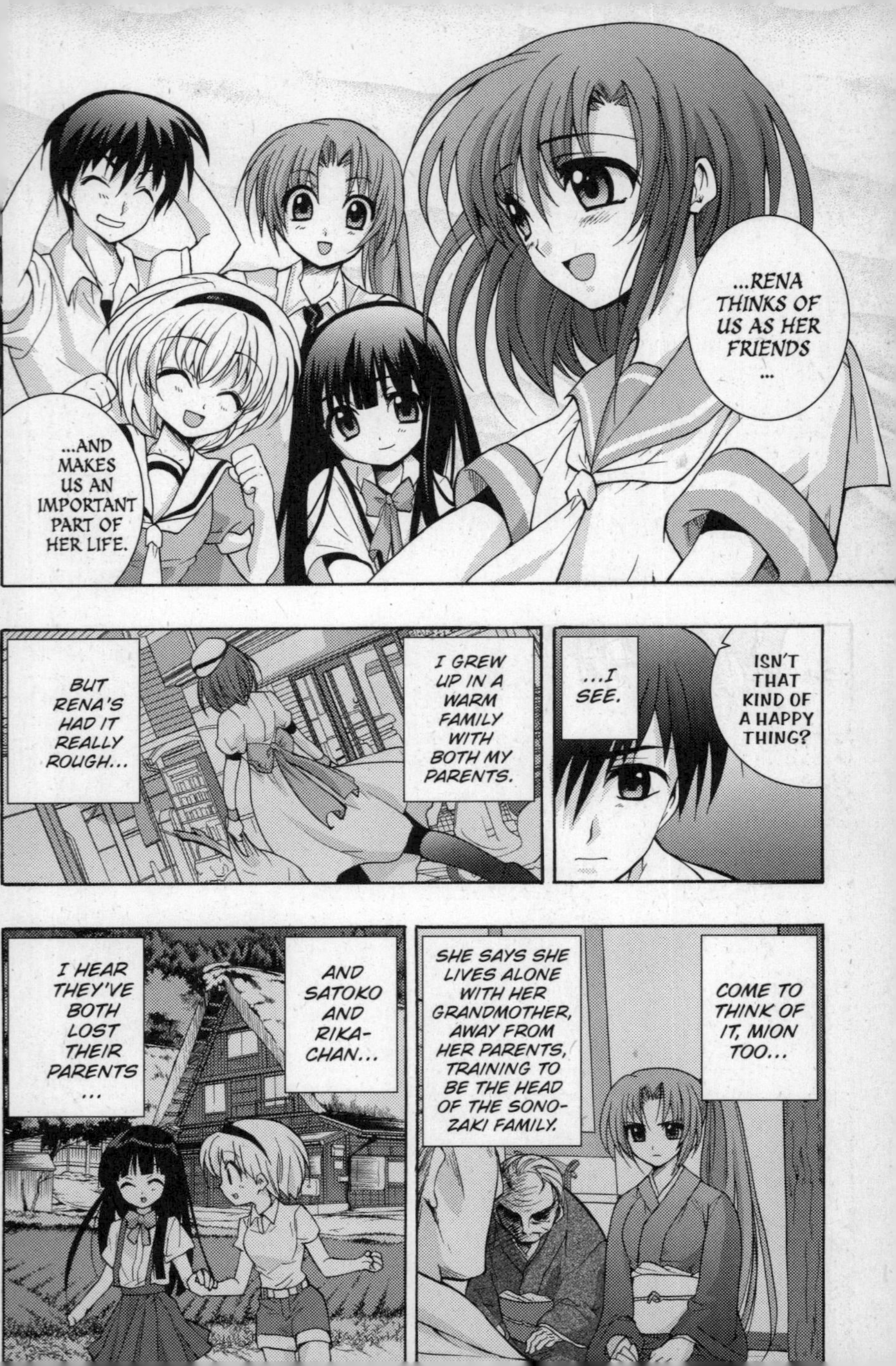
...RENA THINKS OF US AS HER FRIENDS ...
...AND MAKES US AN IMPORTANT PART OF HER LIFE.
ISN'T THAT KIND OF A HAPPY THING?
...I SEE.
I GREW UP IN A WARM FAMILY WITH BOTH MY PARENTS.
BUT RENA'S HAD IT REALLY ROUGH...
COME TO THINK OF IT, MION TOO...
SHE SAYS SHE LIVES ALONE WITH HER GRANDMOTHER, AWAY FROM HER PARENTS, TRAINING TO BE THE HEAD OF THE SONO-ZAKI FAMILY.
AND SATOKO AND RIKA-CHAN...
I HEAR THEY'VE BOTH LOST THEIR PARENTS ...

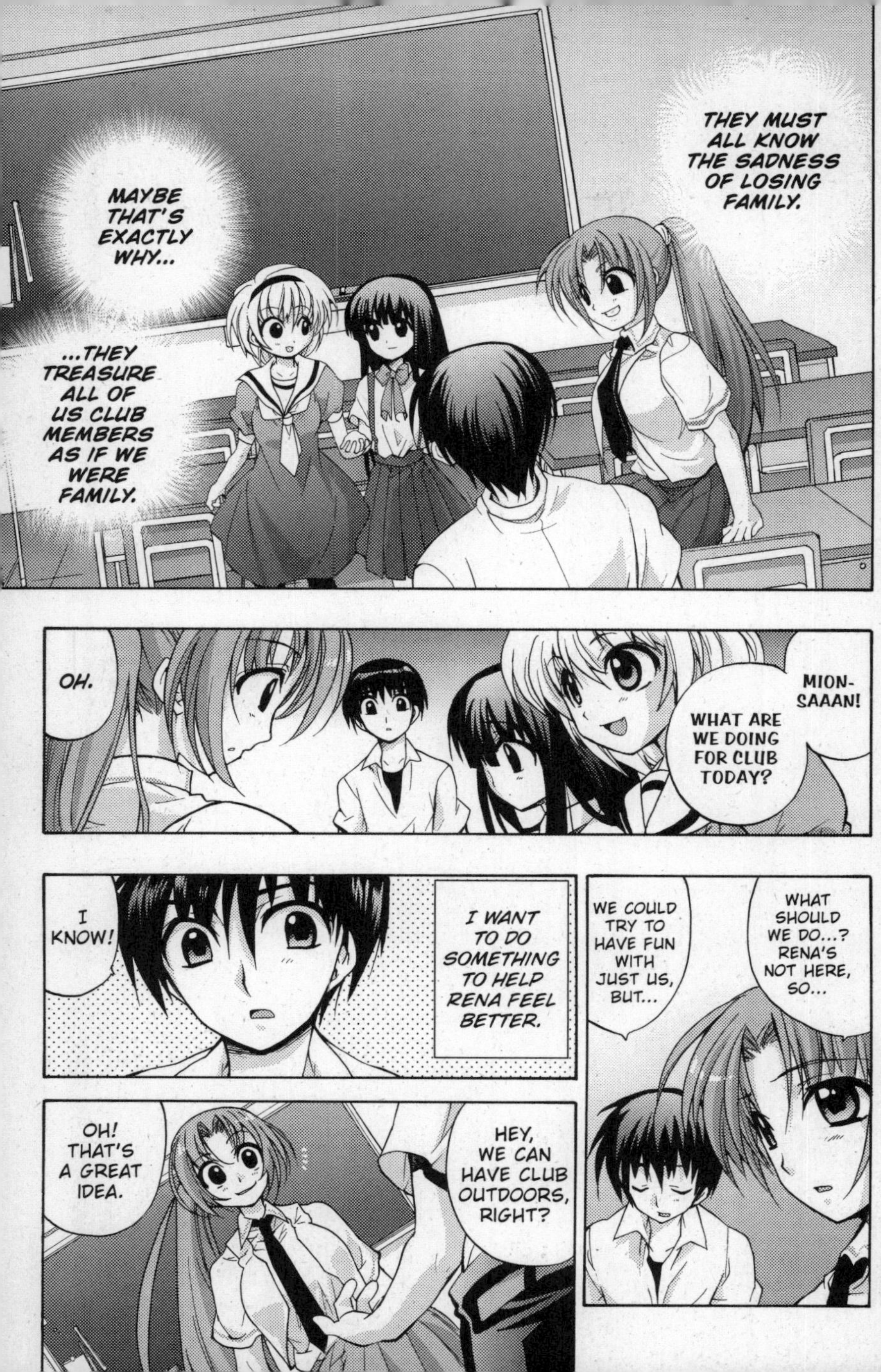
THEY MUST ALL KNOW THE SADNESS OF LOSING FAMILY.
MAYBE THAT'S EXACTLY WHY...
...THEY TREASURE ALL OF US CLUB MEMBERS AS IF WE WERE FAMILY.
MION-SAAAN!
WHAT ARE WE DOING FOR CLUB TODAY?
OH.
WHAT SHOULD WE DO...? RENA'S NOT HERE, SO...
WE COULD TRY TO HAVE FUN WITH JUST US, BUT...
I WANT TO DO SOMETHING TO HELP RENA FEEL BETTER.
I KNOW!
HEY, WE CAN HAVE CLUB OUTDOORS, RIGHT?
OH! THAT'S A GREAT IDEA.

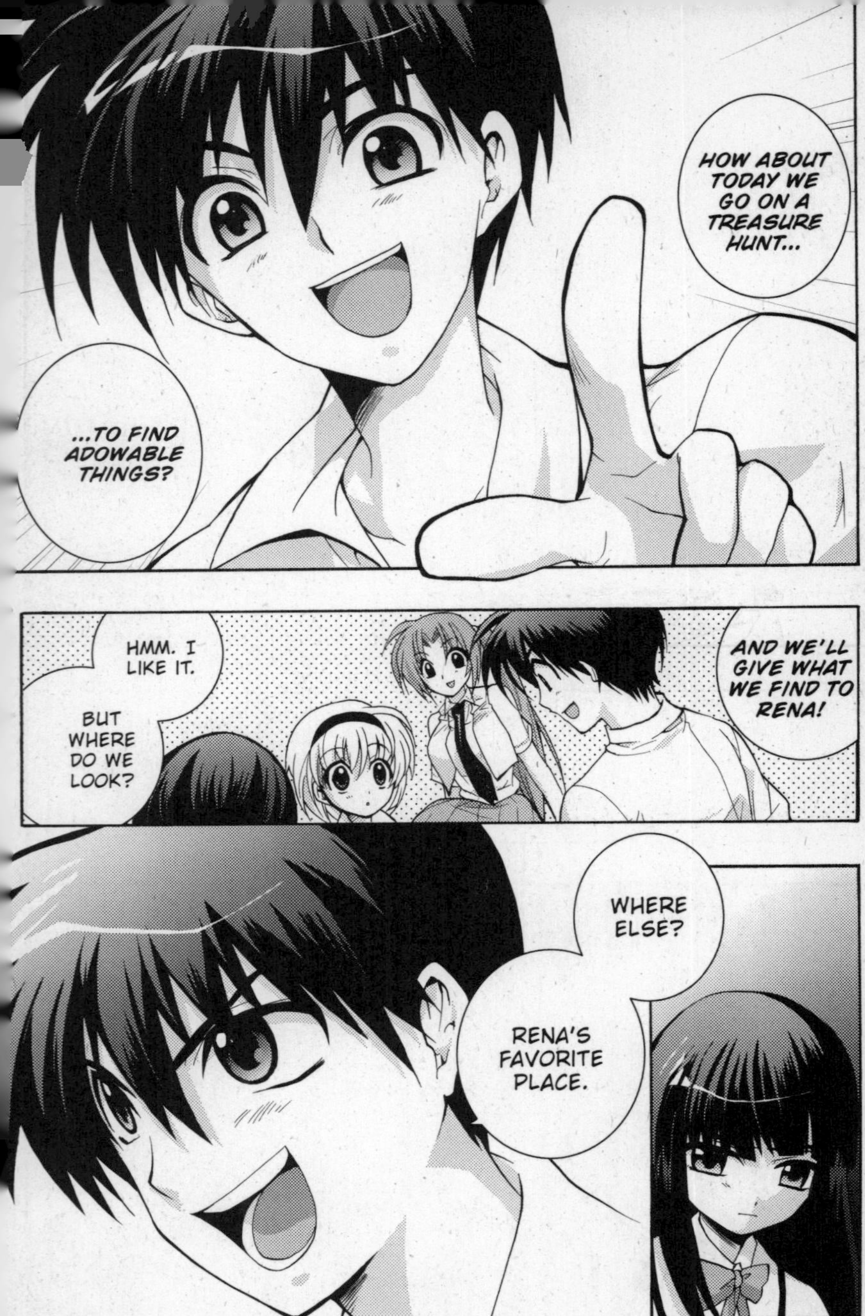
HOW ABOUT TODAY WE GO ON A TREASURE HUNT...
...TO FIND ADOWABLE THINGS?
AND WE'LL GIVE WHAT WE FIND TO RENA!
HMM. I LIKE IT.
BUT WHERE DO WE LOOK?
WHERE ELSE?
RENA'S FAVORITE PLACE.

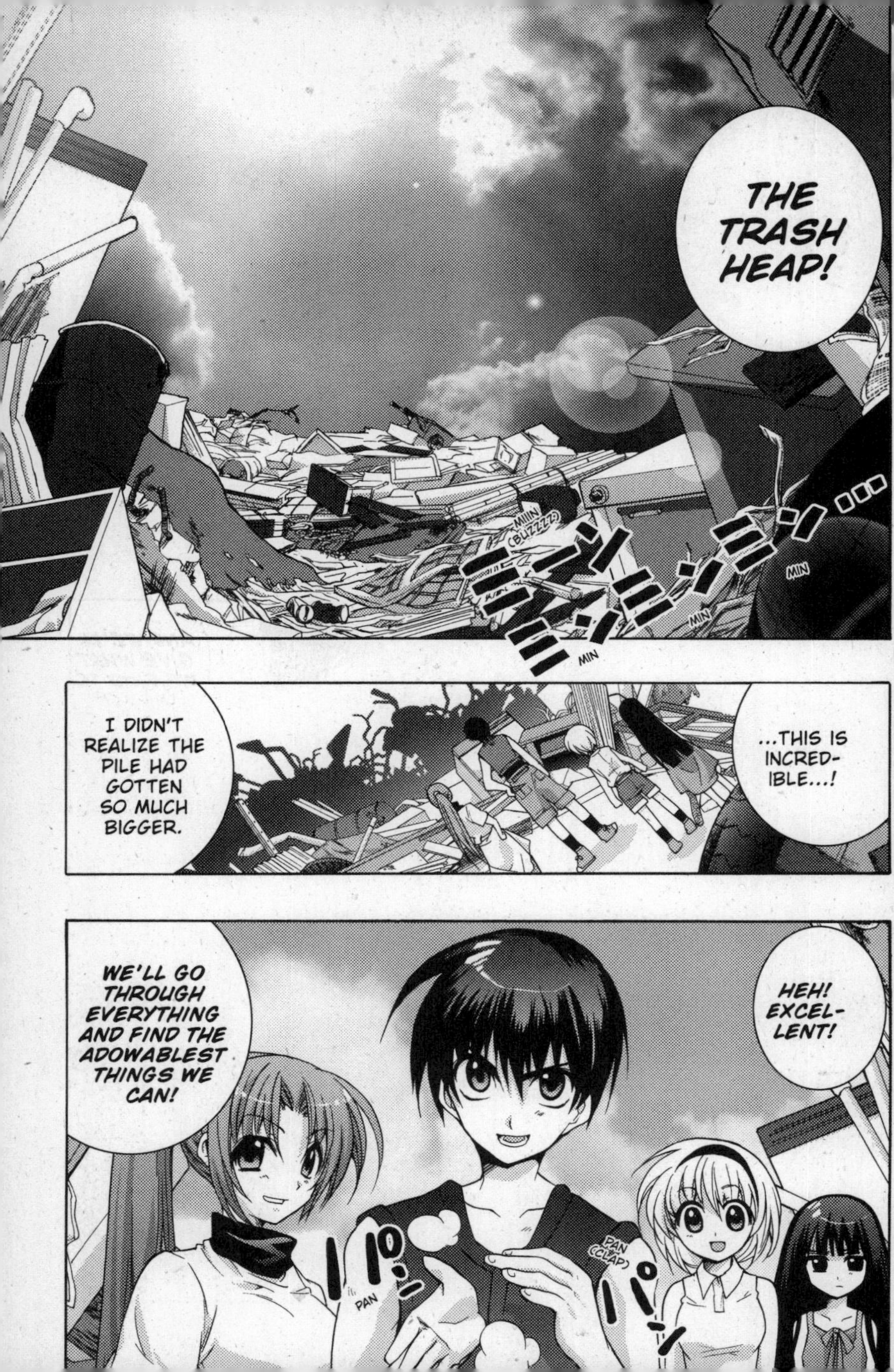
THE TRASH HEAP!
MIIIN (BUZZZZ)
MIN
MIN
MIN
...THIS IS INCRED-IBLE...!
I DIDN'T REALIZE THE PILE HAD GOTTEN SO MUCH BIGGER.
HEH! EXCEL-LENT!
WE'LL GO THROUGH EVERYTHING AND FIND THE ADOWABLEST THINGS WE CAN!
PAN (CLAP)
PAN

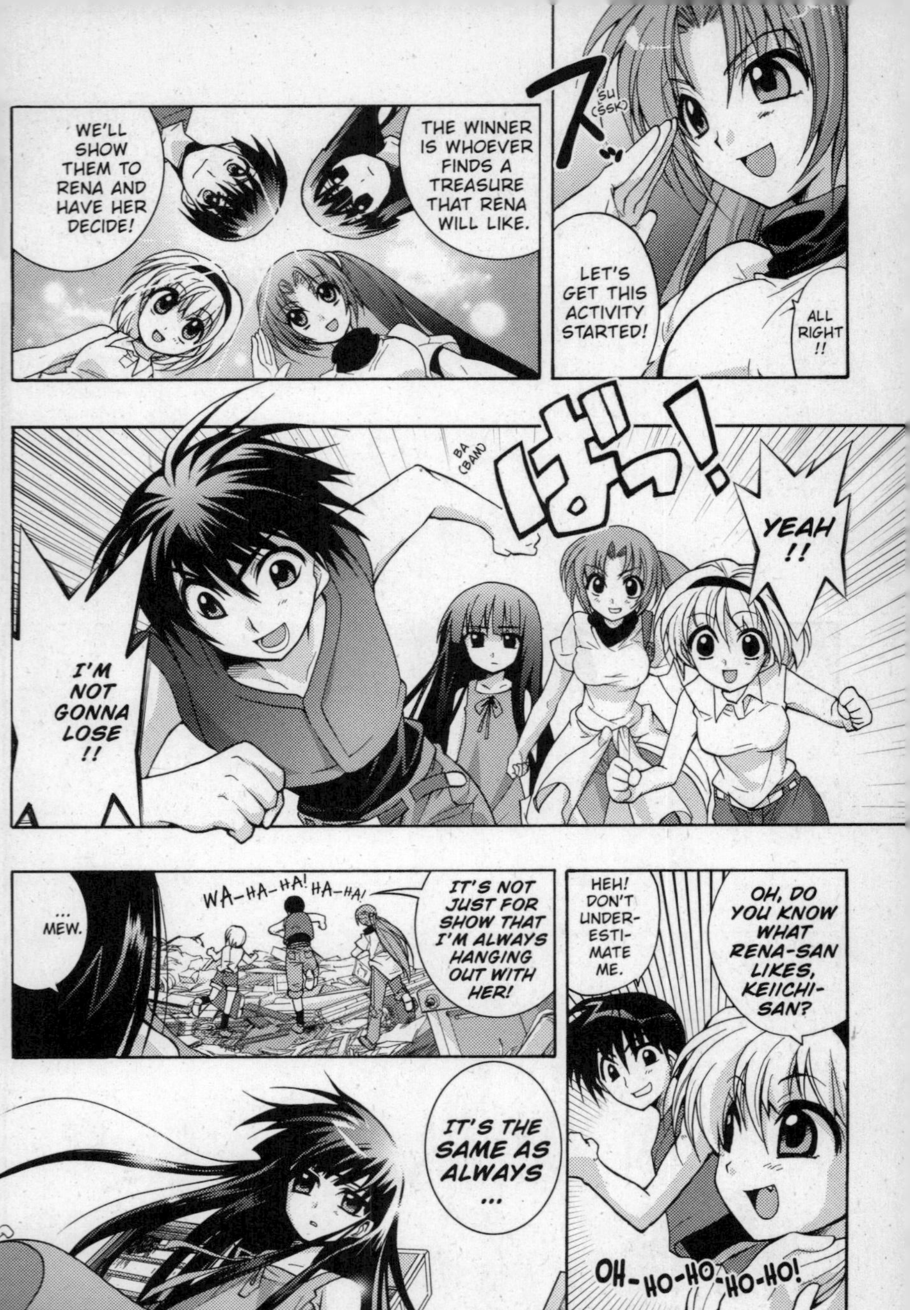
SU (SSK)
LET'S GET THIS ACTIVITY STARTED!
ALL RIGHT !!
THE WINNER IS WHOEVER FINDS A TREASURE THAT RENA WILL LIKE.
WE'LL SHOW THEM TO RENA AND HAVE HER DECIDE!
BA (BAM)
YEAH !!
I'M NOT GONNA LOSE !!
OH, DO YOU KNOW WHAT RENA-SAN LIKES, KEIICHI-SAN?
HEH! DON'T UNDER-ESTI-MATE ME.
OH-HO-HO-HO-HO!
IT'S NOT JUST FOR SHOW THAT I'M ALWAYS HANGING OUT WITH HER!
WA-HA-HA! HA-HA!
... MEW.
IT'S THE SAME AS ALWAYS ...

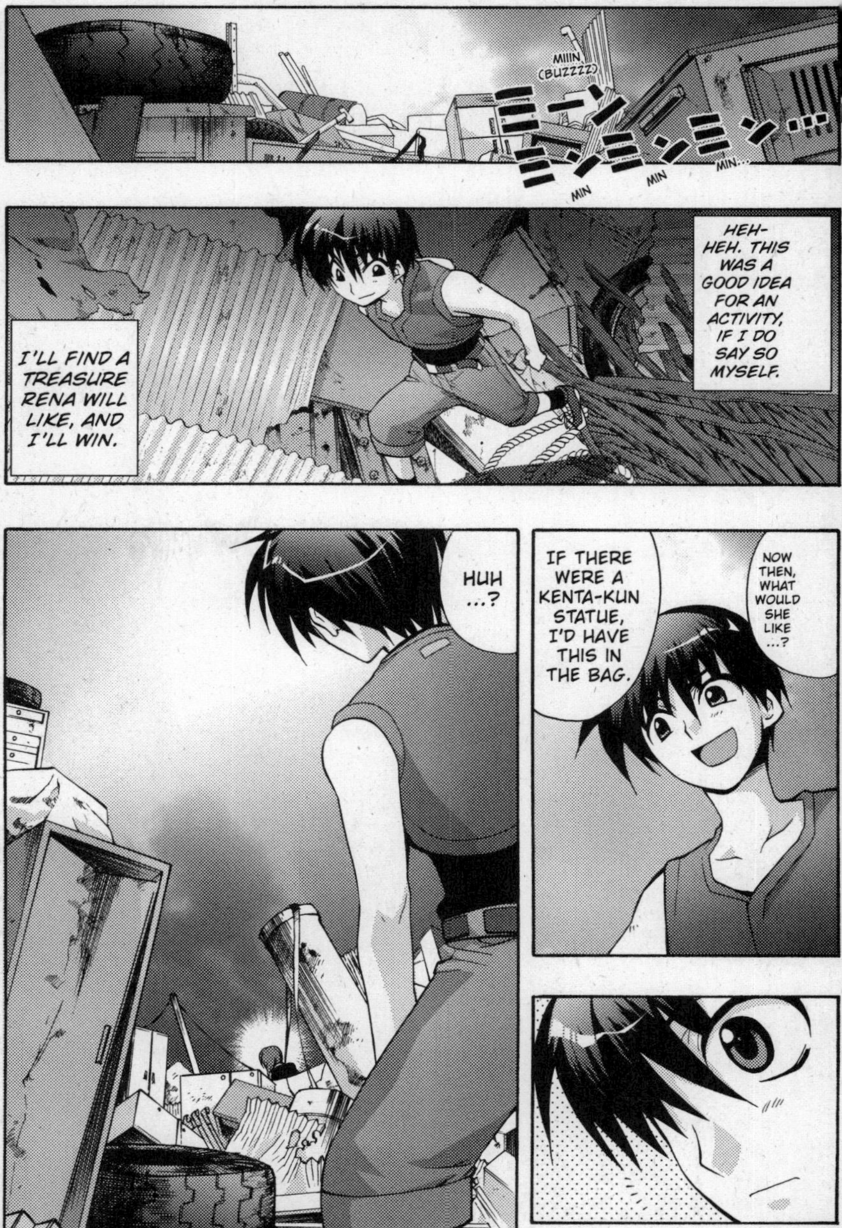
MIIN (BUZZZZ)
MIN MIN MIN...
HEH-HEH. THIS WAS A GOOD IDEA FOR AN ACTIVITY, IF I DO SAY SO MYSELF.
I'LL FIND A TREASURE RENA WILL LIKE, AND I'LL WIN.
NOW THEN, WHAT WOULD SHE LIKE ...?
IF THERE WERE A KENTA-KUN STATUE, I'D HAVE THIS IN THE BAG.
HUH ...?

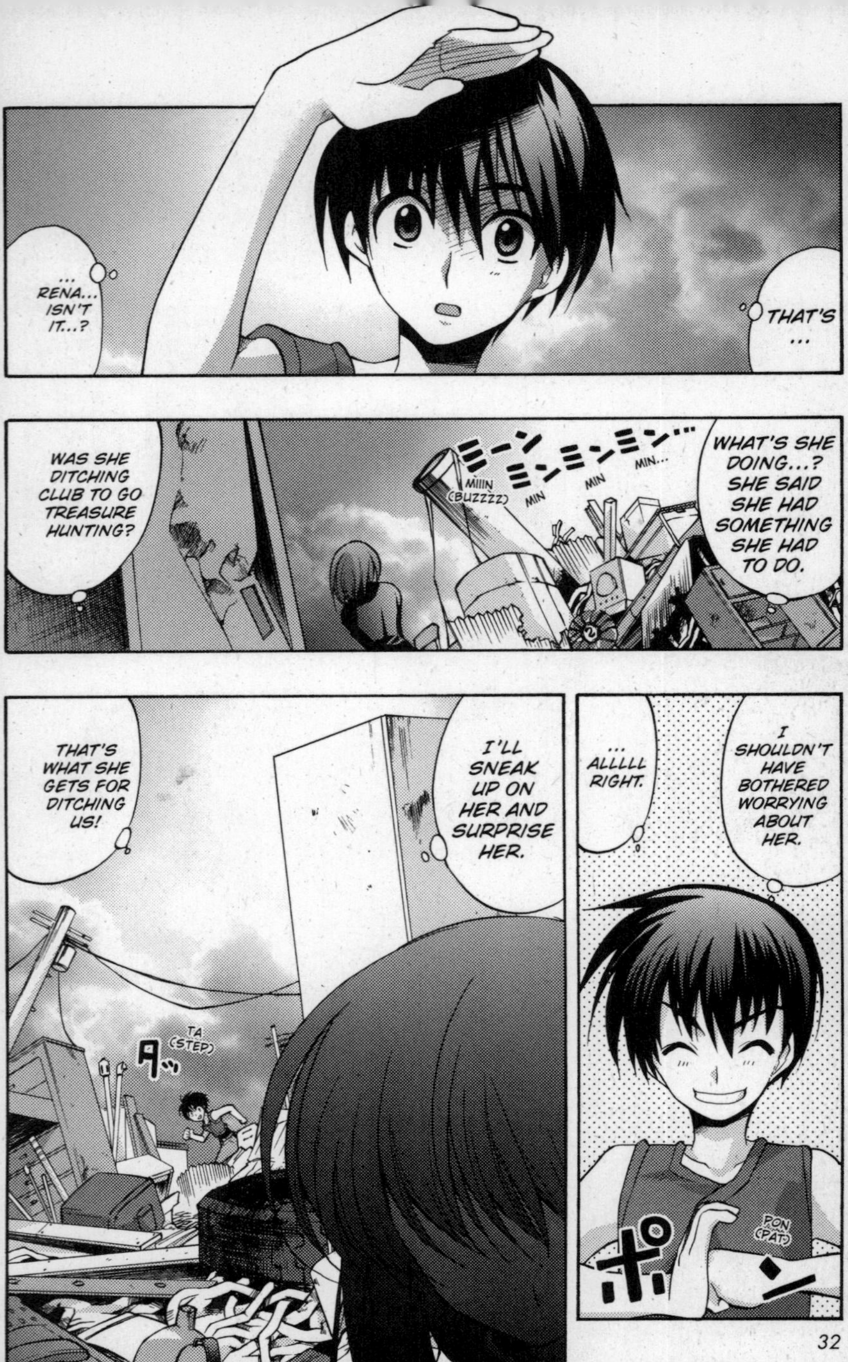
THAT'S ...
... RENA... ISN'T IT...?
WHAT'S SHE DOING...? SHE SAID SHE HAD SOMETHING SHE HAD TO DO.
MIIN (BUZZZZ) MIN MIN MIN...
WAS SHE DITCHING CLUB TO GO TREASURE HUNTING?
I SHOULDN'T HAVE BOTHERED WORRYING ABOUT HER.
... ALLLLL RIGHT.
PON (PAT)
I'LL SNEAK UP ON HER AND SURPRISE HER.
THAT'S WHAT SHE GETS FOR DITCHING US!
TA (STEP)

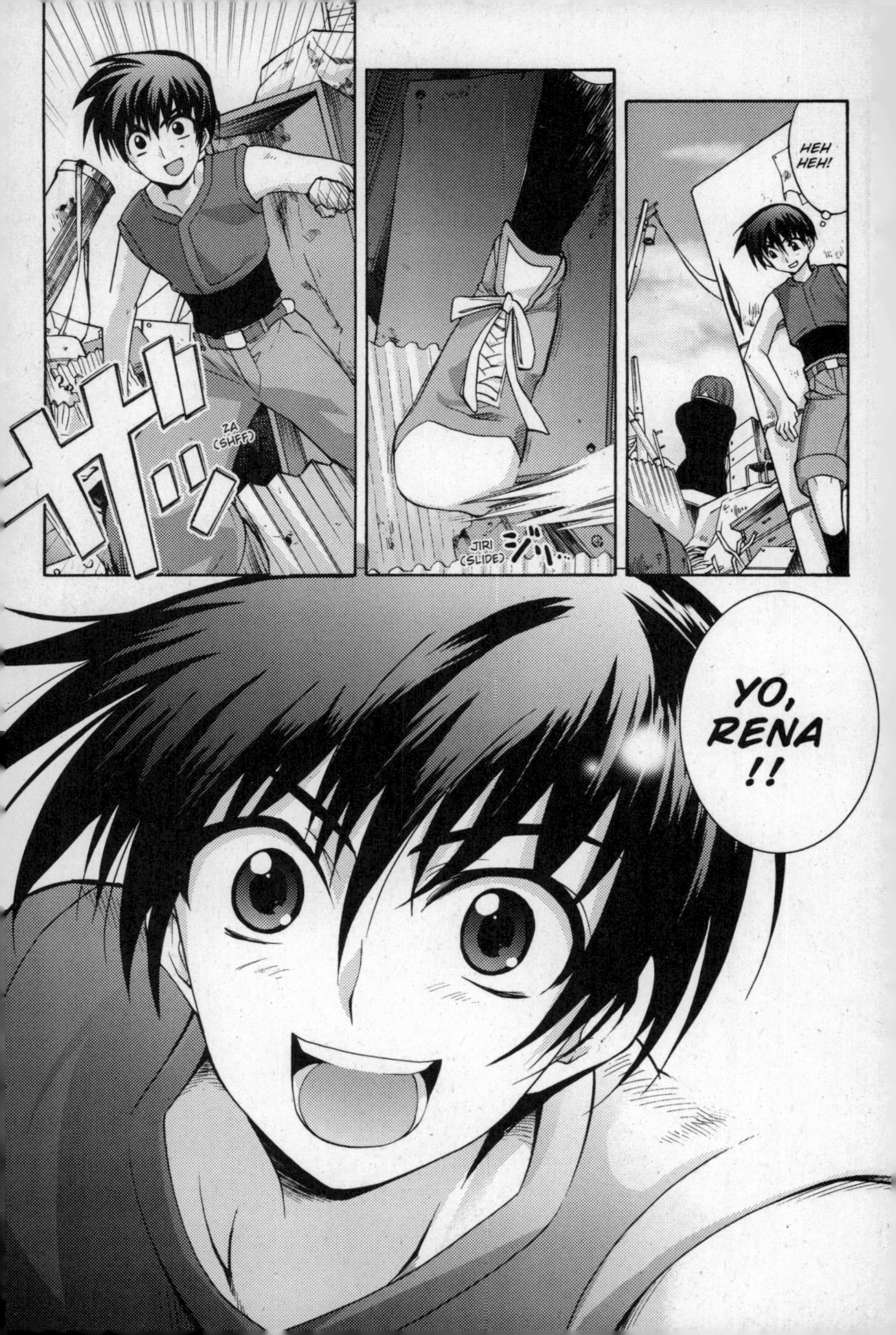
HEH HEH!
JIRI (SLIDE)
ZA (SHFF)
YO, RENA!!

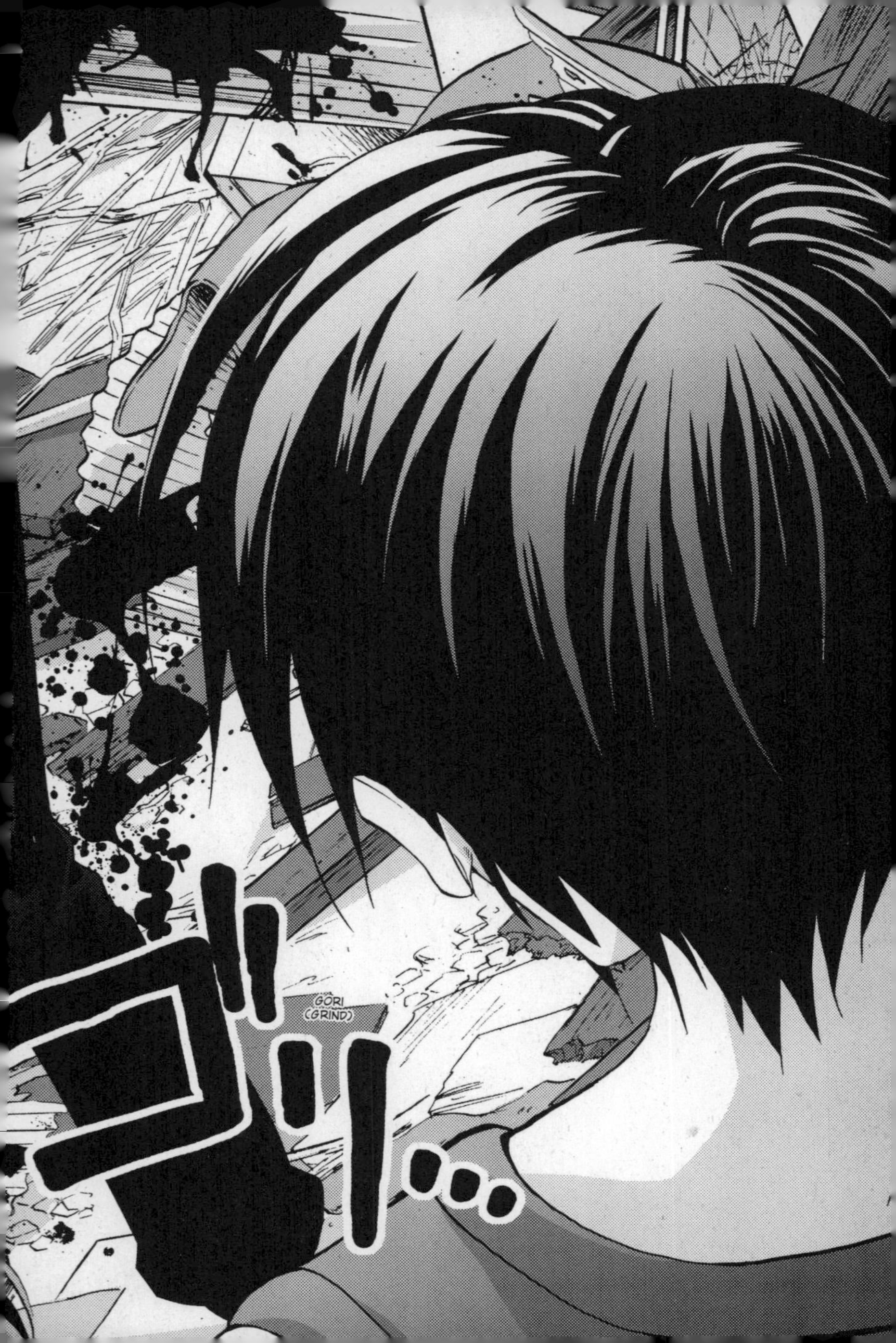
GORI
(GRIND)

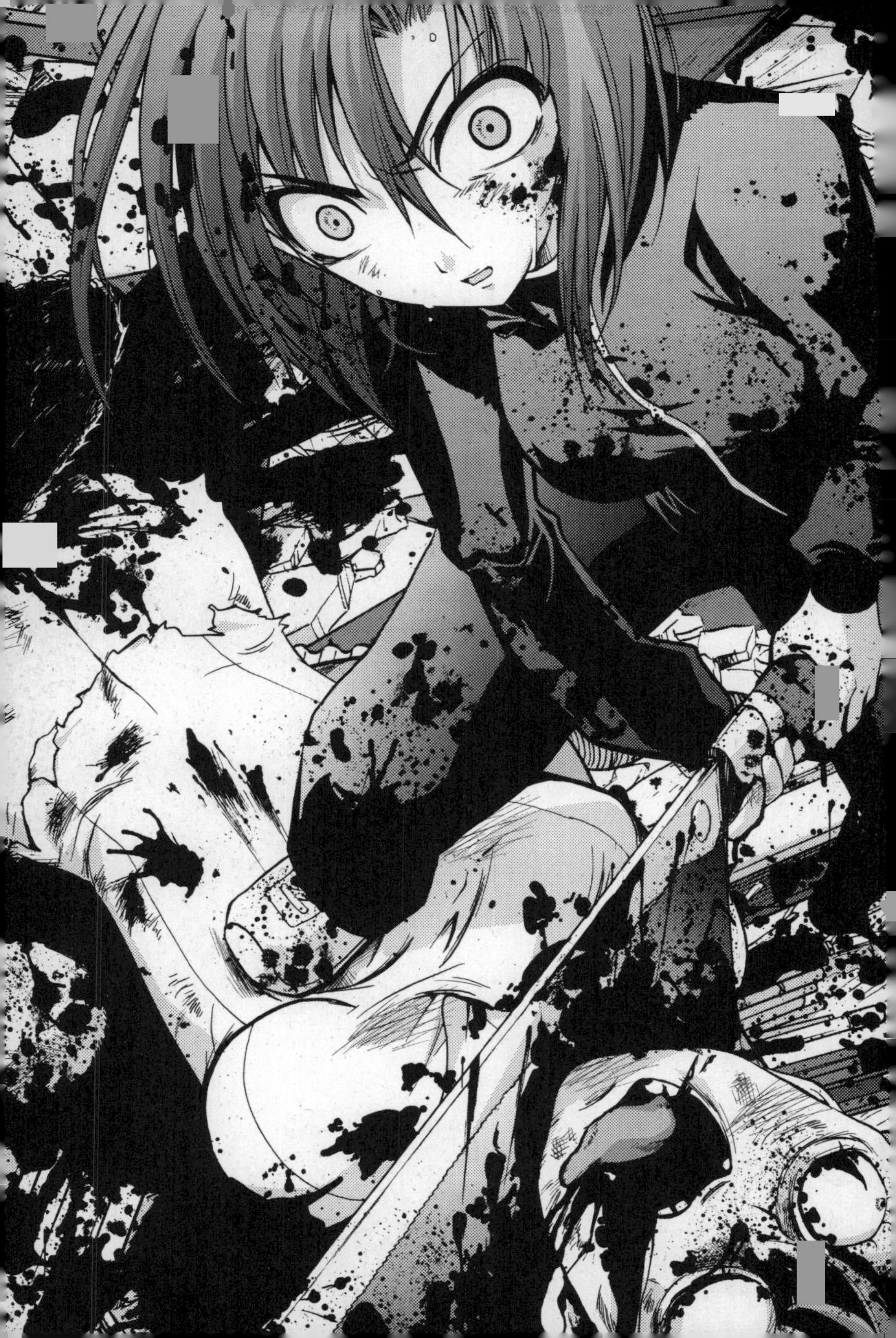

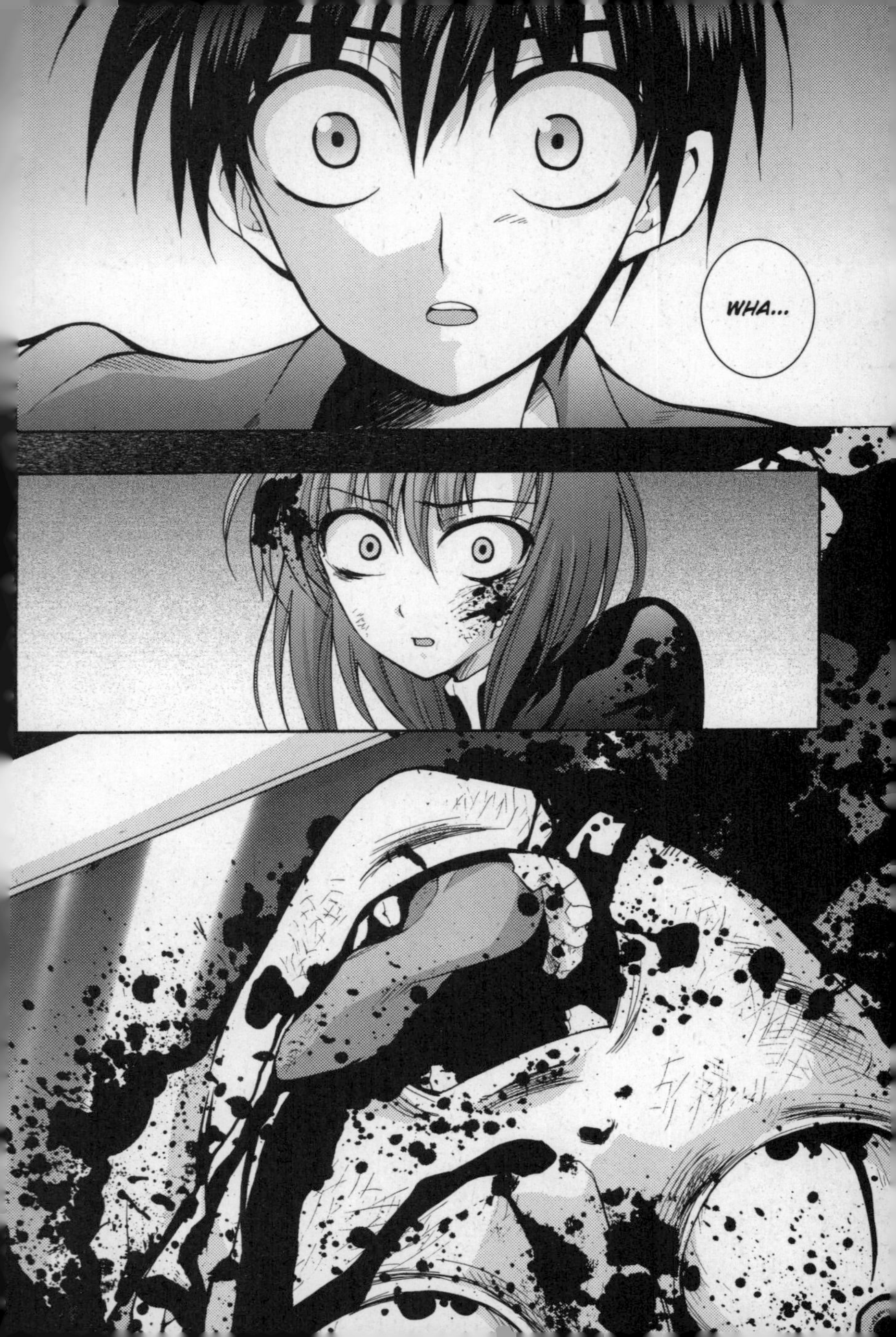
WHA...

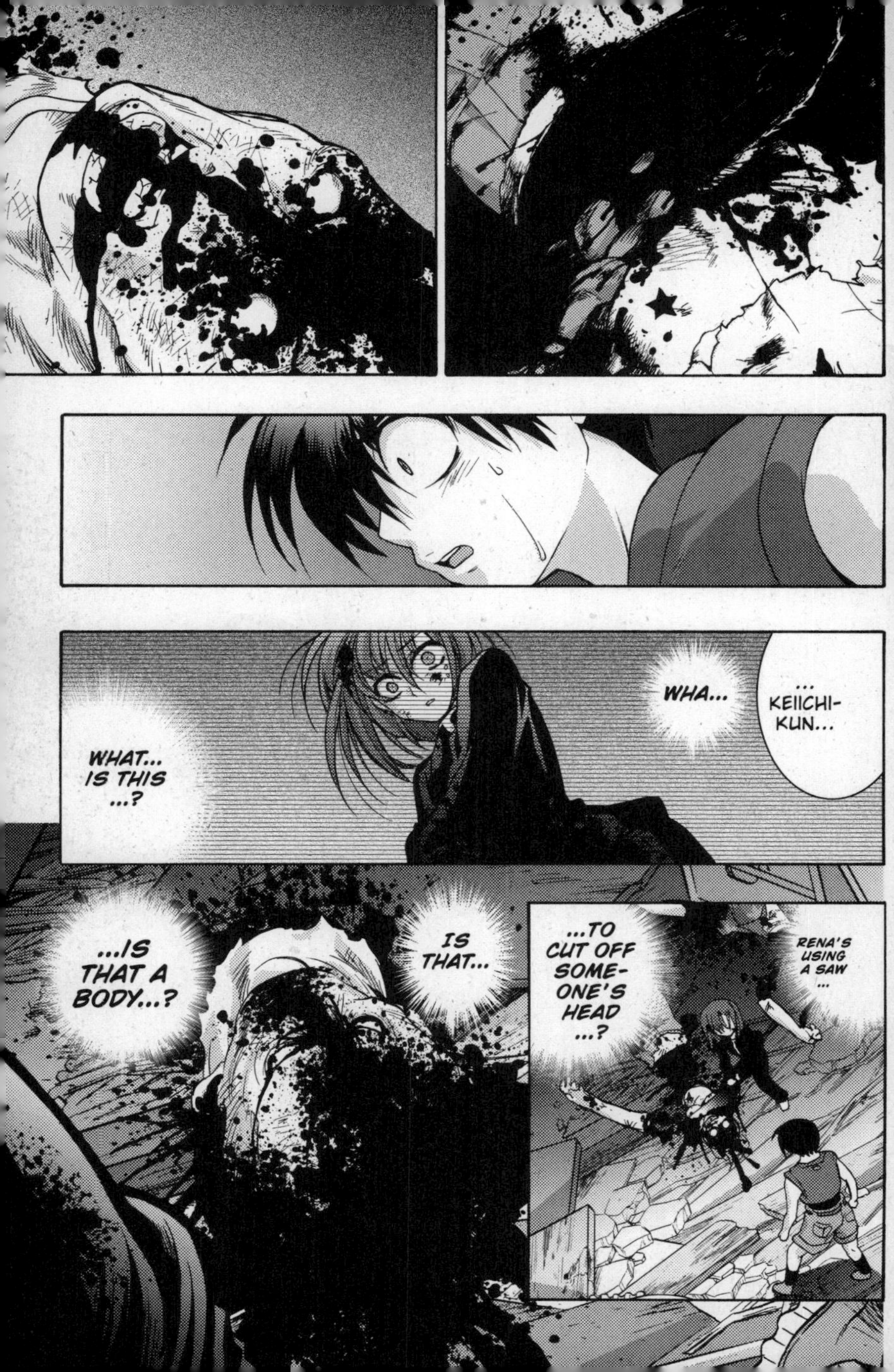
...KEIICHI-KUN...
WHA...
WHAT... IS THIS ...?
RENA'S USING A SAW ...
...TO CUT OFF SOME-ONE'S HEAD ...?
IS THAT...
...IS THAT A BODY...?

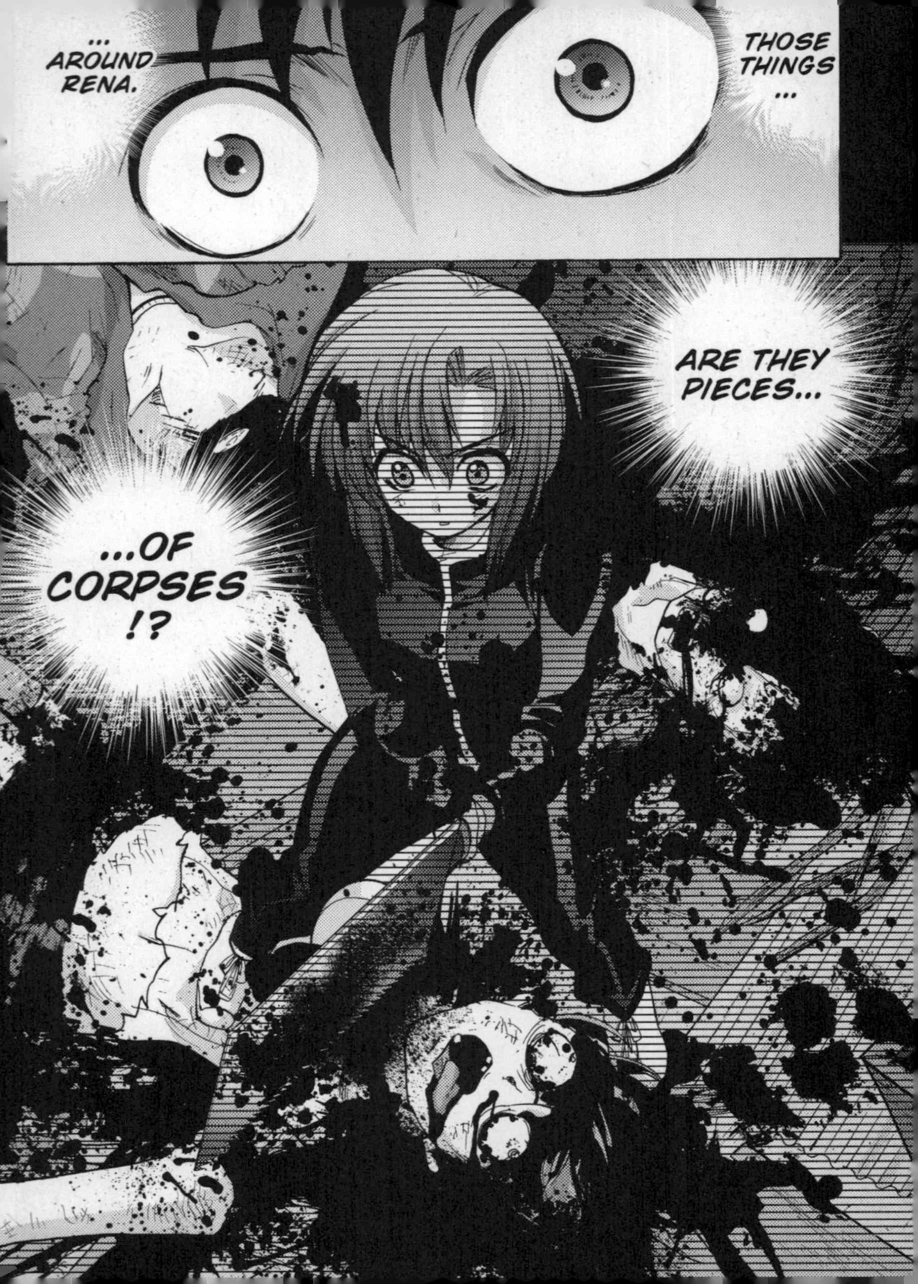
THOSE THINGS ...
... AROUND RENA.
ARE THEY PIECES...
...OF CORPSES !?

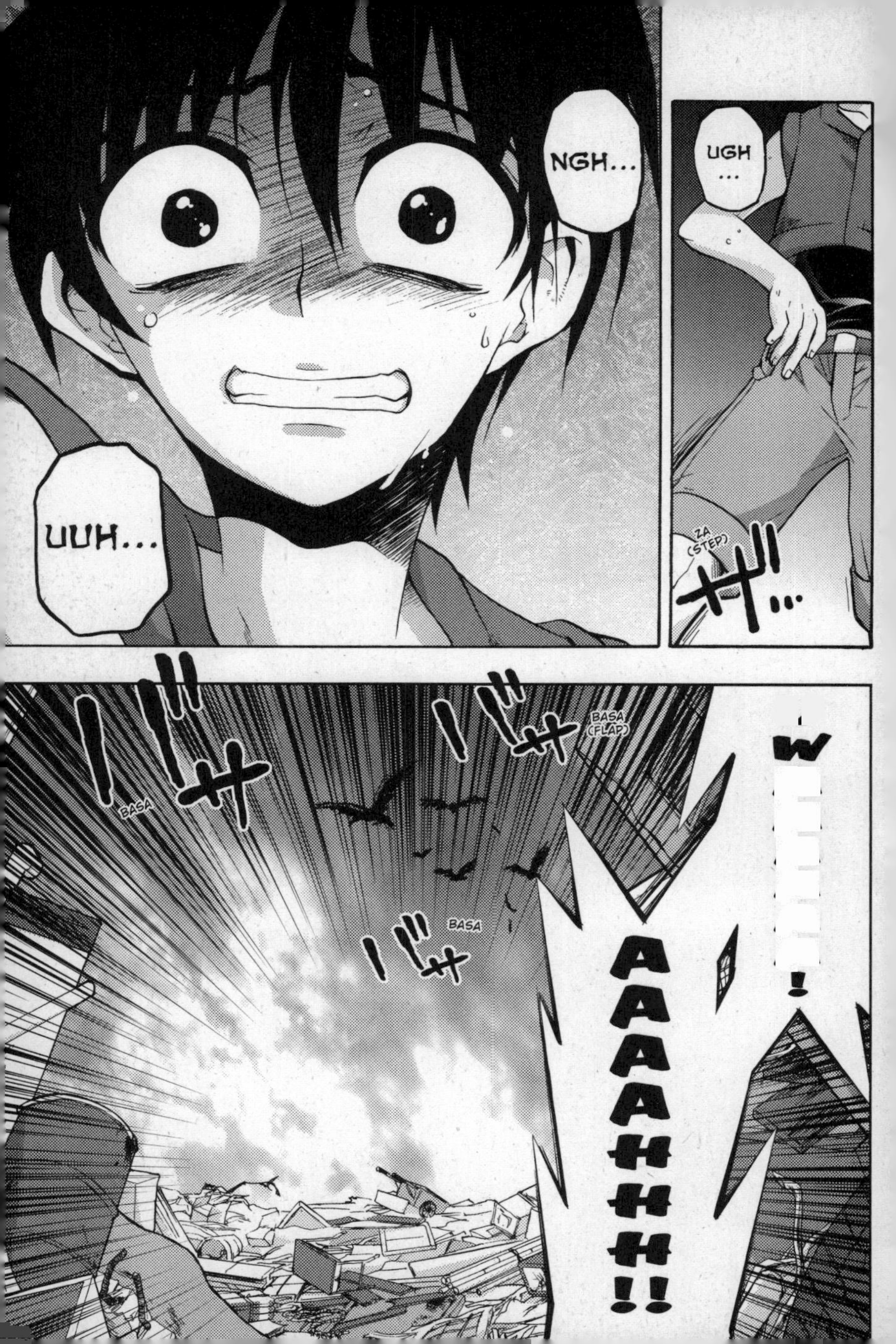
UGH
...
ZA
(STEP)
NGH...
UUH...
W!
AAAAHHH!!
BASA
(FLAP)
BASA
BASA

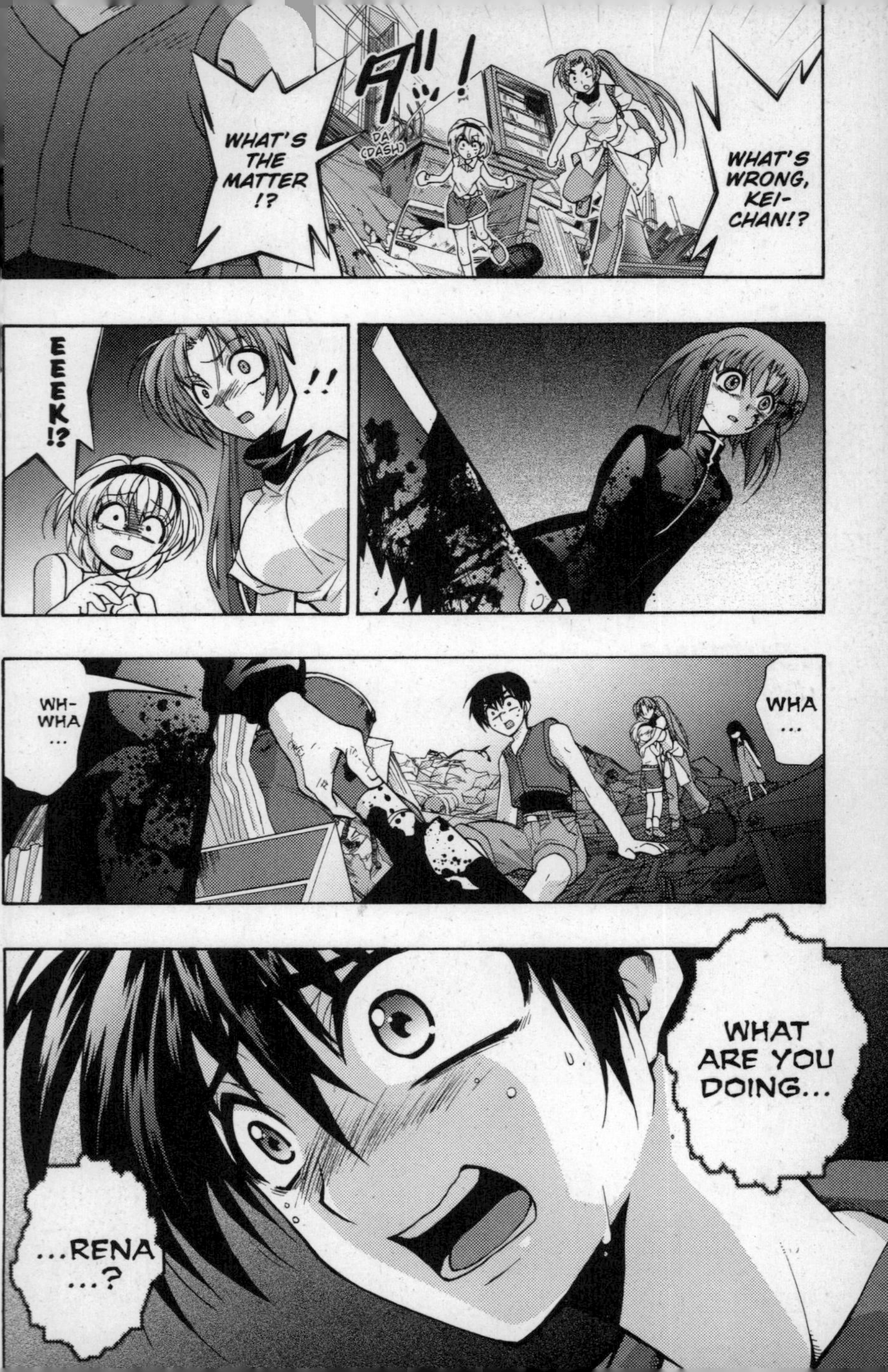
WHAT'S WRONG, KEI-CHAN!?
DA (DASH)
WHAT'S THE MATTER !?
!!
EEEK !?
WHA ...
WH-WHA ...
WHAT ARE YOU DOING...
...RENA ...?

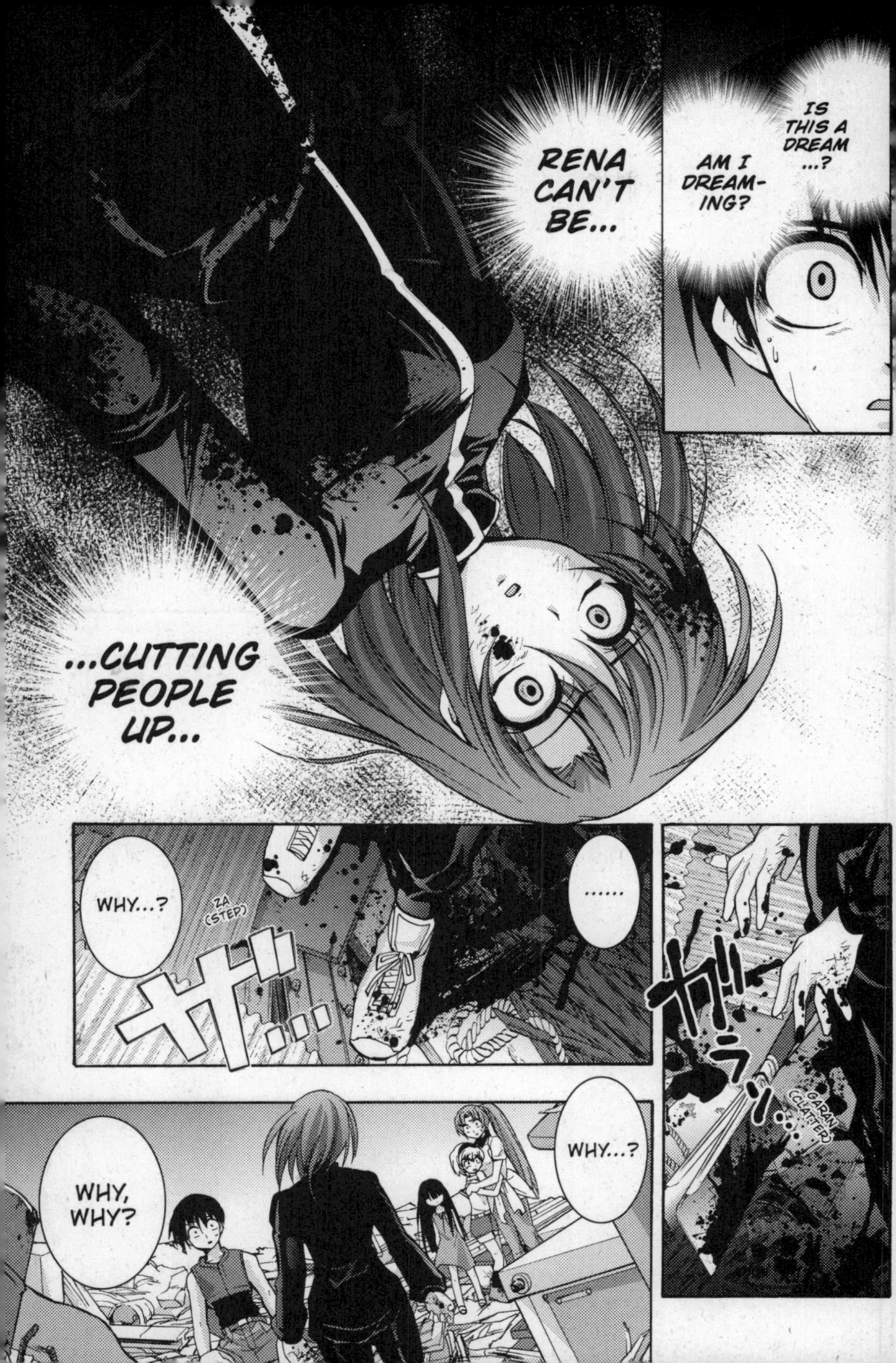
IS THIS A DREAM ...?
AM I DREAMING?
RENA CAN'T BE...
...CUTTING PEOPLE UP...
GARAN (CLATTER)
......
ZA (STEP)
WHY...?
WHY...?
WHY, WHY?

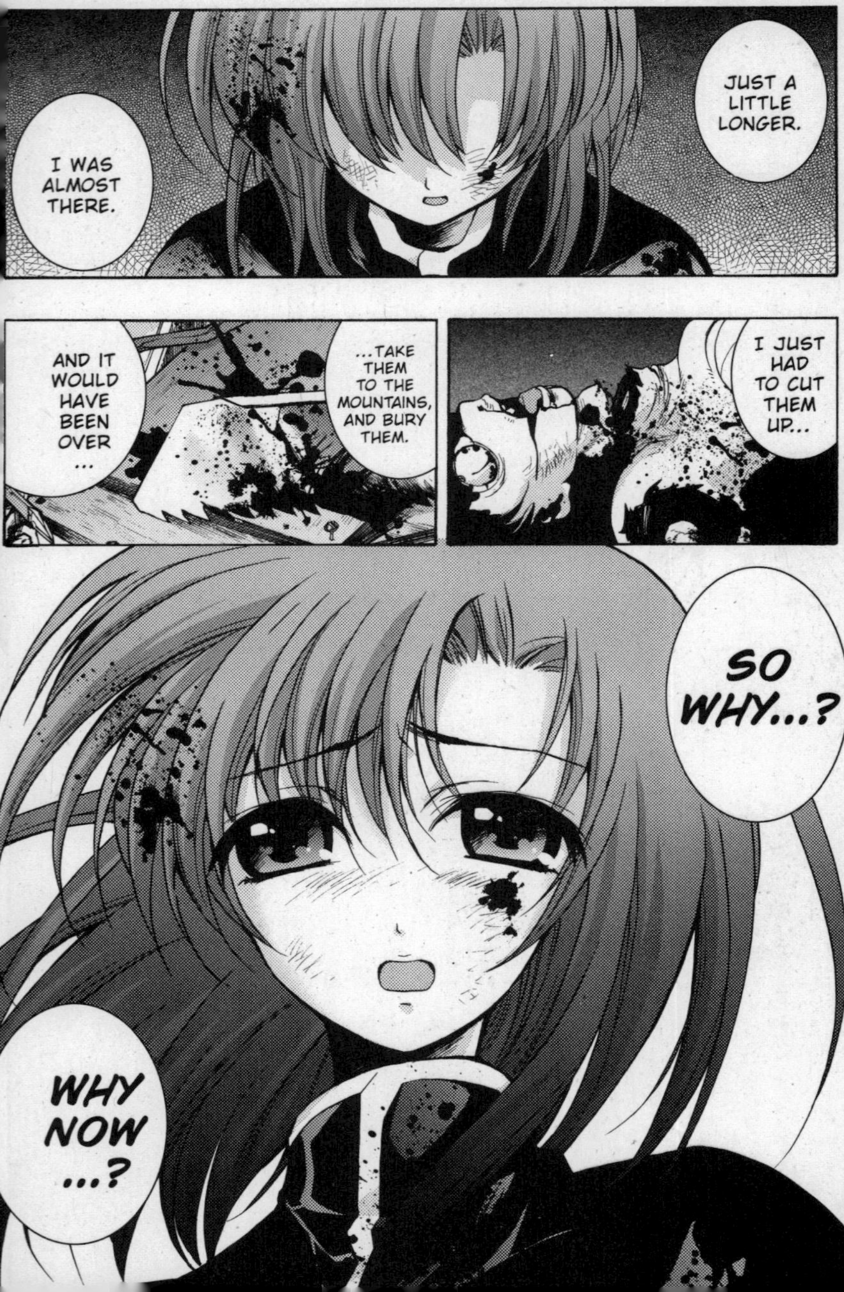
JUST A LITTLE LONGER.
I WAS ALMOST THERE.
I JUST HAD TO CUT THEM UP...
...TAKE THEM TO THE MOUNTAINS, AND BURY THEM.
AND IT WOULD HAVE BEEN OVER ...
SO WHY...?
WHY NOW ...?

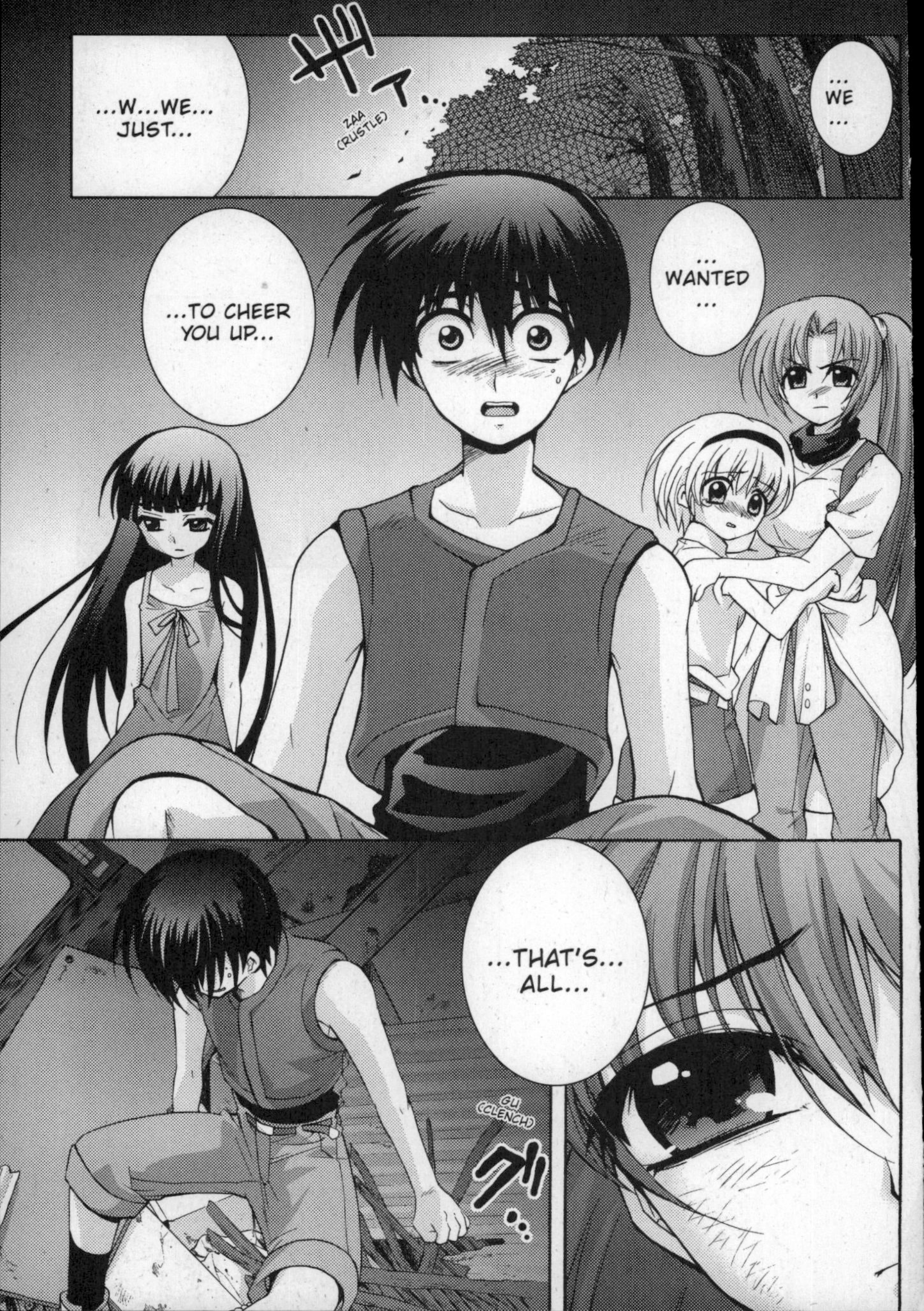
...WE...
ZAA (RUSTLE)
...W...WE... JUST...
...WANTED...
...TO CHEER YOU UP...
...THAT'S... ALL...
GU (CLENCH)

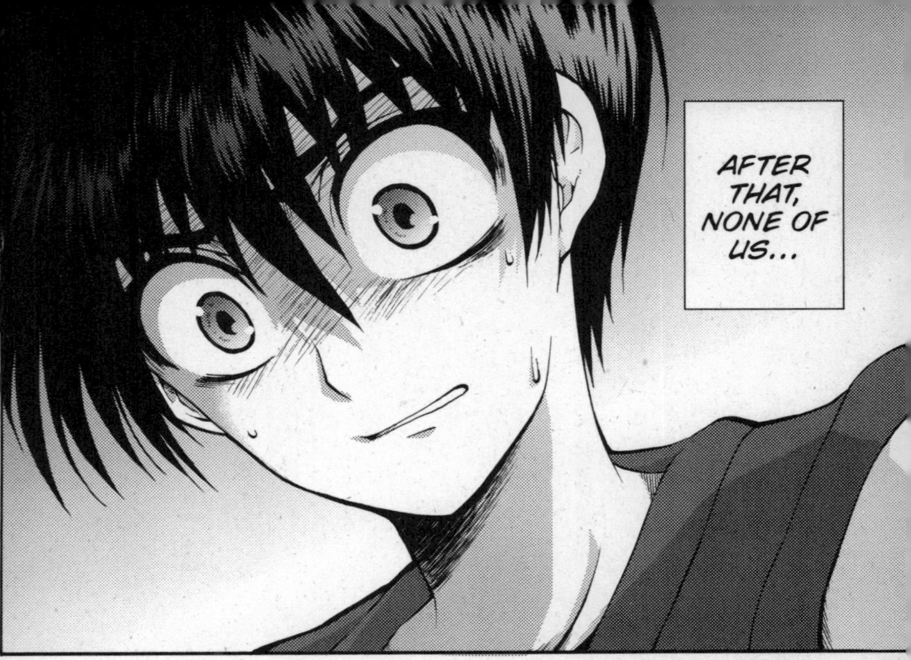
AFTER THAT, NONE OF US...

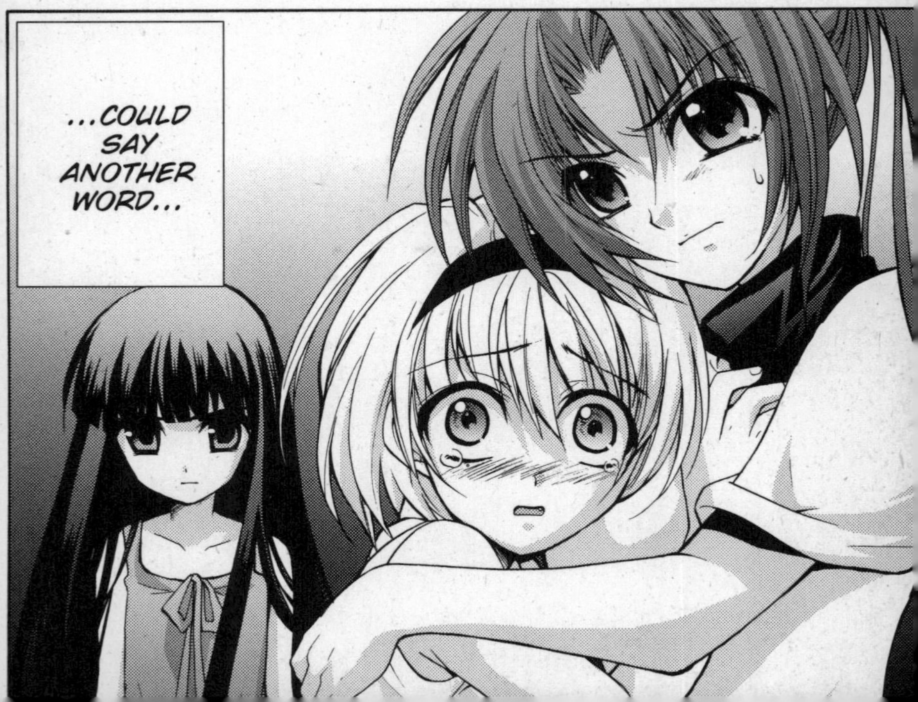
...COULD SAY ANOTHER WORD...

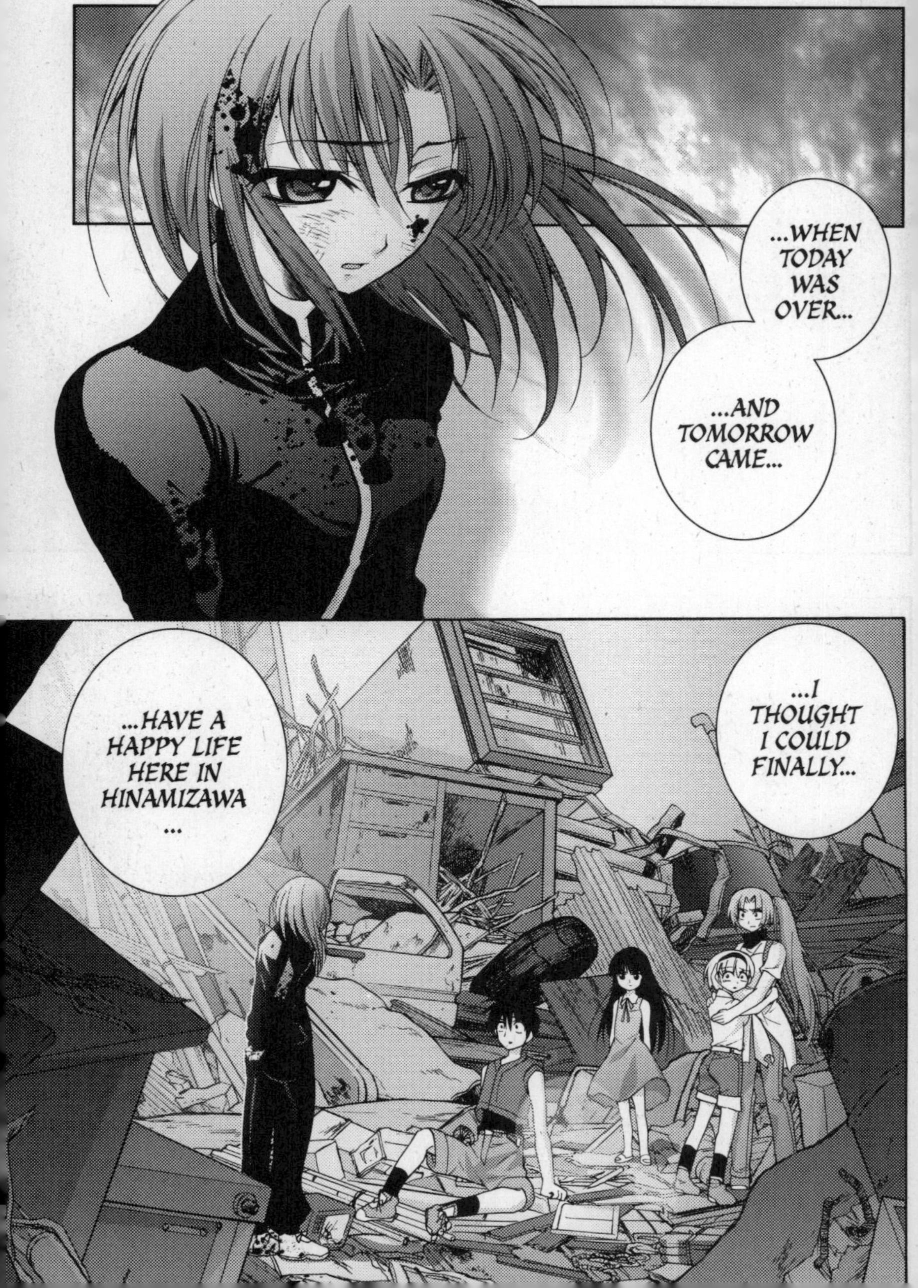
...WHEN TODAY WAS OVER...
...AND TOMORROW CAME...
...I THOUGHT I COULD FINALLY...
...HAVE A HAPPY LIFE HERE IN HINAMIZAWA ...

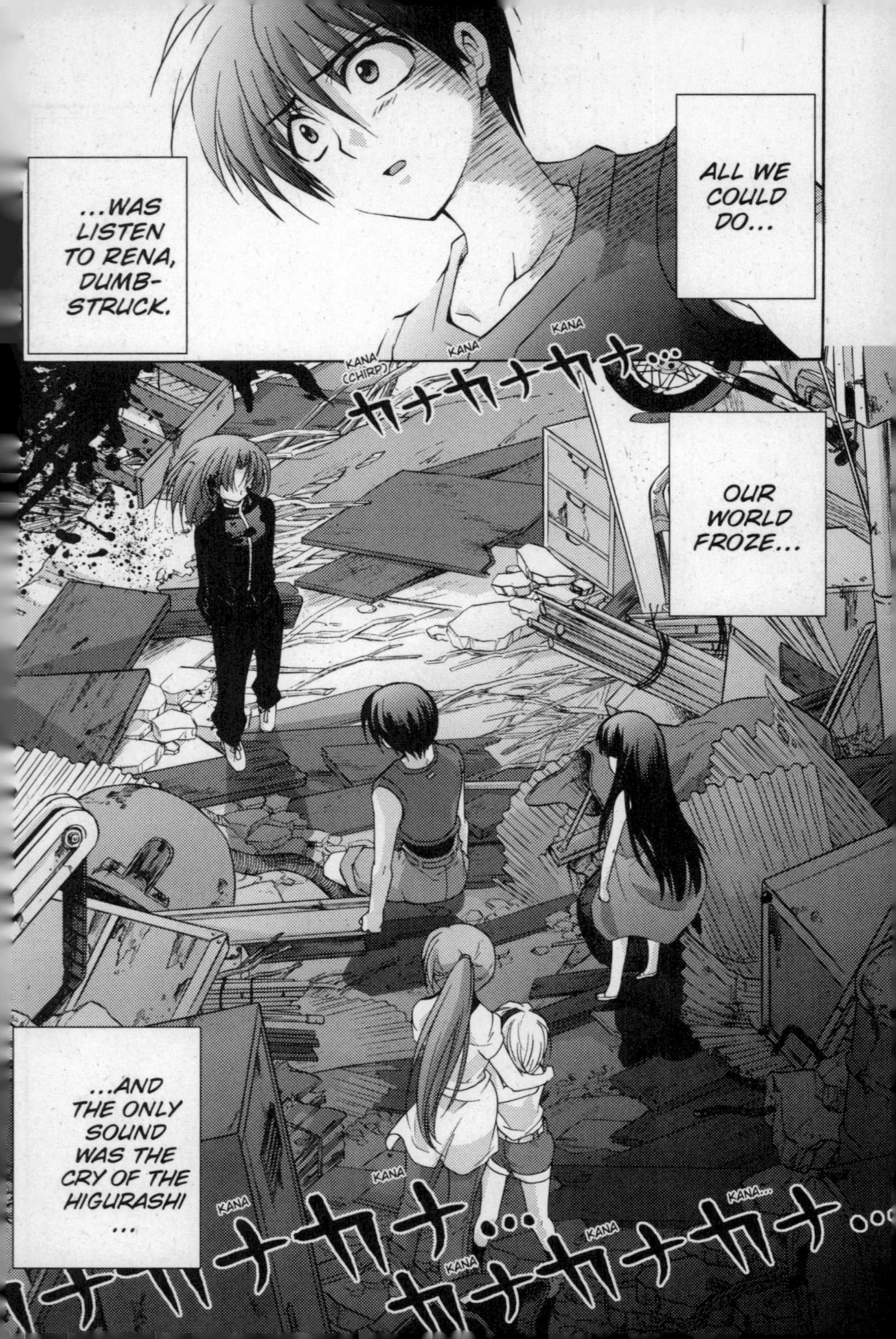
ALL WE COULD DO...
...WAS LISTEN TO RENA, DUMB-STRUCK.
KANA
KANA
KANA (CHIRP)
OUR WORLD FROZE...
...AND THE ONLY SOUND WAS THE CRY OF THE HIGURASHI ...
KANA...
KANA
KANA
KANA
KANA

THE MELANCHOLY OF RIKA FURUDE - PART ONE -

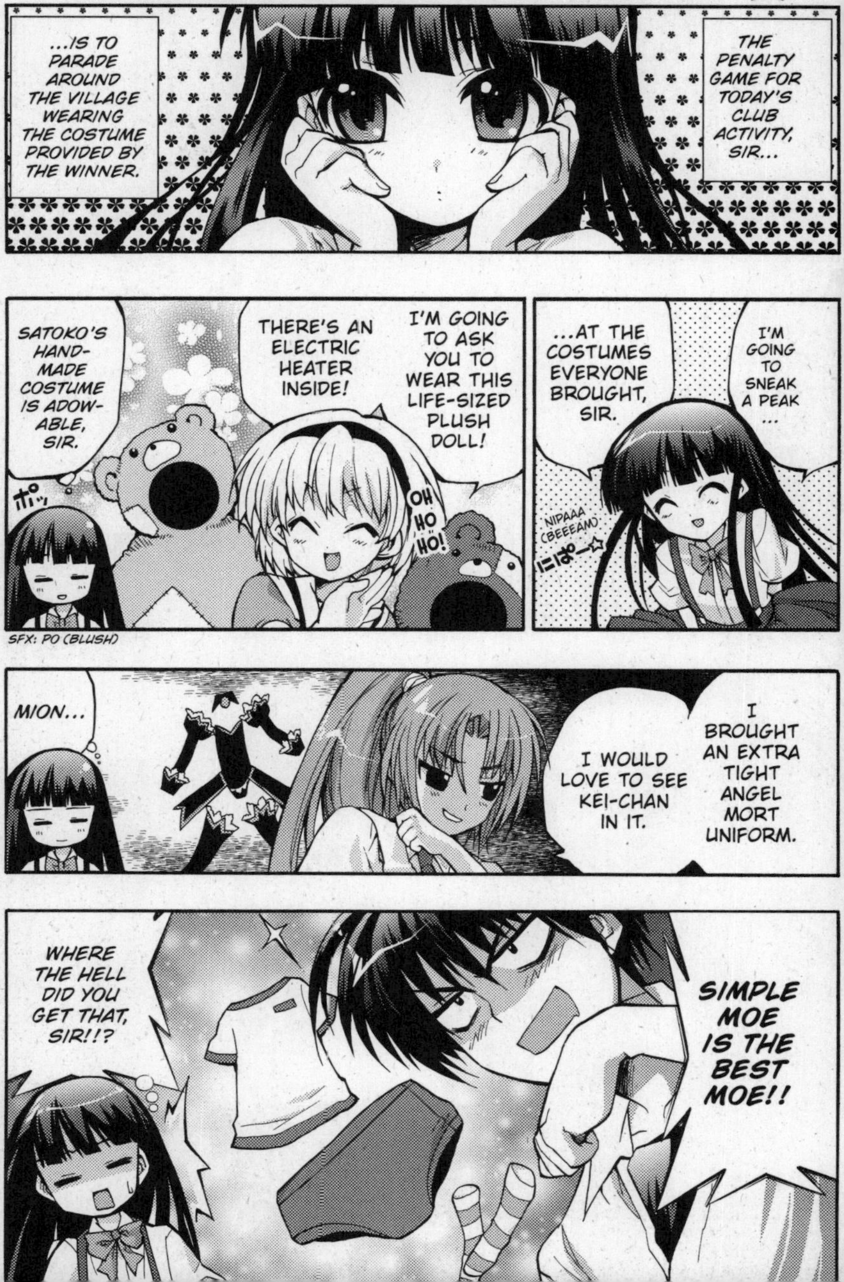
THE PENALTY GAME FOR TODAY'S CLUB ACTIVITY, SIR...
...IS TO PARADE AROUND THE VILLAGE WEARING THE COSTUME PROVIDED BY THE WINNER.
I'M GOING TO SNEAK A PEAK...
...AT THE COSTUMES EVERYONE BROUGHT, SIR.
NIPAAA (BEEEAM)
にぱー☆
I'M GOING TO ASK YOU TO WEAR THIS LIFE-SIZED PLUSH DOLL!
THERE'S AN ELECTRIC HEATER INSIDE!
OH HO HO!
SATOKO'S HAND-MADE COSTUME IS ADOWABLE, SIR.
ポッ
SFX: PO (BLUSH)
I BROUGHT AN EXTRA TIGHT ANGEL MORT UNIFORM.
I WOULD LOVE TO SEE KEI-CHAN IN IT.
MION...
SIMPLE MOE IS THE BEST MOE!!
WHERE THE HELL DID YOU GET THAT, SIR!!?

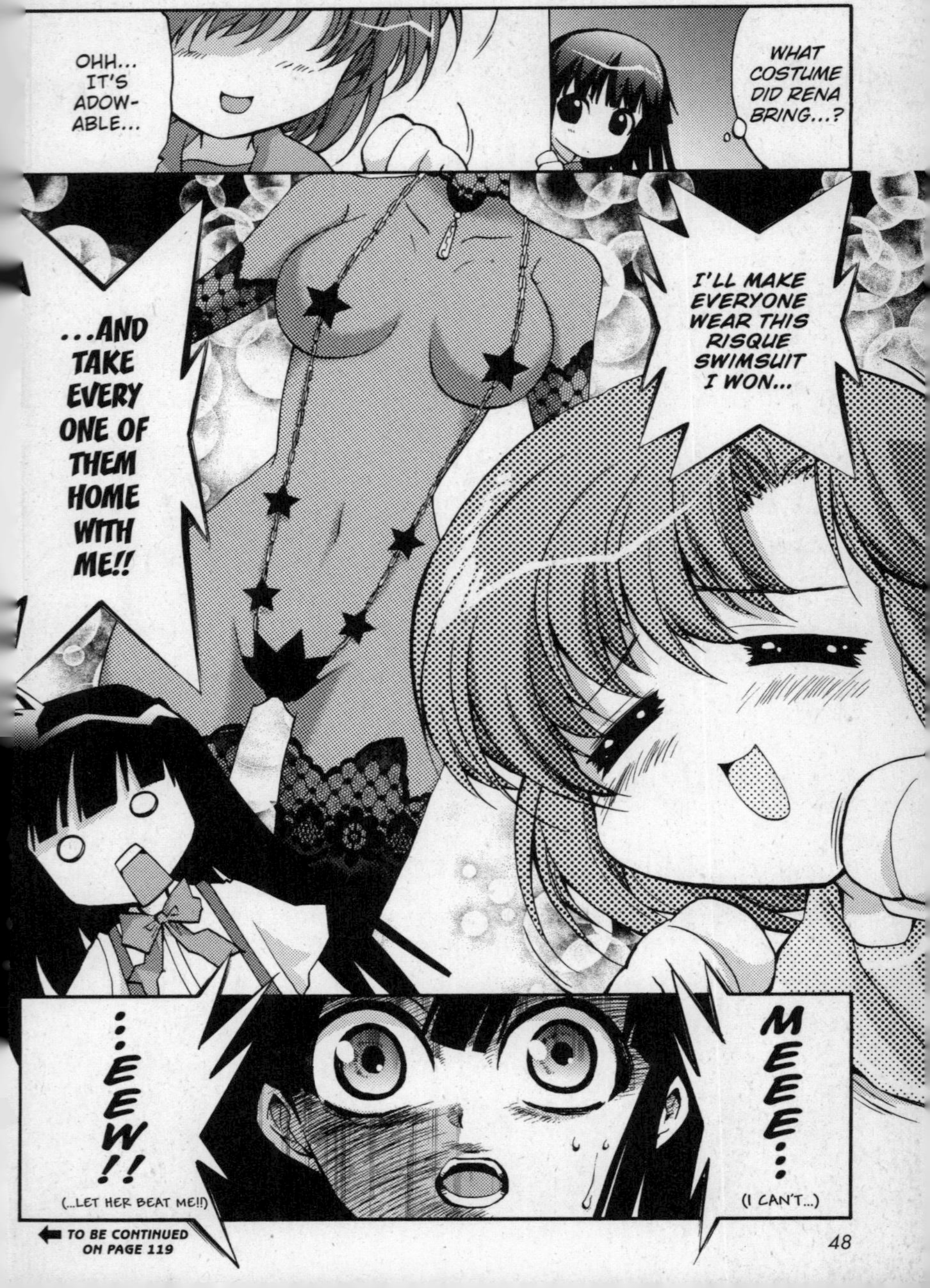
WHAT COSTUME DID RENA BRING...?
OHH... IT'S ADOW-ABLE...
I'LL MAKE EVERYONE WEAR THIS RISQUE SWIMSUIT I WON...
...AND TAKE EVERY ONE OF THEM HOME WITH ME!!
MEEE...
(I CAN'T...)
...EEEW!!
(...LET HER BEAT ME!!)

TO BE CONTINUED ON PAGE 119

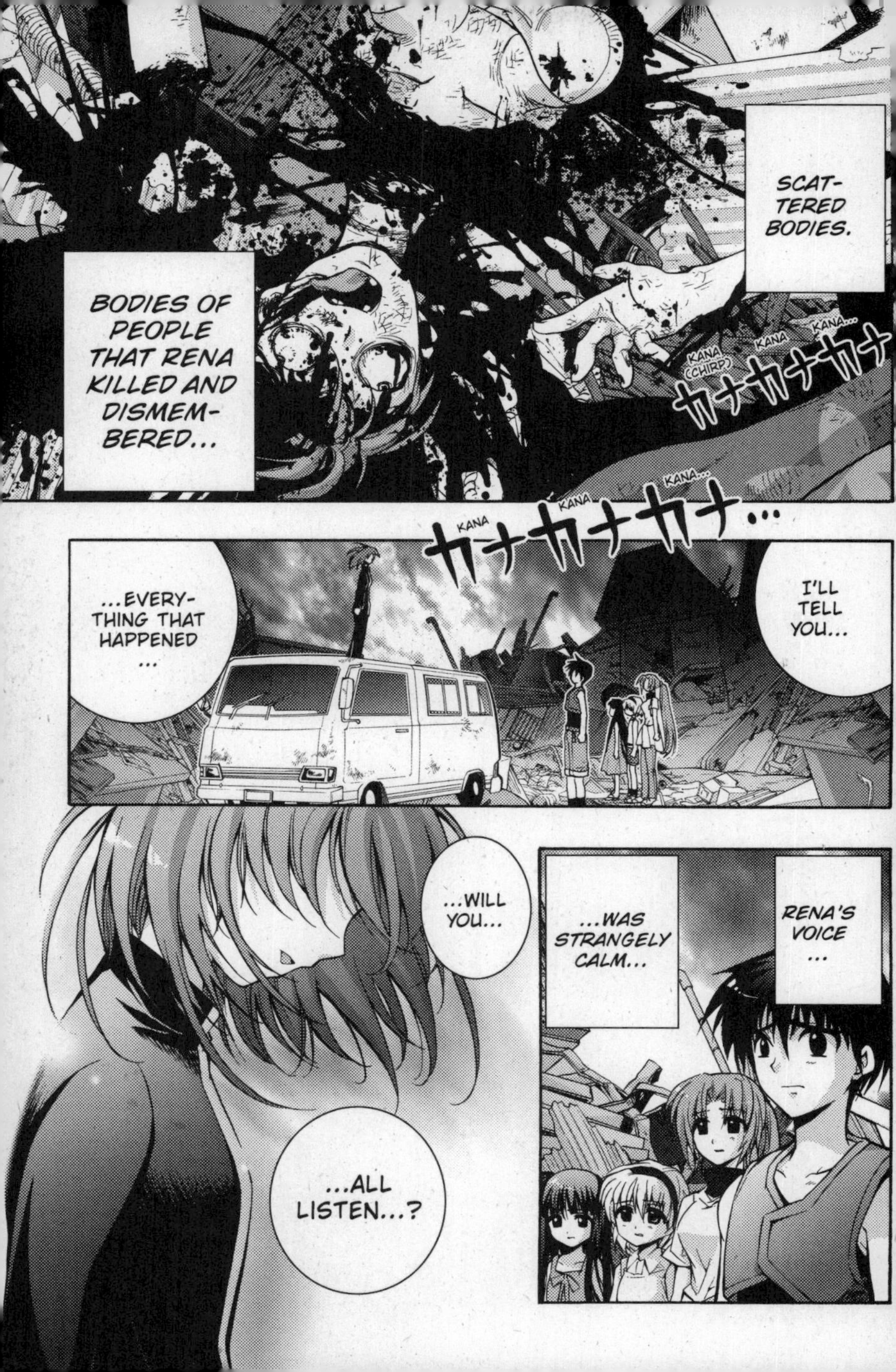
SCAT-
TERED
BODIES.
KANA (CHIRP) KANA KANA...
カナカナカナ
BODIES OF PEOPLE THAT RENA KILLED AND DISMEM-BERED...
KANA KANA KANA...
カナカナカナ...
I'LL TELL YOU...
...EVERY-THING THAT HAPPENED...
RENA'S VOICE...
...WAS STRANGELY CALM...
...WILL YOU...
...ALL LISTEN...?

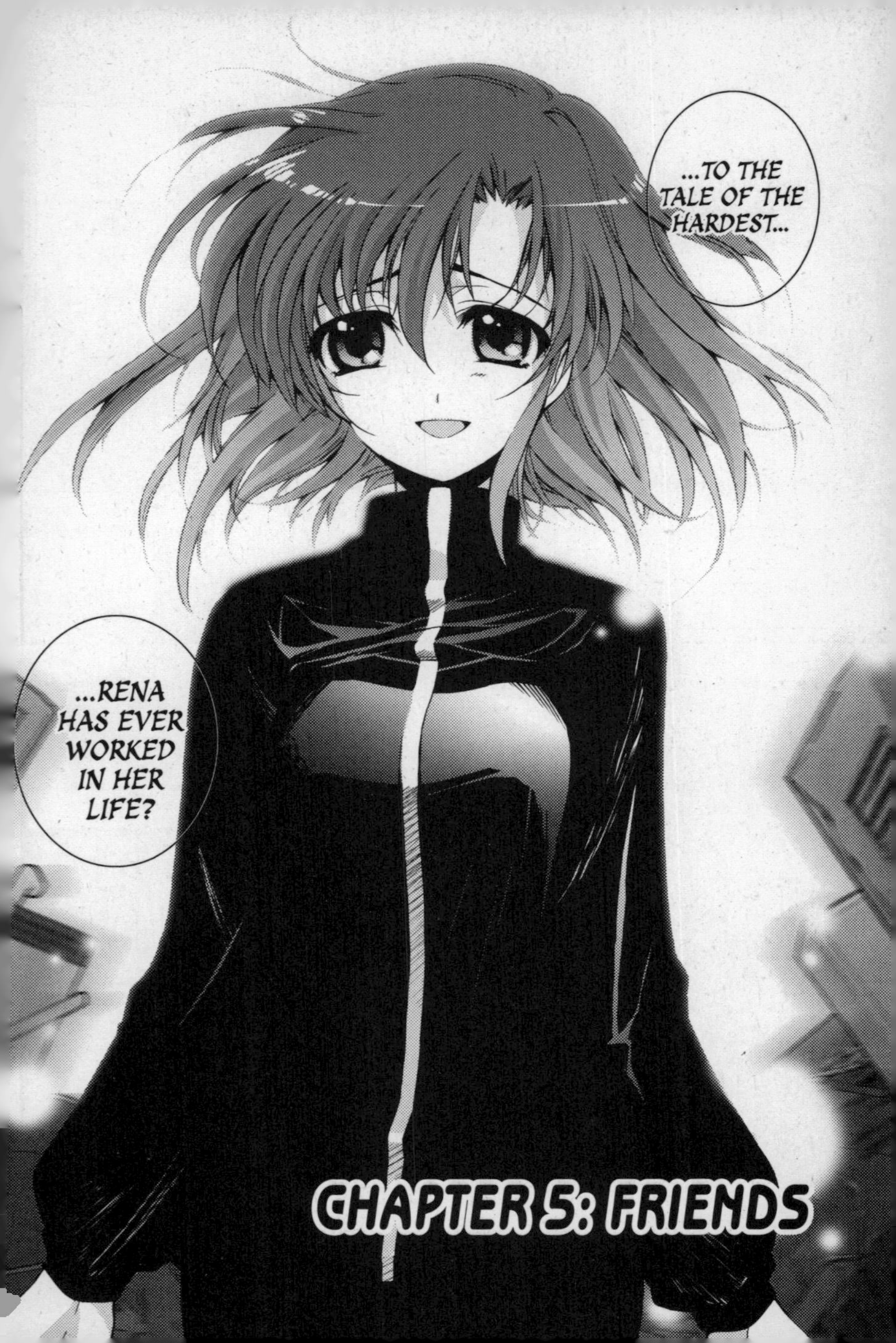
...TO THE TALE OF THE HARDEST...
...RENA HAS EVER WORKED IN HER LIFE?
CHAPTER 5: FRIENDS

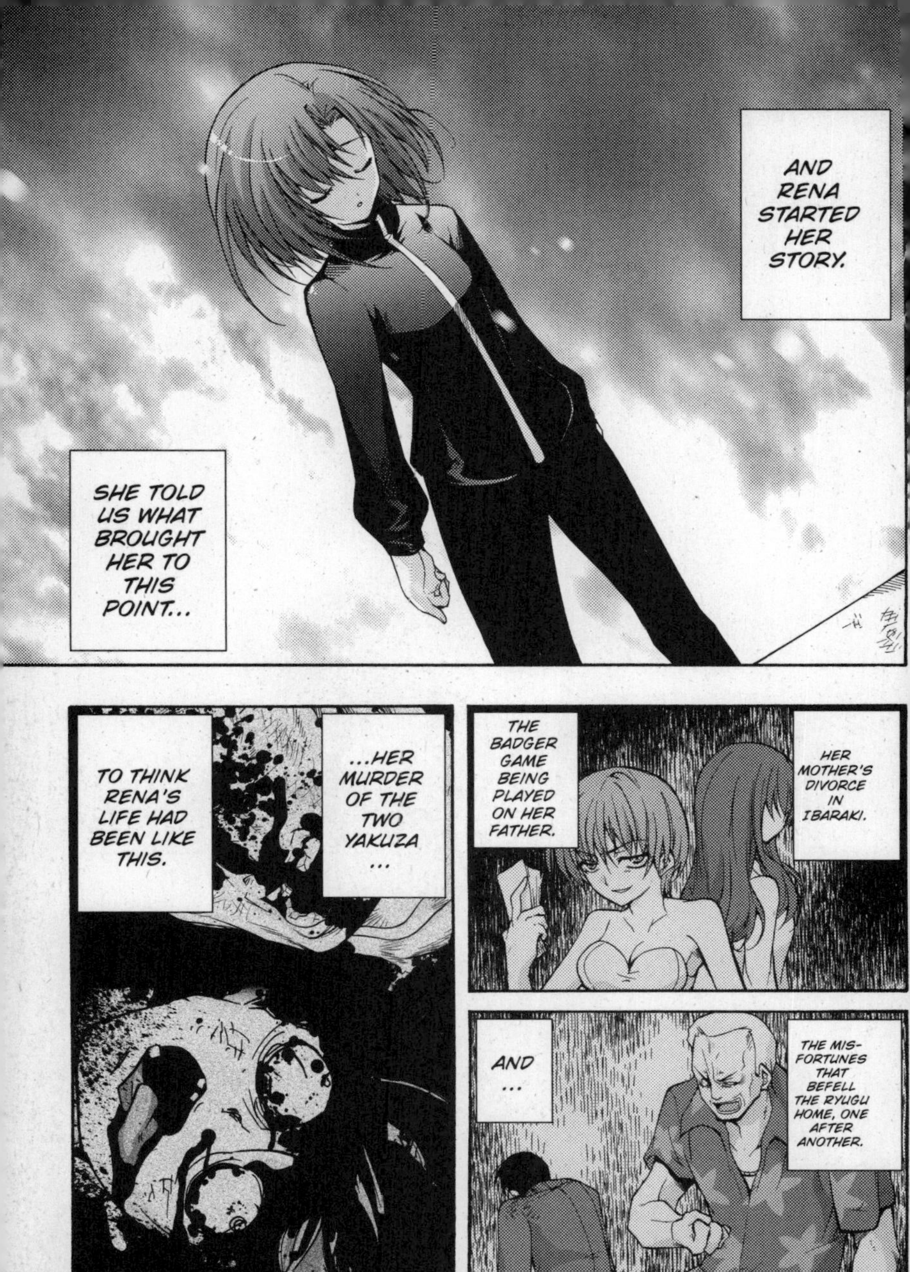
AND RENA STARTED HER STORY.
SHE TOLD US WHAT BROUGHT HER TO THIS POINT...
HER MOTHER'S DIVORCE IN IBARAKI.
THE BADGER GAME BEING PLAYED ON HER FATHER.
THE MIS-FORTUNES THAT BEFELL THE RYUGU HOME, ONE AFTER ANOTHER.
AND ...
...HER MURDER OF THE TWO YAKUZA ...
TO THINK RENA'S LIFE HAD BEEN LIKE THIS.

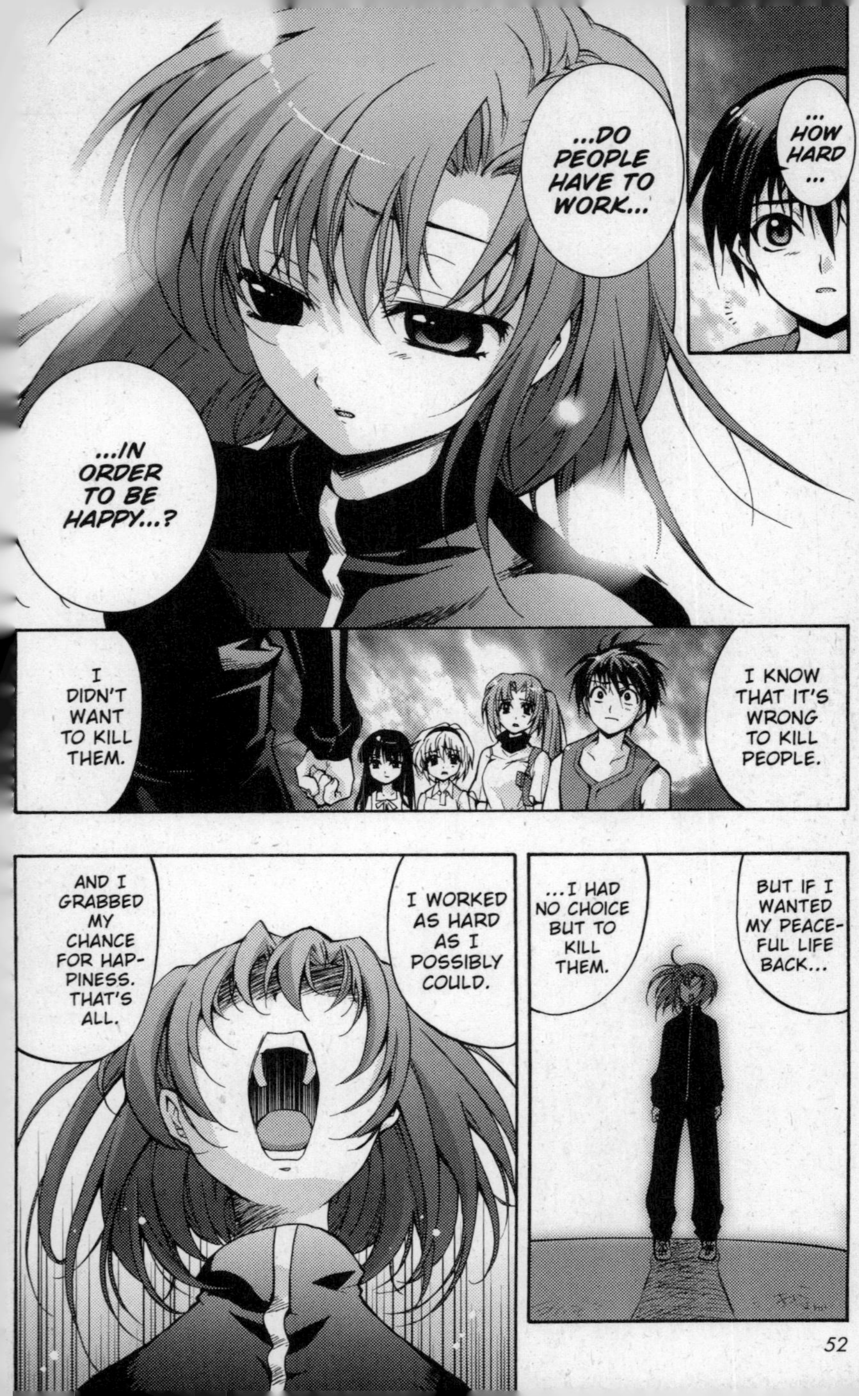
...HOW HARD...
...DO PEOPLE HAVE TO WORK...
...IN ORDER TO BE HAPPY...?
I KNOW THAT IT'S WRONG TO KILL PEOPLE.
I DIDN'T WANT TO KILL THEM.
BUT IF I WANTED MY PEACE-FUL LIFE BACK...
...I HAD NO CHOICE BUT TO KILL THEM.
I WORKED AS HARD AS I POSSIBLY COULD.
AND I GRABBED MY CHANCE FOR HAP-PINESS. THAT'S ALL.

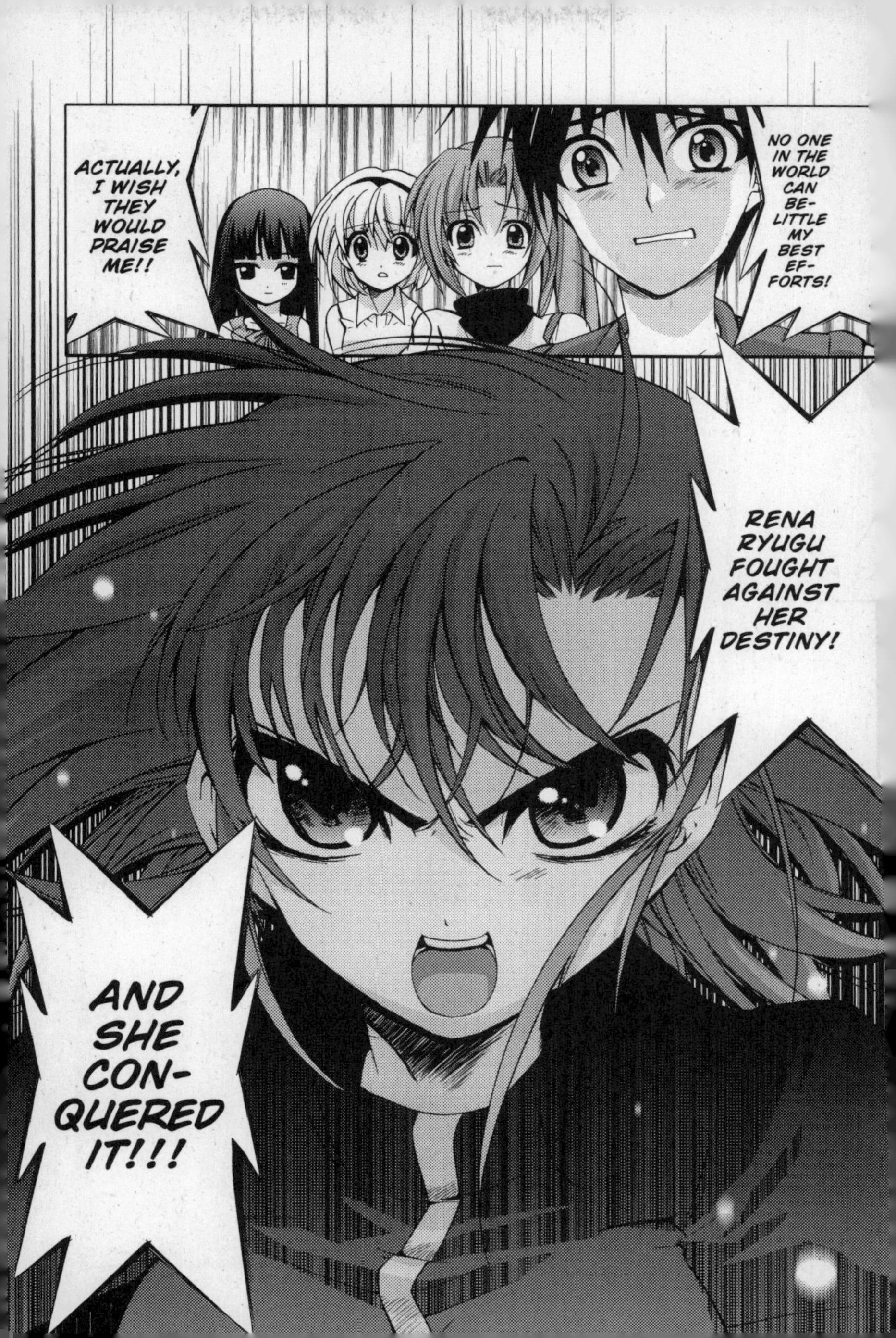
NO ONE IN THE WORLD CAN BE-LITTLE MY BEST EF-FORTS!
ACTUALLY, I WISH THEY WOULD PRAISE ME!!
RENA RYUGU FOUGHT AGAINST HER DESTINY!
AND SHE CON-QUERED IT!!!

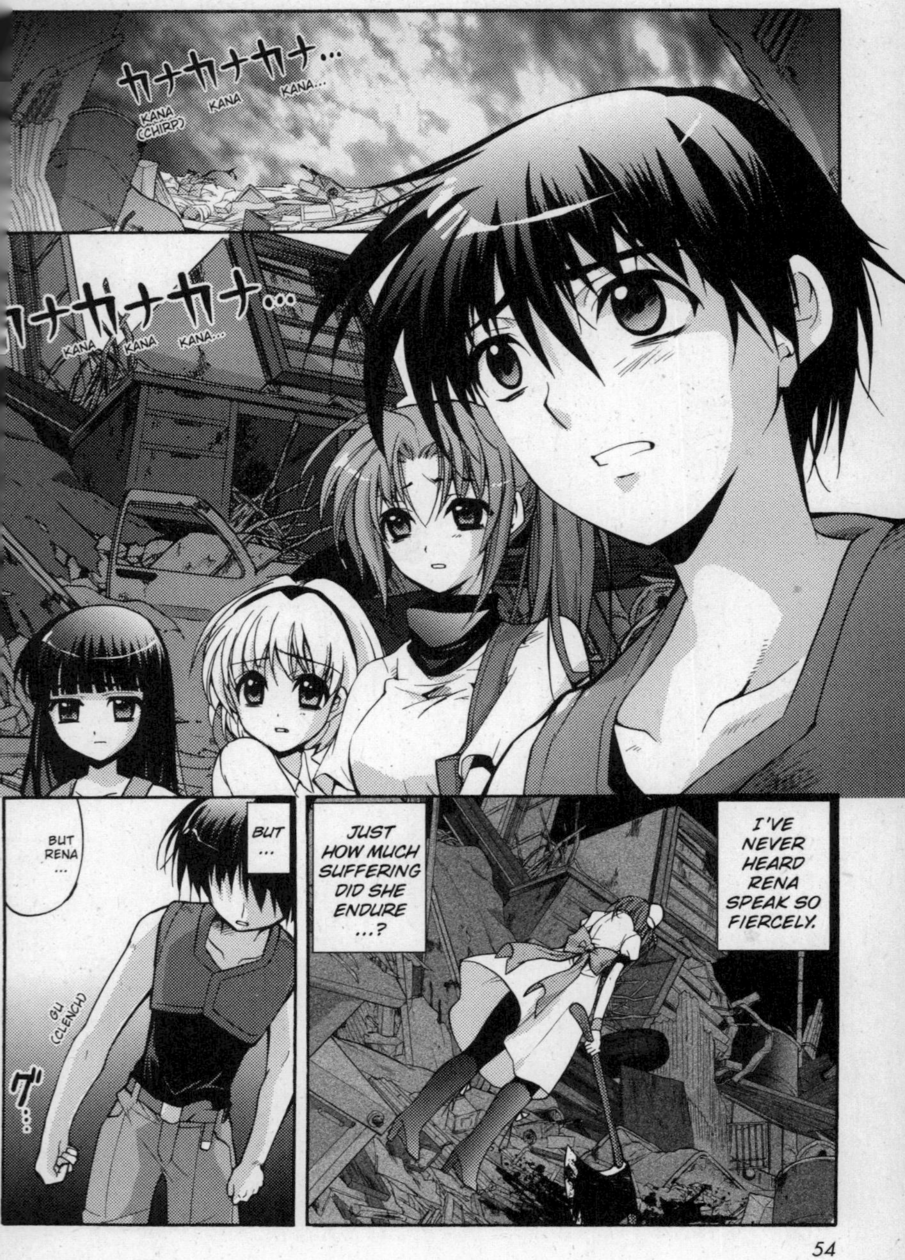
カナカナカナ…
KANA (CHIRP) KANA KANA...
カナガナカナ…
KANA KANA KANA...
I'VE NEVER HEARD RENA SPEAK SO FIERCELY.
JUST HOW MUCH SUFFERING DID SHE ENDURE ...?
BUT ...
BUT RENA ...
グ…
GU (CLENCH)

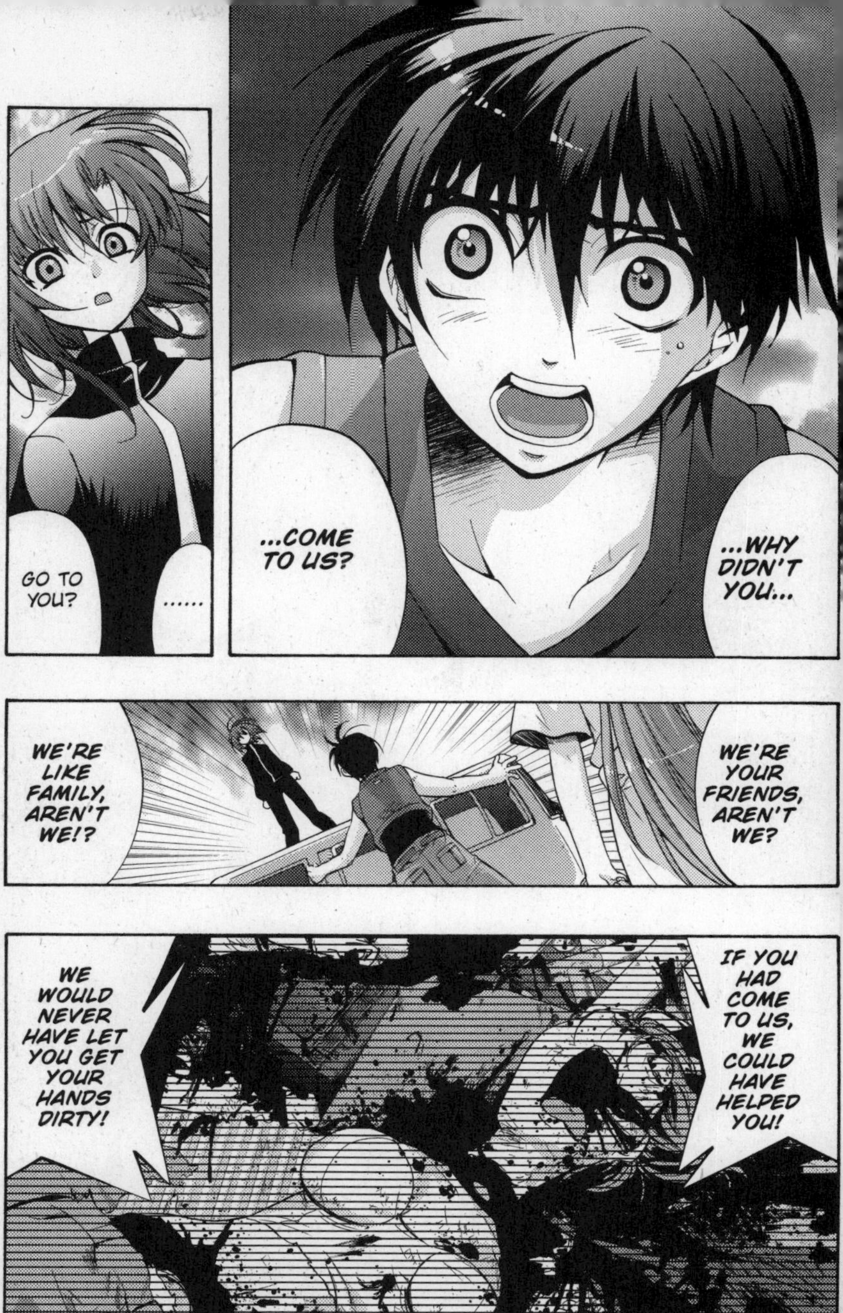
...WHY DIDN'T YOU...
...COME TO US?
......
GO TO YOU?
WE'RE YOUR FRIENDS, AREN'T WE?
WE'RE LIKE FAMILY, AREN'T WE!?
IF YOU HAD COME TO US, WE COULD HAVE HELPED YOU!
WE WOULD NEVER HAVE LET YOU GET YOUR HANDS DIRTY!

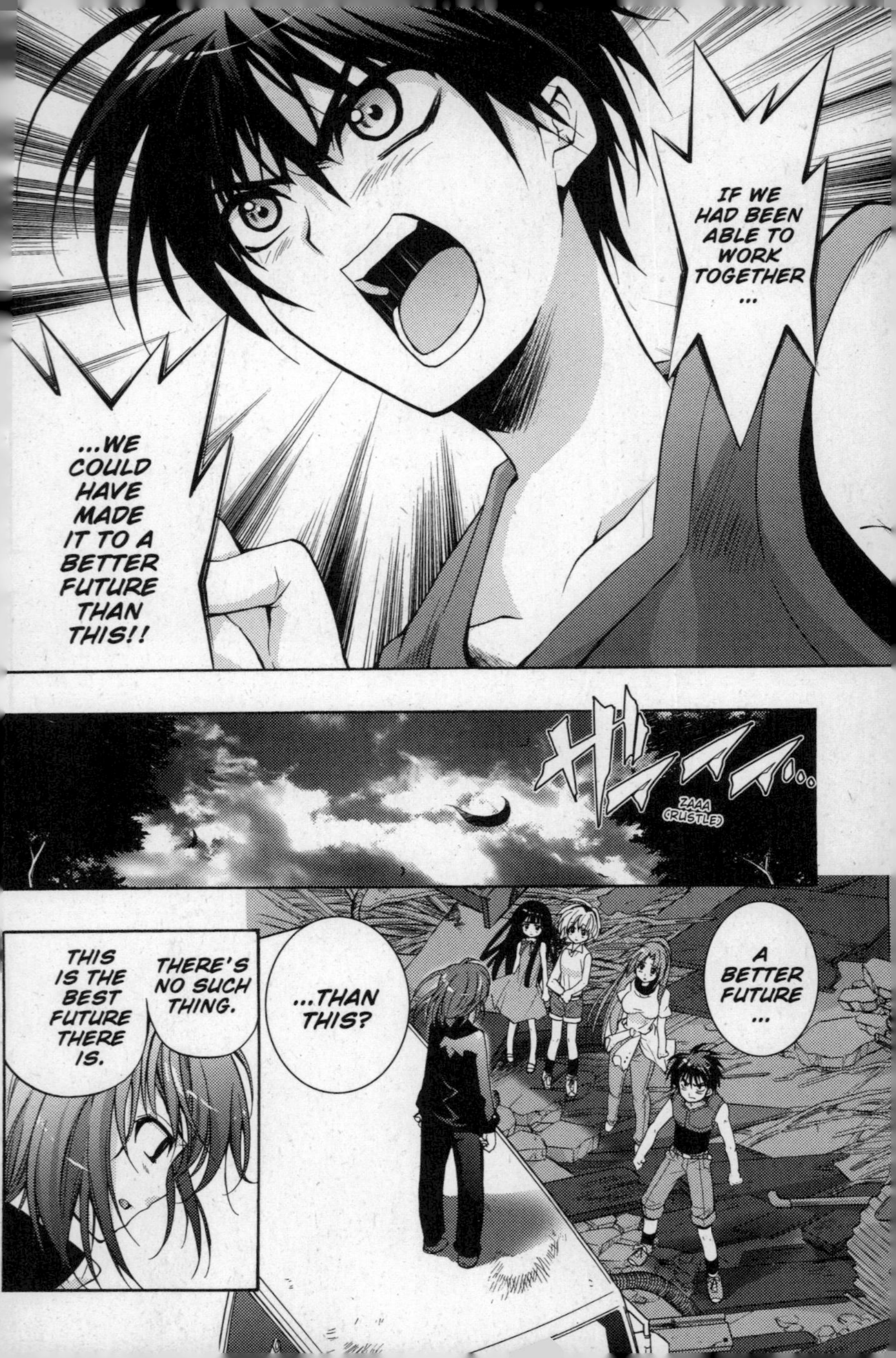
IF WE HAD BEEN ABLE TO WORK TOGETHER ...
...WE COULD HAVE MADE IT TO A BETTER FUTURE THAN THIS!!
ZAAA (RUSTLE)
A BETTER FUTURE ...
...THAN THIS?
THERE'S NO SUCH THING.
THIS IS THE BEST FUTURE THERE IS.

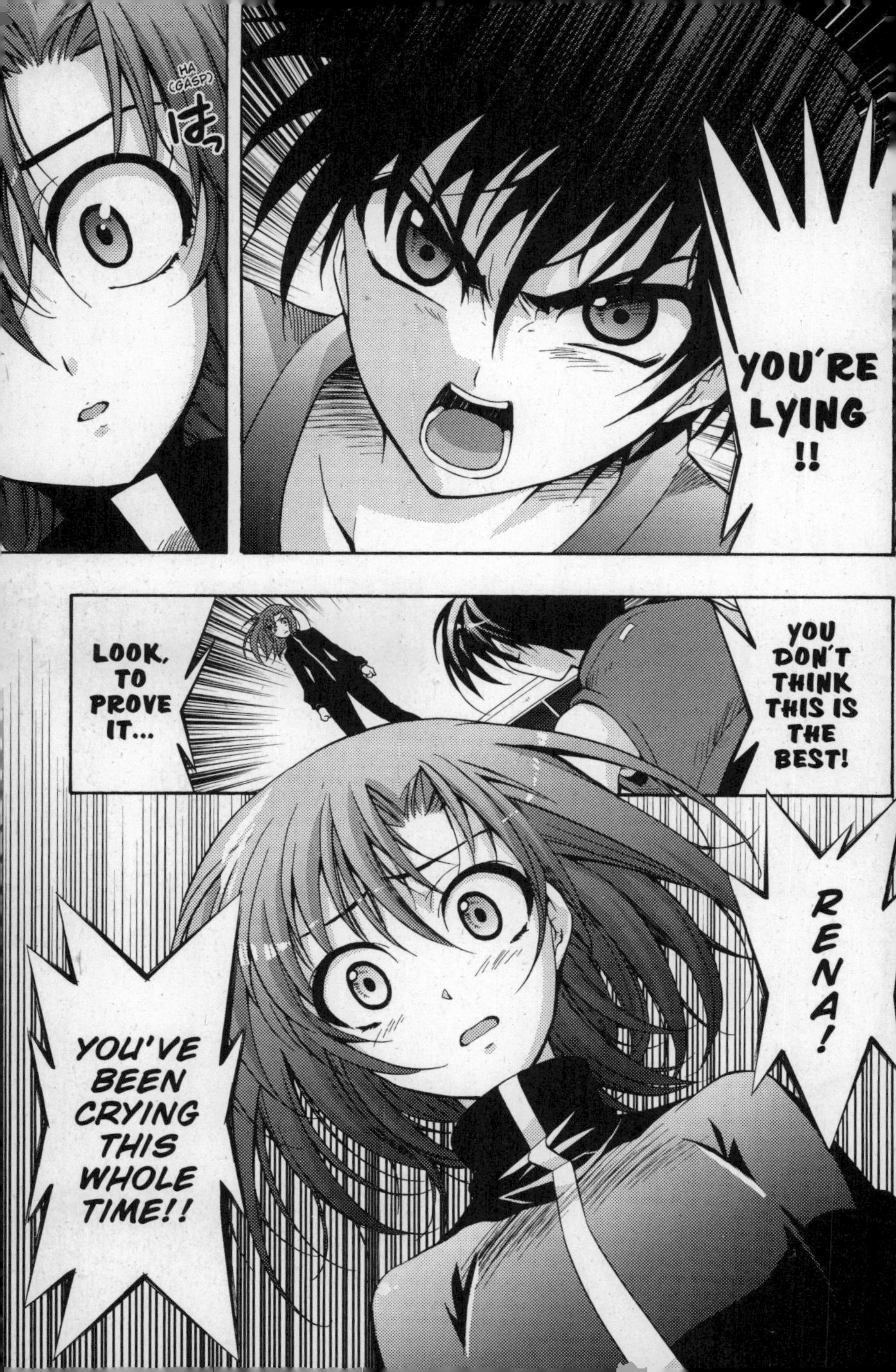
YOU'RE LYING !!
HA (GASP)
はっ
YOU DON'T THINK THIS IS THE BEST!
LOOK, TO PROVE IT...
RENA!
YOU'VE BEEN CRYING THIS WHOLE TIME!!

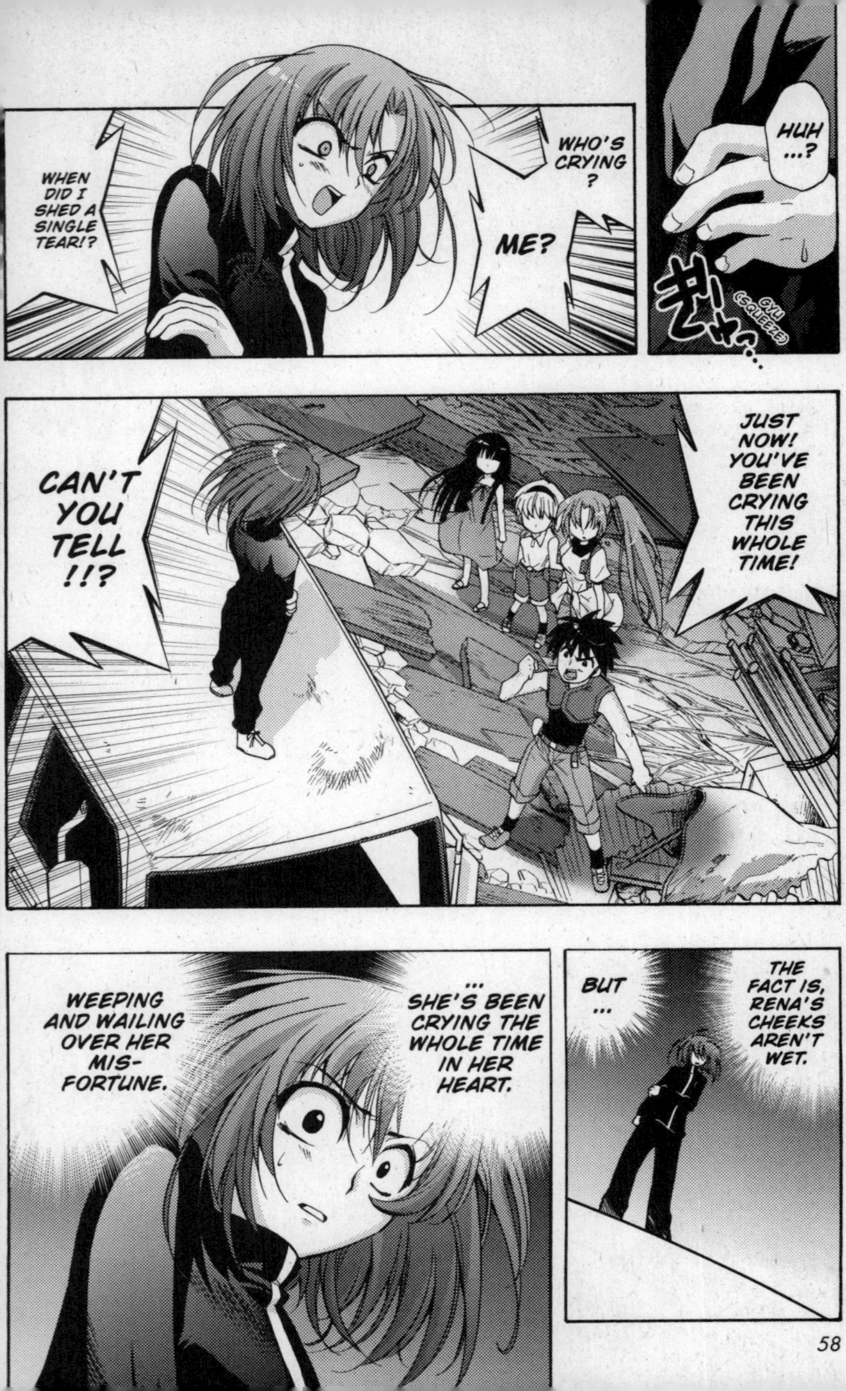
HUH ...?
ぎゅっ…
GYU (SQUEEZE)
WHO'S CRYING ?
ME?
WHEN DID I SHED A SINGLE TEAR!?
JUST NOW! YOU'VE BEEN CRYING THIS WHOLE TIME!
CAN'T YOU TELL !!?
THE FACT IS, RENA'S CHEEKS AREN'T WET.
BUT ...
... SHE'S BEEN CRYING THE WHOLE TIME IN HER HEART.
WEEPING AND WAILING OVER HER MIS-FORTUNE.

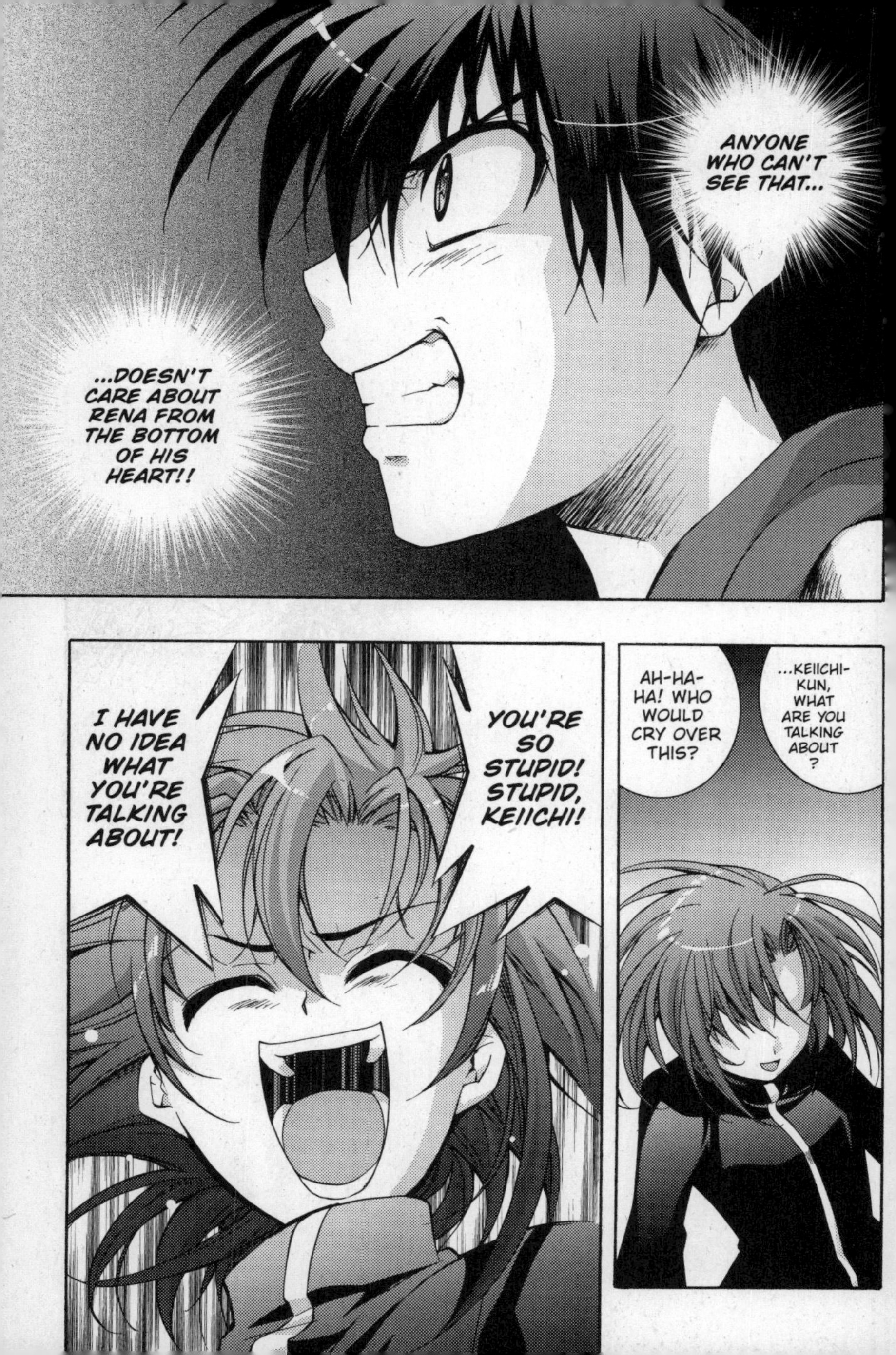
ANYONE WHO CAN'T SEE THAT...
...DOESN'T CARE ABOUT RENA FROM THE BOTTOM OF HIS HEART!!
...KEIICHI-KUN, WHAT ARE YOU TALKING ABOUT?
AH-HA-HA! WHO WOULD CRY OVER THIS?
YOU'RE SO STUPID! STUPID, KEIICHI!
I HAVE NO IDEA WHAT YOU'RE TALKING ABOUT!

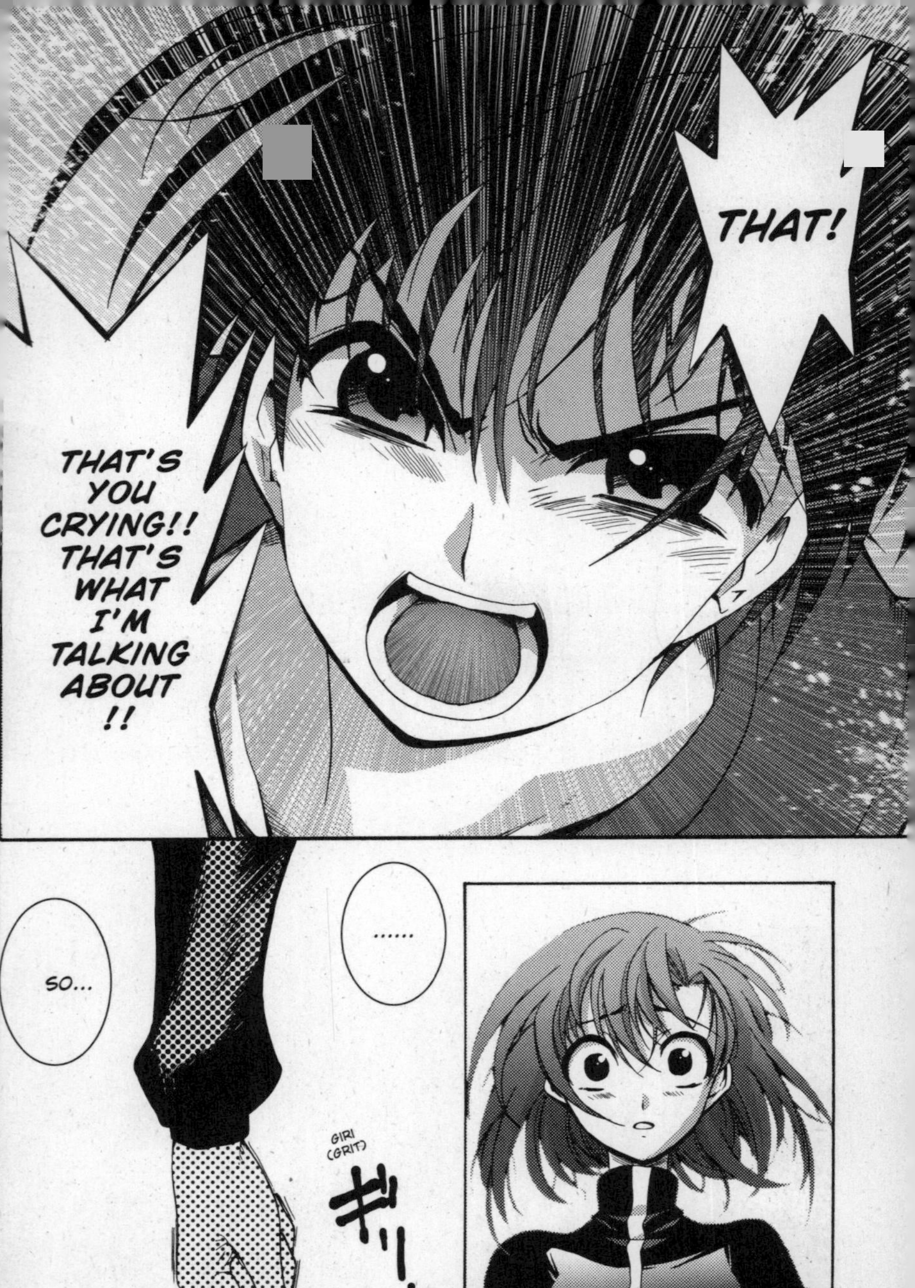
THAT!
THAT'S YOU CRYING!! THAT'S WHAT I'M TALKING ABOUT!!
......
SO...
GIRI (GRIT)

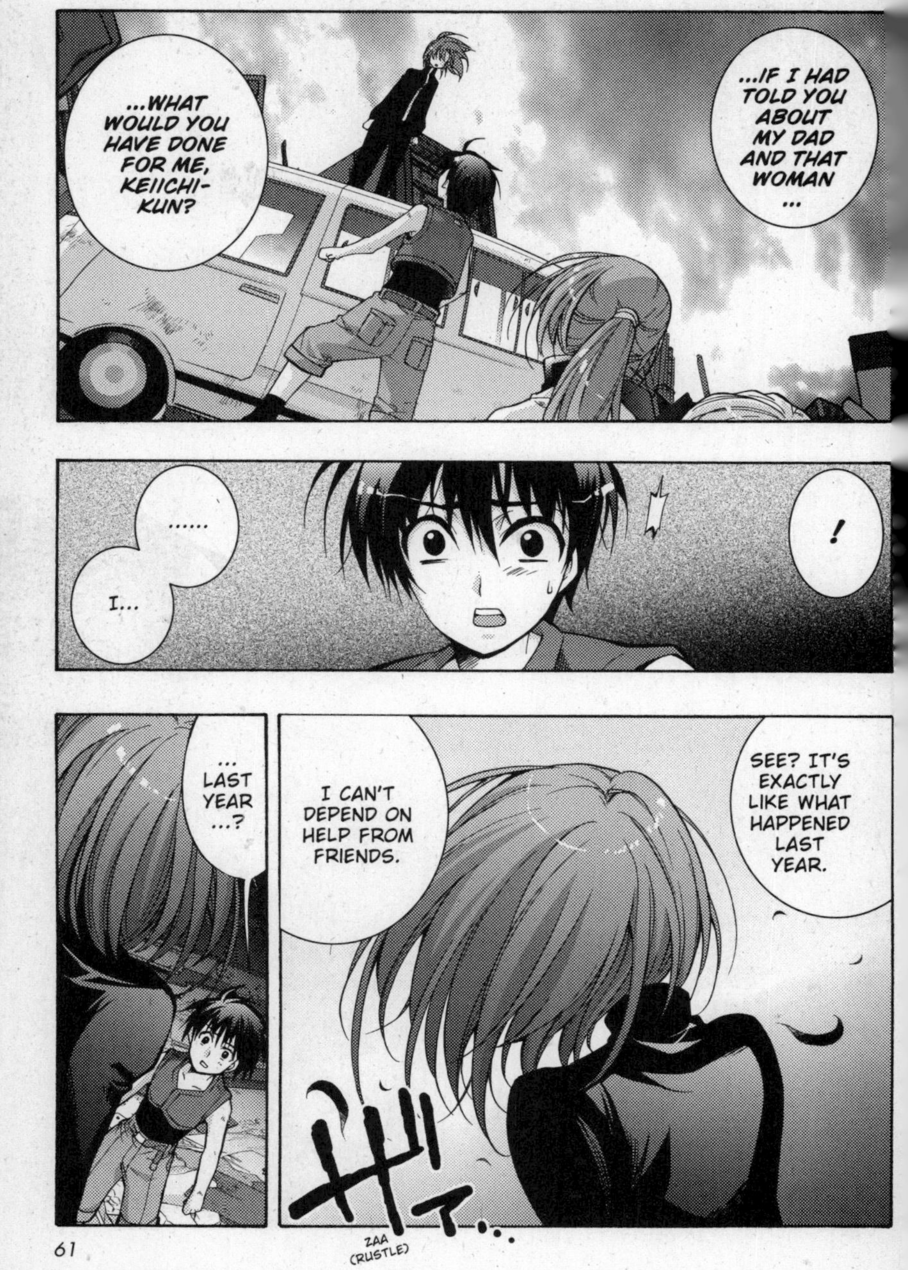
...IF I HAD TOLD YOU ABOUT MY DAD AND THAT WOMAN ...
...WHAT WOULD YOU HAVE DONE FOR ME, KEIICHI-KUN?
!
......
I...
SEE? IT'S EXACTLY LIKE WHAT HAPPENED LAST YEAR.
I CAN'T DEPEND ON HELP FROM FRIENDS.
ZAA (RUSTLE)
... LAST YEAR ...?

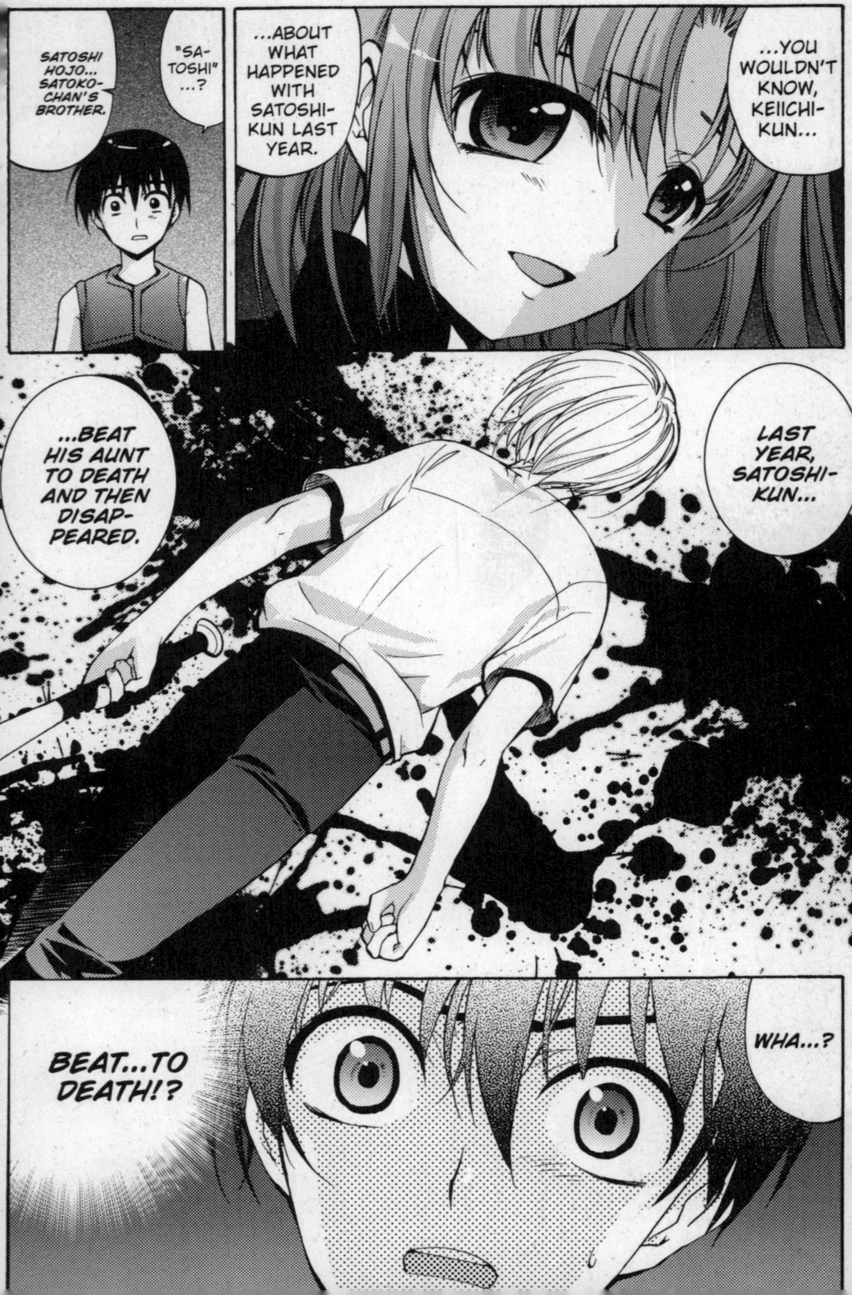
...YOU WOULDN'T KNOW, KEIICHI-KUN...
...ABOUT WHAT HAPPENED WITH SATOSHI-KUN LAST YEAR.
"SA-TOSHI" ...?
SATOSHI HOJO... SATOKO-CHAN'S BROTHER.
LAST YEAR, SATOSHI-KUN...
...BEAT HIS AUNT TO DEATH AND THEN DISAPPEARED.
WHA...?
BEAT...TO DEATH!?

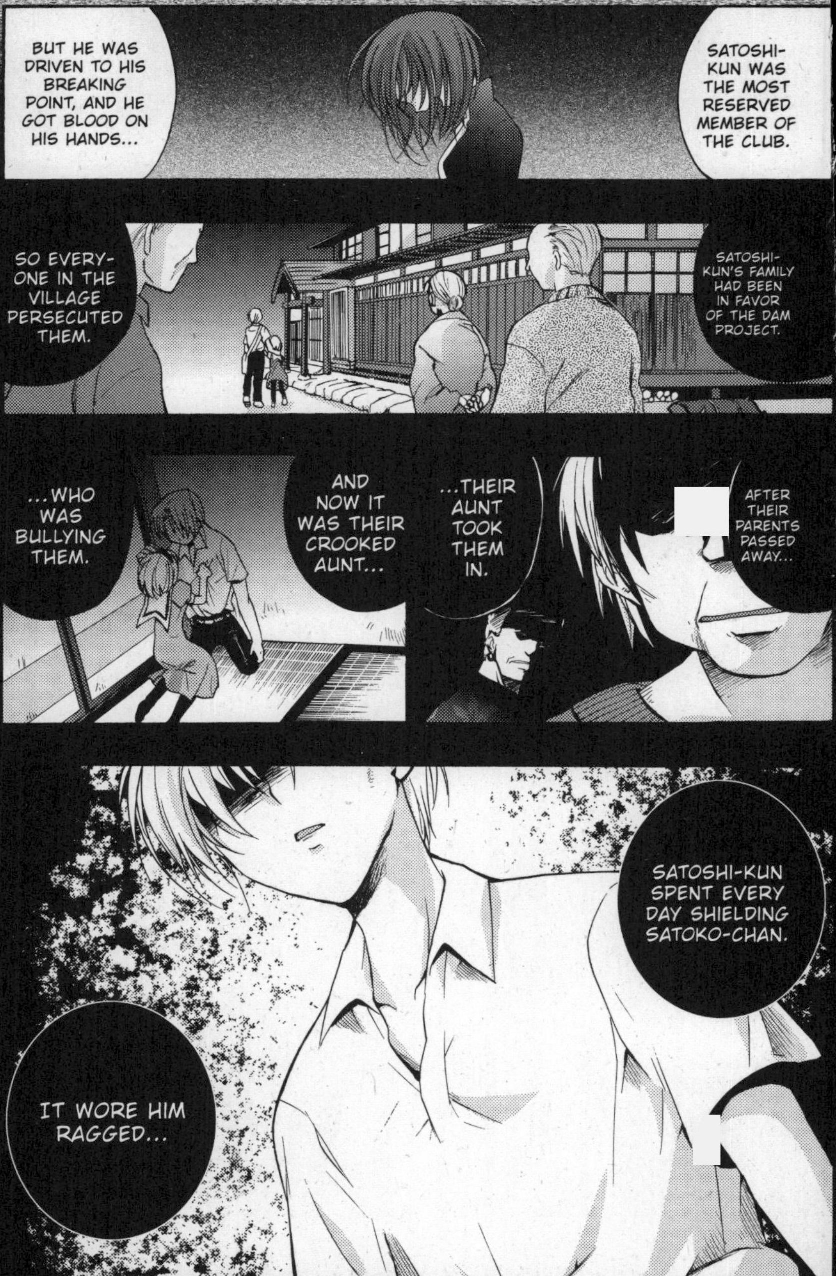
SATOSHI-KUN WAS THE MOST RESERVED MEMBER OF THE CLUB.
BUT HE WAS DRIVEN TO HIS BREAKING POINT, AND HE GOT BLOOD ON HIS HANDS...
SATOSHI-KUN'S FAMILY HAD BEEN IN FAVOR OF THE DAM PROJECT.
SO EVERY-ONE IN THE VILLAGE PERSECUTED THEM.
AFTER THEIR PARENTS PASSED AWAY...
...THEIR AUNT TOOK THEM IN.
AND NOW IT WAS THEIR CROOKED AUNT...
...WHO WAS BULLYING THEM.
SATOSHI-KUN SPENT EVERY DAY SHIELDING SATOKO-CHAN.
IT WORE HIM RAGGED...

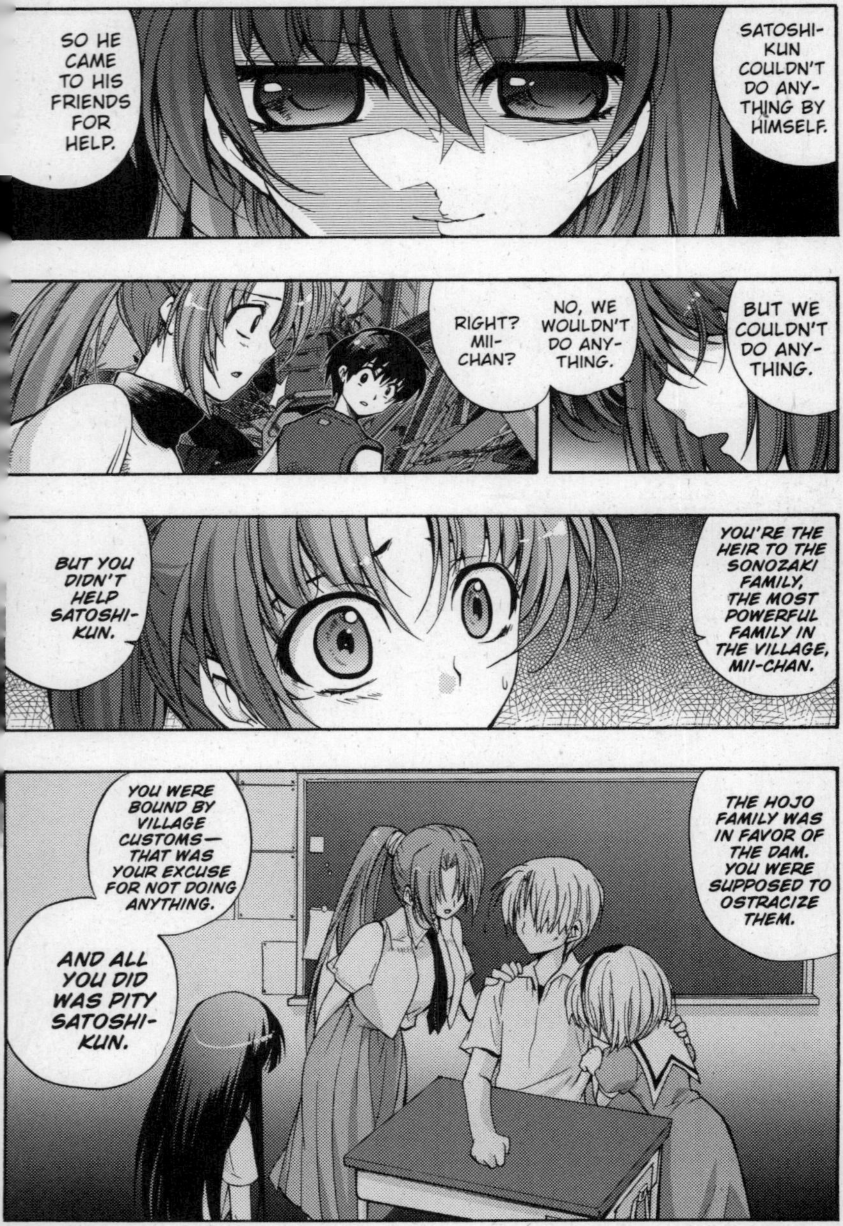

SATOSHI-KUN COULDN'T DO ANY-THING BY HIMSELF.
SO HE CAME TO HIS FRIENDS FOR HELP.
BUT WE COULDN'T DO ANY-THING.
NO, WE WOULDN'T DO ANY-THING.
RIGHT? MII-CHAN?
YOU'RE THE HEIR TO THE SONOZAKI FAMILY, THE MOST POWERFUL FAMILY IN THE VILLAGE, MII-CHAN.
BUT YOU DIDN'T HELP SATOSHI-KUN.
THE HOJO FAMILY WAS IN FAVOR OF THE DAM. YOU WERE SUPPOSED TO OSTRACIZE THEM.
YOU WERE BOUND BY VILLAGE CUSTOMS—THAT WAS YOUR EXCUSE FOR NOT DOING ANYTHING.
AND ALL YOU DID WAS PITY SATOSHI-KUN.

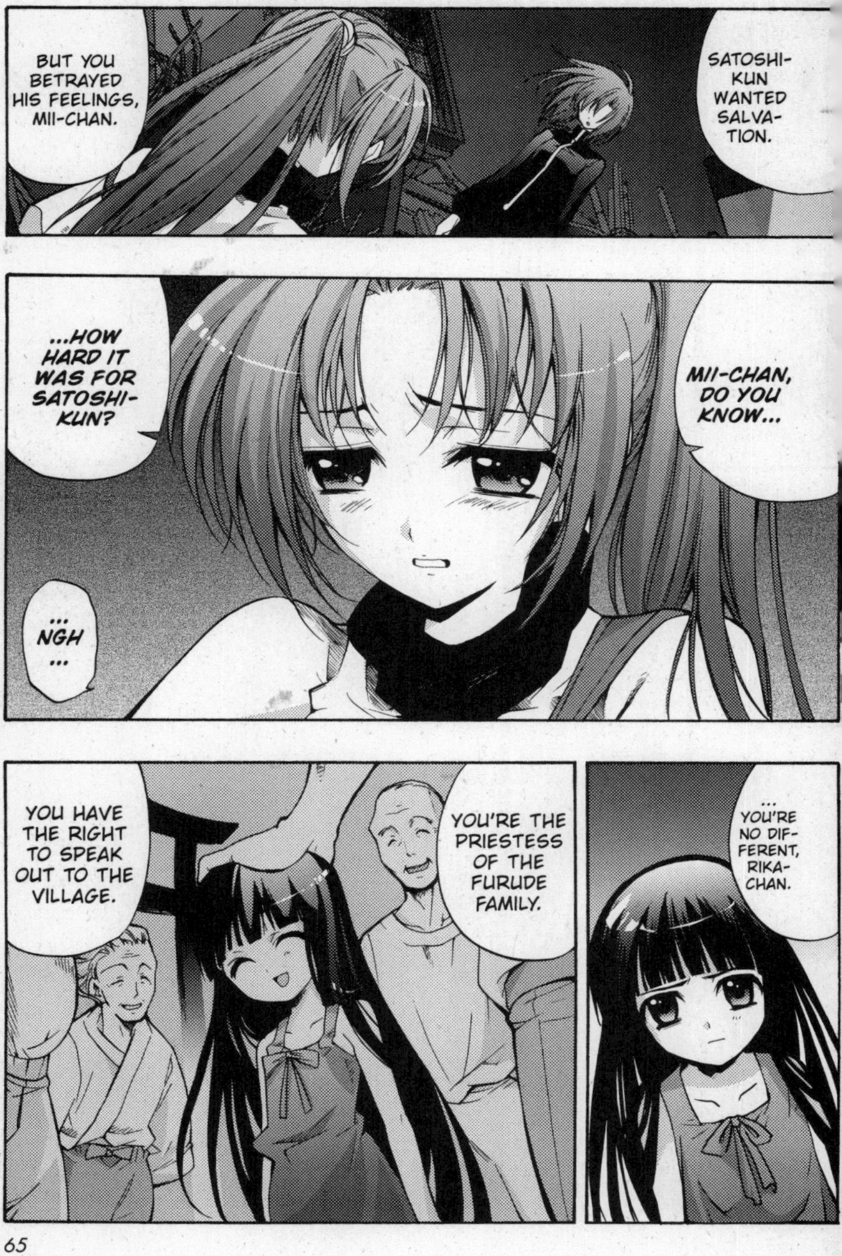
SATOSHI-KUN WANTED SALVATION.
BUT YOU BETRAYED HIS FEELINGS, MII-CHAN.
MII-CHAN, DO YOU KNOW...
...HOW HARD IT WAS FOR SATOSHI-KUN?
...NGH...
...YOU'RE NO DIFFERENT, RIKA-CHAN.
YOU'RE THE PRIESTESS OF THE FURUDE FAMILY.
YOU HAVE THE RIGHT TO SPEAK OUT TO THE VILLAGE.

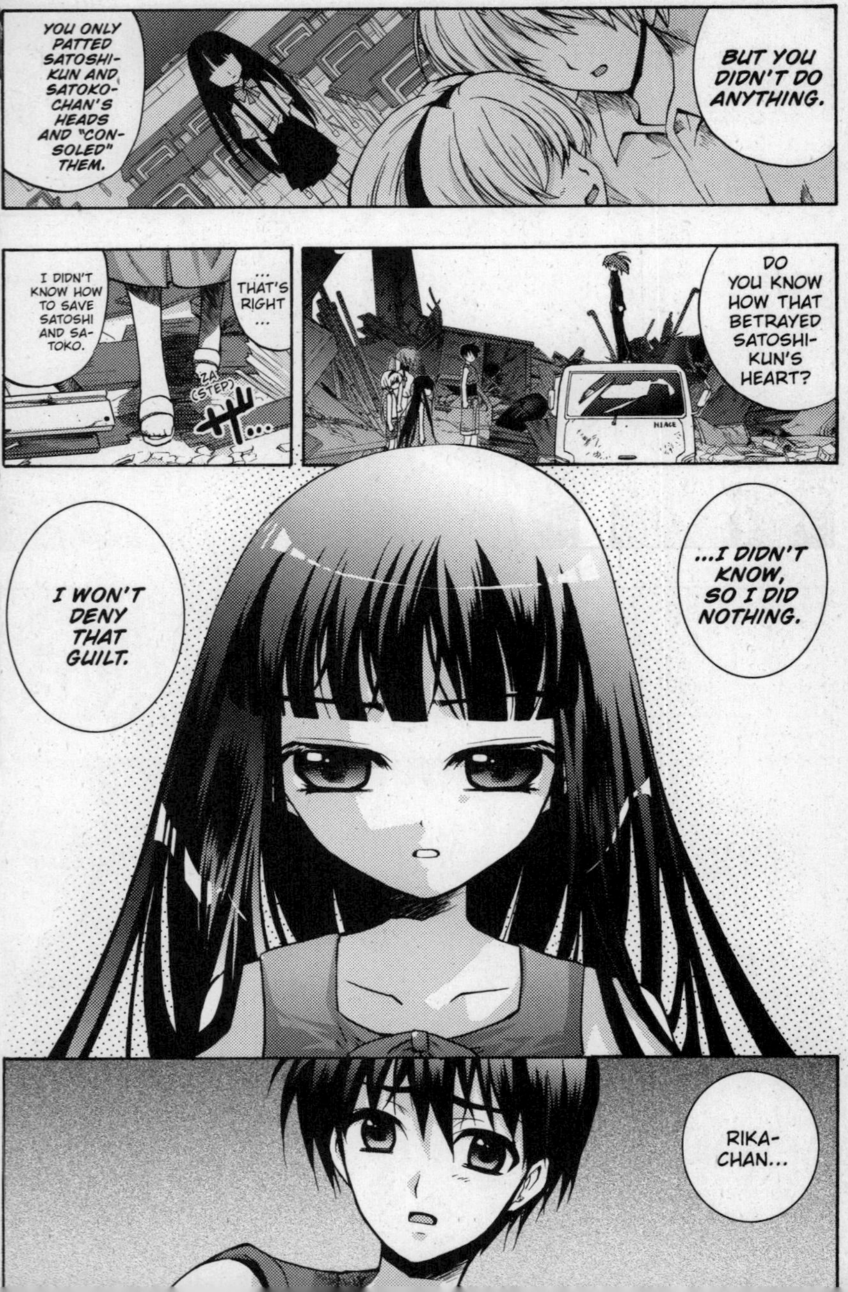
BUT YOU DIDN'T DO ANYTHING.
YOU ONLY PATTED SATOSHI-KUN AND SATOKO-CHAN'S HEADS AND "CONSOLED" THEM.
DO YOU KNOW HOW THAT BETRAYED SATOSHI-KUN'S HEART?
... THAT'S RIGHT ...
I DIDN'T KNOW HOW TO SAVE SATOSHI AND SA-TOKO.
ZA (STEP)
...I DIDN'T KNOW, SO I DID NOTHING.
I WON'T DENY THAT GUILT.
RIKA-CHAN...

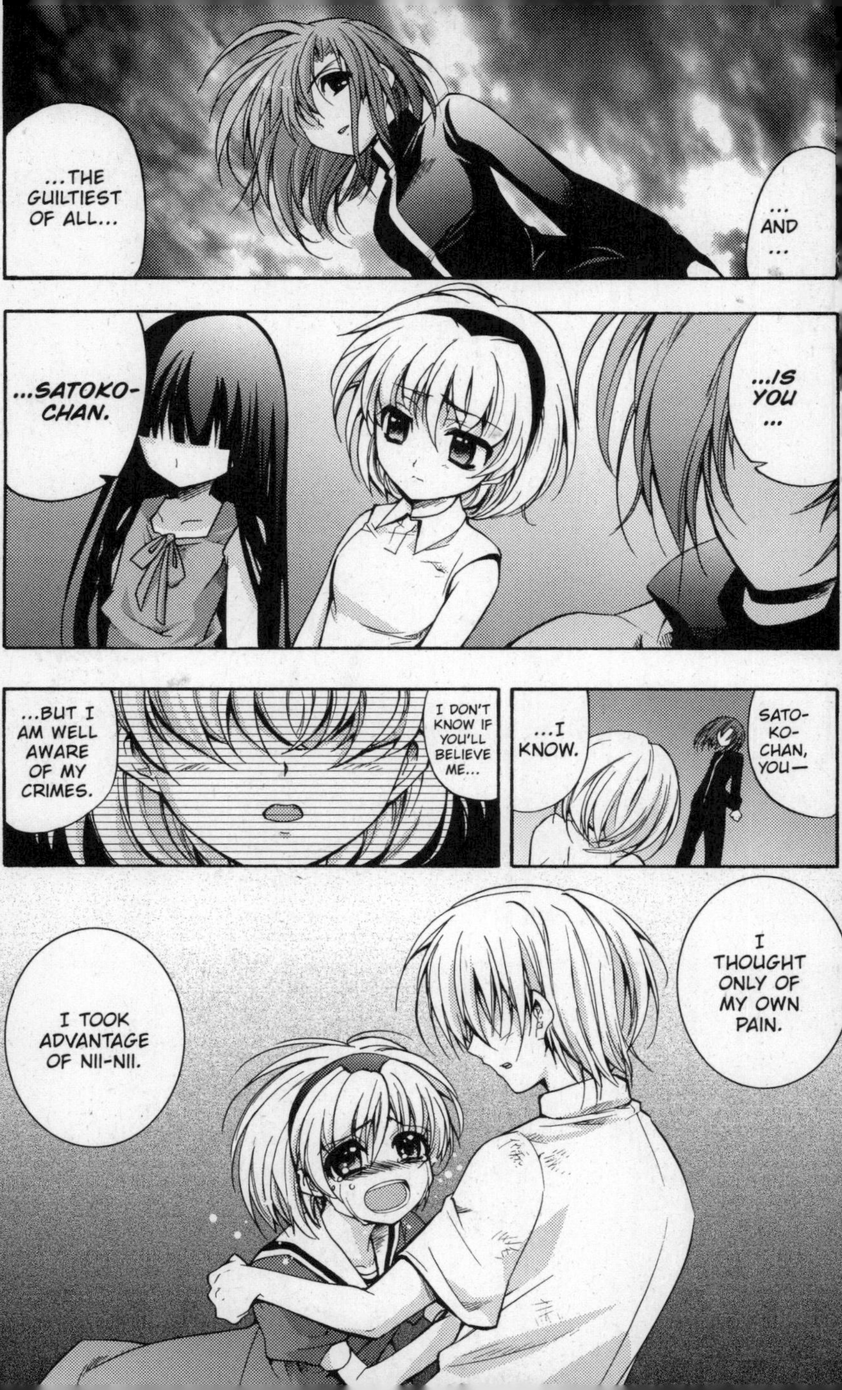
... AND ...
...THE GUILTIEST OF ALL...
...IS YOU ...
...SATOKO-CHAN.
SATO-KO-CHAN, YOU—
...I KNOW.
I DON'T KNOW IF YOU'LL BELIEVE ME...
...BUT I AM WELL AWARE OF MY CRIMES.
I THOUGHT ONLY OF MY OWN PAIN.
I TOOK ADVANTAGE OF NII-NII.

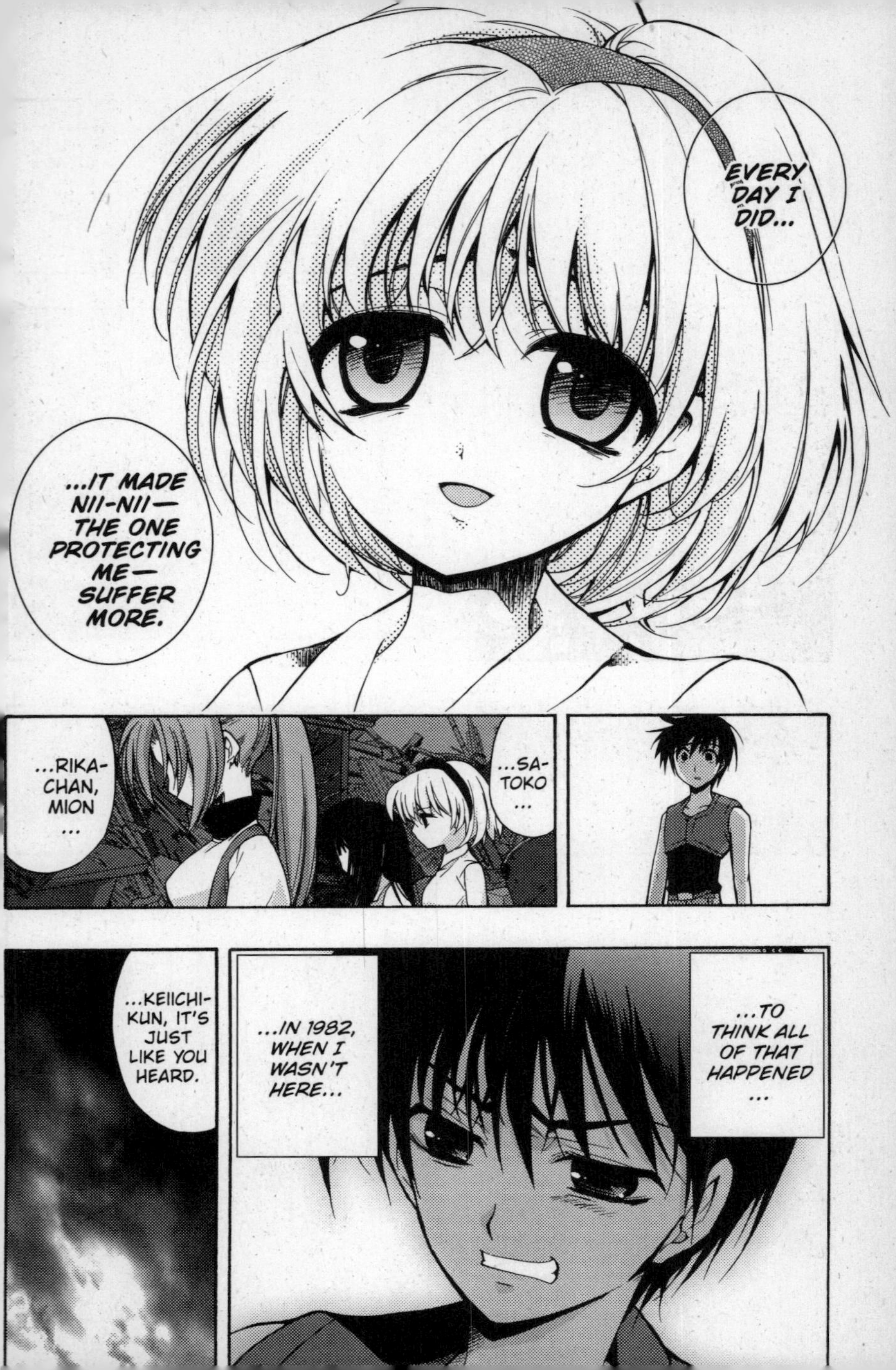
EVERY DAY I DID...
...IT MADE NII-NII—THE ONE PROTECTING ME—SUFFER MORE.
...SATOKO...
...RIKA-CHAN, MION...
...TO THINK ALL OF THAT HAPPENED...
...IN 1982, WHEN I WASN'T HERE...
...KEIICHI-KUN, IT'S JUST LIKE YOU HEARD.

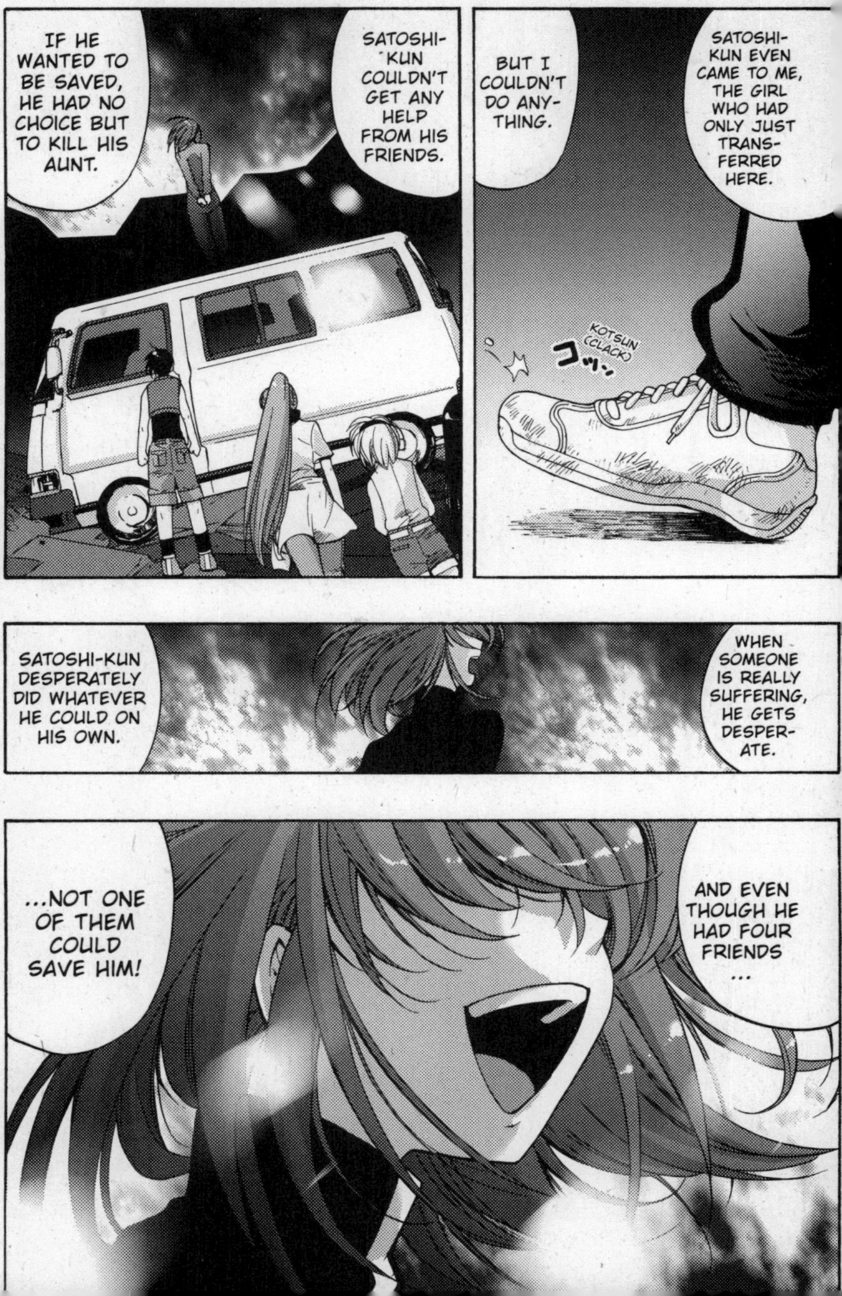
SATOSHI-KUN EVEN CAME TO ME, THE GIRL WHO HAD ONLY JUST TRANSFERRED HERE.
BUT I COULDN'T DO ANYTHING.
KOTSUN (CLACK)
コッ
SATOSHI-KUN COULDN'T GET ANY HELP FROM HIS FRIENDS.
IF HE WANTED TO BE SAVED, HE HAD NO CHOICE BUT TO KILL HIS AUNT.
WHEN SOMEONE IS REALLY SUFFERING, HE GETS DESPERATE.
SATOSHI-KUN DESPERATELY DID WHATEVER HE COULD ON HIS OWN.
AND EVEN THOUGH HE HAD FOUR FRIENDS...
...NOT ONE OF THEM COULD SAVE HIM!

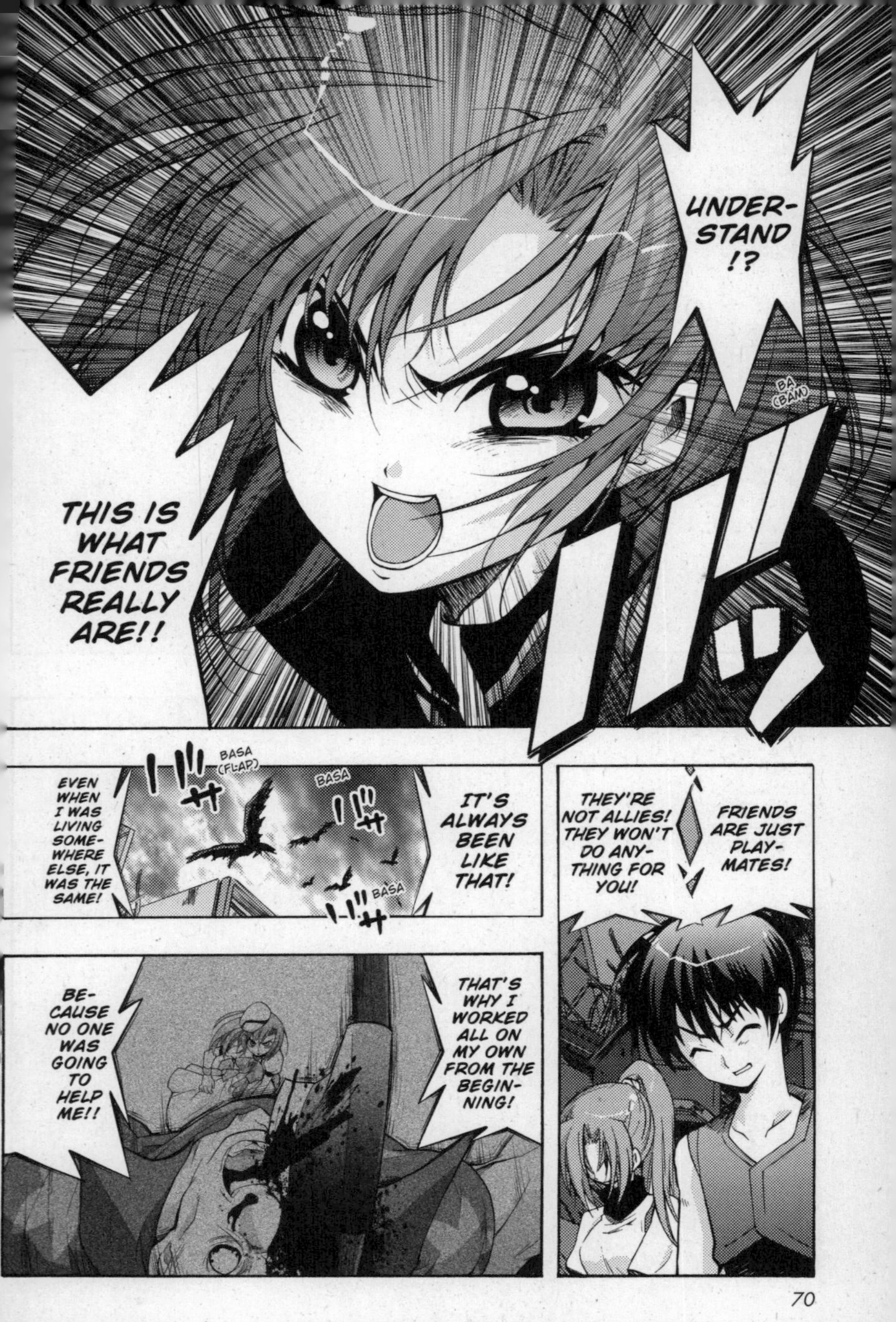
UNDER-STAND!?
BA (BAM)
THIS IS WHAT FRIENDS REALLY ARE!!
FRIENDS ARE JUST PLAY-MATES!
THEY'RE NOT ALLIES! THEY WON'T DO ANY-THING FOR YOU!
IT'S ALWAYS BEEN LIKE THAT!
BASA (FLAP)
BASA
BASA
EVEN WHEN I WAS LIVING SOME-WHERE ELSE, IT WAS THE SAME!
THAT'S WHY I WORKED ALL ON MY OWN FROM THE BEGIN-NING!
BE-CAUSE NO ONE WAS GOING TO HELP ME!!

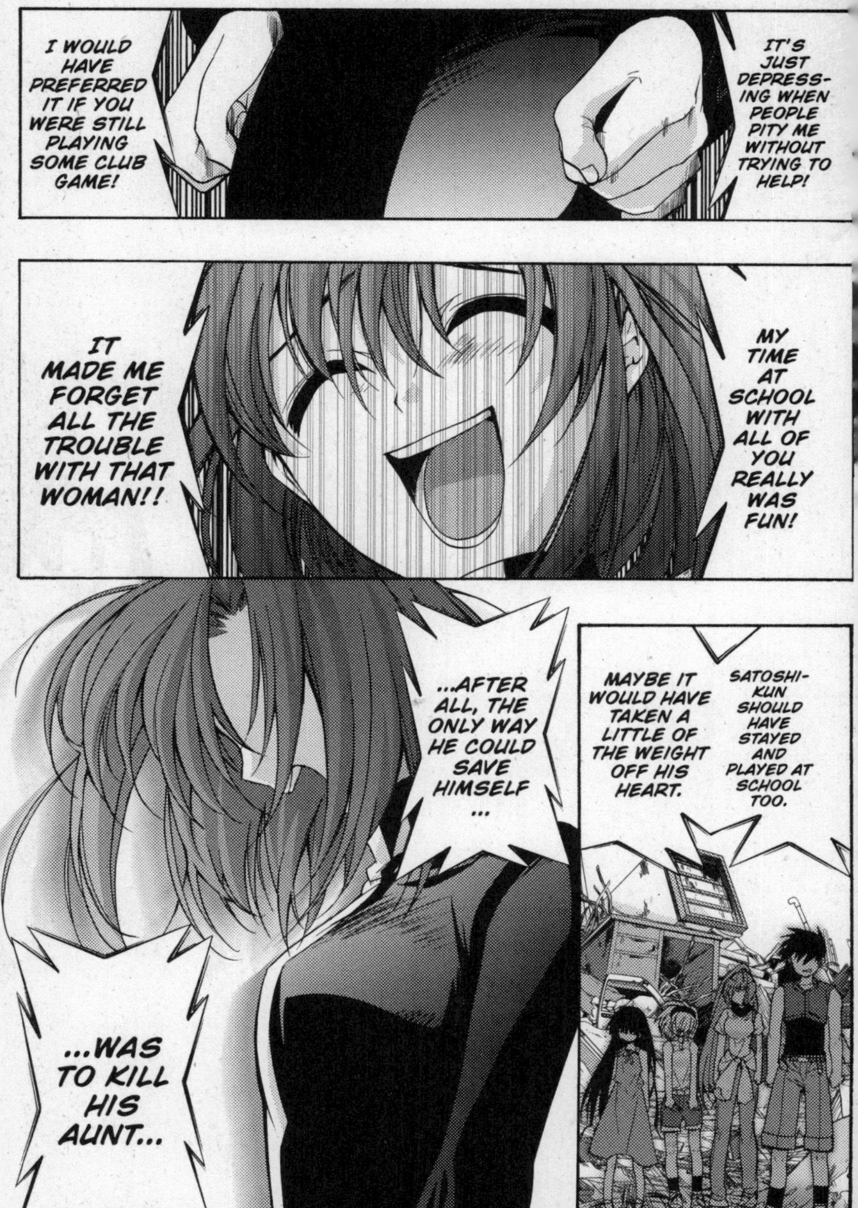
IT'S JUST DEPRESSING WHEN PEOPLE PITY ME WITHOUT TRYING TO HELP!
I WOULD HAVE PREFERRED IT IF YOU WERE STILL PLAYING SOME CLUB GAME!
MY TIME AT SCHOOL WITH ALL OF YOU REALLY WAS FUN!
IT MADE ME FORGET ALL THE TROUBLE WITH THAT WOMAN!!
SATOSHI-KUN SHOULD HAVE STAYED AND PLAYED AT SCHOOL TOO.
MAYBE IT WOULD HAVE TAKEN A LITTLE OF THE WEIGHT OFF HIS HEART.
...AFTER ALL, THE ONLY WAY HE COULD SAVE HIMSELF ...
...WAS TO KILL HIS AUNT...

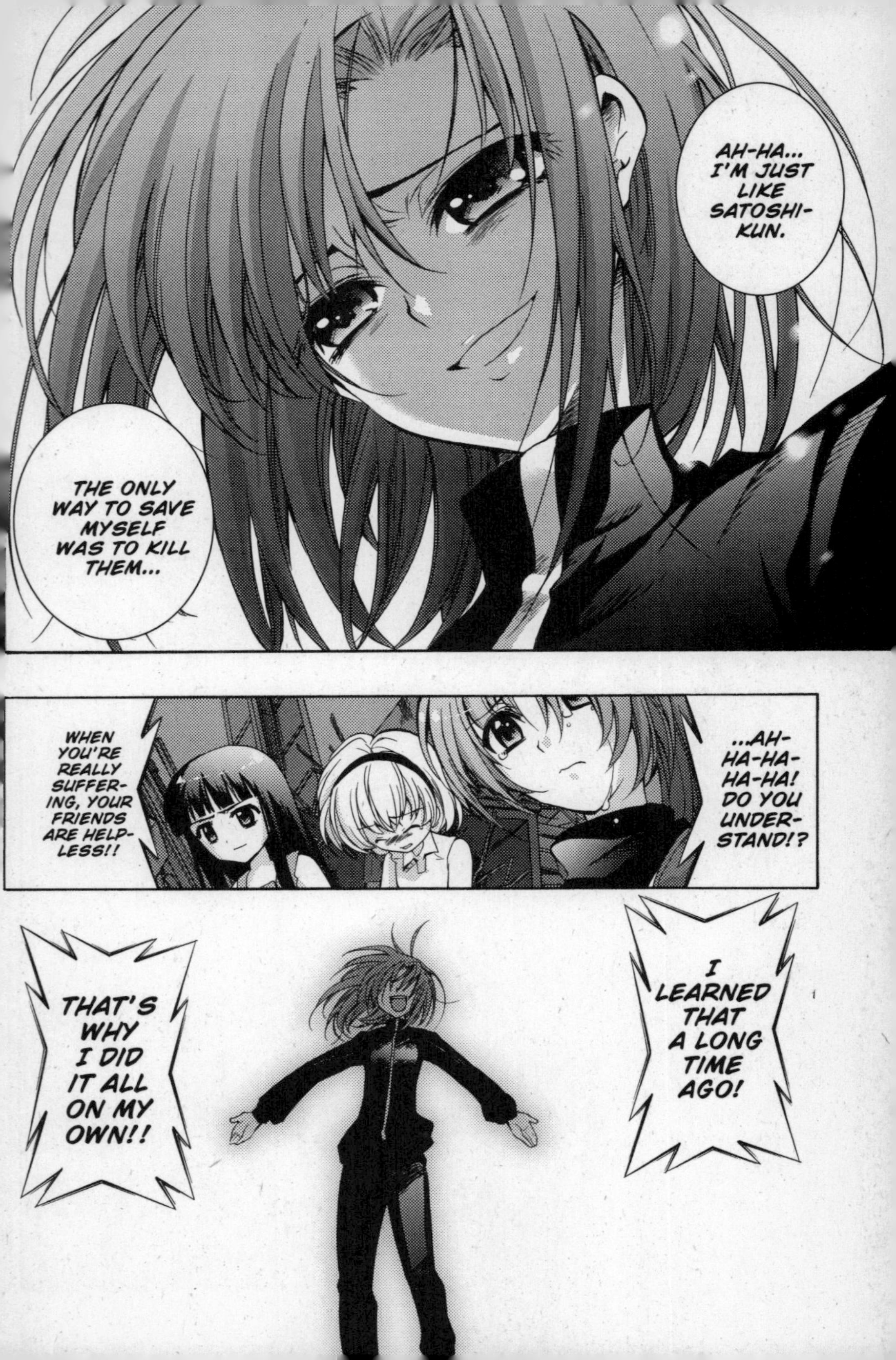
AH-HA... I'M JUST LIKE SATOSHI-KUN.
THE ONLY WAY TO SAVE MYSELF WAS TO KILL THEM...
...AH-HA-HA-HA-HA! DO YOU UNDERSTAND!?
WHEN YOU'RE REALLY SUFFERING, YOUR FRIENDS ARE HELPLESS!!
I LEARNED THAT A LONG TIME AGO!
THAT'S WHY I DID IT ALL ON MY OWN!!

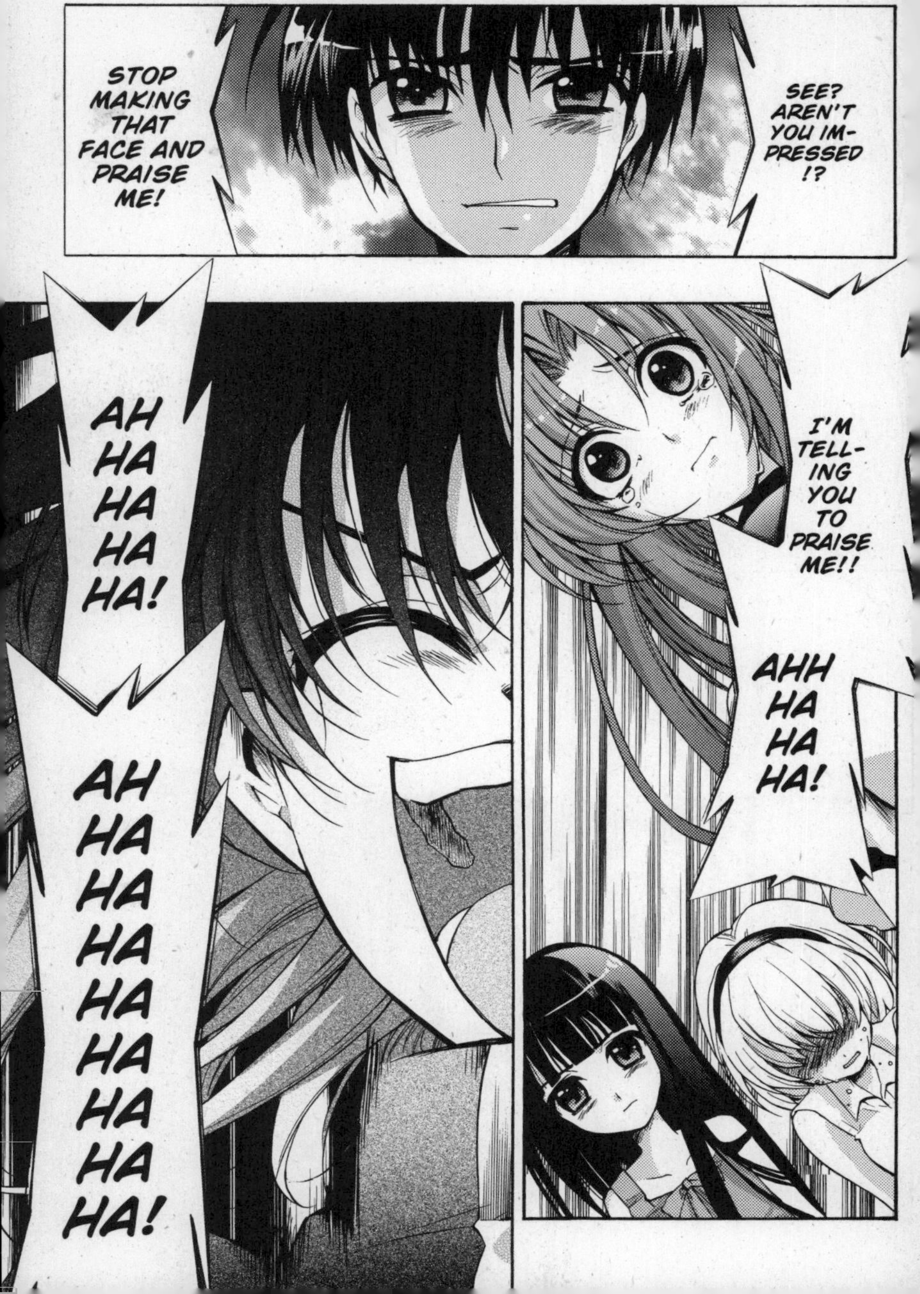
SEE? AREN'T YOU IM-PRESSED !?
STOP MAKING THAT FACE AND PRAISE ME!
I'M TELLING YOU TO PRAISE ME!!
AHH HA HA HA!
AH HA HA HA HA!
AH HA HA HA HA HA HA HA HA HA!

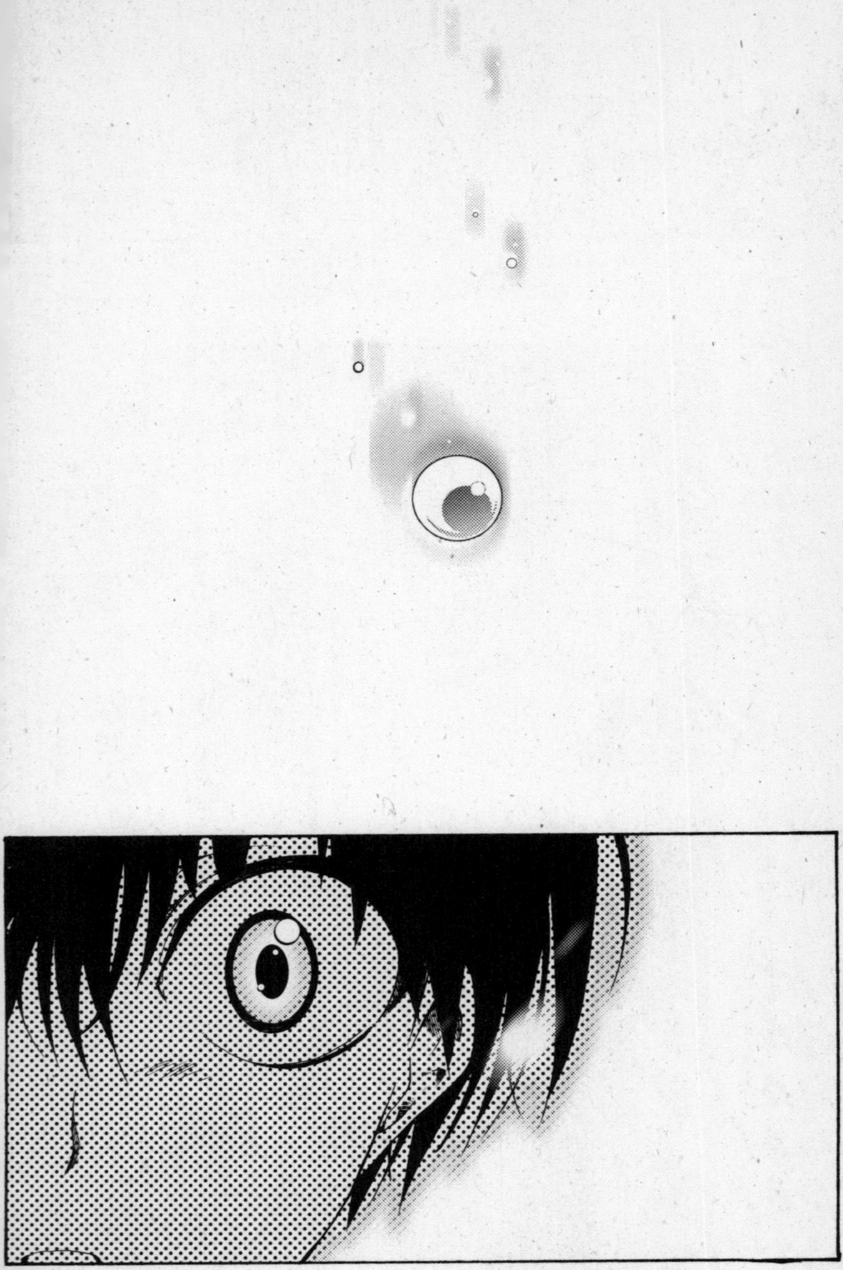

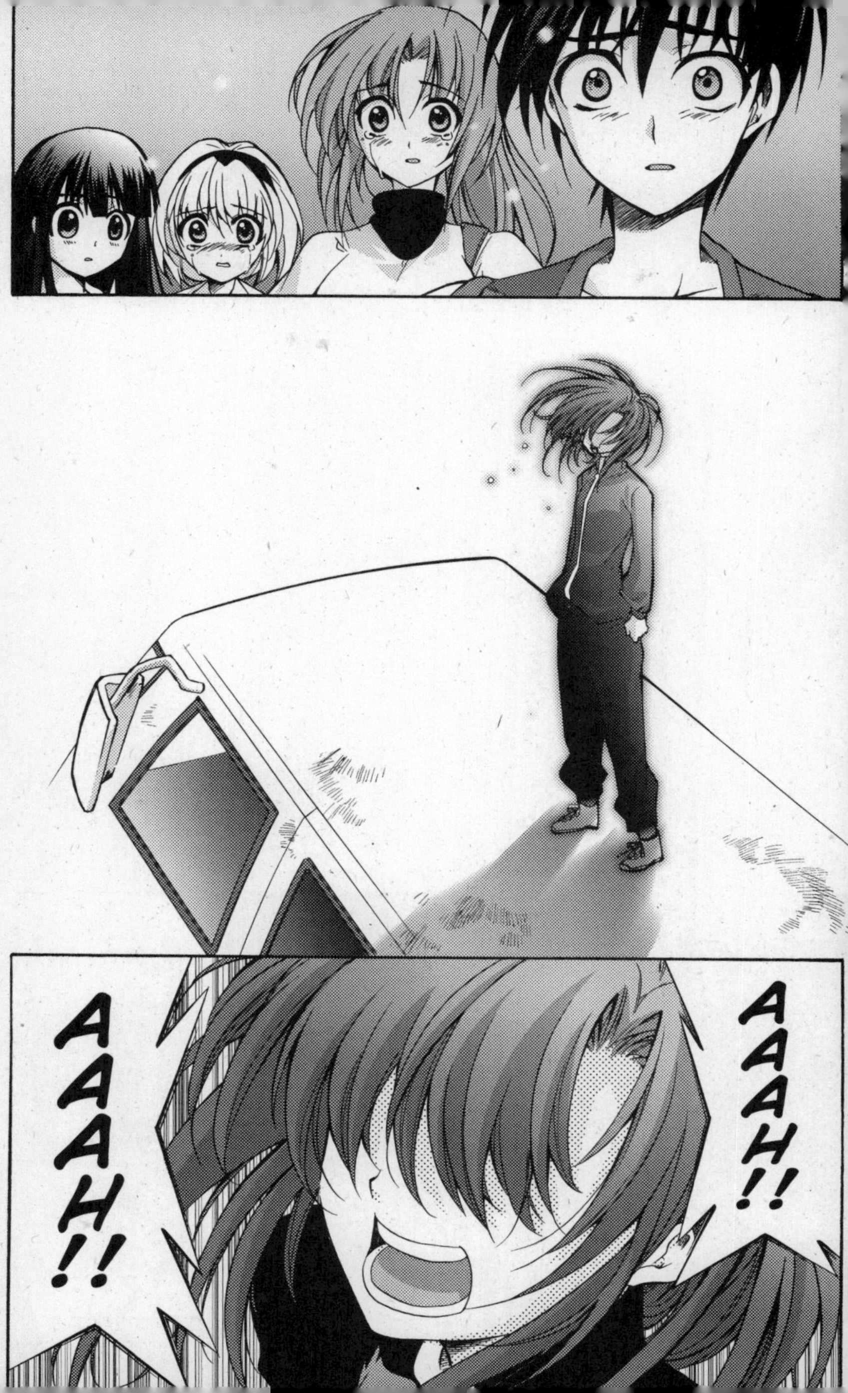
AAAH!!
AAAH!!

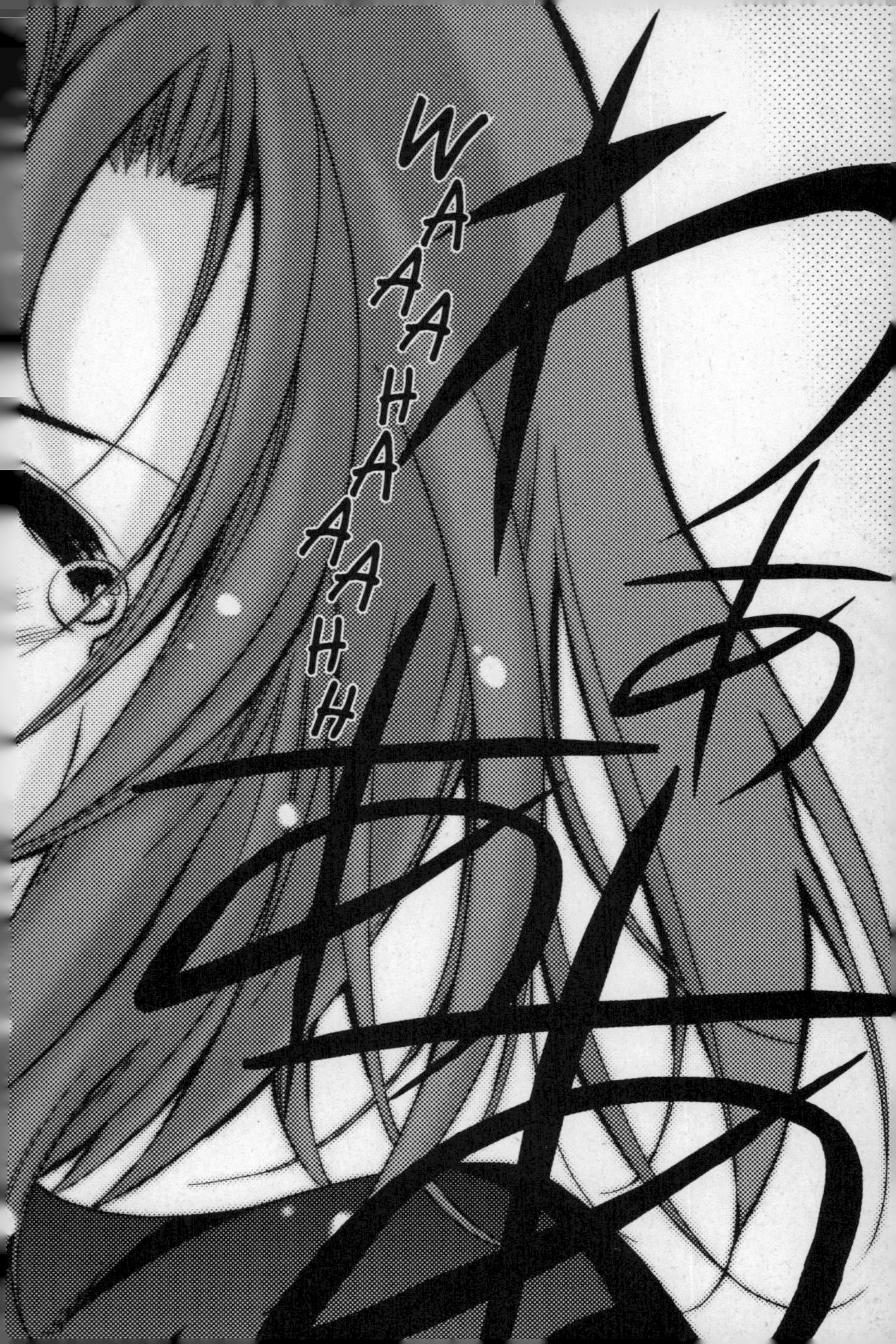
WAAAHAAAAHH

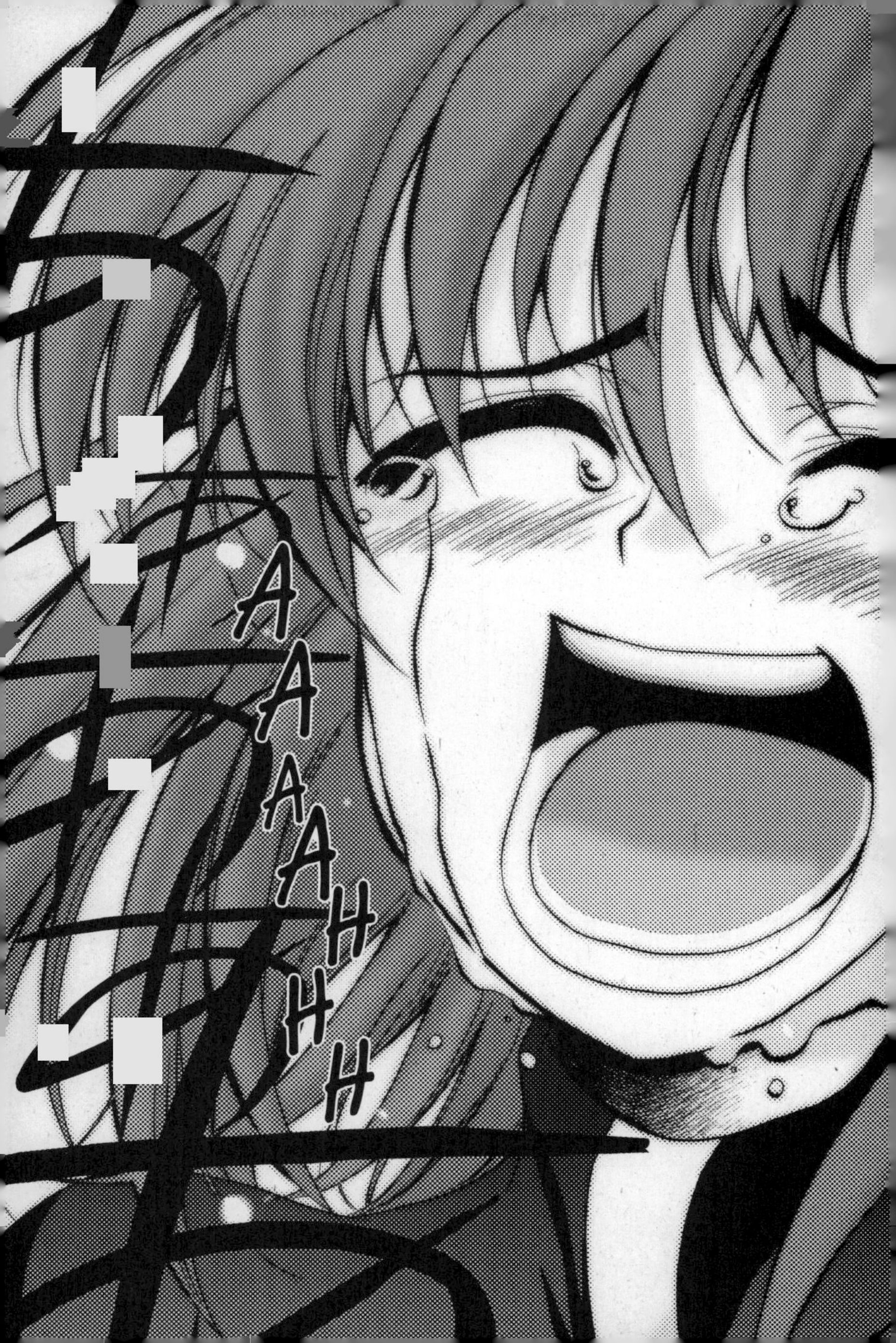
AAAAAHHH

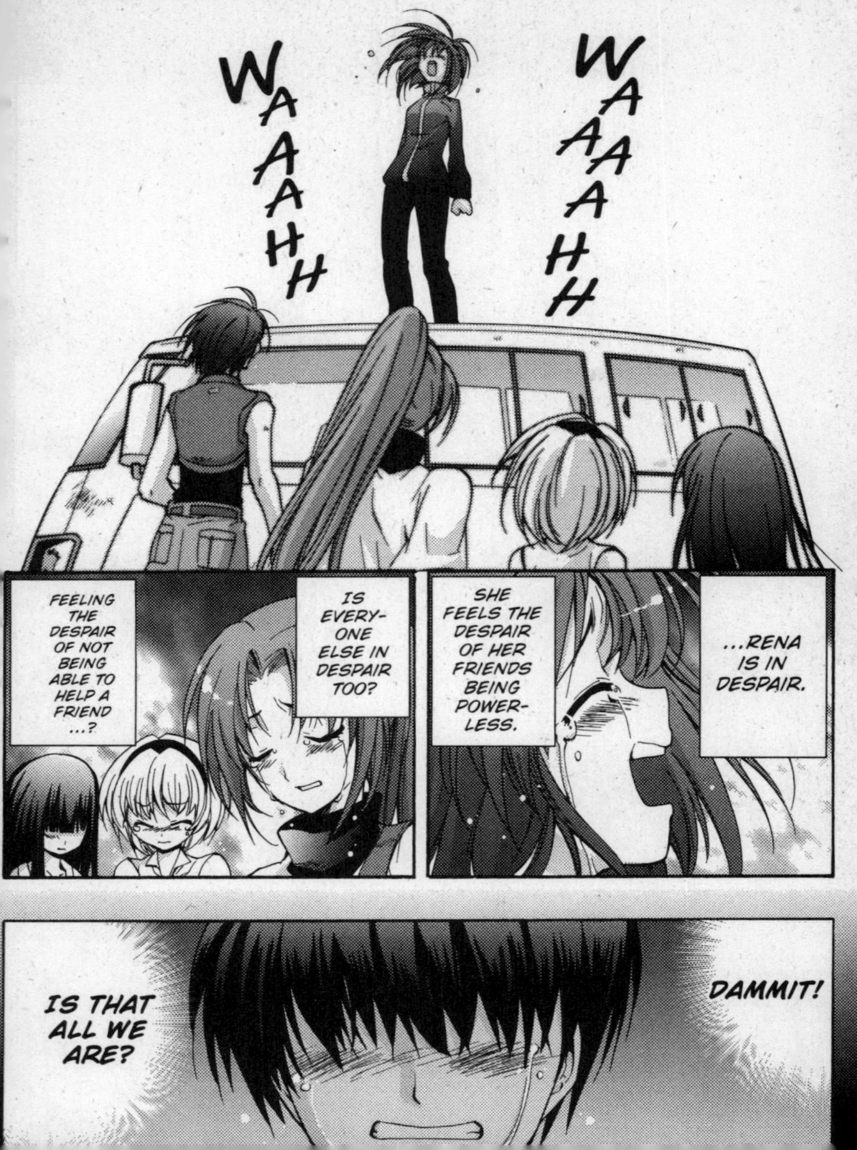
WAAAAHH
WAAAHH
...RENA IS IN DESPAIR.
SHE FEELS THE DESPAIR OF HER FRIENDS BEING POWER-LESS.
IS EVERY-ONE ELSE IN DESPAIR TOO?
FEELING THE DESPAIR OF NOT BEING ABLE TO HELP A FRIEND ...?
DAMMIT!
IS THAT ALL WE ARE?

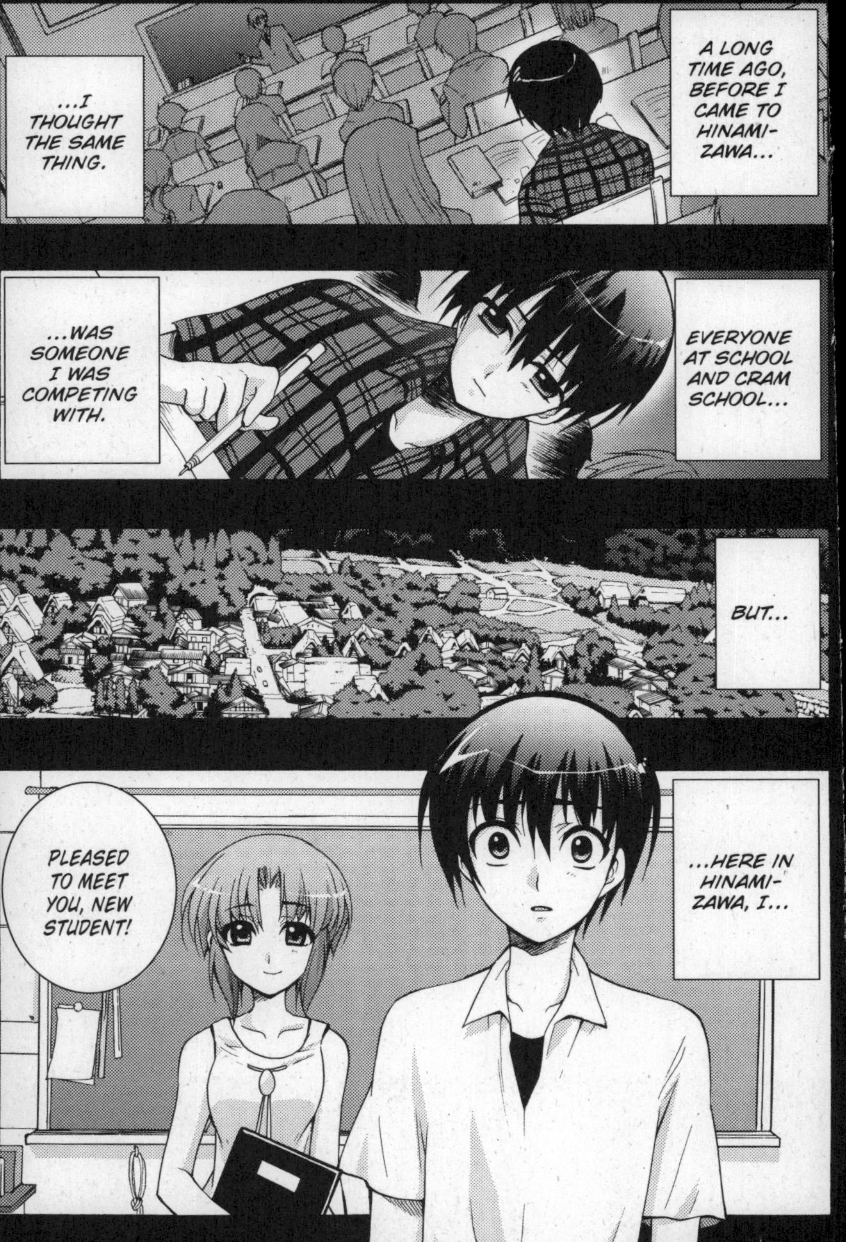
A LONG TIME AGO, BEFORE I CAME TO HINAMI-ZAWA...
...I THOUGHT THE SAME THING.
EVERYONE AT SCHOOL AND CRAM SCHOOL...
...WAS SOMEONE I WAS COMPETING WITH.
BUT...
...HERE IN HINAMI-ZAWA, I...
PLEASED TO MEET YOU, NEW STUDENT!

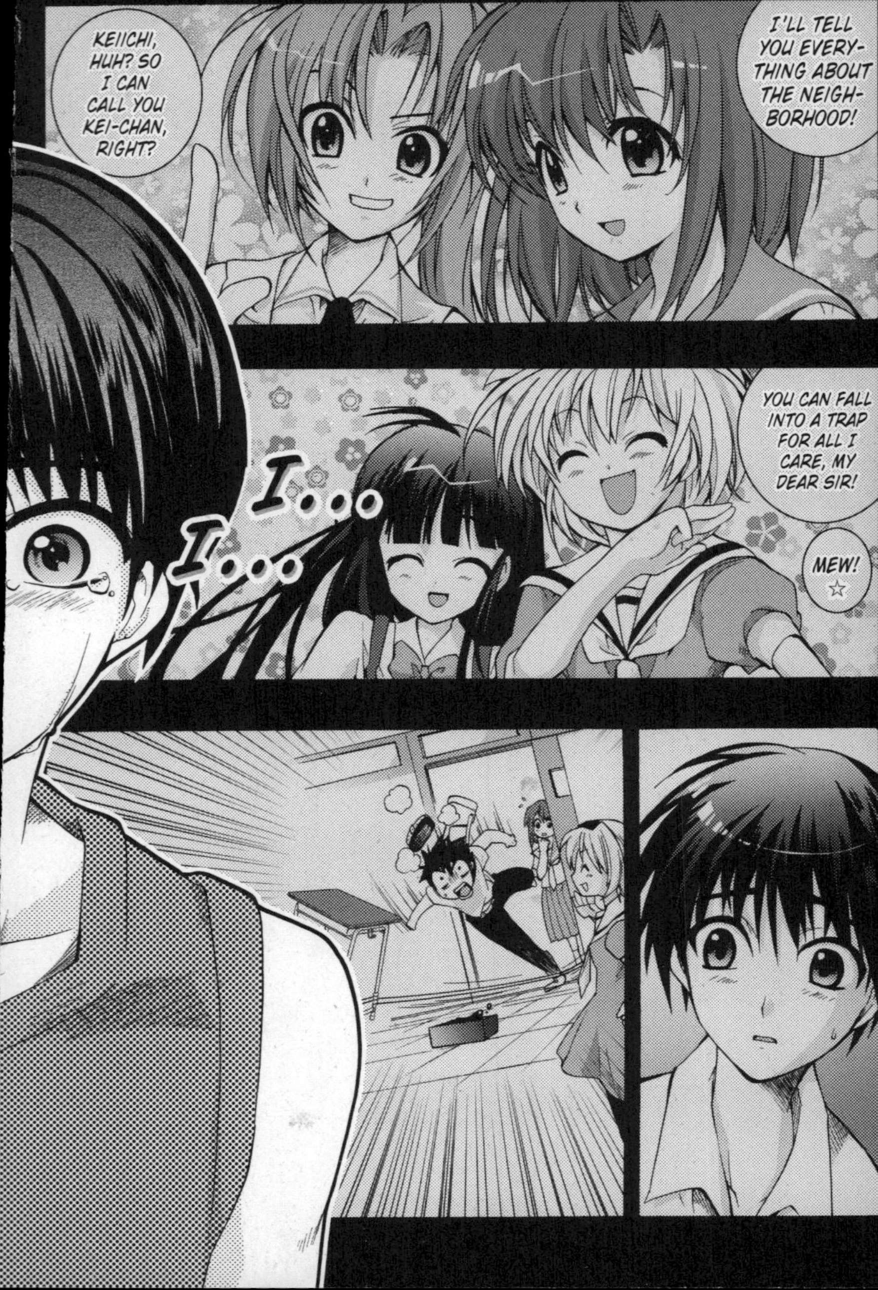
I'LL TELL YOU EVERYTHING ABOUT THE NEIGHBORHOOD!
KEIICHI, HUH? SO I CAN CALL YOU KEI-CHAN, RIGHT?
YOU CAN FALL INTO A TRAP FOR ALL I CARE, MY DEAR SIR!
MEW! ☆
I...
I...

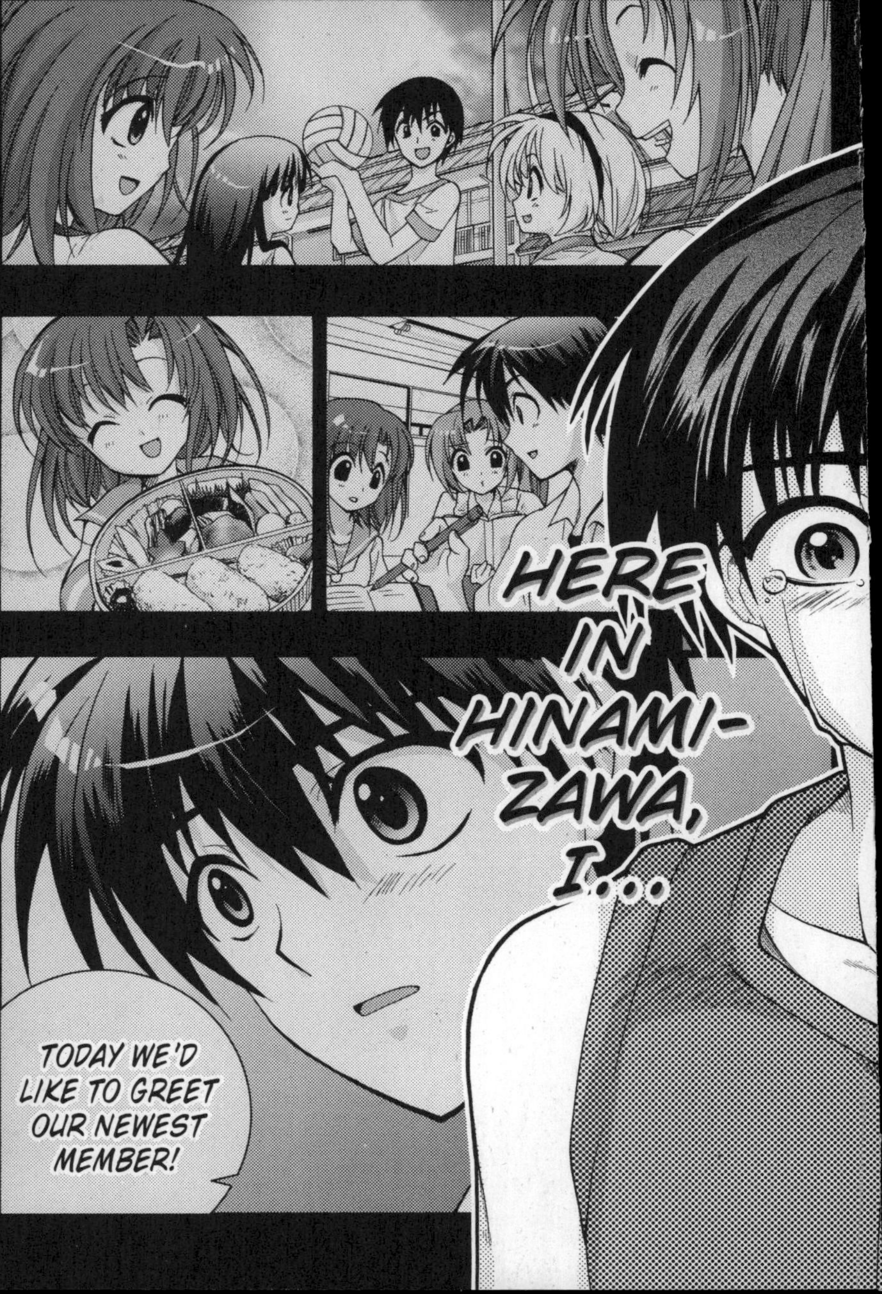
HERE IN HINAMI-ZAWA, I...
TODAY WE'D LIKE TO GREET OUR NEWEST MEMBER!

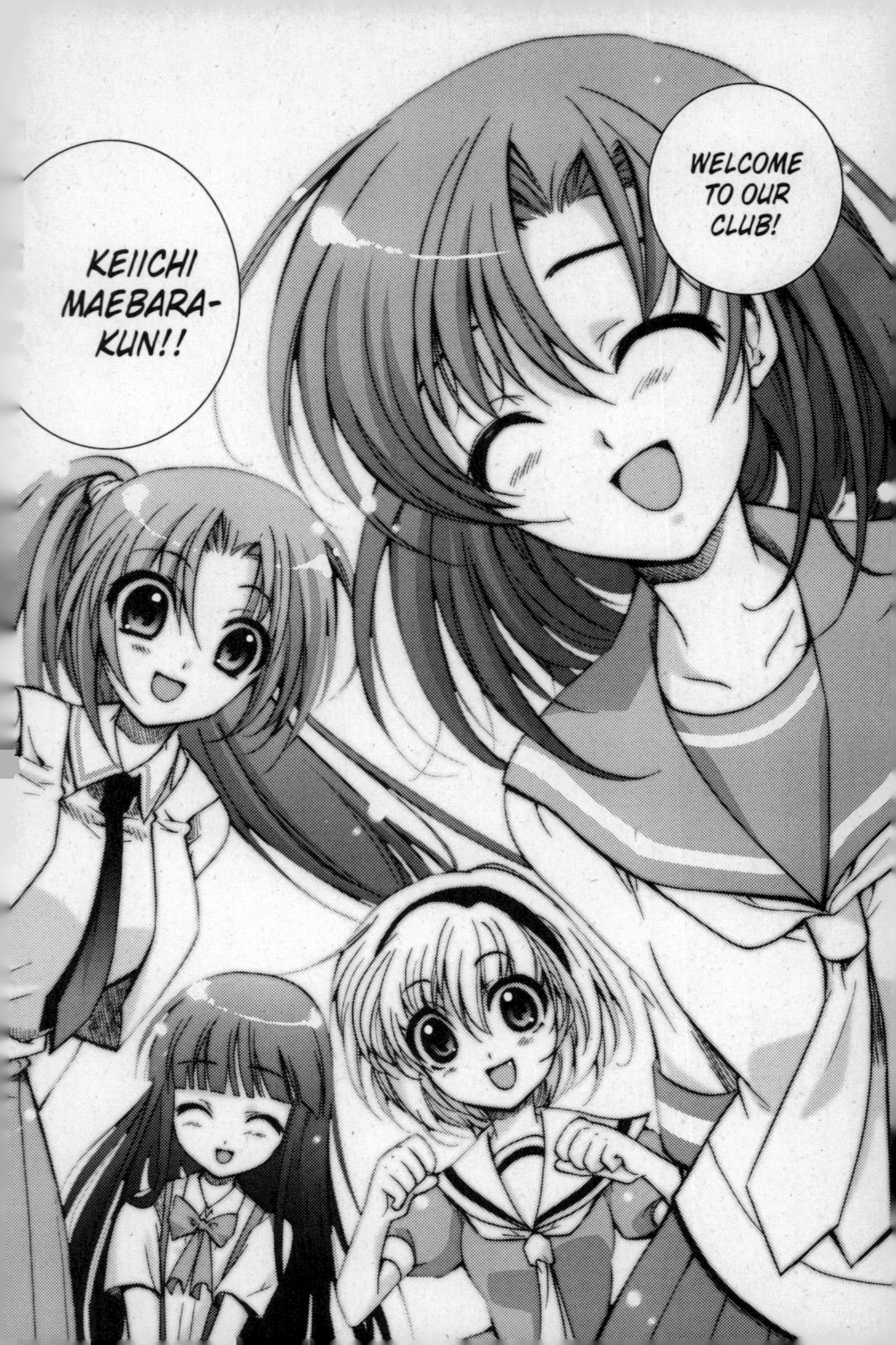
WELCOME TO OUR CLUB!
KEIICHI MAEBARA-KUN!!

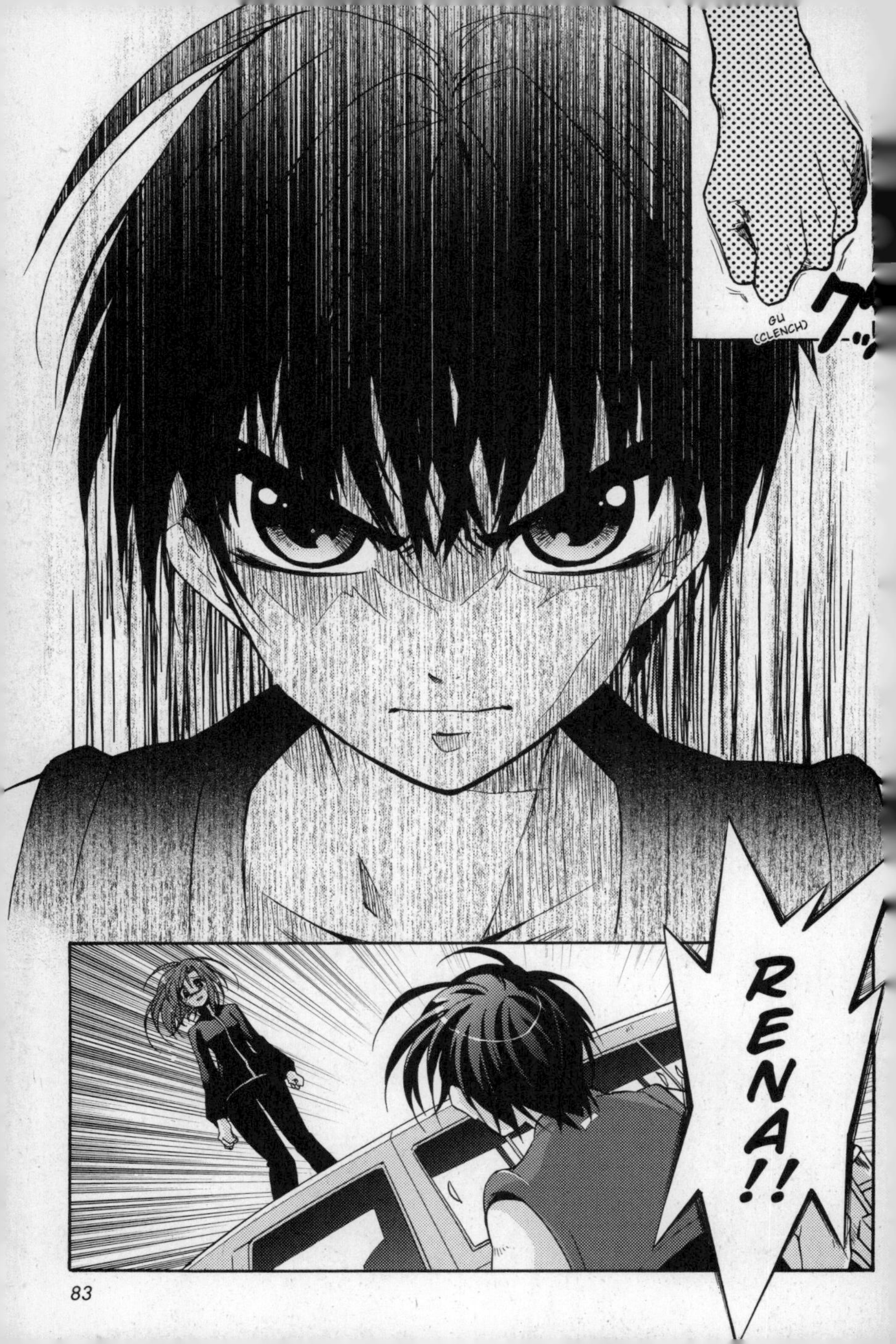
GU (CLENCH)
RENA!!

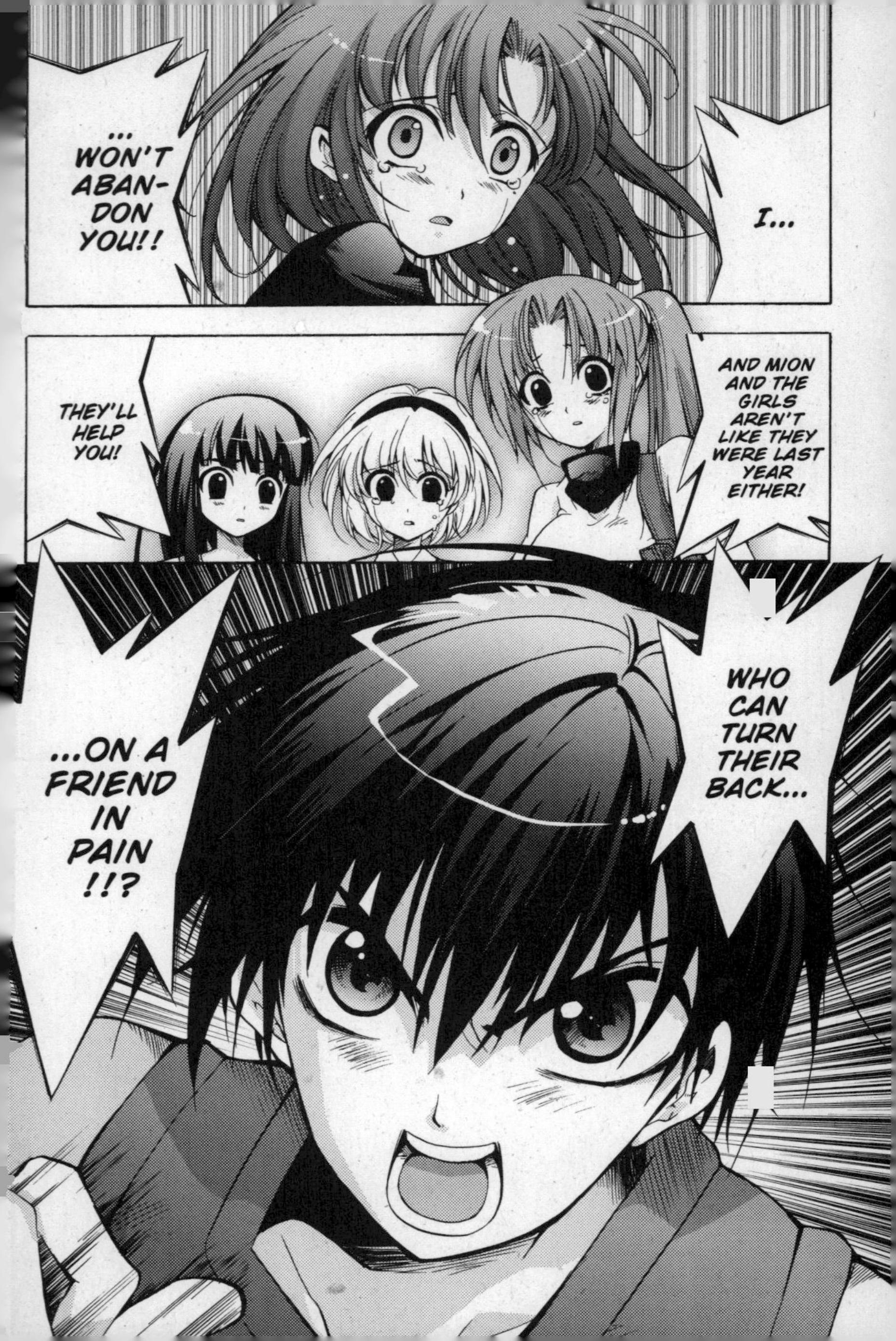
I...
...WON'T ABAN-DON YOU!!
AND MION AND THE GIRLS AREN'T LIKE THEY WERE LAST YEAR EITHER!
THEY'LL HELP YOU!
WHO CAN TURN THEIR BACK...
...ON A FRIEND IN PAIN!!?

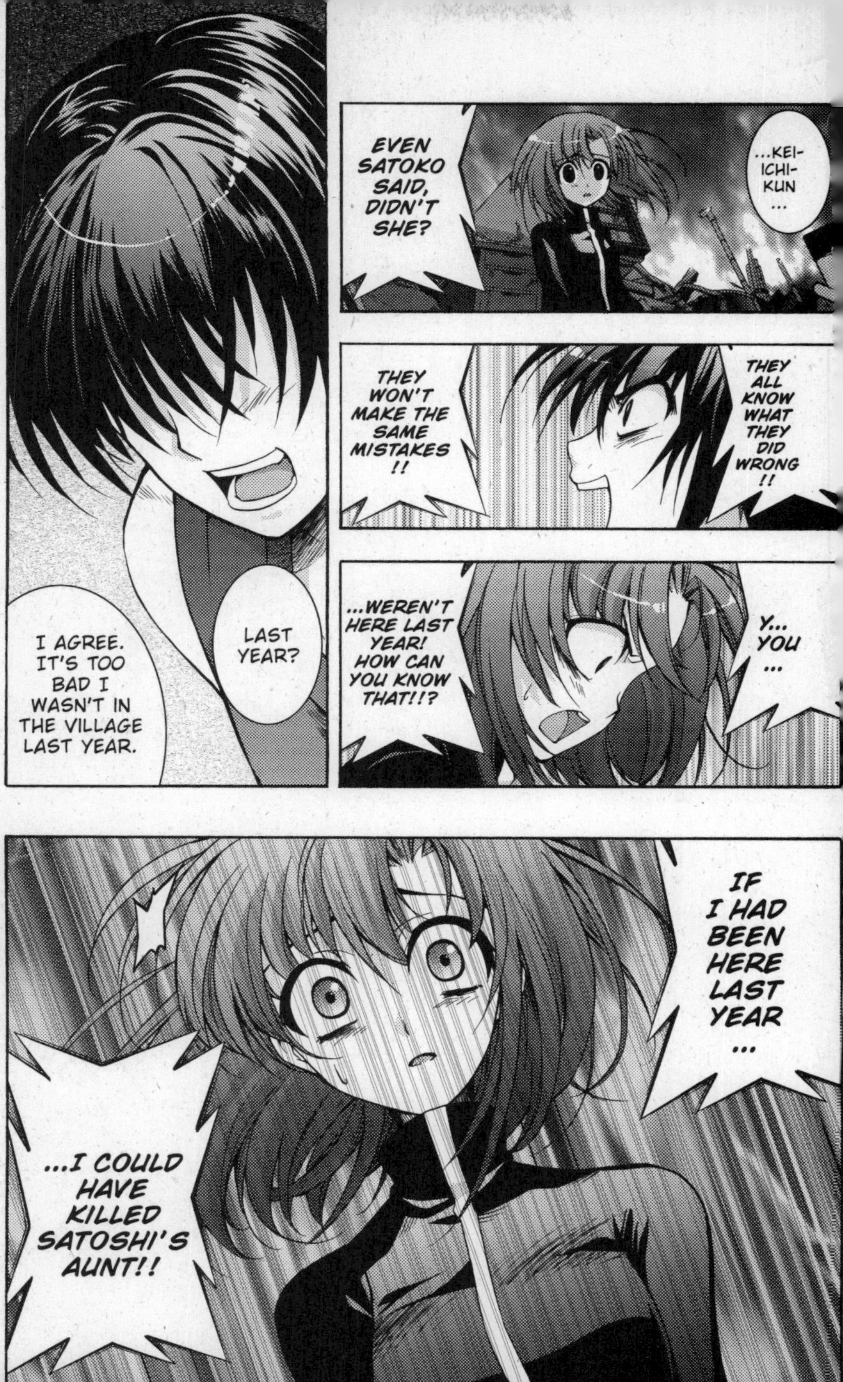
...KEI-ICHI-KUN ...
EVEN SATOKO SAID, DIDN'T SHE?
THEY ALL KNOW WHAT THEY DID WRONG!!
THEY WON'T MAKE THE SAME MISTAKES!!
Y... YOU ...
...WEREN'T HERE LAST YEAR! HOW CAN YOU KNOW THAT!!?
LAST YEAR?
I AGREE. IT'S TOO BAD I WASN'T IN THE VILLAGE LAST YEAR.
IF I HAD BEEN HERE LAST YEAR ...
...I COULD HAVE KILLED SATOSHI'S AUNT!!

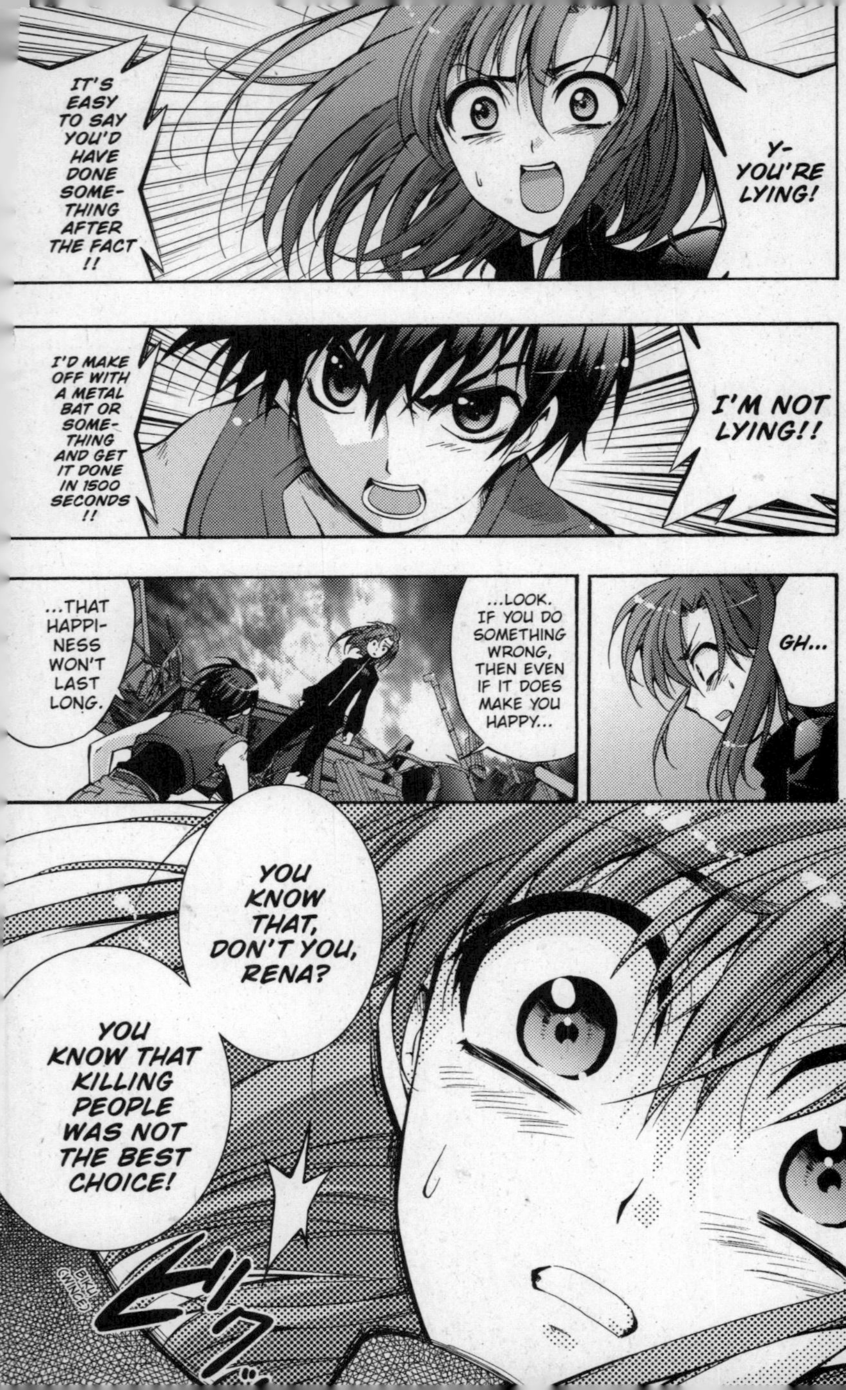
Y- YOU'RE LYING!
IT'S EASY TO SAY YOU'D HAVE DONE SOME-THING AFTER THE FACT !!
I'M NOT LYING!!
I'D MAKE OFF WITH A METAL BAT OR SOME-THING AND GET IT DONE IN 1500 SECONDS !!
GH...
...LOOK. IF YOU DO SOMETHING WRONG, THEN EVEN IF IT DOES MAKE YOU HAPPY...
...THAT HAPPI-NESS WON'T LAST LONG.
YOU KNOW THAT, DON'T YOU, RENA?
YOU KNOW THAT KILLING PEOPLE WAS NOT THE BEST CHOICE!
BIKU (WINCE)

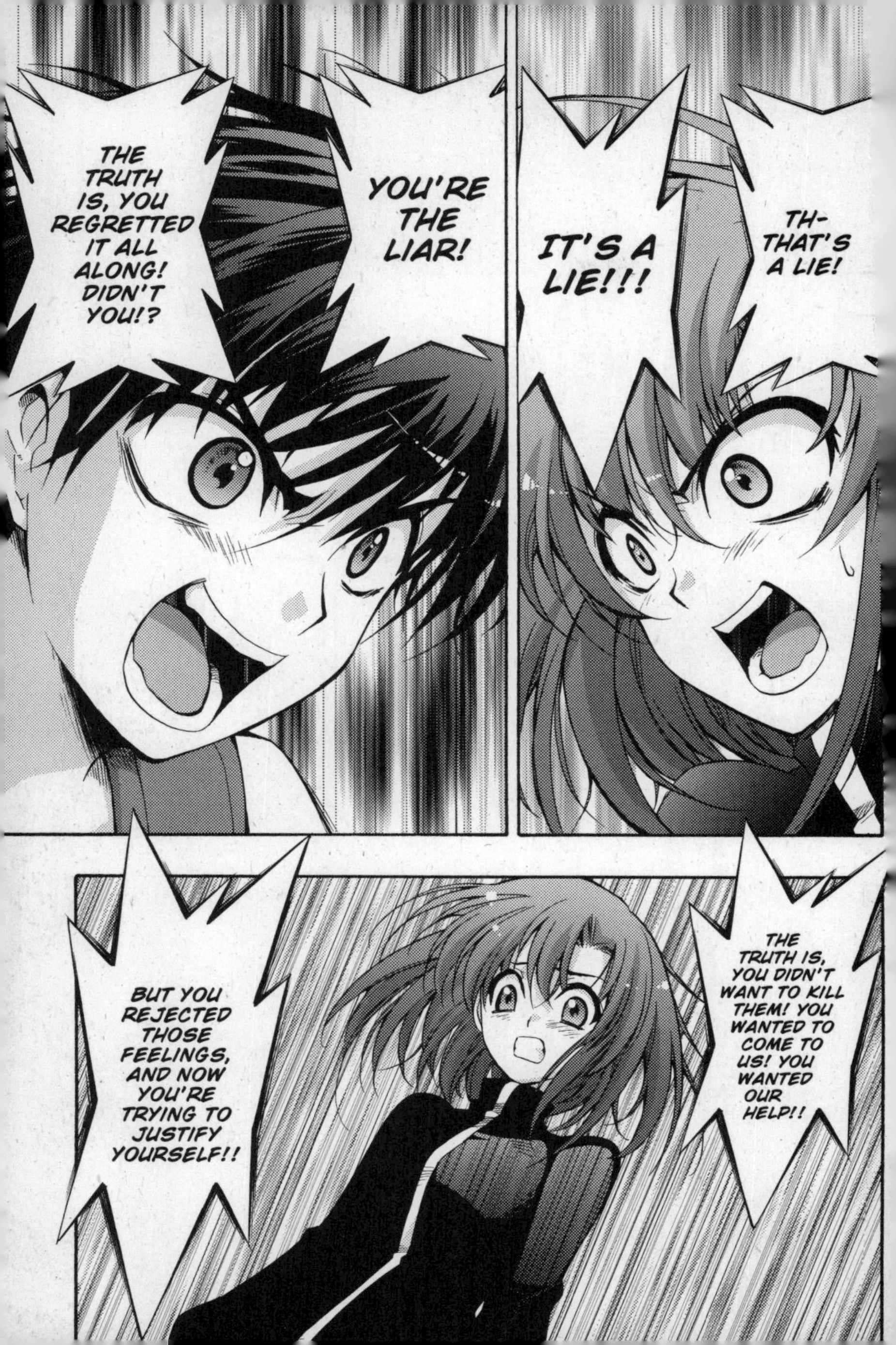
TH- THAT'S A LIE!
IT'S A LIE!!!
YOU'RE THE LIAR!
THE TRUTH IS, YOU REGRETTED IT ALL ALONG! DIDN'T YOU!?
THE TRUTH IS, YOU DIDN'T WANT TO KILL THEM! YOU WANTED TO COME TO US! YOU WANTED OUR HELP!!
BUT YOU REJECTED THOSE FEELINGS, AND NOW YOU'RE TRYING TO JUSTIFY YOURSELF!!

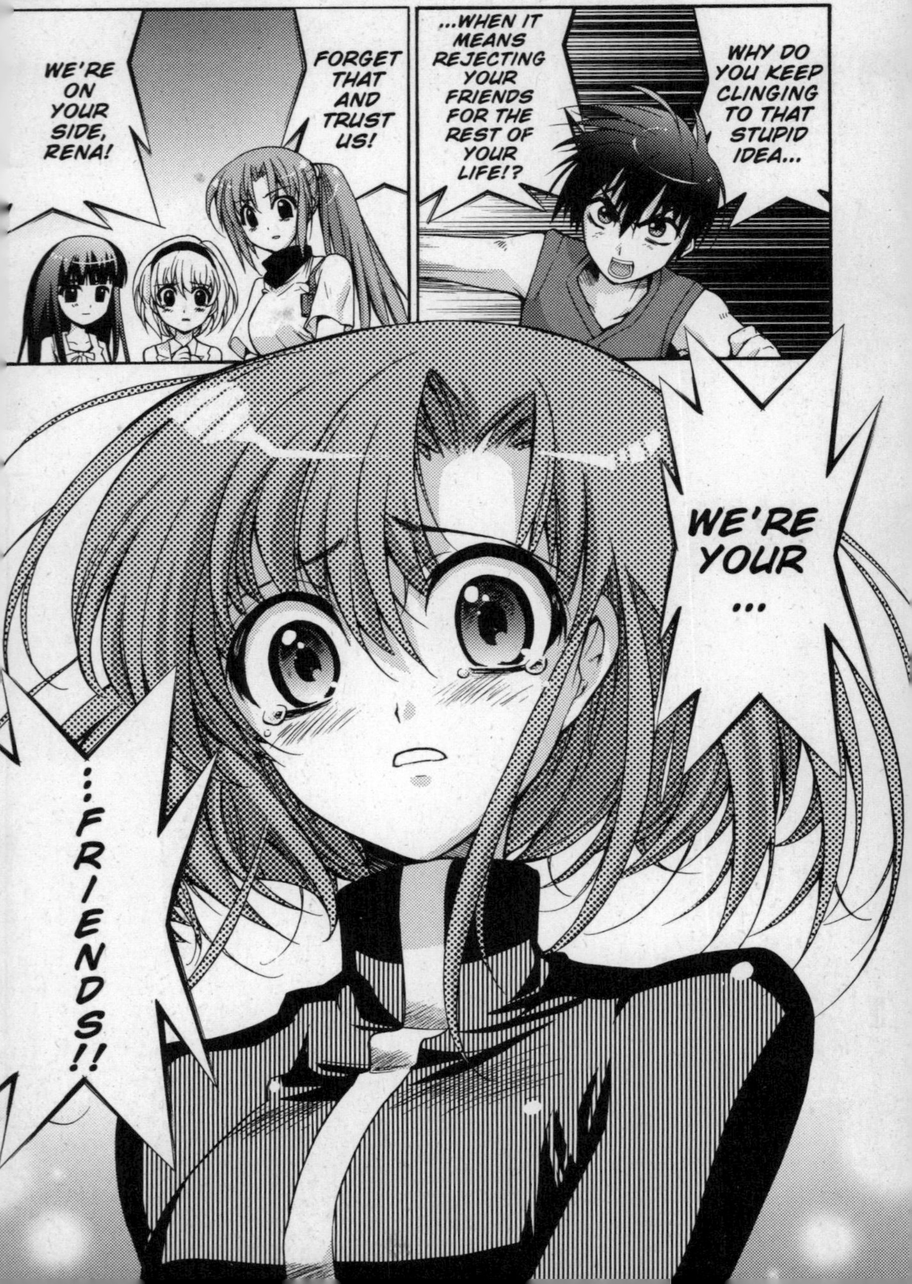
WHY DO YOU KEEP CLINGING TO THAT STUPID IDEA...
...WHEN IT MEANS REJECTING YOUR FRIENDS FOR THE REST OF YOUR LIFE!?
FORGET THAT AND TRUST US!
WE'RE ON YOUR SIDE, RENA!
WE'RE YOUR ...
...FRIENDS!!

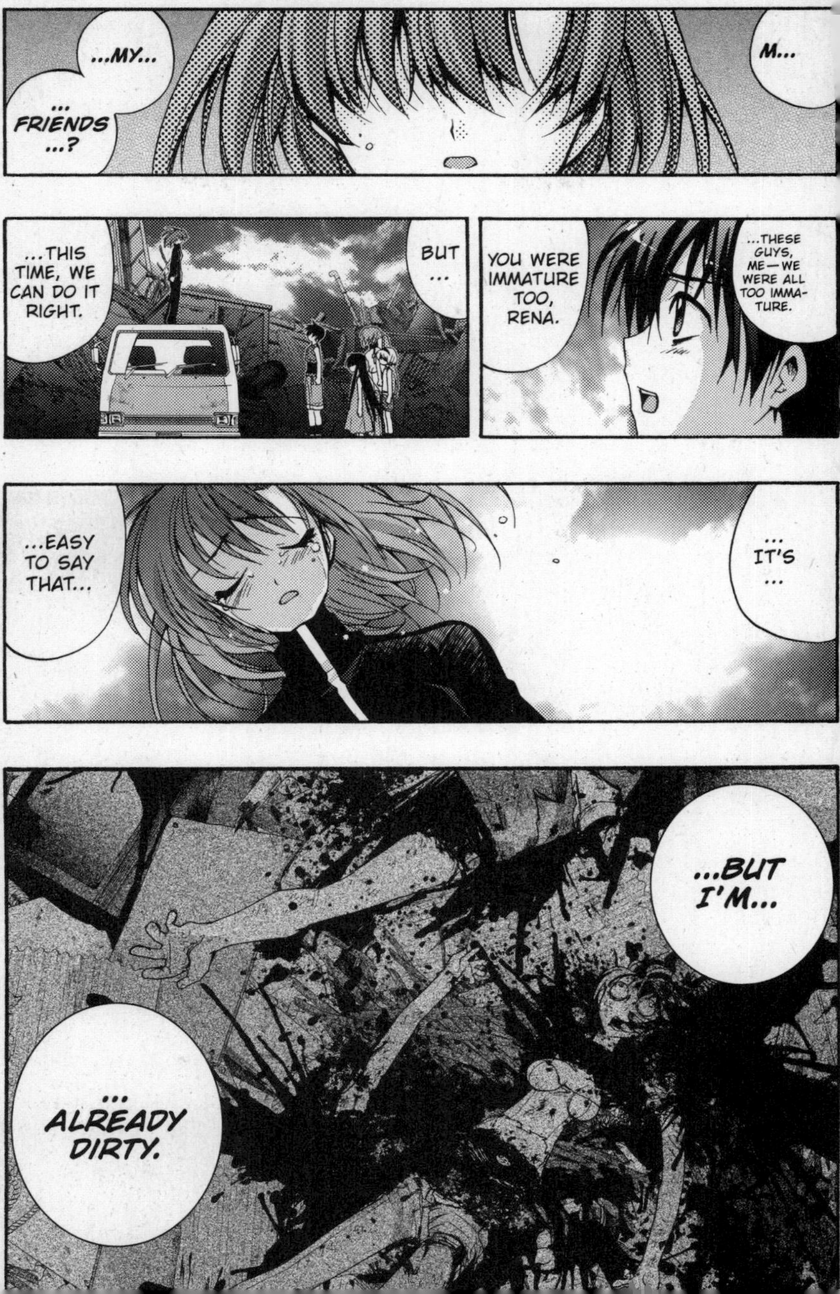
M...
...MY...
... FRIENDS ...?
...THESE GUYS, ME—WE WERE ALL TOO IMMATURE.
YOU WERE IMMATURE TOO, RENA.
BUT ...
...THIS TIME, WE CAN DO IT RIGHT.
... IT'S ...
...EASY TO SAY THAT...
...BUT I'M...
... ALREADY DIRTY.

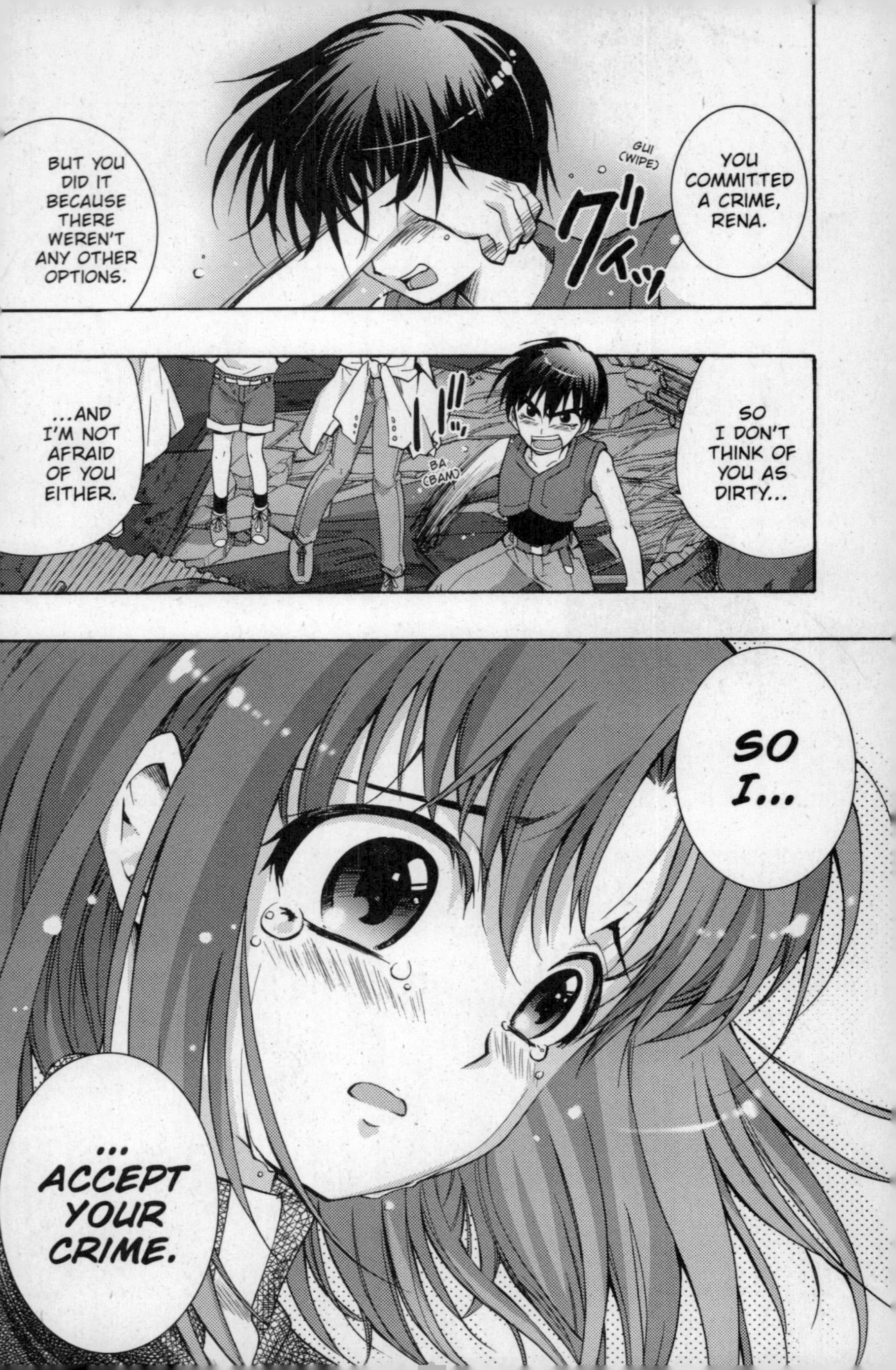
YOU COMMITTED A CRIME, RENA.
GUI (WIPE)
BUT YOU DID IT BECAUSE THERE WEREN'T ANY OTHER OPTIONS.
SO I DON'T THINK OF YOU AS DIRTY...
BA (BAM)
...AND I'M NOT AFRAID OF YOU EITHER.
SO I...
...ACCEPT YOUR CRIME.

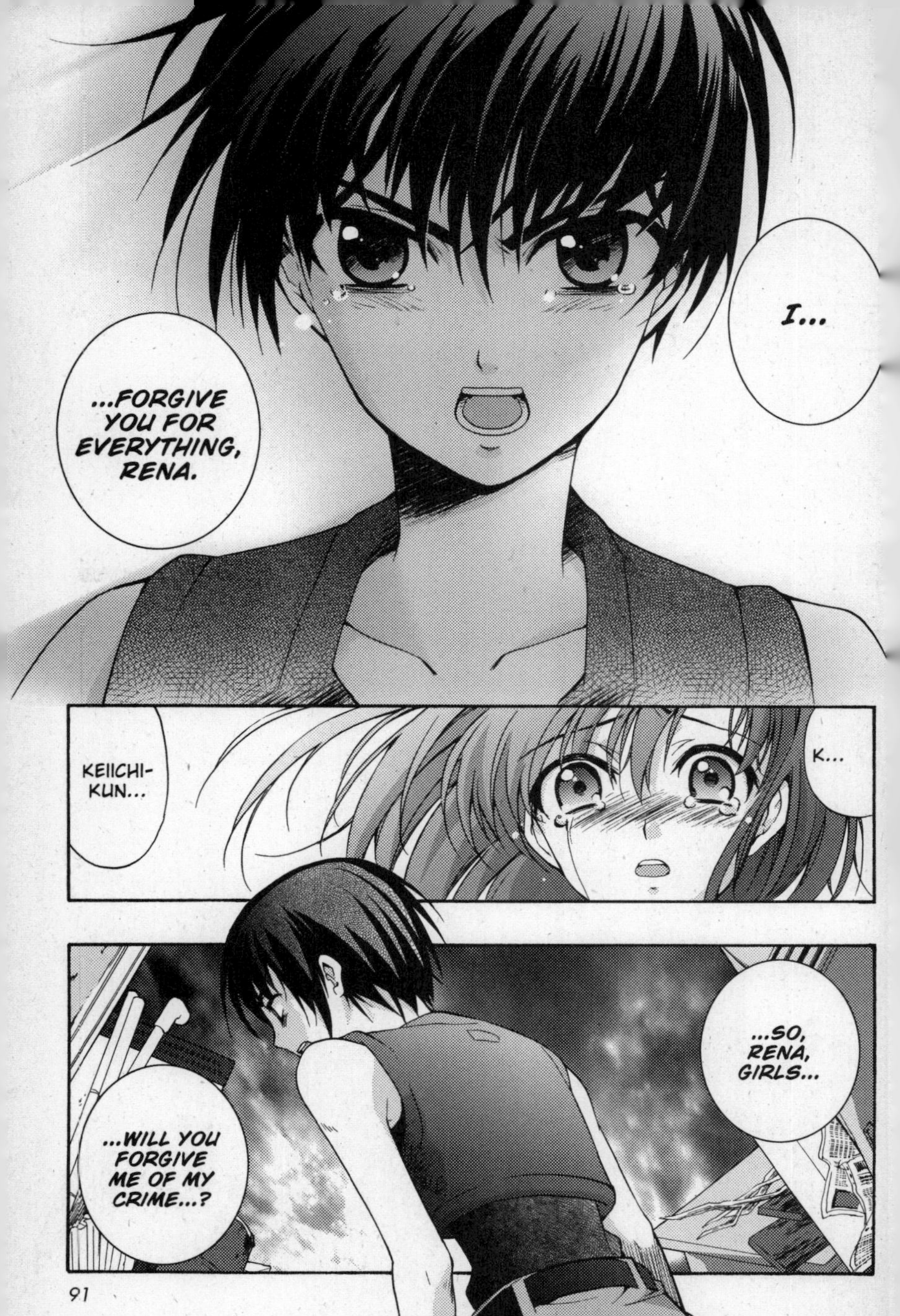
I...
...FORGIVE YOU FOR EVERYTHING, RENA.
K...
KEIICHI-KUN...
...SO, RENA, GIRLS...
...WILL YOU FORGIVE ME OF MY CRIME...?

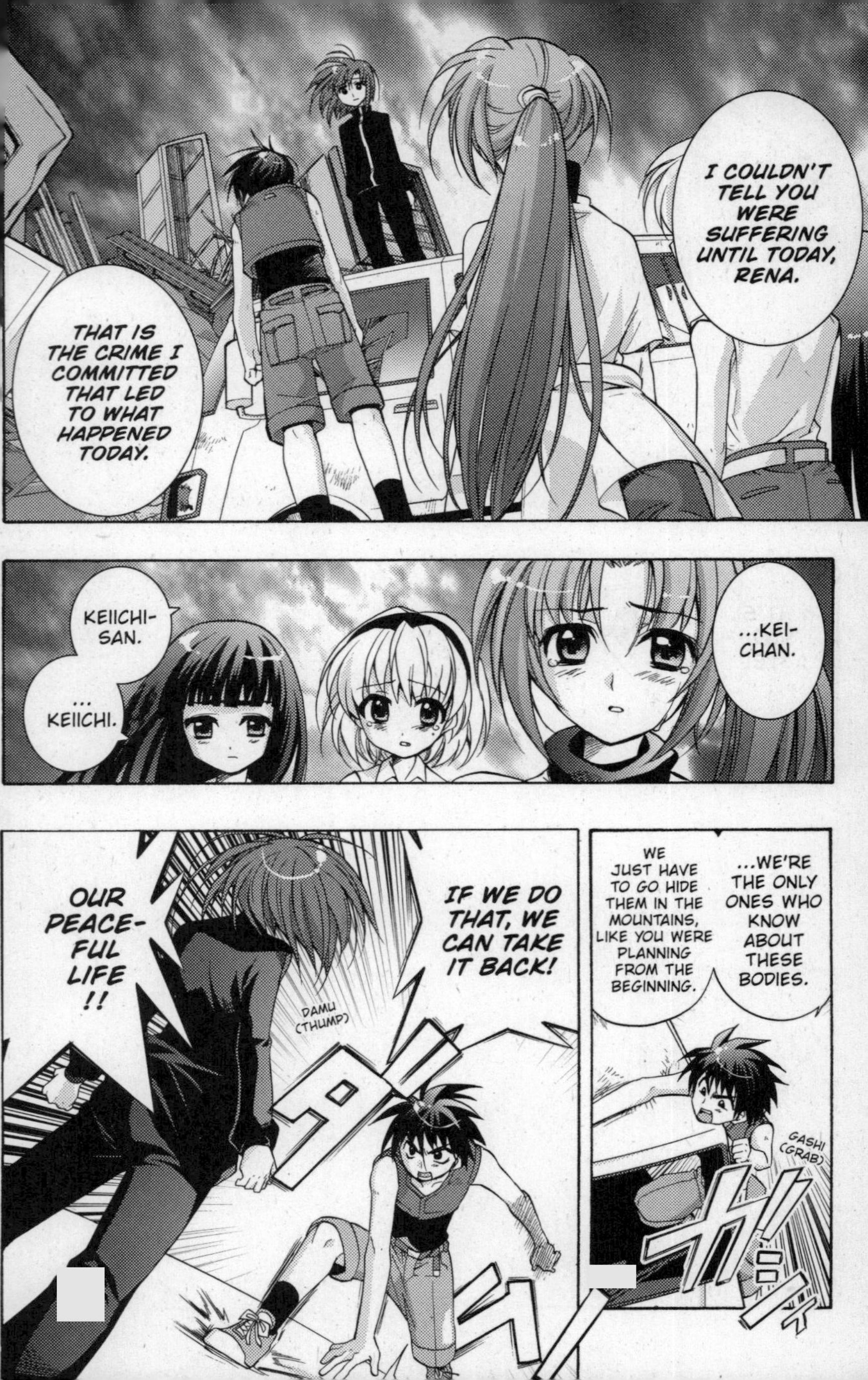
I COULDN'T TELL YOU WERE SUFFERING UNTIL TODAY, RENA.
THAT IS THE CRIME I COMMITTED THAT LED TO WHAT HAPPENED TODAY.
...KEI-CHAN.
KEIICHI-SAN.
... KEIICHI.
...WE'RE THE ONLY ONES WHO KNOW ABOUT THESE BODIES.
WE JUST HAVE TO GO HIDE THEM IN THE MOUNTAINS, LIKE YOU WERE PLANNING FROM THE BEGINNING.
GASHI (GRAB)
IF WE DO THAT, WE CAN TAKE IT BACK!
DAMU (THUMP)
OUR PEACE-FUL LIFE !!

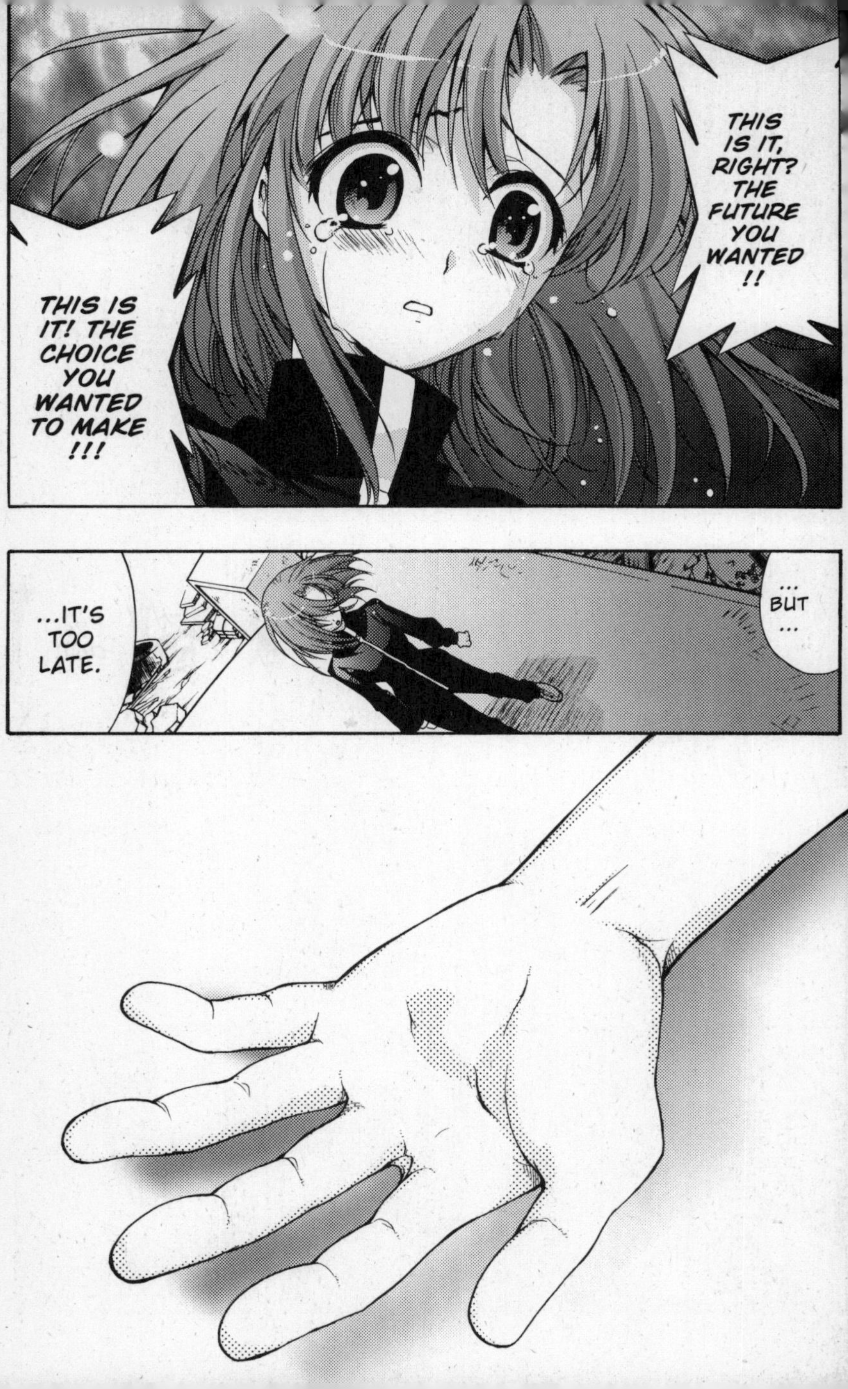
THIS IS IT, RIGHT? THE FUTURE YOU WANTED !!
THIS IS IT! THE CHOICE YOU WANTED TO MAKE !!!
...BUT...
...IT'S TOO LATE.

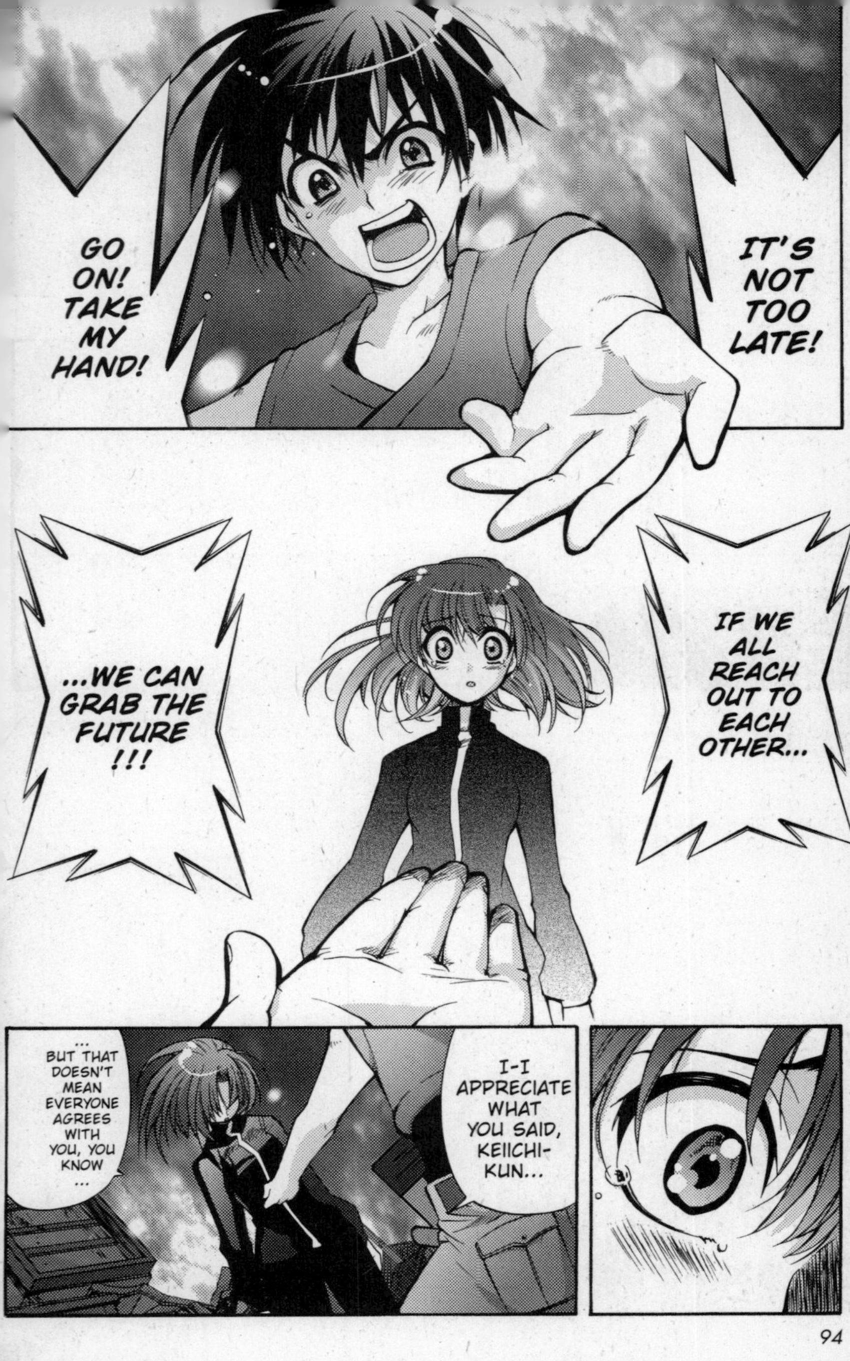
IT'S NOT TOO LATE!
GO ON! TAKE MY HAND!
IF WE ALL REACH OUT TO EACH OTHER...
...WE CAN GRAB THE FUTURE!!!
I-I APPRECIATE WHAT YOU SAID, KEIICHI-KUN...
...BUT THAT DOESN'T MEAN EVERYONE AGREES WITH YOU, YOU KNOW...

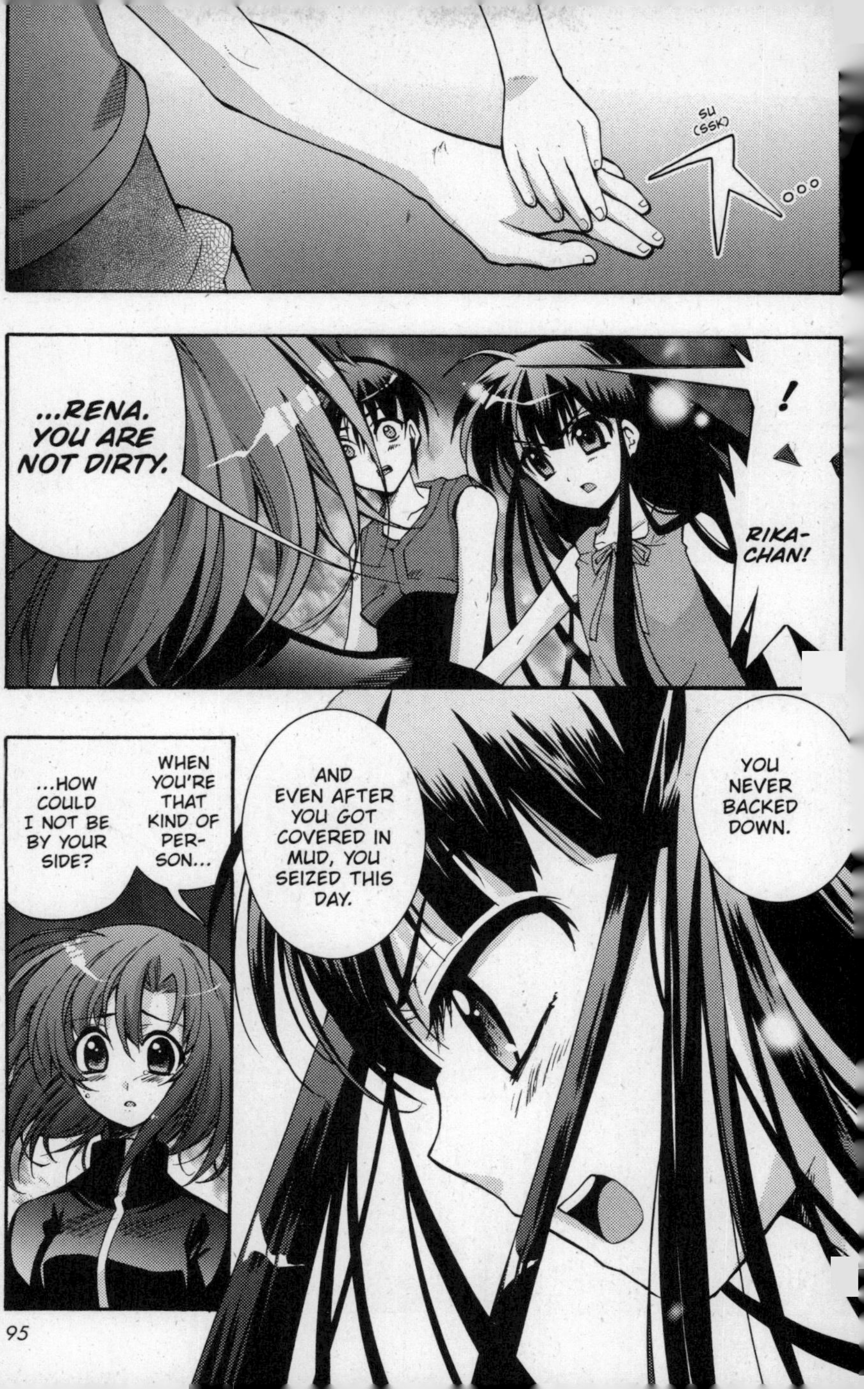

SU (SSK)
...
!
RIKA-CHAN!
...RENA. YOU ARE NOT DIRTY.
YOU NEVER BACKED DOWN.
AND EVEN AFTER YOU GOT COVERED IN MUD, YOU SEIZED THIS DAY.
WHEN YOU'RE THAT KIND OF PER-SON...
...HOW COULD I NOT BE BY YOUR SIDE?

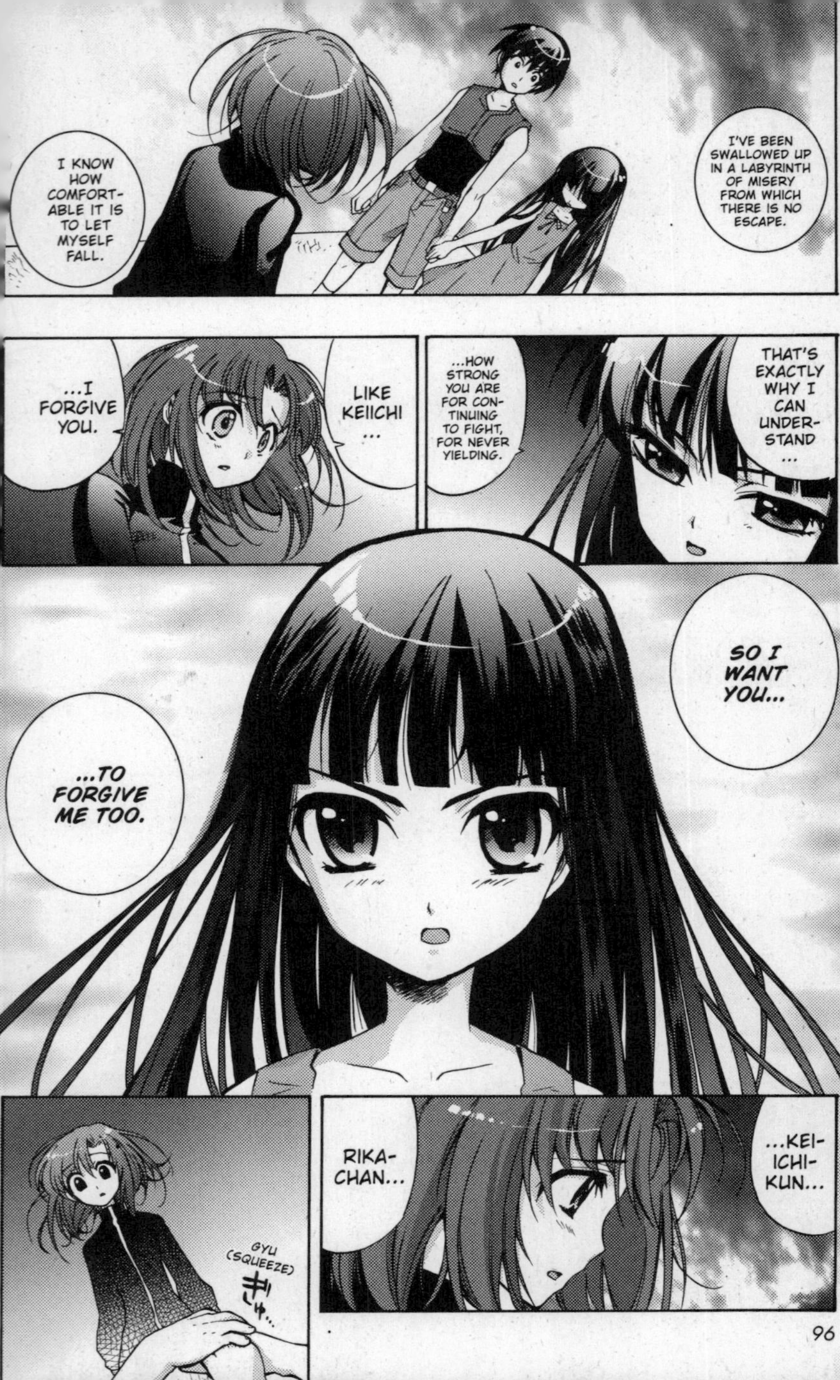
I'VE BEEN SWALLOWED UP IN A LABYRINTH OF MISERY FROM WHICH THERE IS NO ESCAPE.
I KNOW HOW COMFORTABLE IT IS TO LET MYSELF FALL.
THAT'S EXACTLY WHY I CAN UNDERSTAND...
...HOW STRONG YOU ARE FOR CONTINUING TO FIGHT, FOR NEVER YIELDING.
LIKE KEIICHI...
...I FORGIVE YOU.
SO I WANT YOU...
...TO FORGIVE ME TOO.
...KEIICHI-KUN...
RIKA-CHAN...
GYU (SQUEEZE)
きゅ…

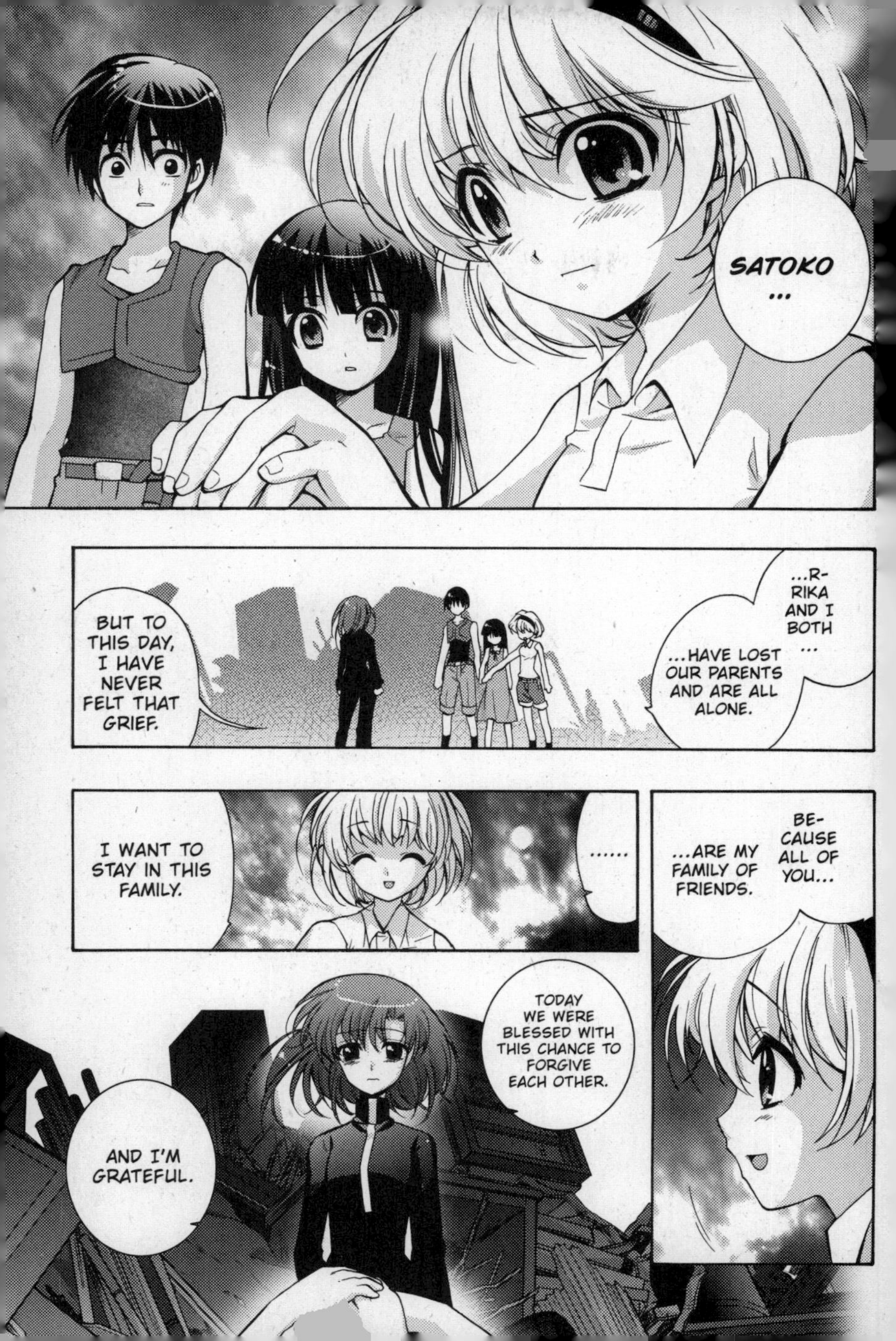
SATOKO ...
...R-RIKA AND I BOTH ...
...HAVE LOST OUR PARENTS AND ARE ALL ALONE.
BUT TO THIS DAY, I HAVE NEVER FELT THAT GRIEF.
BE-CAUSE ALL OF YOU...
...ARE MY FAMILY OF FRIENDS.
......
I WANT TO STAY IN THIS FAMILY.
TODAY WE WERE BLESSED WITH THIS CHANCE TO FORGIVE EACH OTHER.
AND I'M GRATEFUL.

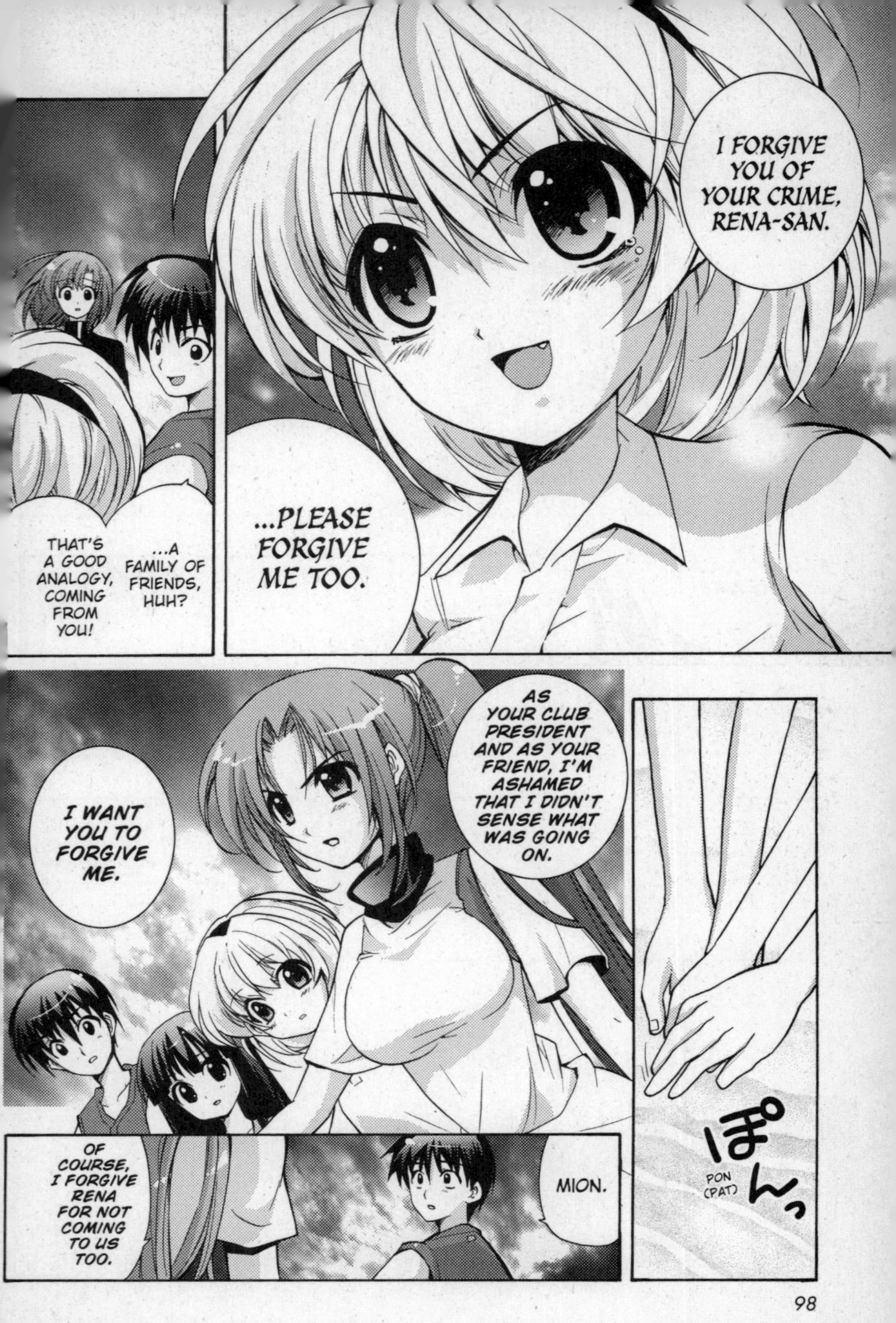
I FORGIVE YOU OF YOUR CRIME, RENA-SAN.
...PLEASE FORGIVE ME TOO.
...A FAMILY OF FRIENDS, HUH?
THAT'S A GOOD ANALOGY, COMING FROM YOU!
ぽんっ
PON (PAT)
AS YOUR CLUB PRESIDENT AND AS YOUR FRIEND, I'M ASHAMED THAT I DIDN'T SENSE WHAT WAS GOING ON.
I WANT YOU TO FORGIVE ME.
MION.
OF COURSE, I FORGIVE RENA FOR NOT COMING TO US TOO.

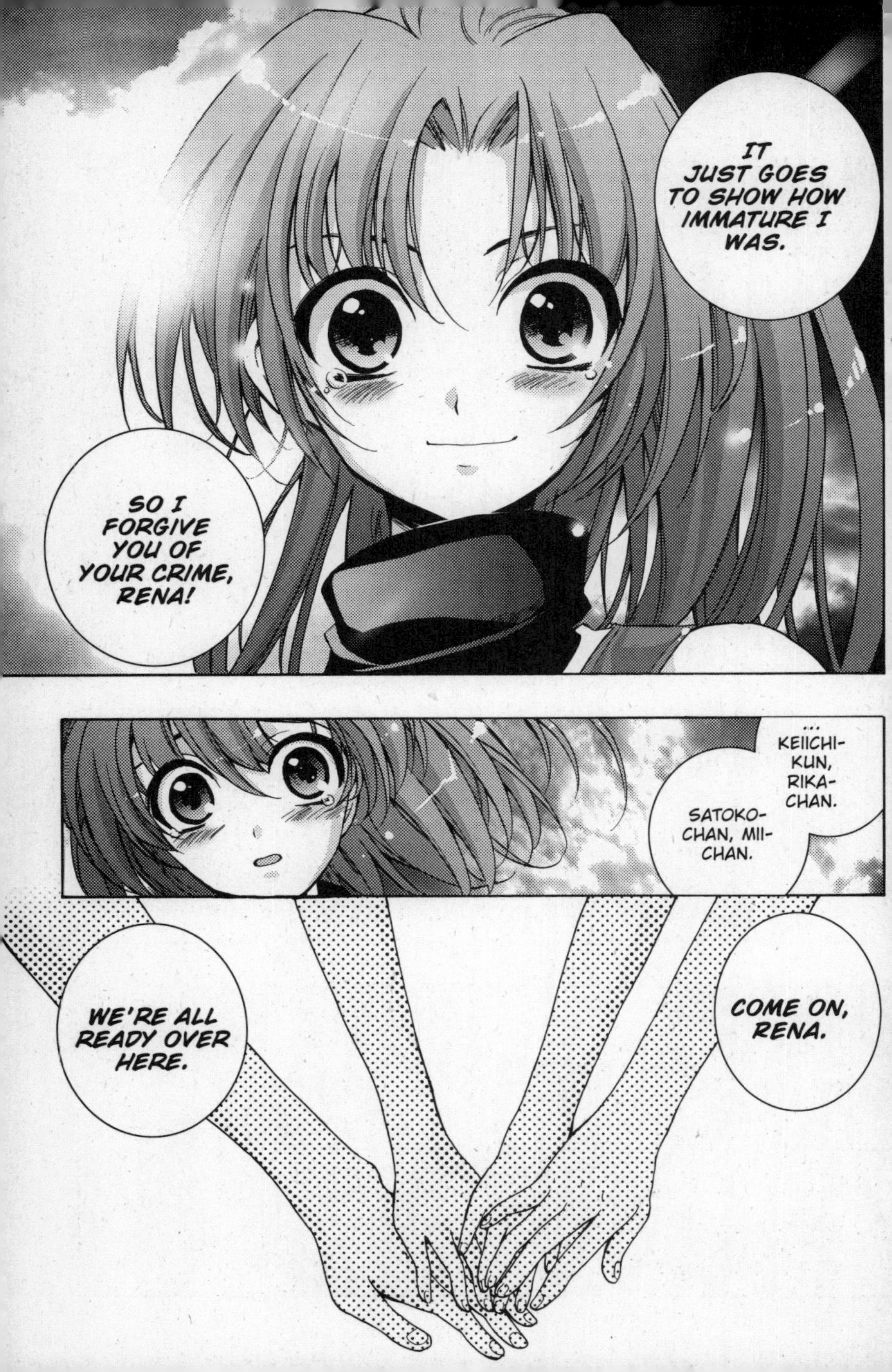
IT JUST GOES TO SHOW HOW IMMATURE I WAS.
SO I FORGIVE YOU OF YOUR CRIME, RENA!
... KEIICHI-KUN, RIKA-CHAN.
SATOKO-CHAN, MII-CHAN.
COME ON, RENA.
WE'RE ALL READY OVER HERE.

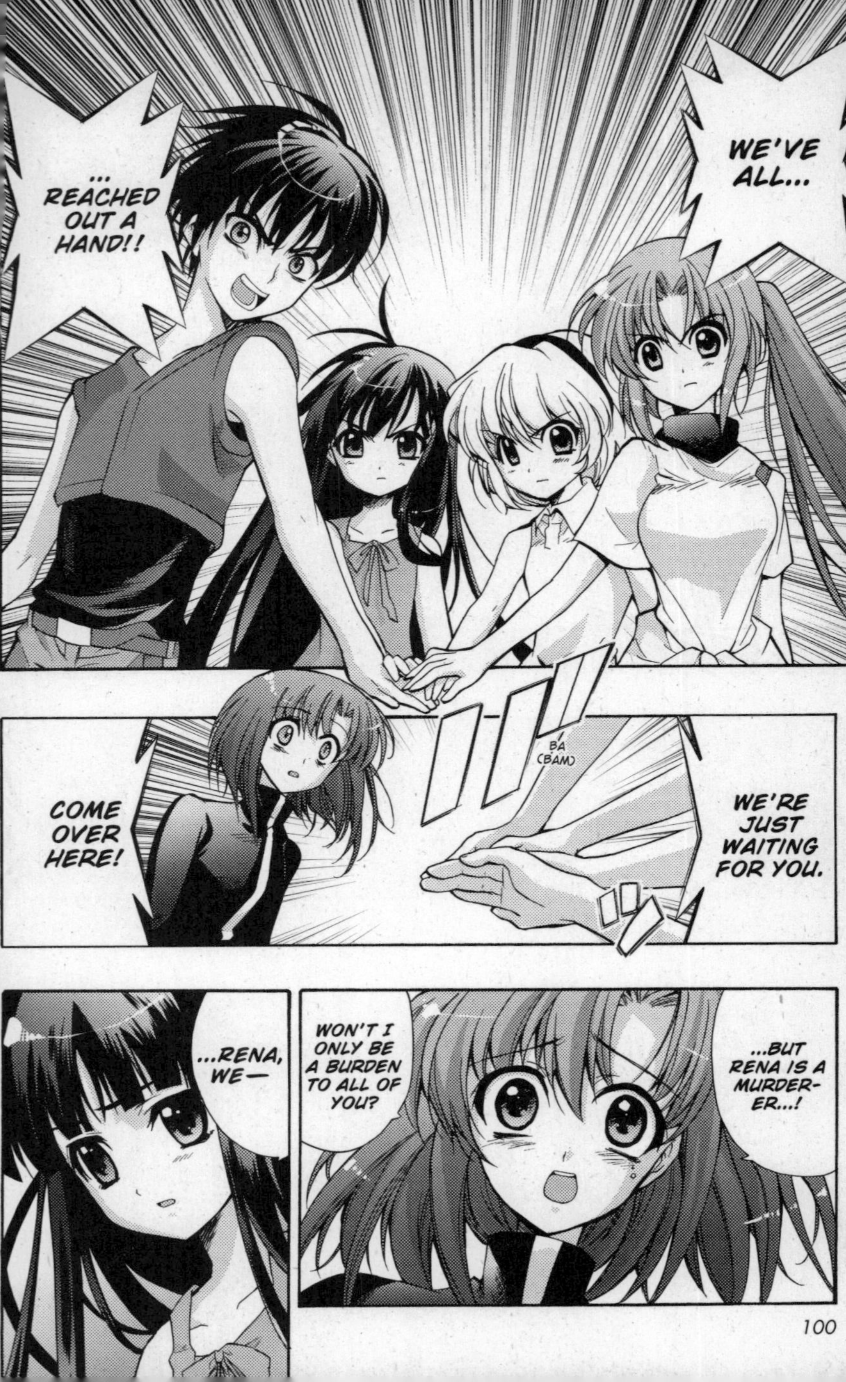
WE'VE ALL...
...REACHED OUT A HAND!!
WE'RE JUST WAITING FOR YOU.
BA (BAM)
COME OVER HERE!
...BUT RENA IS A MURDERER...!
WON'T I ONLY BE A BURDEN TO ALL OF YOU?
...RENA, WE—

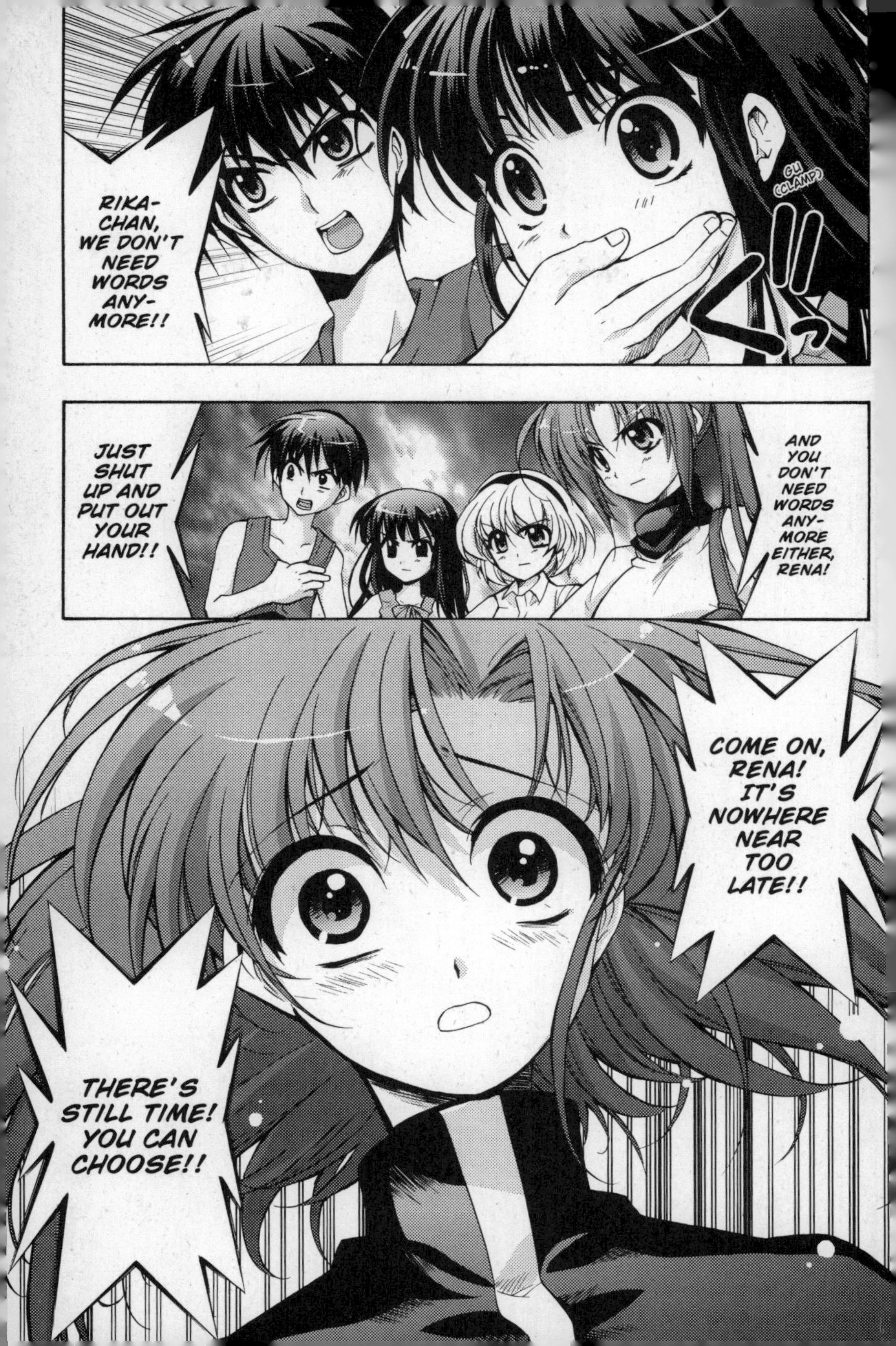
GU (CLAMP)
RIKA-CHAN, WE DON'T NEED WORDS ANYMORE!!
AND YOU DON'T NEED WORDS ANYMORE EITHER, RENA!
JUST SHUT UP AND PUT OUT YOUR HAND!!
COME ON, RENA! IT'S NOWHERE NEAR TOO LATE!!
THERE'S STILL TIME! YOU CAN CHOOSE!!

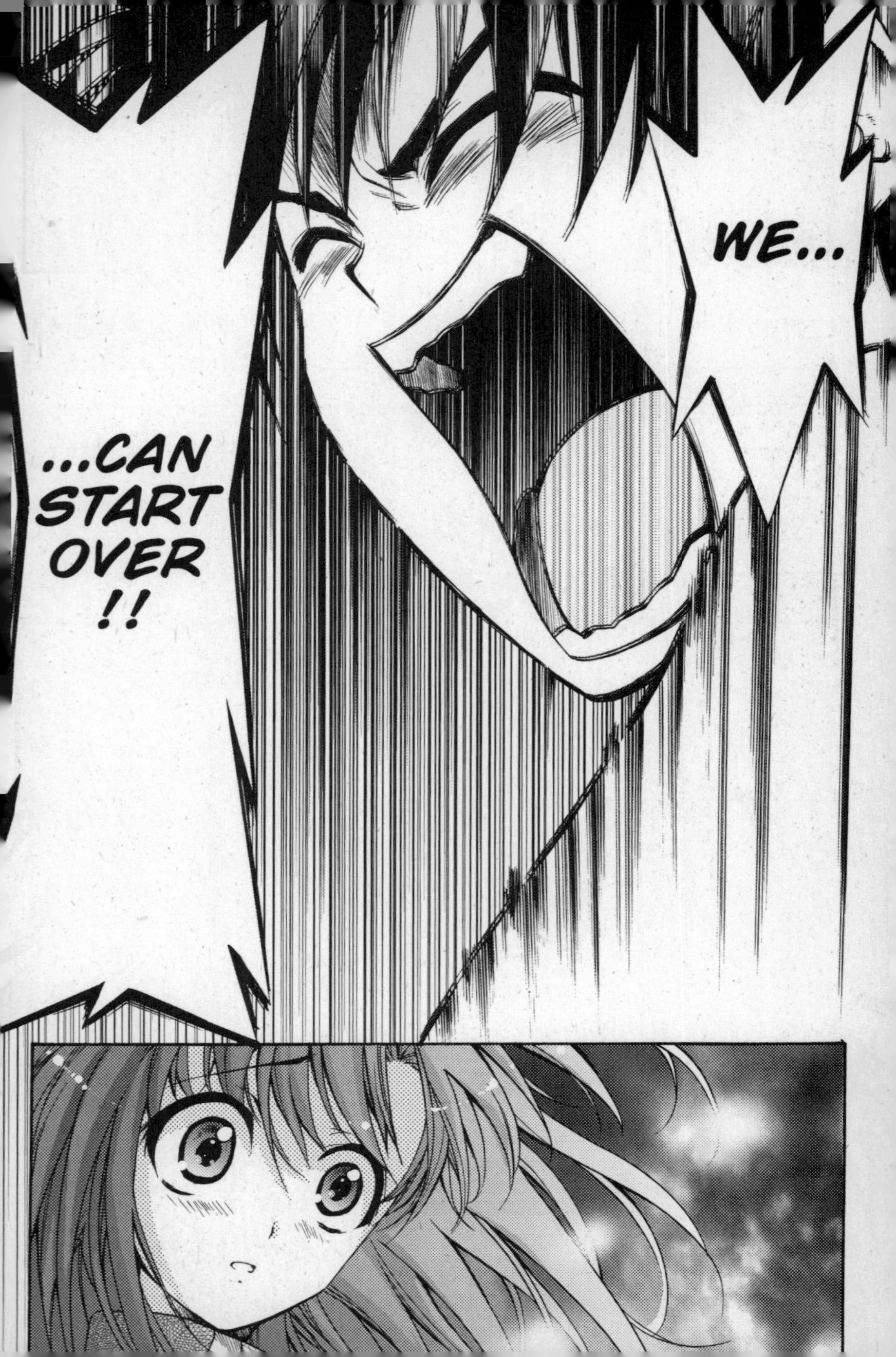
WE...
...CAN START OVER!!

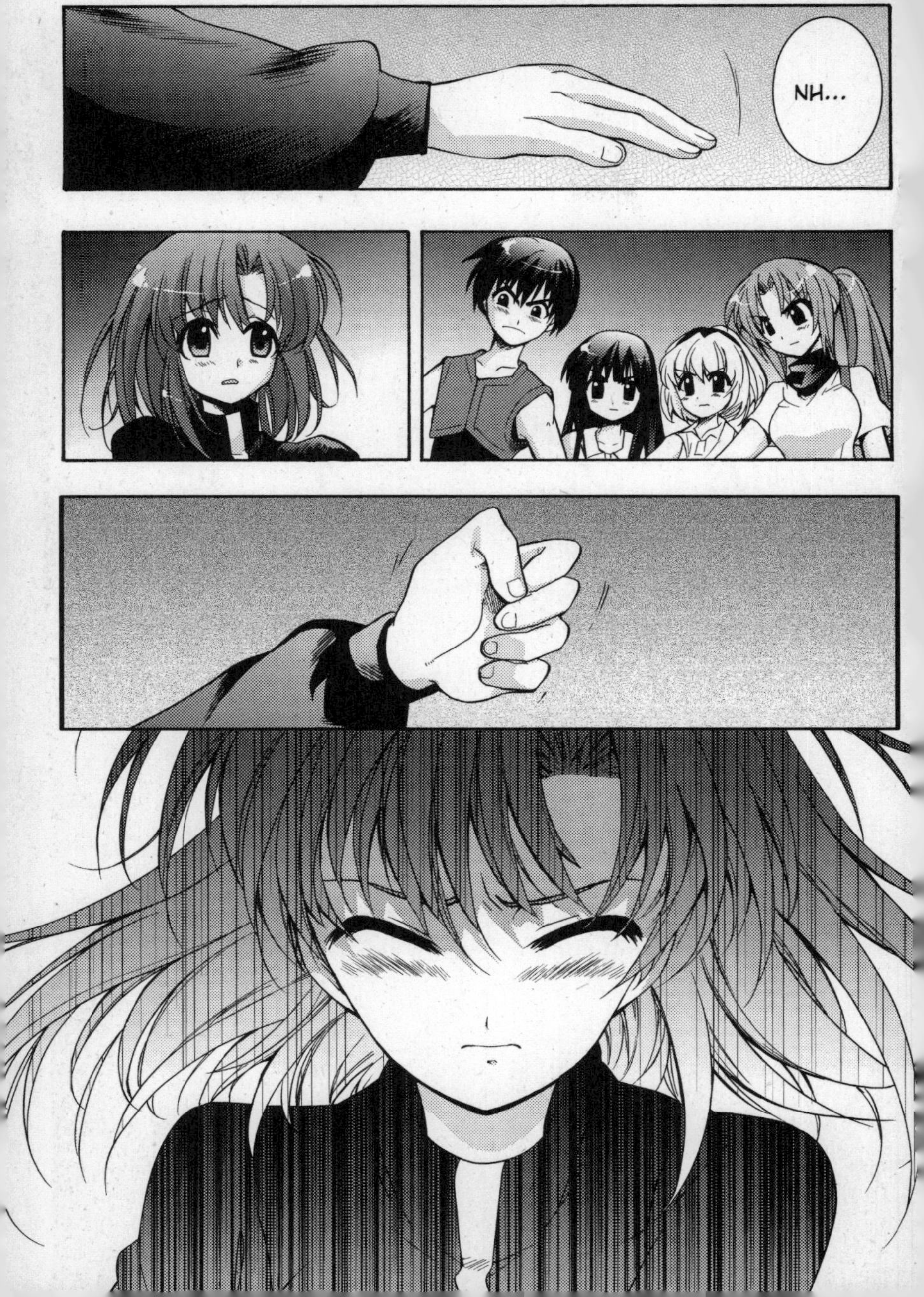
NH...

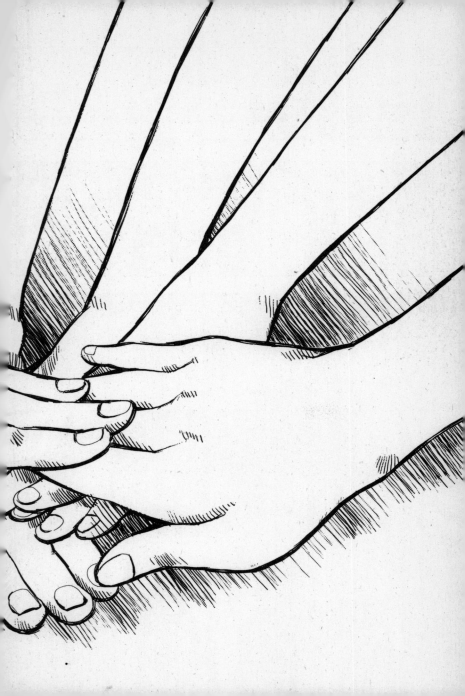

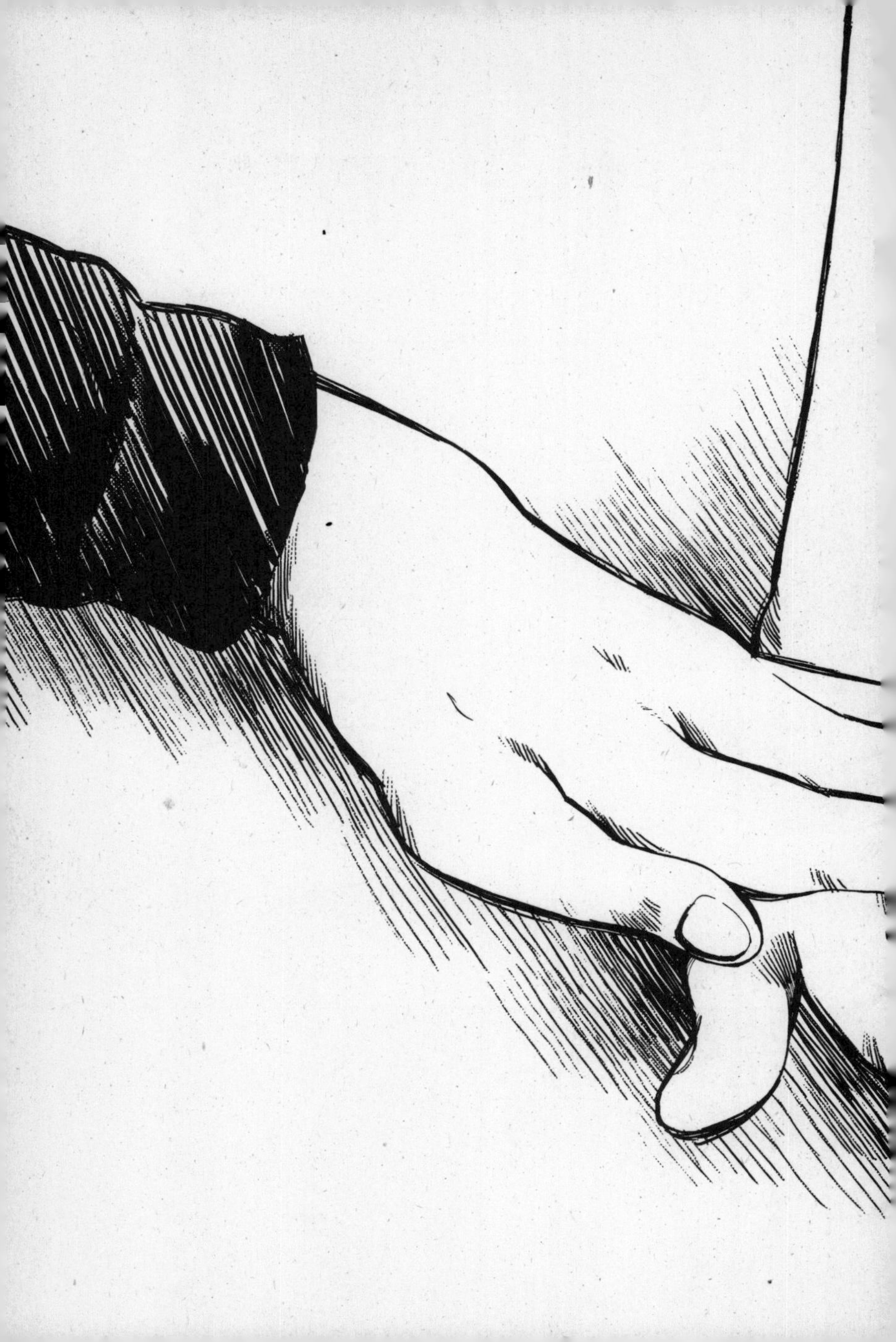

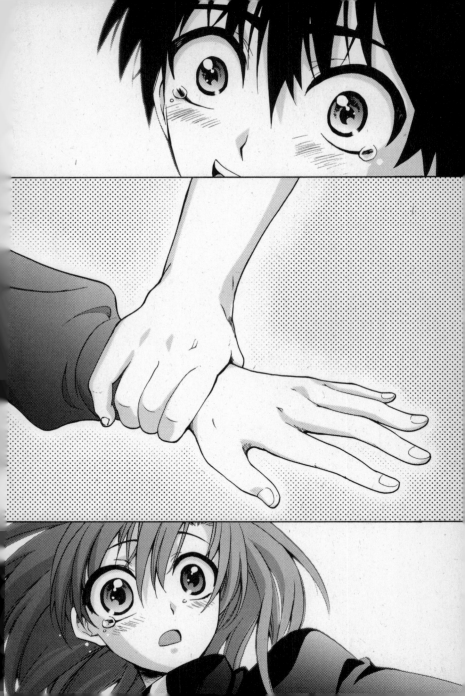

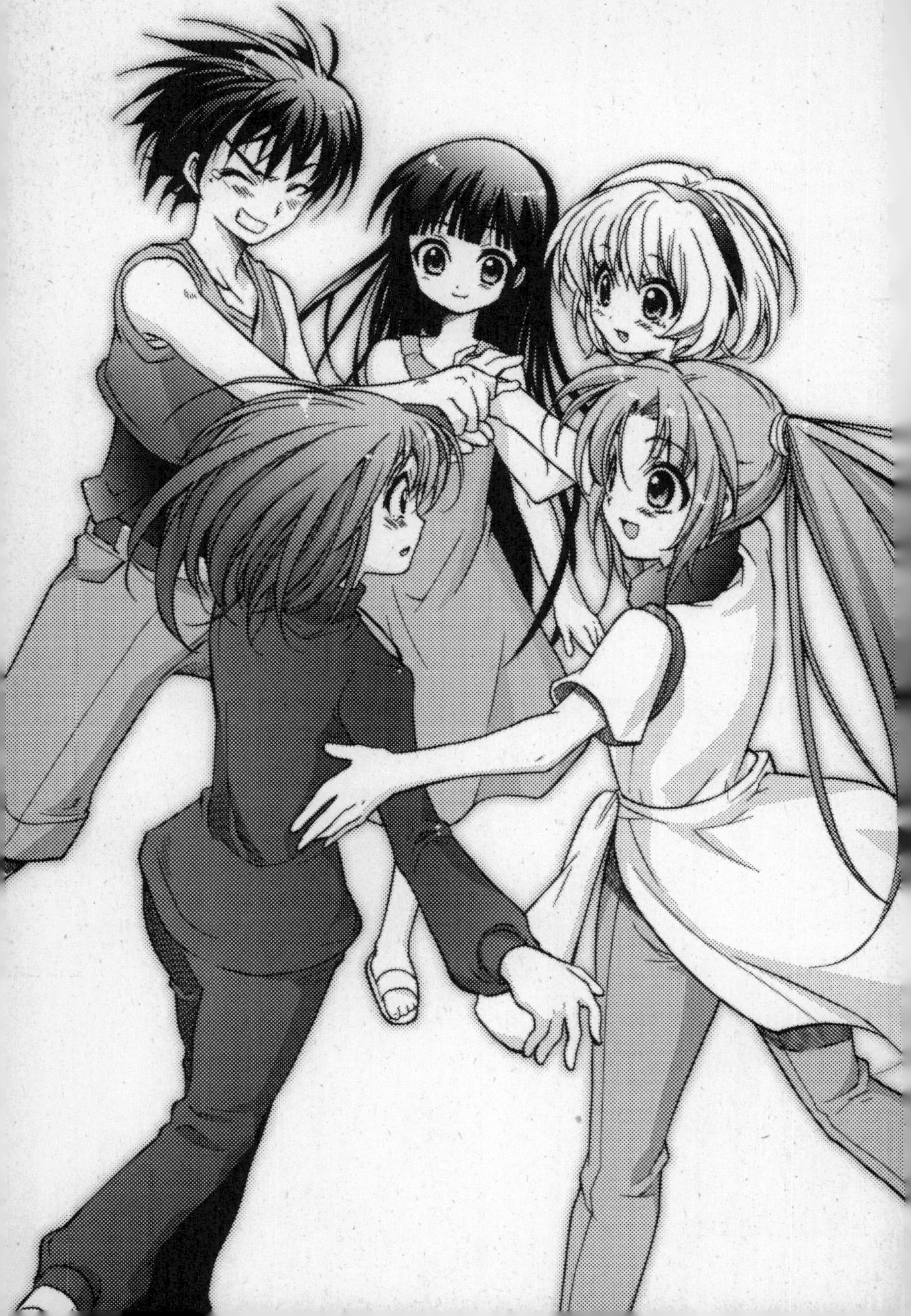

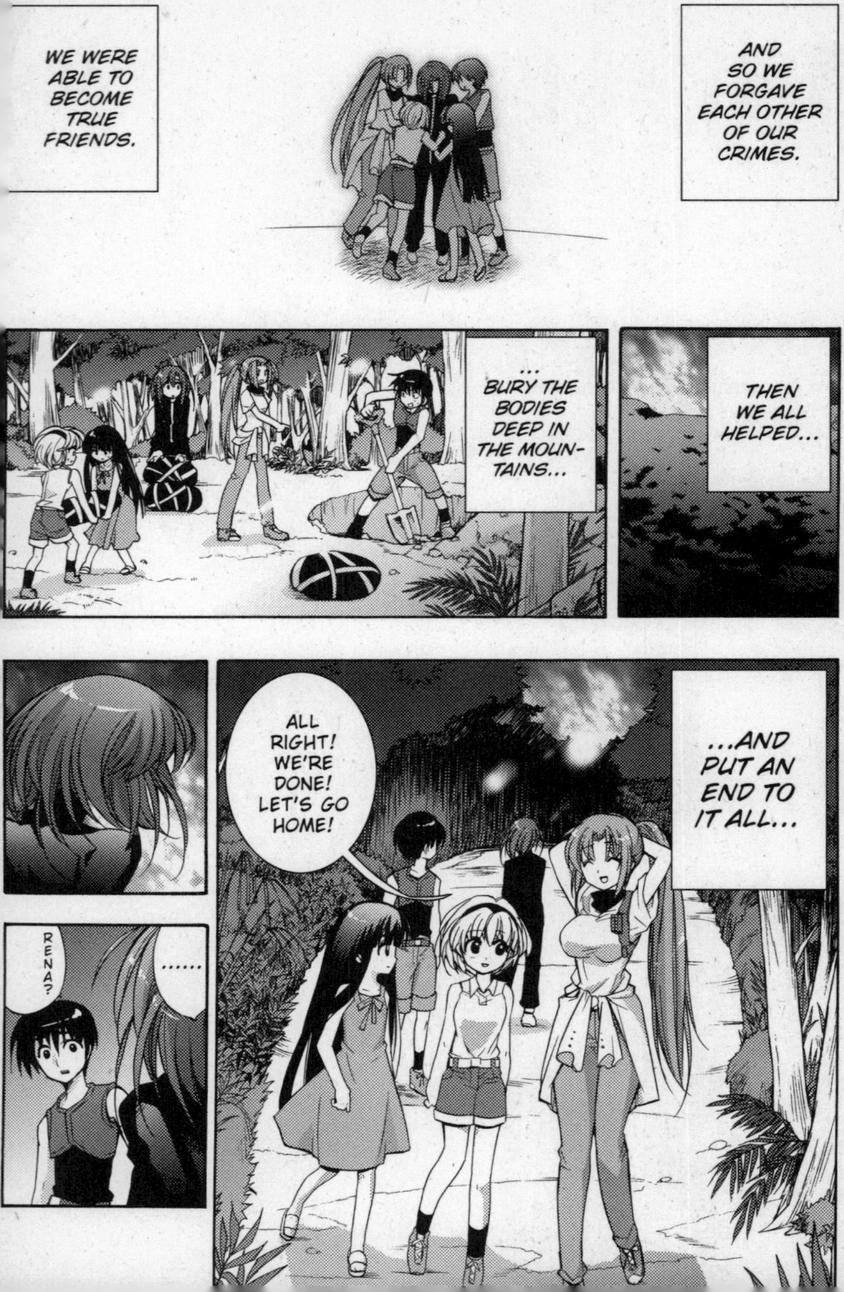
AND SO WE FORGAVE EACH OTHER OF OUR CRIMES.
WE WERE ABLE TO BECOME TRUE FRIENDS.
THEN WE ALL HELPED...
... BURY THE BODIES DEEP IN THE MOUN-TAINS...
...AND PUT AN END TO IT ALL...
ALL RIGHT! WE'RE DONE! LET'S GO HOME!
......
RENA?

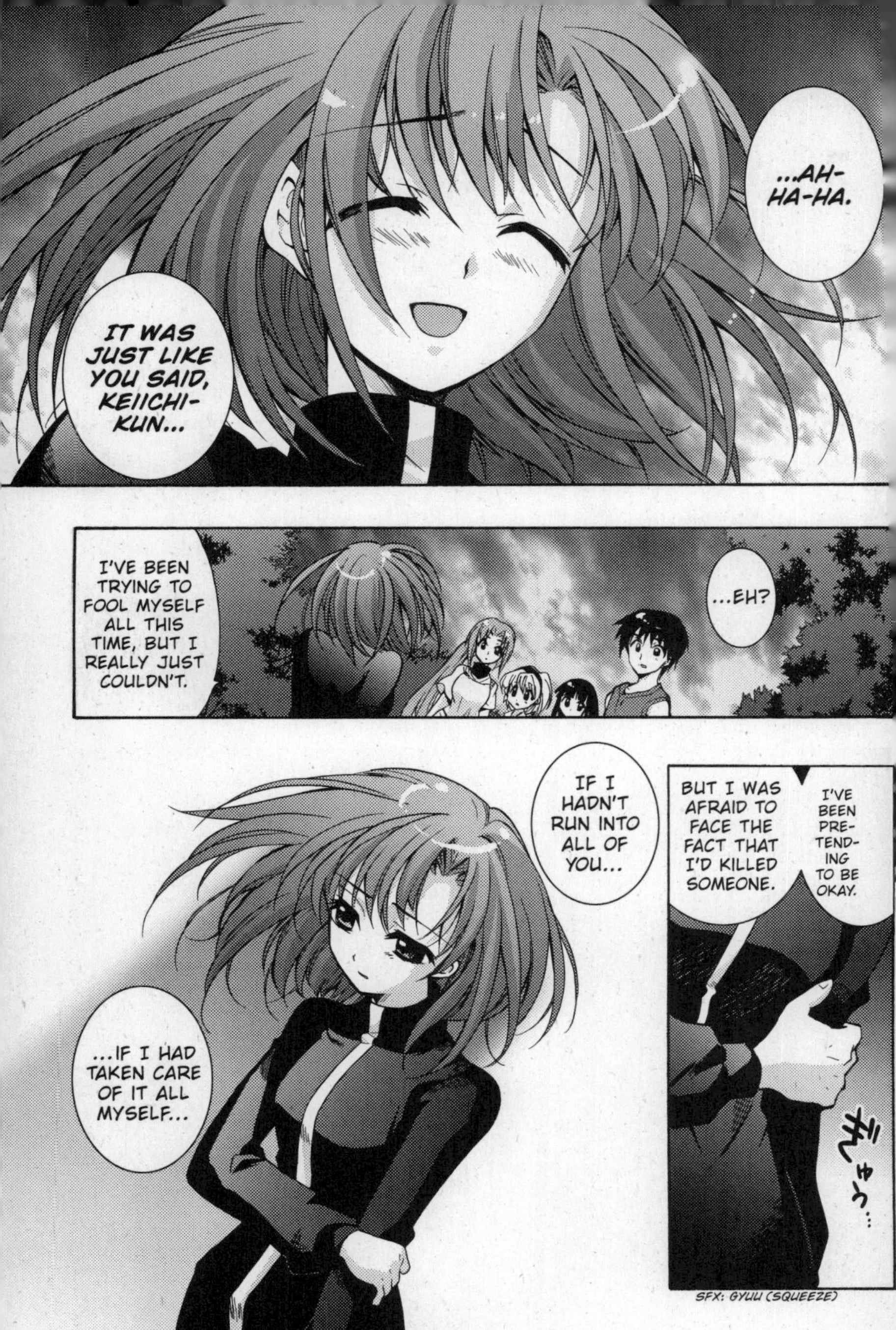
...AH-HA-HA.
IT WAS JUST LIKE YOU SAID, KEIICHI-KUN...
...EH?
I'VE BEEN TRYING TO FOOL MYSELF ALL THIS TIME, BUT I REALLY JUST COULDN'T.
I'VE BEEN PRE-TEND-ING TO BE OKAY.
BUT I WAS AFRAID TO FACE THE FACT THAT I'D KILLED SOMEONE.
ぎゅう…
IF I HADN'T RUN INTO ALL OF YOU...
...IF I HAD TAKEN CARE OF IT ALL MYSELF...
SFX: GYUU (SQUEEZE)

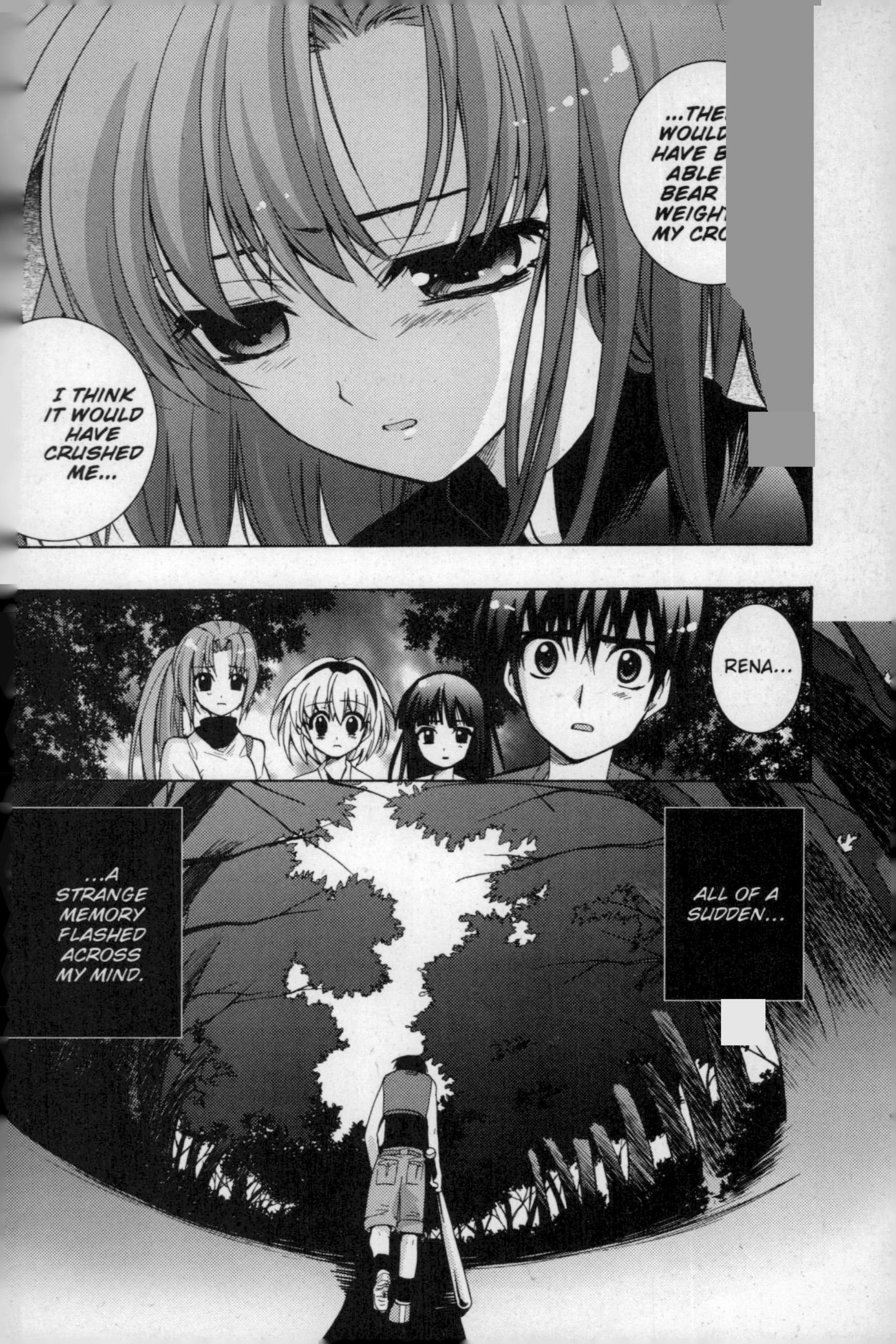
...THE WOULD HAVE B ABLE BEAR WEIGHT MY CRO
I THINK IT WOULD HAVE CRUSHED ME...
RENA...
ALL OF A SUDDEN...
...A STRANGE MEMORY FLASHED ACROSS MY MIND.

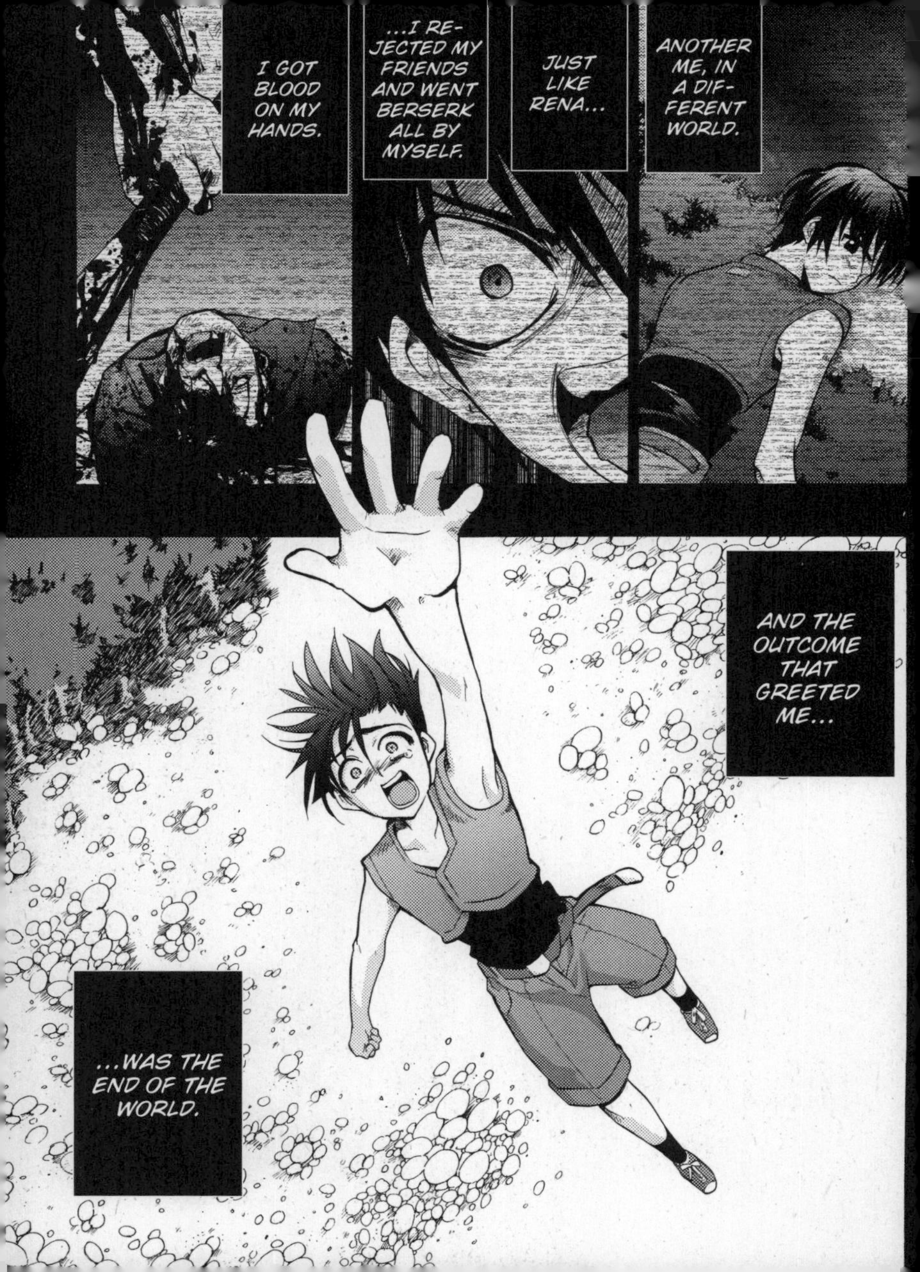
ANOTHER ME, IN A DIF-FERENT WORLD.
JUST LIKE RENA...
...I RE-JECTED MY FRIENDS AND WENT BERSERK ALL BY MYSELF.
I GOT BLOOD ON MY HANDS.
AND THE OUTCOME THAT GREETED ME...
...WAS THE END OF THE WORLD.

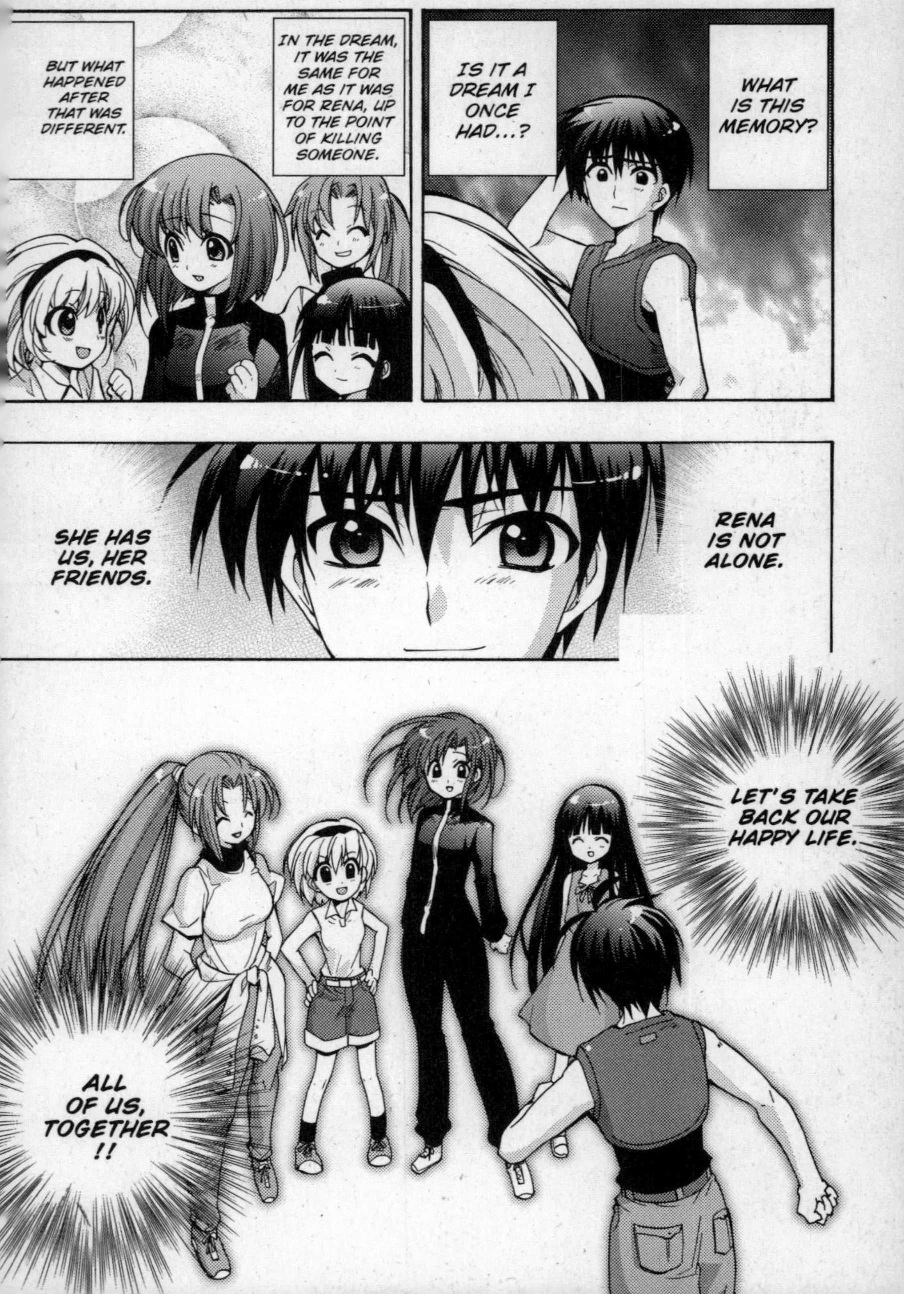
WHAT IS THIS MEMORY?
IS IT A DREAM I ONCE HAD...?
IN THE DREAM, IT WAS THE SAME FOR ME AS IT WAS FOR RENA, UP TO THE POINT OF KILLING SOMEONE.
BUT WHAT HAPPENED AFTER THAT WAS DIFFERENT.
RENA IS NOT ALONE.
SHE HAS US, HER FRIENDS.
LET'S TAKE BACK OUR HAPPY LIFE.
ALL OF US, TOGETHER!!

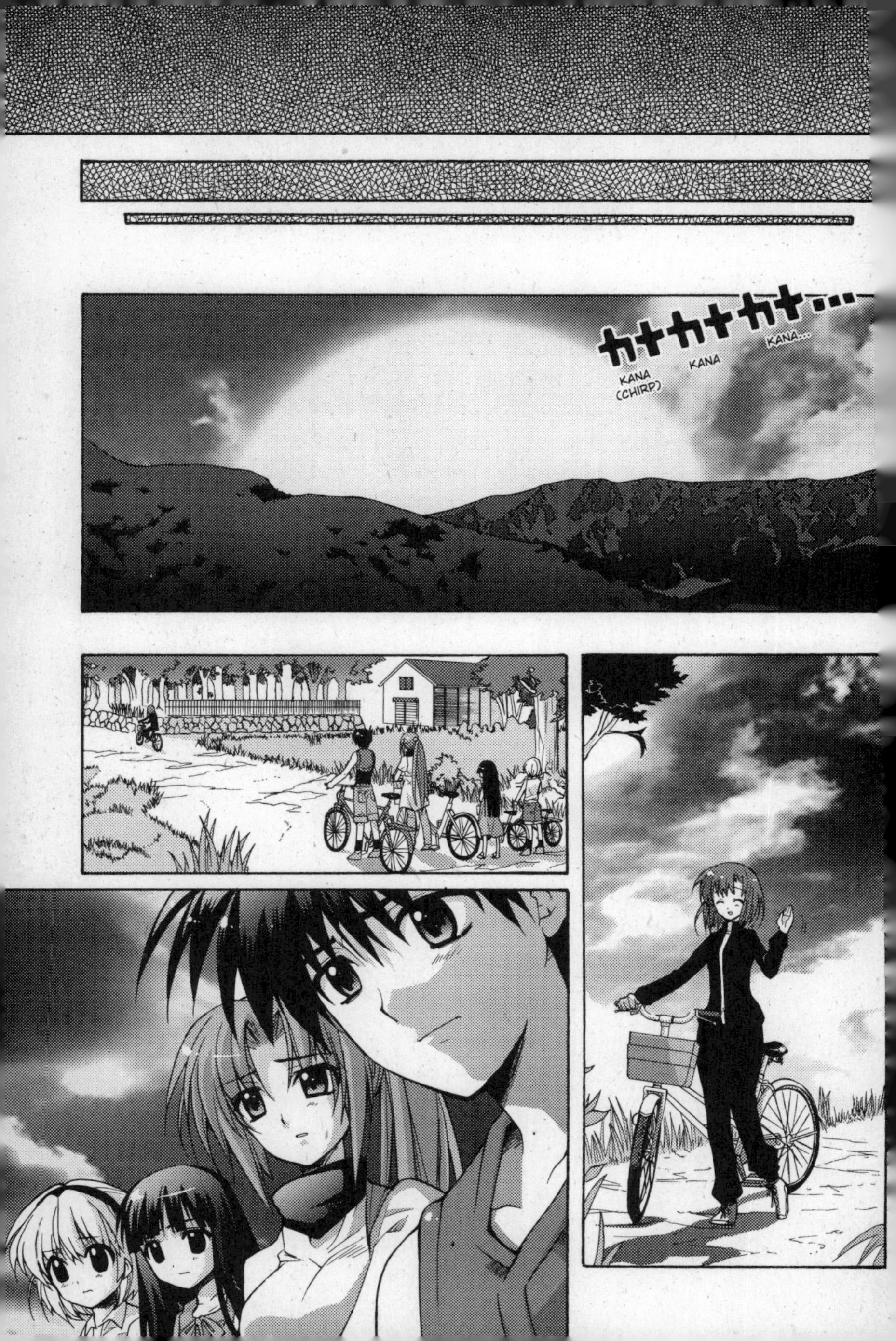
カナカナカナ…
KANA (CHIRP)
KANA
KANA…

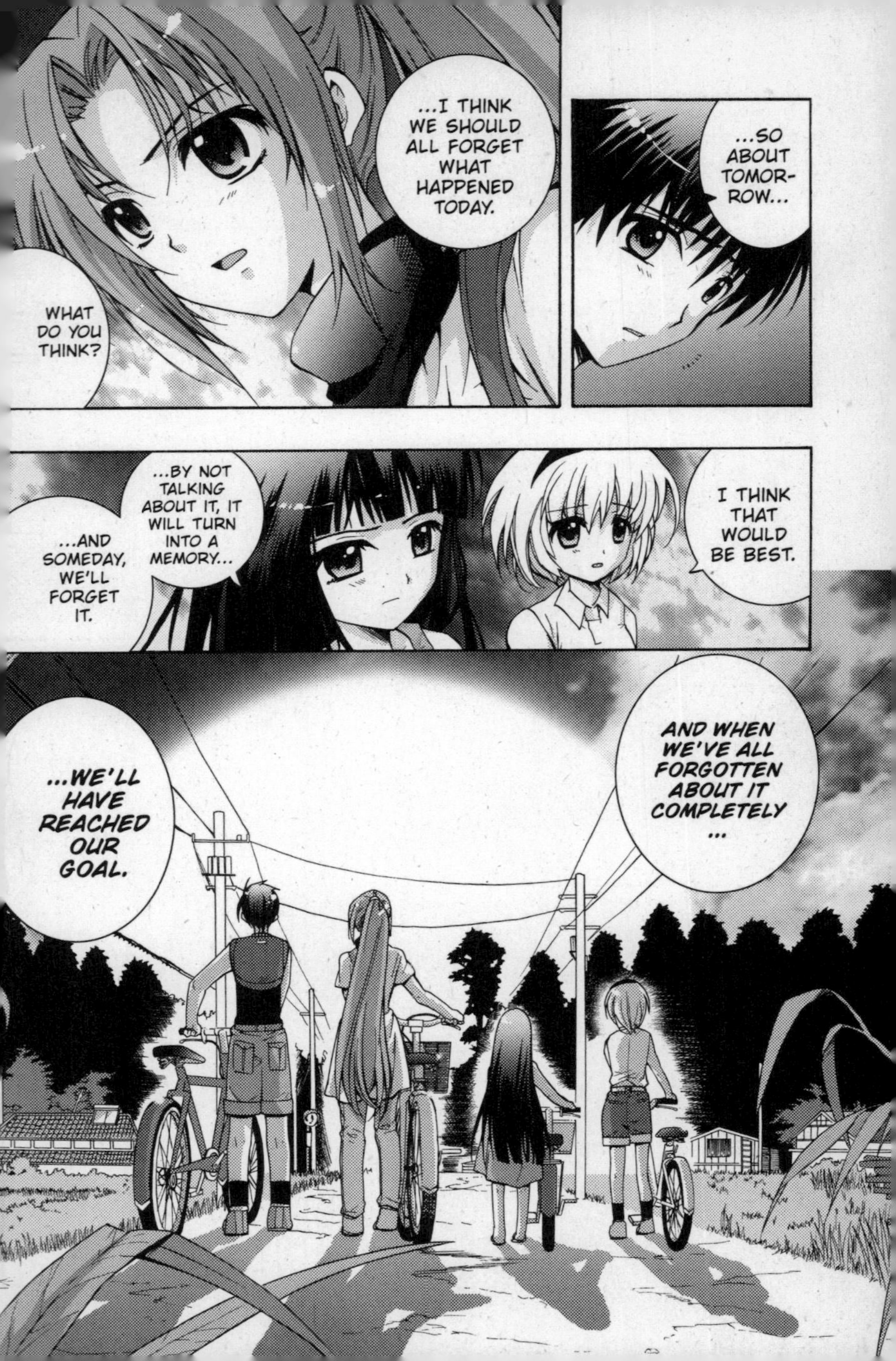
...SO ABOUT TOMORROW...
...I THINK WE SHOULD ALL FORGET WHAT HAPPENED TODAY.
WHAT DO YOU THINK?
I THINK THAT WOULD BE BEST.
...BY NOT TALKING ABOUT IT, IT WILL TURN INTO A MEMORY...
...AND SOMEDAY, WE'LL FORGET IT.
AND WHEN WE'VE ALL FORGOTTEN ABOUT IT COMPLETELY...
...WE'LL HAVE REACHED OUR GOAL.

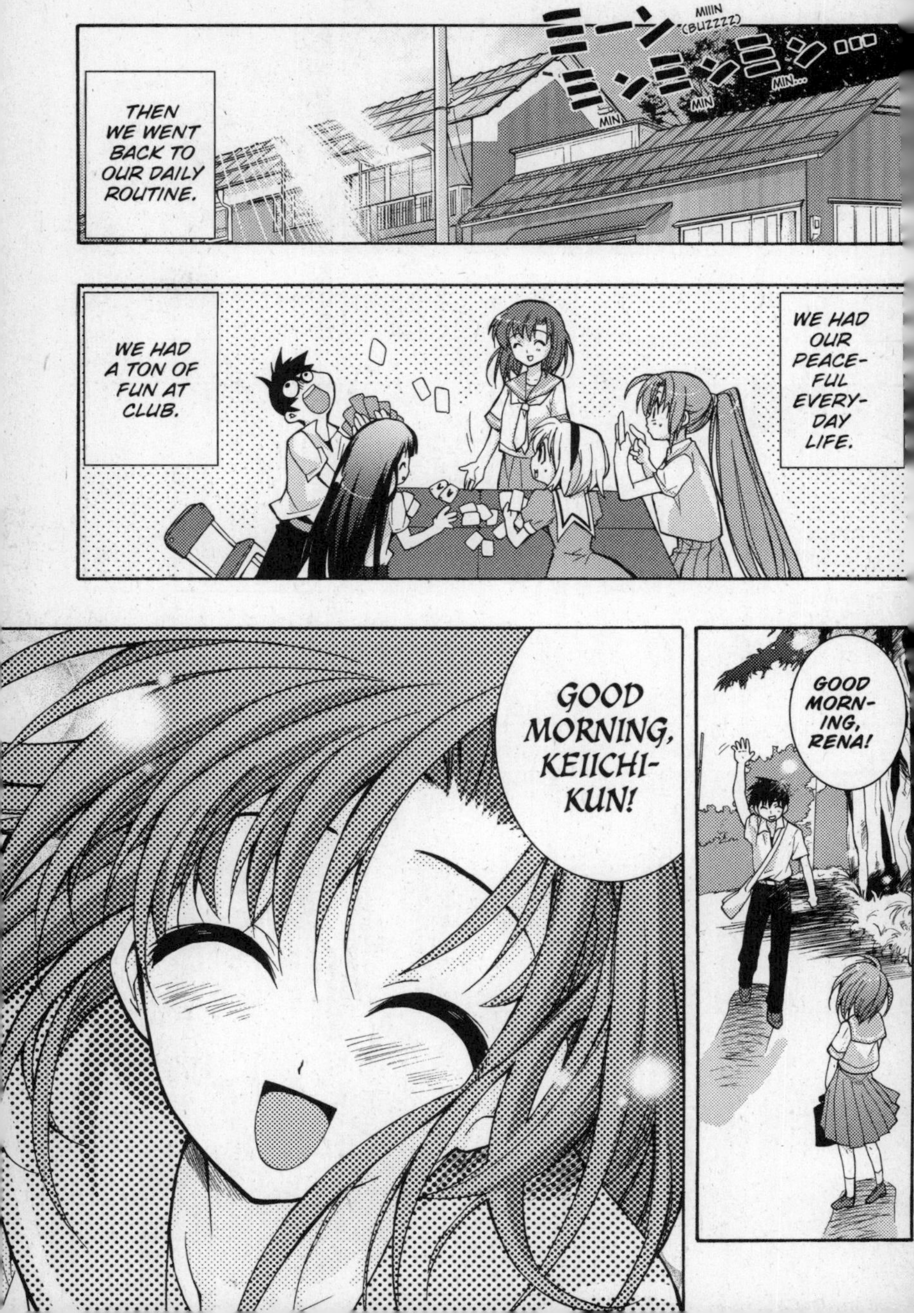
MIIN (BUZZZZ)
MIN
MIN
MIN...
THEN WE WENT BACK TO OUR DAILY ROUTINE.
WE HAD OUR PEACE-FUL EVERY-DAY LIFE.
WE HAD A TON OF FUN AT CLUB.
GOOD MORN-ING, RENA!
GOOD MORNING, KEIICHI-KUN!

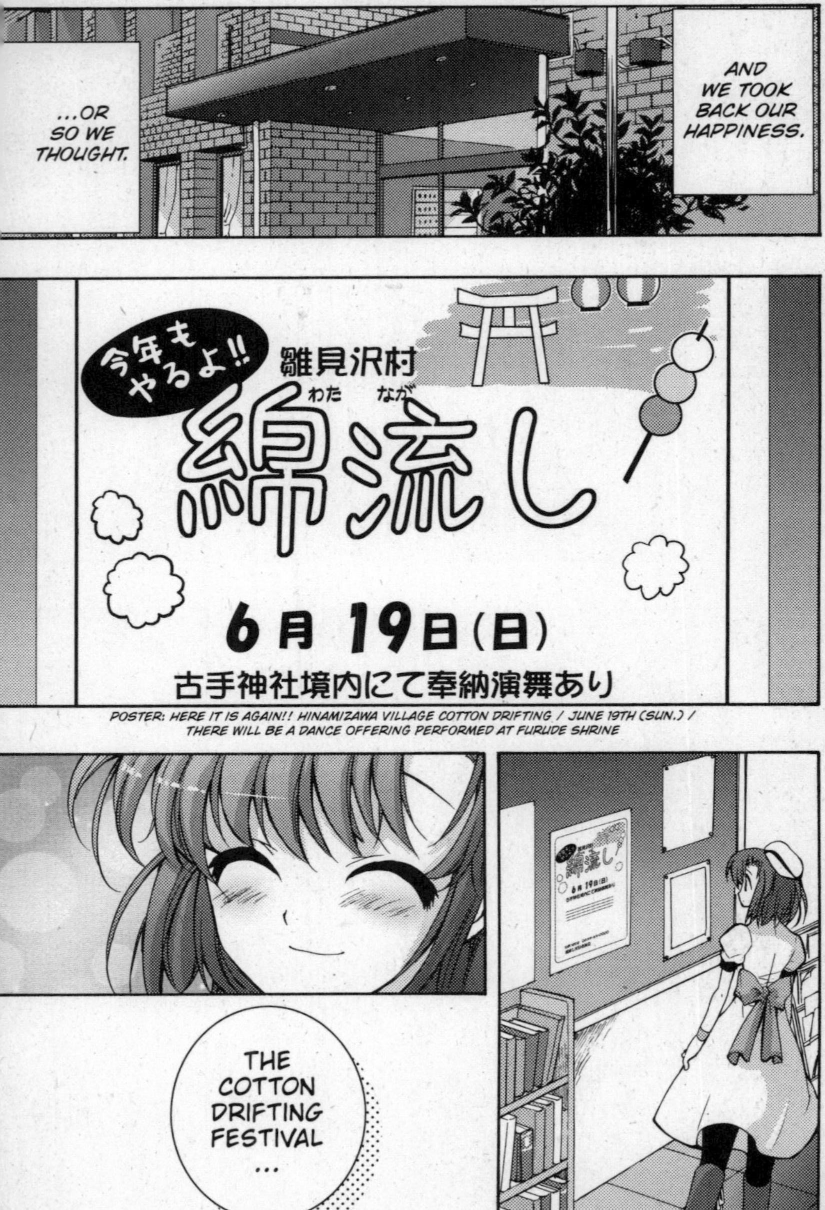
AND WE TOOK BACK OUR HAPPINESS.
...OR SO WE THOUGHT.
今年もやるよ!!
雛見沢村
綿流し
わた なが
6月 19日(日)
古手神社境内にて奉納演舞あり
POSTER: HERE IT IS AGAIN!! HINAMIZAWA VILLAGE COTTON DRIFTING / JUNE 19TH (SUN.) / THERE WILL BE A DANCE OFFERING PERFORMED AT FURUDE SHRINE
THE COTTON DRIFTING FESTIVAL ...

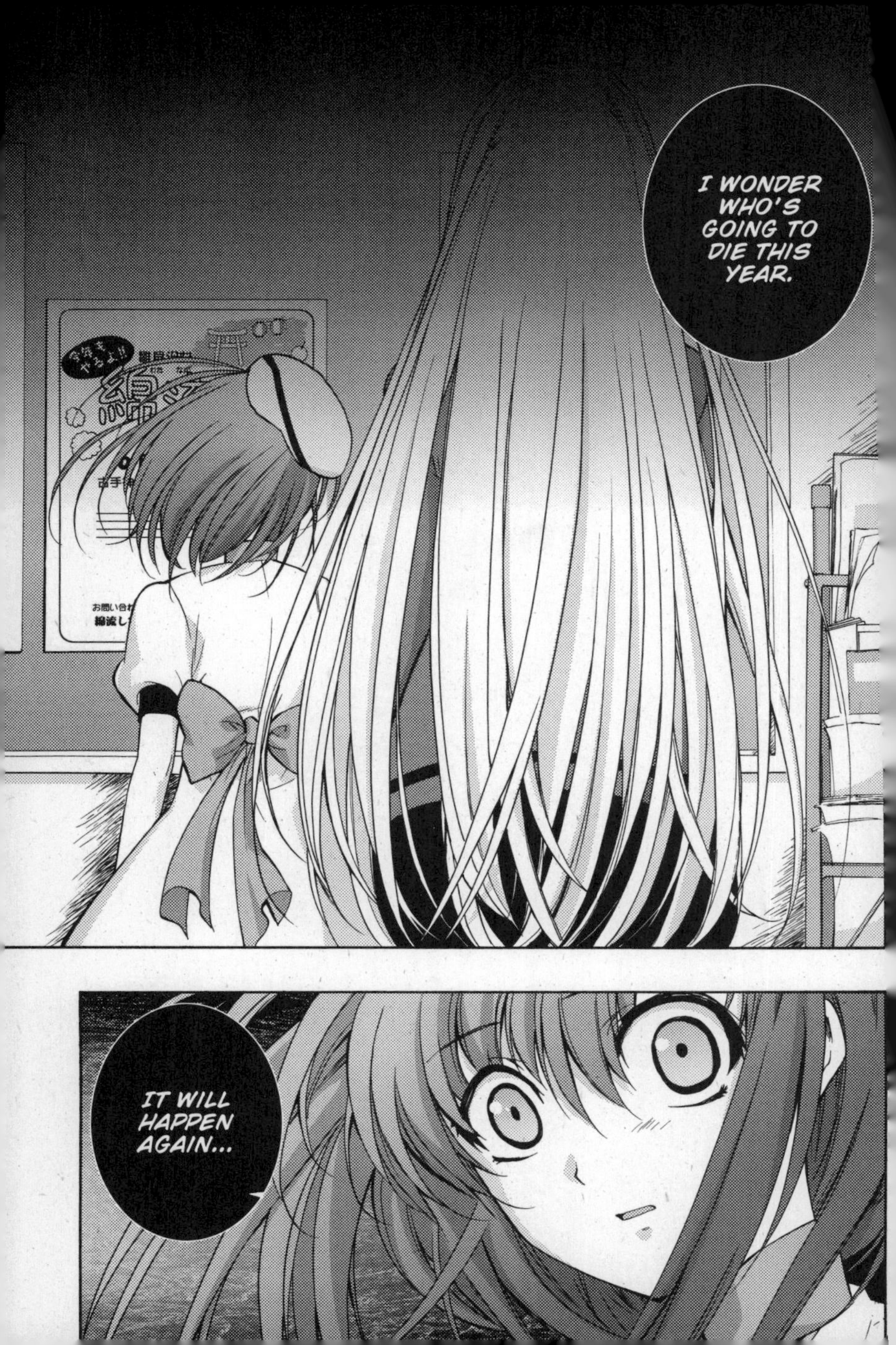
I WONDER WHO'S GOING TO DIE THIS YEAR.
IT WILL HAPPEN AGAIN...

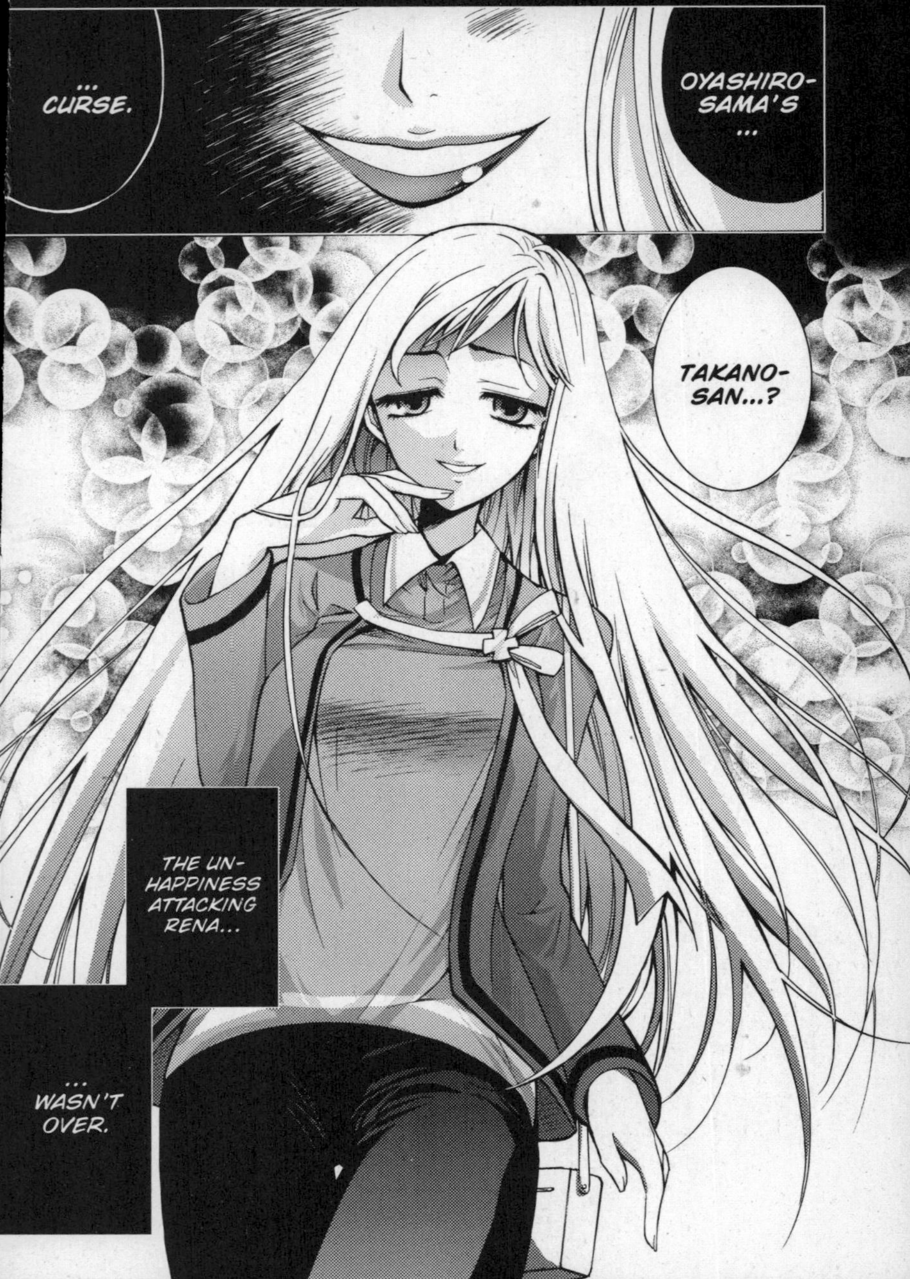
OYASHIRO-SAMA'S ...
... CURSE.
TAKANO-SAN...?
THE UN-HAPPINESS ATTACKING RENA...
... WASN'T OVER.

☆ THE MELANCHOLY OF RIKA FURUDE – PART TWO – ☆

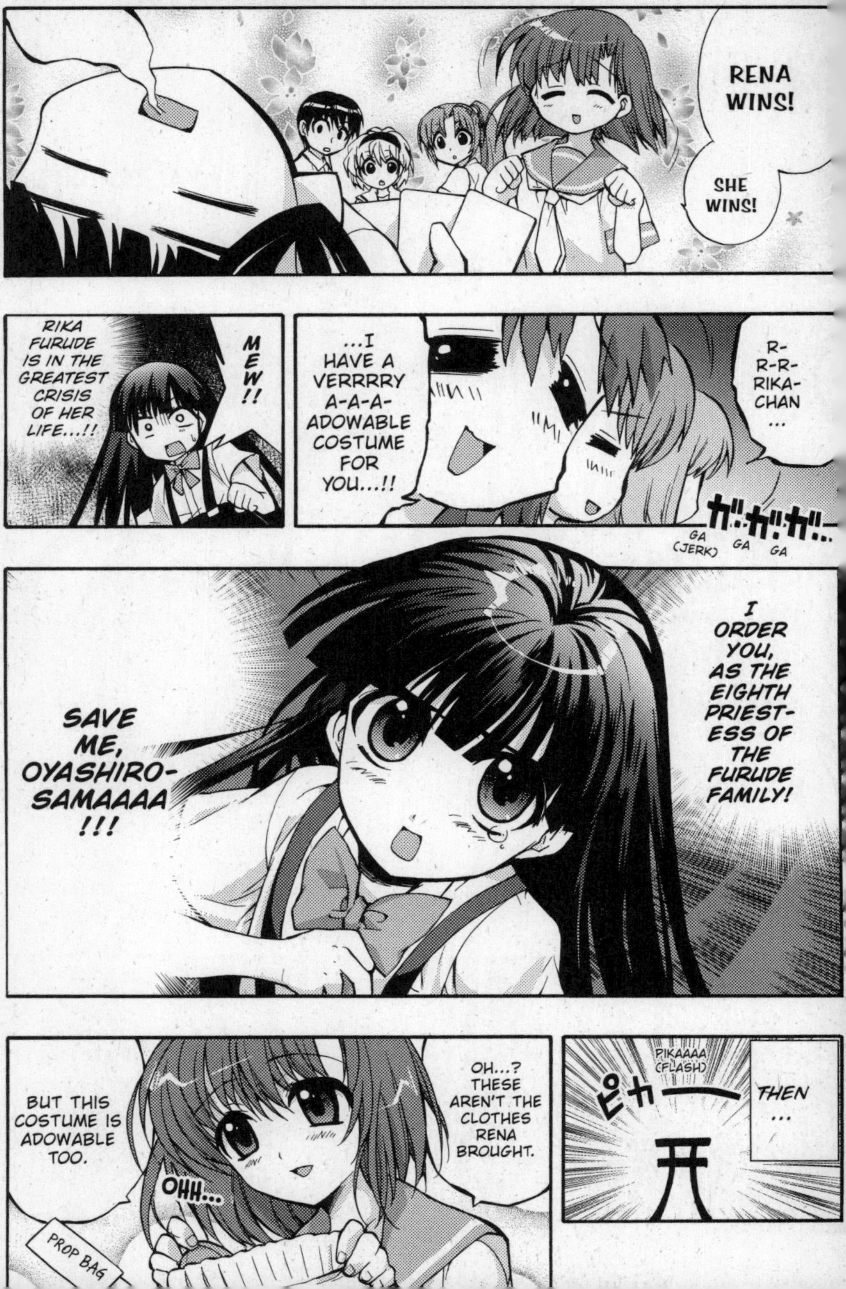
RENA WINS!
SHE WINS!
R-R-R-RIKA-CHAN ...
...I HAVE A VERRRRY A-A-A-ADOWABLE COSTUME FOR YOU...!!
GA (JERK) GA GA
MEW!!
RIKA FURUDE IS IN THE GREATEST CRISIS OF HER LIFE...!!
I ORDER YOU, AS THE EIGHTH PRIEST-ESS OF THE FURUDE FAMILY!
SAVE ME, OYASHIRO-SAMAAAA!!!
THEN ...
PIKAAAA (FLASH)
OH...? THESE AREN'T THE CLOTHES RENA BROUGHT.
BUT THIS COSTUME IS ADOWABLE TOO.
OHH...
PROP BAG

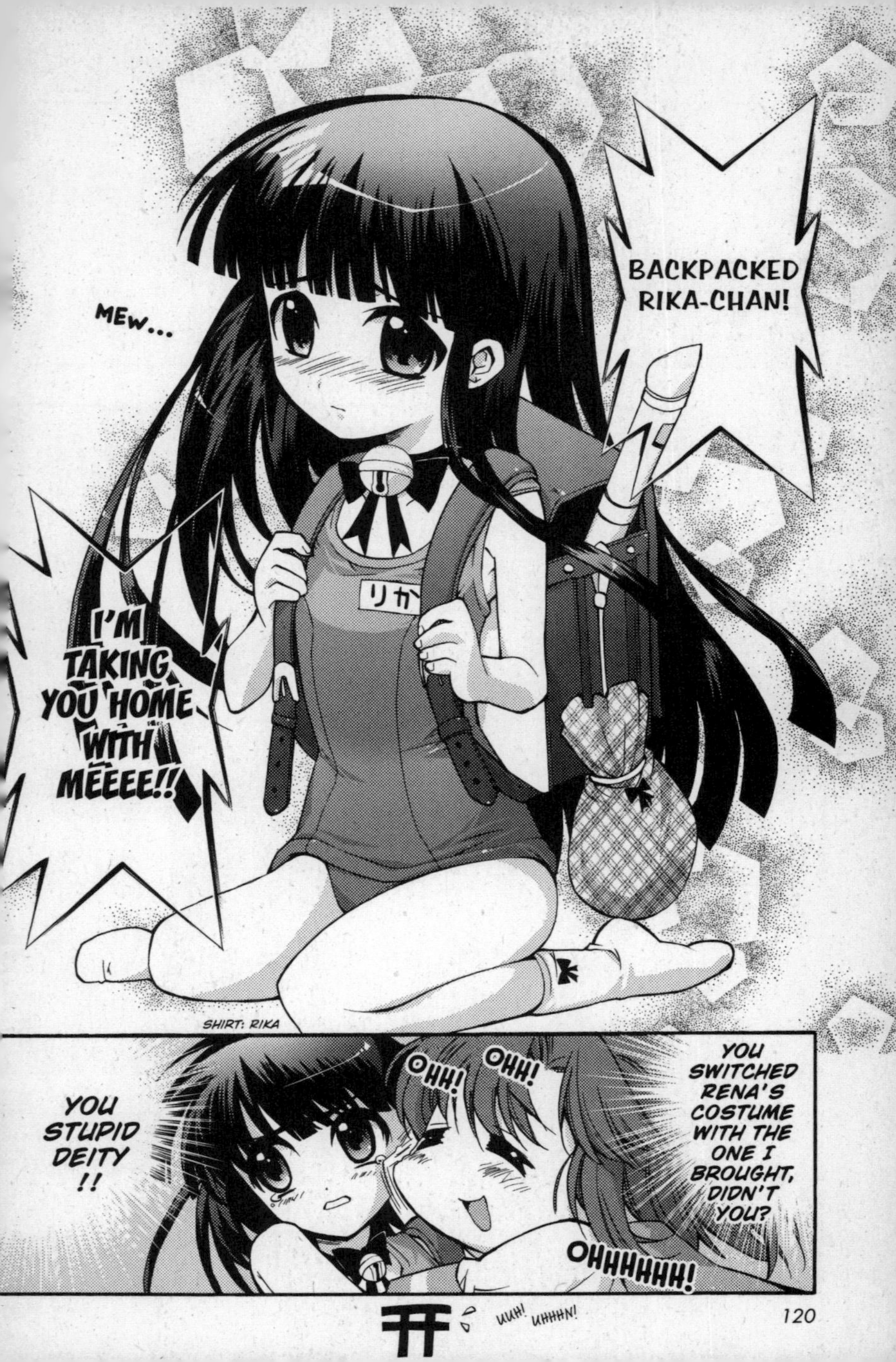
BACKPACKED RIKA-CHAN!
MEW...
I'M TAKING YOU HOME WITH MEEEEE!!
SHIRT: RIKA
YOU SWITCHED RENA'S COSTUME WITH THE ONE I BROUGHT, DIDN'T YOU?
OHH! OHH!
OHHHHHHH!
YOU STUPID DEITY!!
UUH! UHHHN!

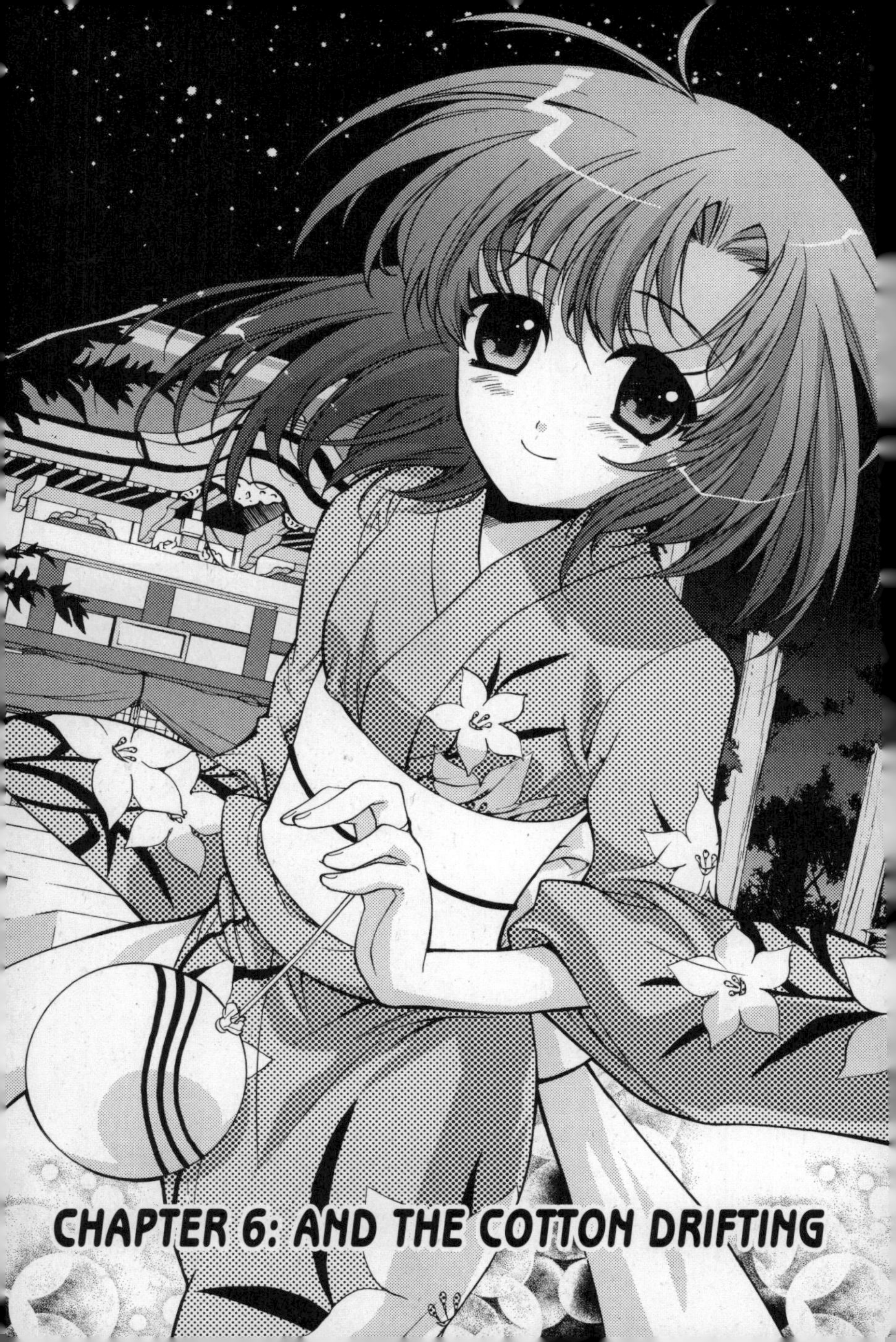
CHAPTER 6: AND THE COTTON DRIFTING

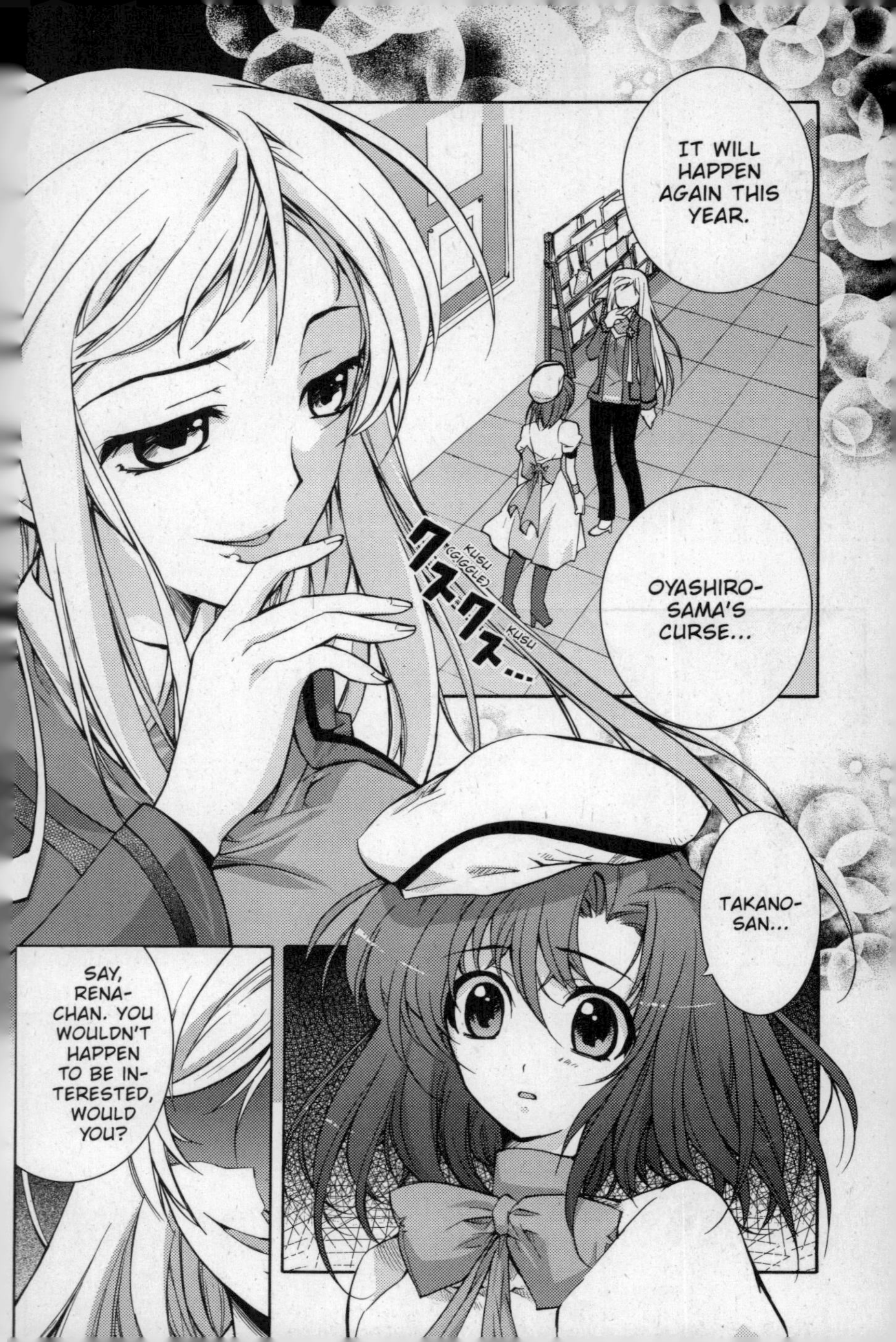
IT WILL HAPPEN AGAIN THIS YEAR.
OYASHIRO-SAMA'S CURSE...
KUSU (GIGGLE)
KUSU
TAKANO-SAN...
SAY, RENA-CHAN. YOU WOULDN'T HAPPEN TO BE INTERESTED, WOULD YOU?

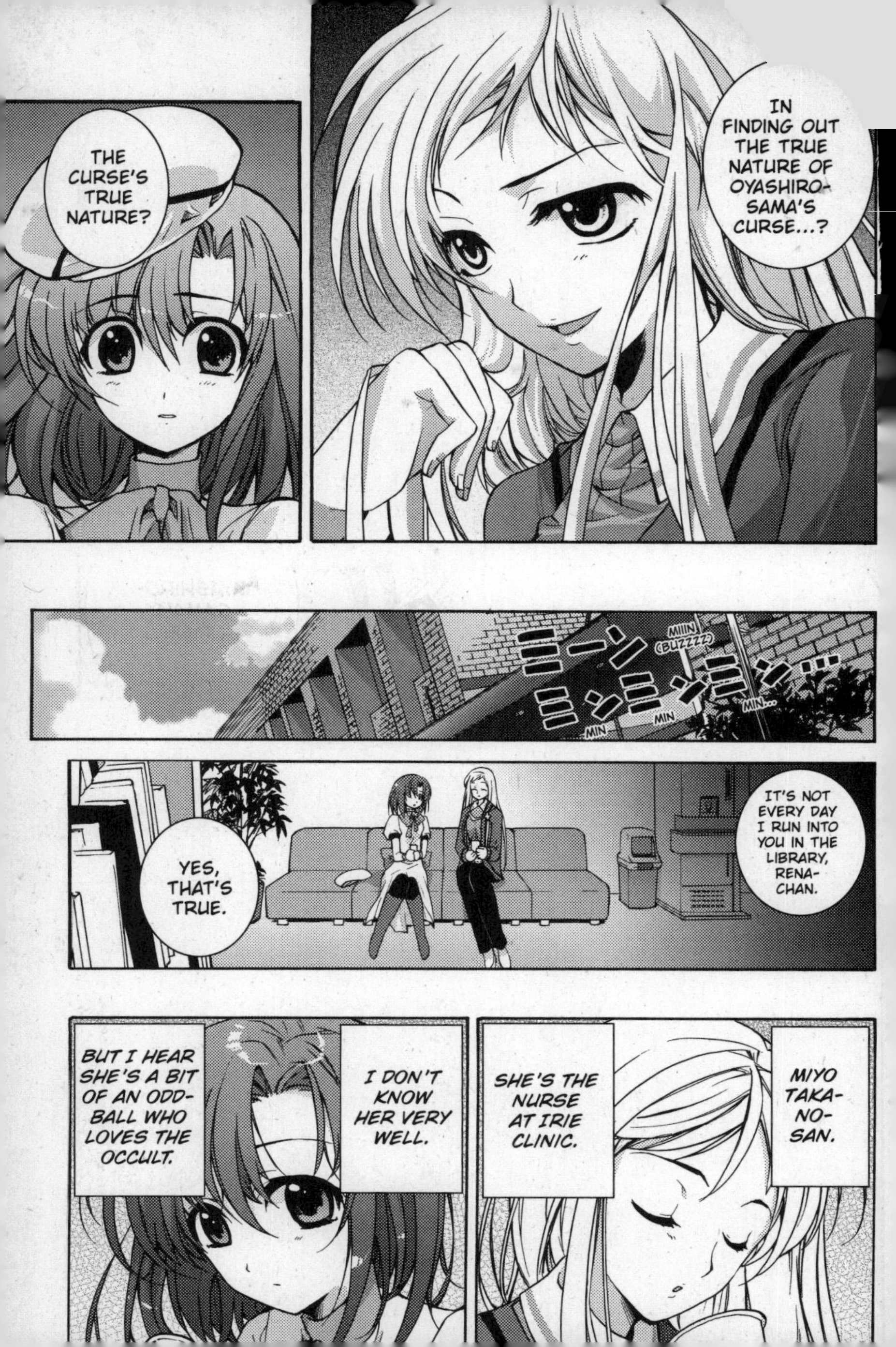
IN FINDING OUT THE TRUE NATURE OF OYASHIRO-SAMA'S CURSE...?
THE CURSE'S TRUE NATURE?
MIIIN (BUZZZZ)
MIN...
MIN
MIN
IT'S NOT EVERY DAY I RUN INTO YOU IN THE LIBRARY, RENA-CHAN.
YES, THAT'S TRUE.
MIYO TAKANO-SAN.
SHE'S THE NURSE AT IRIE CLINIC.
I DON'T KNOW HER VERY WELL.
BUT I HEAR SHE'S A BIT OF AN ODDBALL WHO LOVES THE OCCULT.

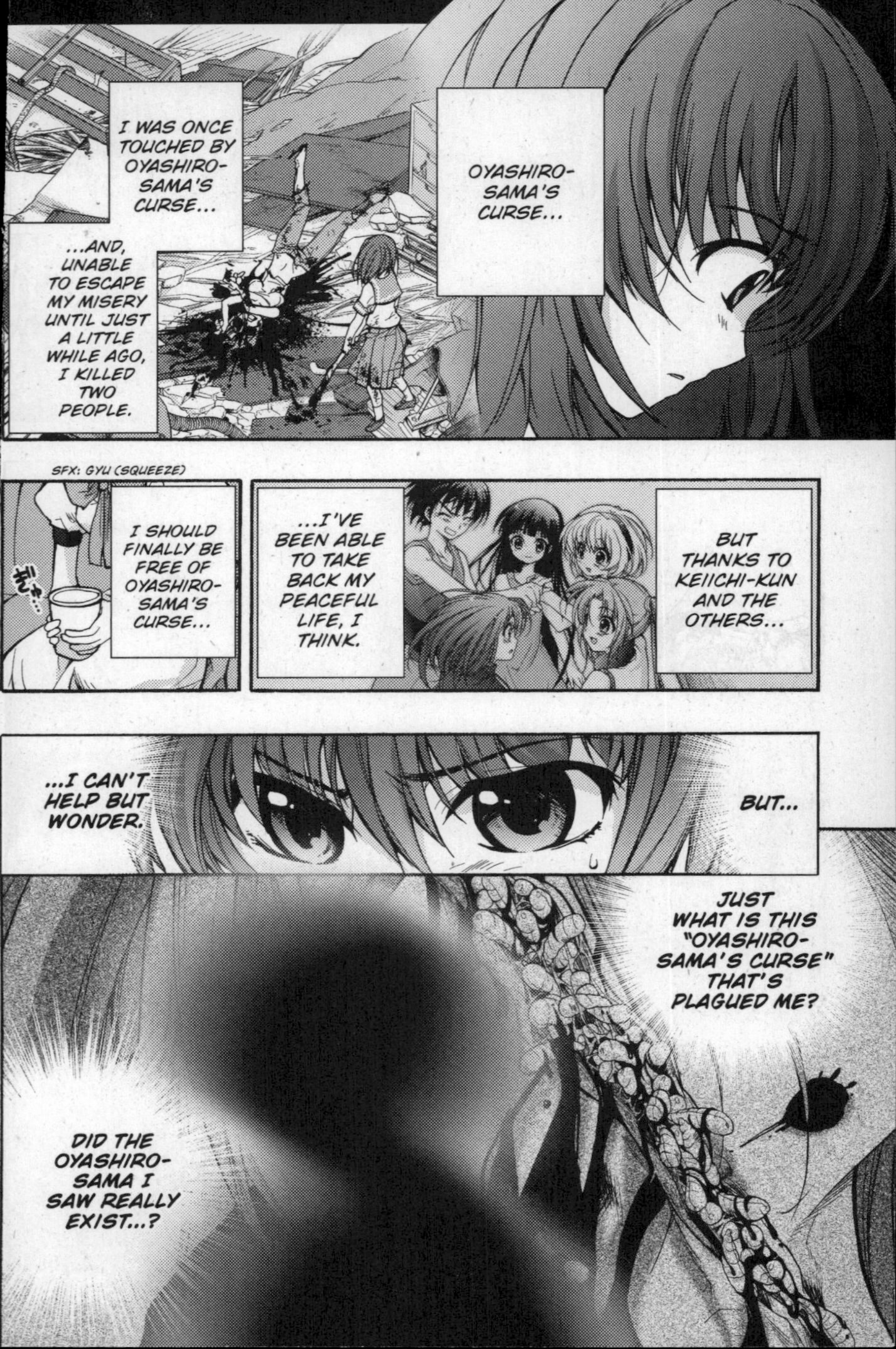
OYASHIRO-SAMA'S CURSE...
I WAS ONCE TOUCHED BY OYASHIRO-SAMA'S CURSE...
...AND, UNABLE TO ESCAPE MY MISERY UNTIL JUST A LITTLE WHILE AGO, I KILLED TWO PEOPLE.
SFX: GYU (SQUEEZE)
BUT THANKS TO KEIICHI-KUN AND THE OTHERS...
...I'VE BEEN ABLE TO TAKE BACK MY PEACEFUL LIFE, I THINK.
I SHOULD FINALLY BE FREE OF OYASHIRO-SAMA'S CURSE...
BUT...
...I CAN'T HELP BUT WONDER.
JUST WHAT IS THIS "OYASHIRO-SAMA'S CURSE" THAT'S PLAGUED ME?
DID THE OYASHIRO-SAMA I SAW REALLY EXIST...?

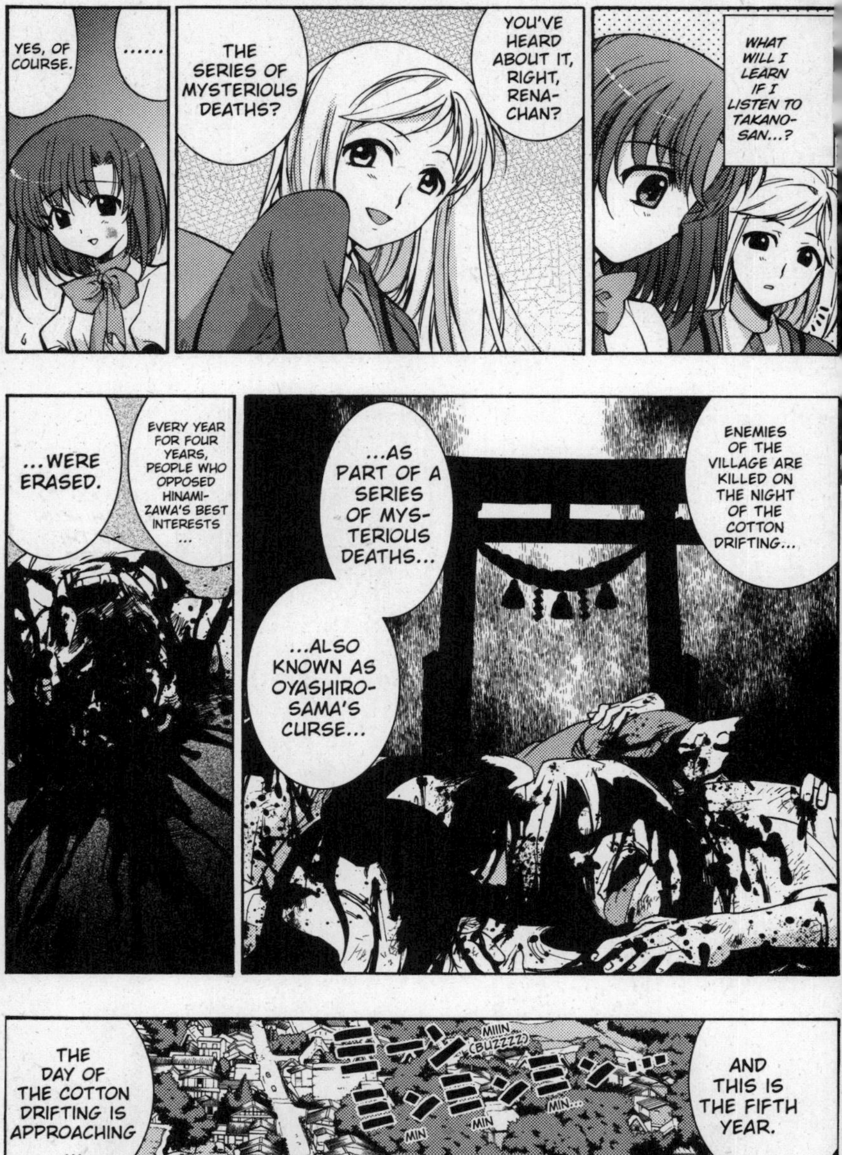
WHAT WILL I LEARN IF I LISTEN TO TAKANO-SAN...?
YOU'VE HEARD ABOUT IT, RIGHT, RENA-CHAN?
THE SERIES OF MYSTERIOUS DEATHS?
......
YES, OF COURSE.
ENEMIES OF THE VILLAGE ARE KILLED ON THE NIGHT OF THE COTTON DRIFTING...
...AS PART OF A SERIES OF MYS-TERIOUS DEATHS...
...ALSO KNOWN AS OYASHIRO-SAMA'S CURSE...
EVERY YEAR FOR FOUR YEARS, PEOPLE WHO OPPOSED HINAMI-ZAWA'S BEST INTERESTS ...
...WERE ERASED.
AND THIS IS THE FIFTH YEAR.
MIIIN (BUZZZZ)
MIN...
MIN
MIN
THE DAY OF THE COTTON DRIFTING IS APPROACHING ...

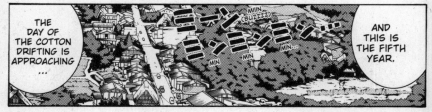

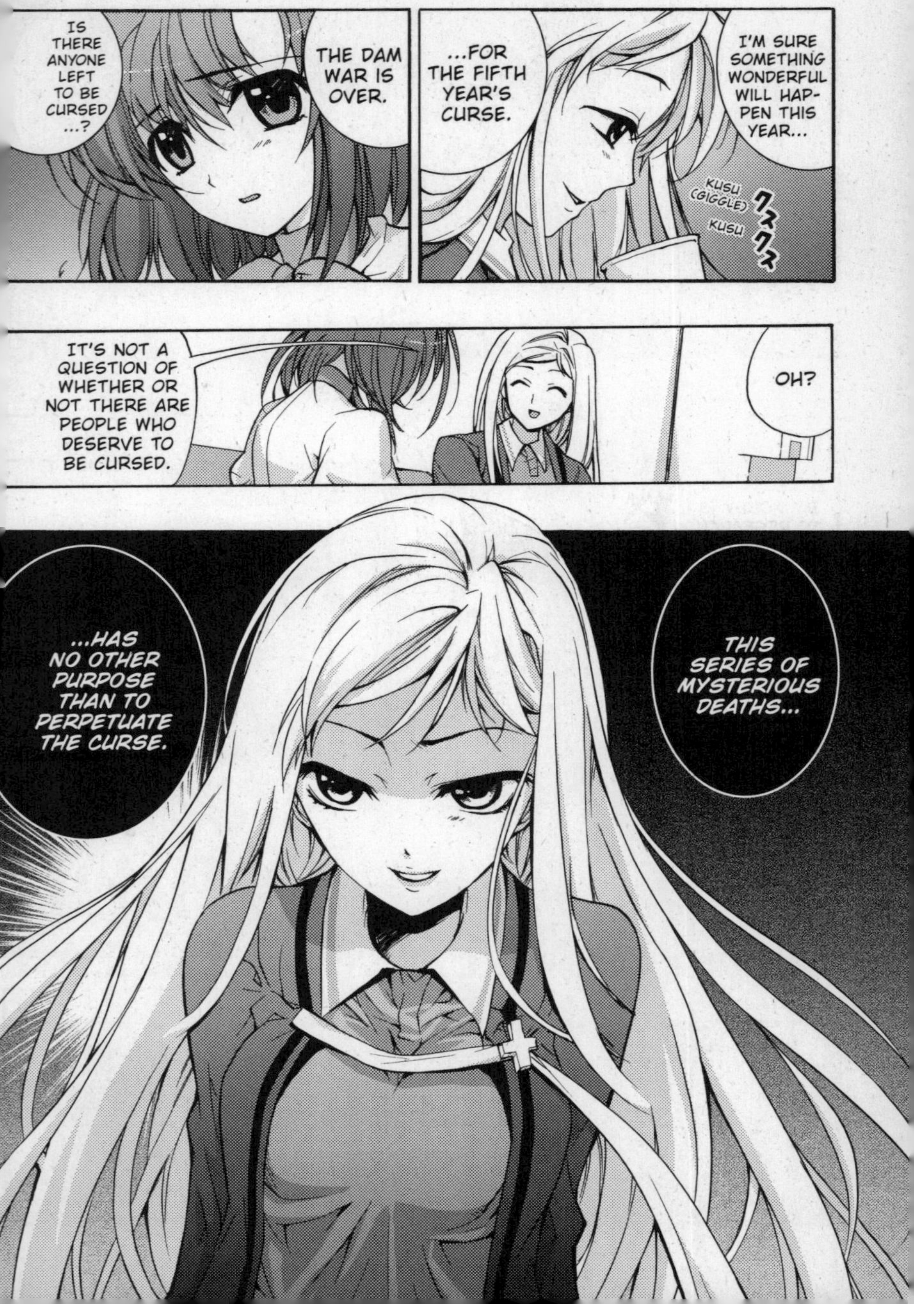
I'M SURE SOMETHING WONDERFUL WILL HAPPEN THIS YEAR...
KUSU (GIGGLE) KUSU
クスクス
...FOR THE FIFTH YEAR'S CURSE.
THE DAM WAR IS OVER.
IS THERE ANYONE LEFT TO BE CURSED ...?
OH?
IT'S NOT A QUESTION OF WHETHER OR NOT THERE ARE PEOPLE WHO DESERVE TO BE CURSED.
THIS SERIES OF MYSTERIOUS DEATHS...
...HAS NO OTHER PURPOSE THAN TO PERPETUATE THE CURSE.

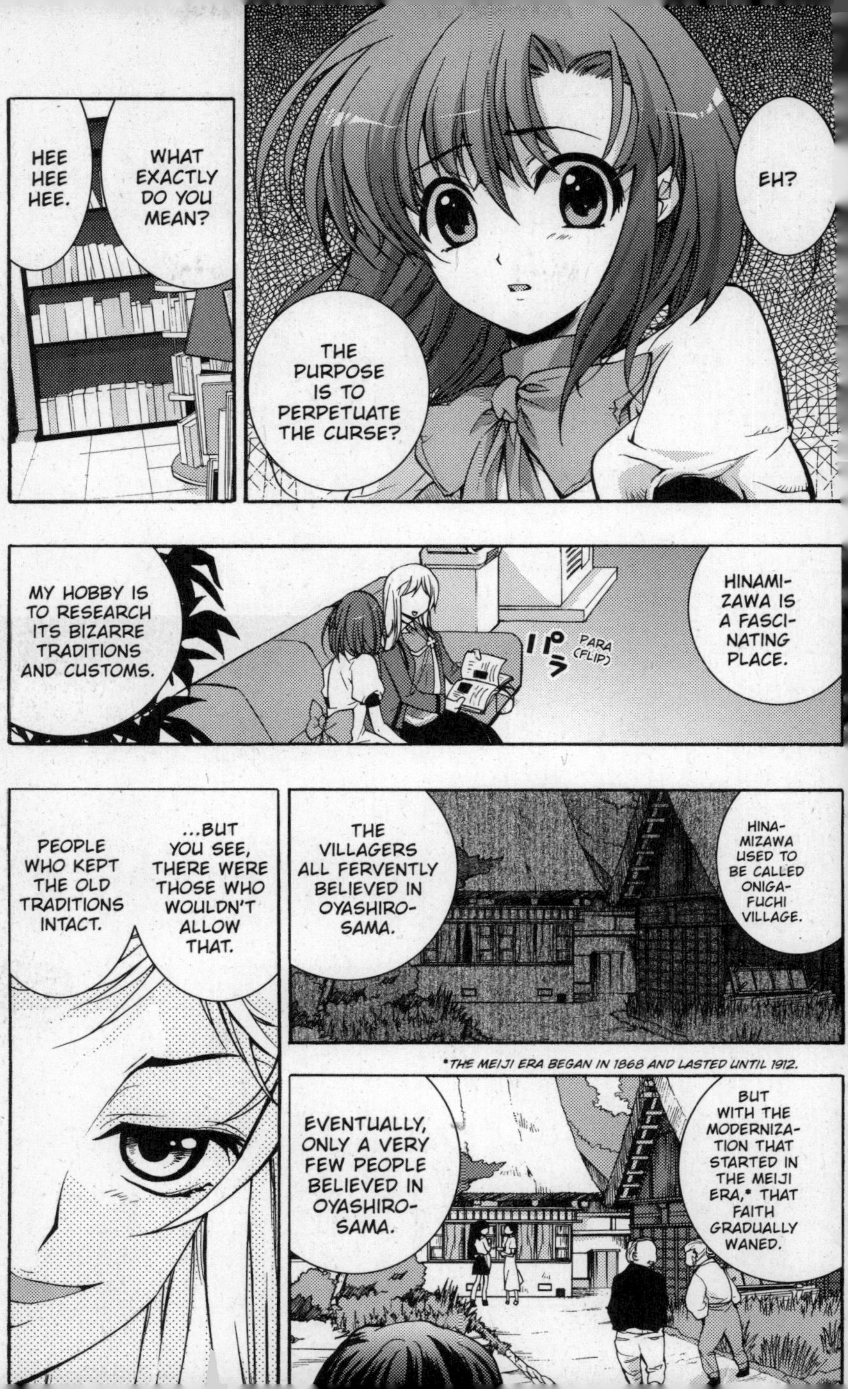
EH?
THE PURPOSE IS TO PERPETUATE THE CURSE?
WHAT EXACTLY DO YOU MEAN?
HEE HEE HEE.
HINAMI-ZAWA IS A FASCI-NATING PLACE.
パラ PARA (FLIP)
MY HOBBY IS TO RESEARCH ITS BIZARRE TRADITIONS AND CUSTOMS.
HINA-MIZAWA USED TO BE CALLED ONIGA-FUCHI VILLAGE.
THE VILLAGERS ALL FERVENTLY BELIEVED IN OYASHIRO-SAMA.
BUT WITH THE MODERNIZA-TION THAT STARTED IN THE MEIJI ERA,* THAT FAITH GRADUALLY WANED.
EVENTUALLY, ONLY A VERY FEW PEOPLE BELIEVED IN OYASHIRO-SAMA.
...BUT YOU SEE, THERE WERE THOSE WHO WOULDN'T ALLOW THAT.
PEOPLE WHO KEPT THE OLD TRADITIONS INTACT.

*THE MEIJI ERA BEGAN IN 1868 AND LASTED UNTIL 1912.

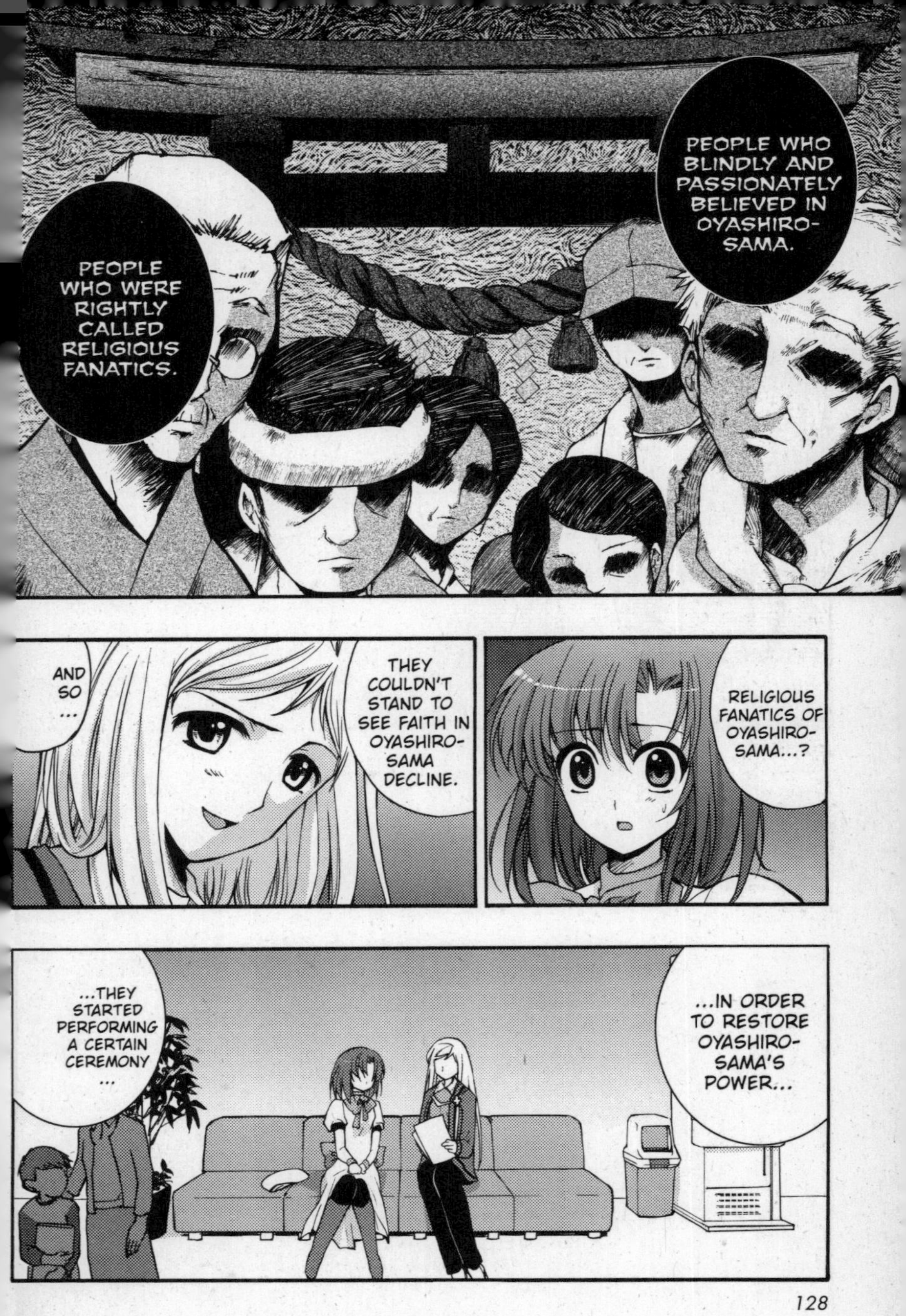
PEOPLE WHO BLINDLY AND PASSIONATELY BELIEVED IN OYASHIRO-SAMA.
PEOPLE WHO WERE RIGHTLY CALLED RELIGIOUS FANATICS.
RELIGIOUS FANATICS OF OYASHIRO-SAMA...?
THEY COULDN'T STAND TO SEE FAITH IN OYASHIRO-SAMA DECLINE.
AND SO ...
...IN ORDER TO RESTORE OYASHIRO-SAMA'S POWER...
...THEY STARTED PERFORMING A CERTAIN CEREMONY ...

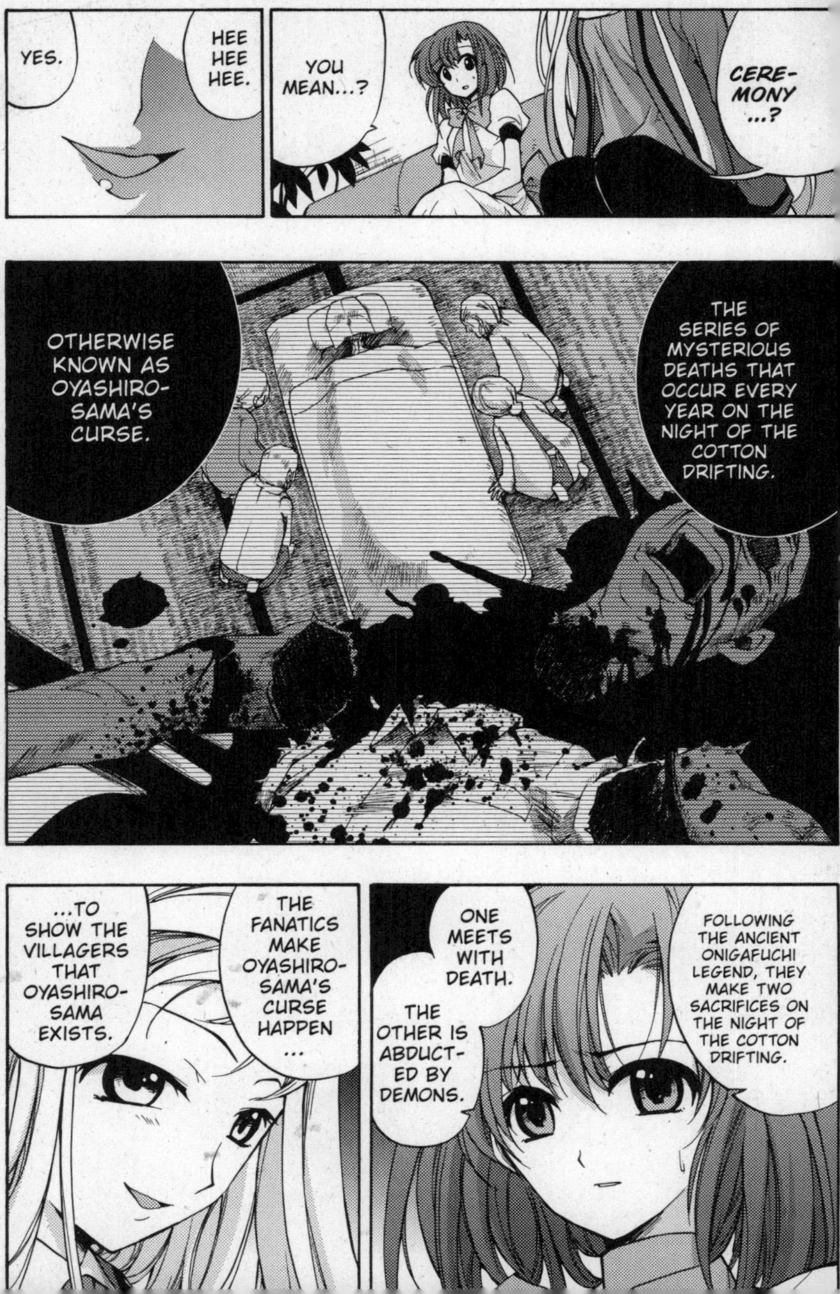
CEREMONY...?
YOU MEAN...?
HEE HEE HEE.
YES.
THE SERIES OF MYSTERIOUS DEATHS THAT OCCUR EVERY YEAR ON THE NIGHT OF THE COTTON DRIFTING.
OTHERWISE KNOWN AS OYASHIRO-SAMA'S CURSE.
FOLLOWING THE ANCIENT ONIGAFUCHI LEGEND, THEY MAKE TWO SACRIFICES ON THE NIGHT OF THE COTTON DRIFTING.
ONE MEETS WITH DEATH.
THE OTHER IS ABDUCTED BY DEMONS.
THE FANATICS MAKE OYASHIRO-SAMA'S CURSE HAPPEN...
...TO SHOW THE VILLAGERS THAT OYASHIRO-SAMA EXISTS.

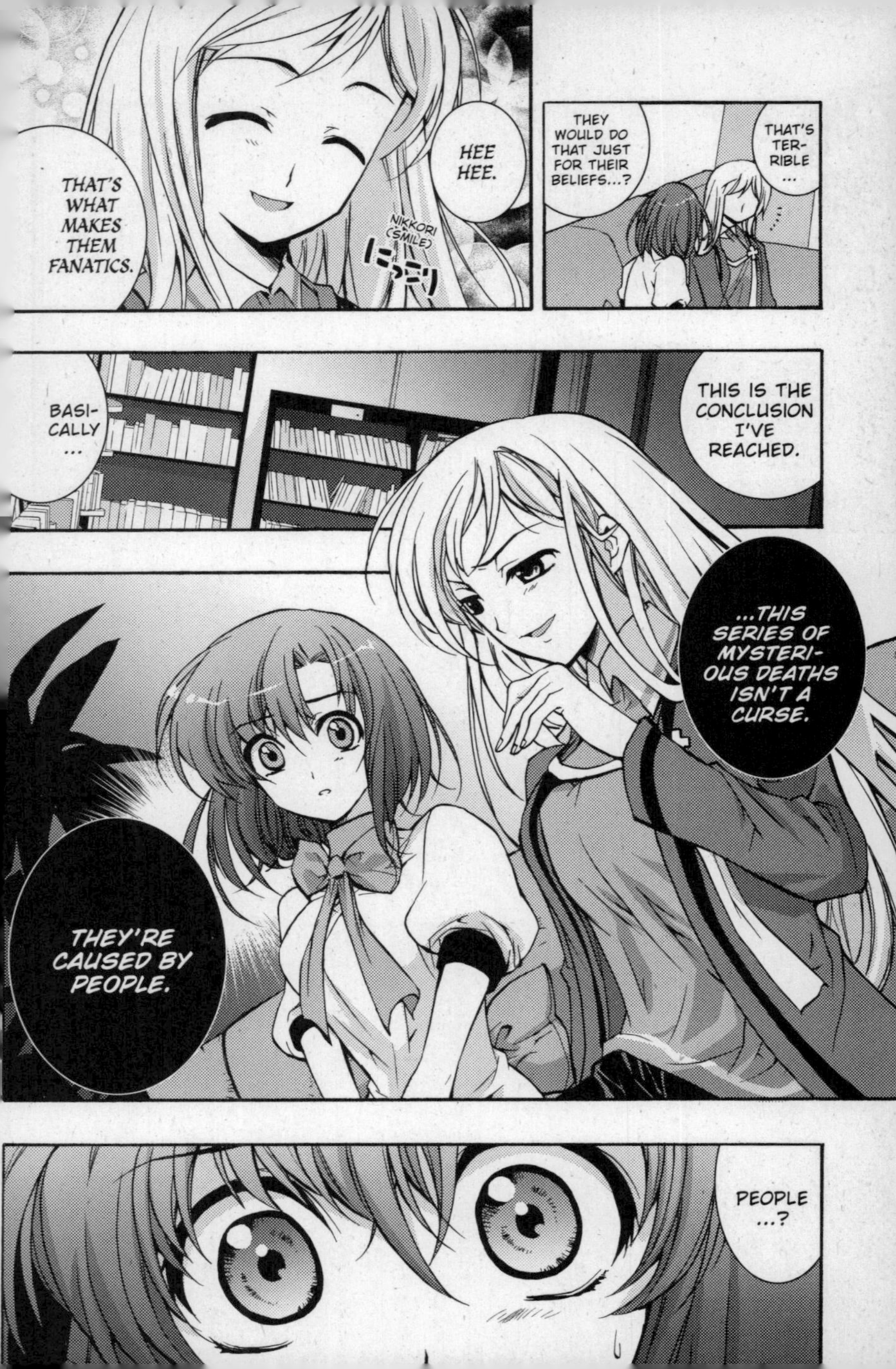
THAT'S TERRIBLE ...
THEY WOULD DO THAT JUST FOR THEIR BELIEFS...?
...
HEE HEE.
NIKKORI (SMILE)
THAT'S WHAT MAKES THEM FANATICS.
THIS IS THE CONCLUSION I'VE REACHED.
BASICALLY ...
...THIS SERIES OF MYSTERIOUS DEATHS ISN'T A CURSE.
THEY'RE CAUSED BY PEOPLE.
PEOPLE ...?

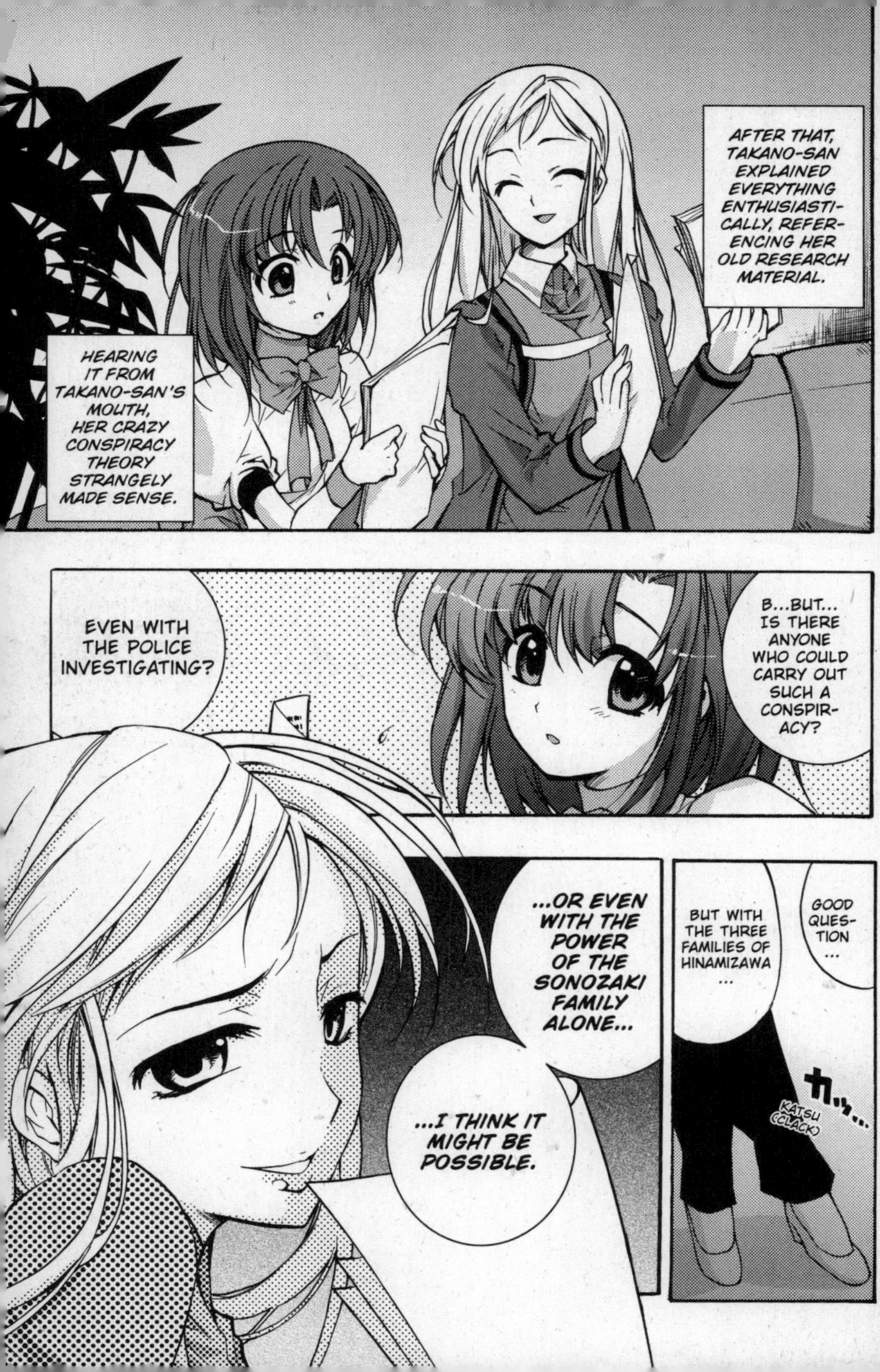
AFTER THAT, TAKANO-SAN EXPLAINED EVERYTHING ENTHUSIASTICALLY, REFERENCING HER OLD RESEARCH MATERIAL.
HEARING IT FROM TAKANO-SAN'S MOUTH, HER CRAZY CONSPIRACY THEORY STRANGELY MADE SENSE.
B...BUT... IS THERE ANYONE WHO COULD CARRY OUT SUCH A CONSPIRACY?
EVEN WITH THE POLICE INVESTIGATING?
GOOD QUESTION...
BUT WITH THE THREE FAMILIES OF HINAMIZAWA...
カッ...
KATSU (CLACK)
...OR EVEN WITH THE POWER OF THE SONOZAKI FAMILY ALONE...
...I THINK IT MIGHT BE POSSIBLE.

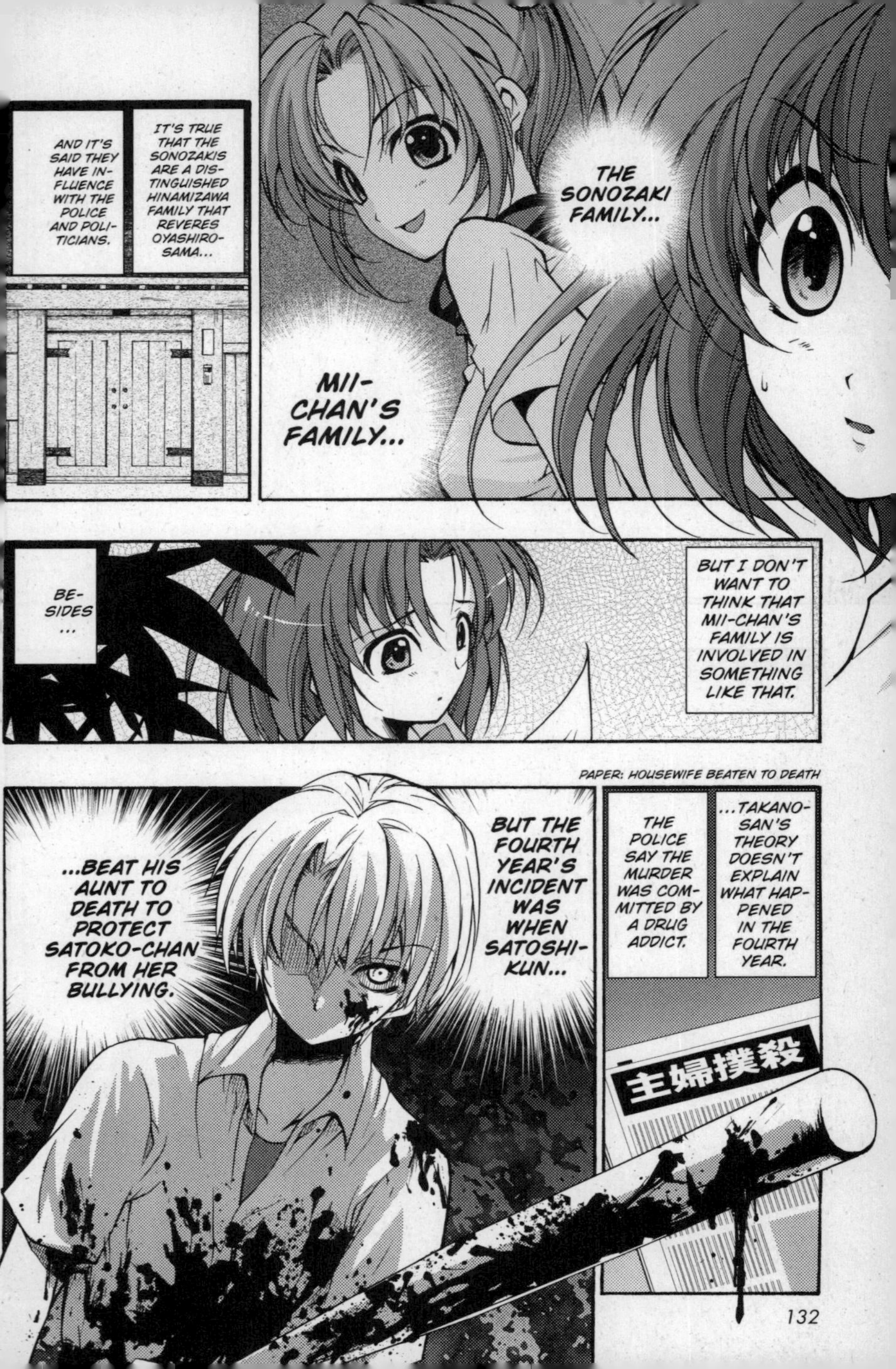
THE SONOZAKI FAMILY...
MII-CHAN'S FAMILY...
IT'S TRUE THAT THE SONOZAKIS ARE A DISTINGUISHED HINAMIZAWA FAMILY THAT REVERES OYASHIRO-SAMA...
AND IT'S SAID THEY HAVE INFLUENCE WITH THE POLICE AND POLITICIANS.
BUT I DON'T WANT TO THINK THAT MII-CHAN'S FAMILY IS INVOLVED IN SOMETHING LIKE THAT.
BESIDES...
PAPER: HOUSEWIFE BEATEN TO DEATH
...TAKANO-SAN'S THEORY DOESN'T EXPLAIN WHAT HAPPENED IN THE FOURTH YEAR.
THE POLICE SAY THE MURDER WAS COMMITTED BY A DRUG ADDICT.
主婦撲殺
BUT THE FOURTH YEAR'S INCIDENT WAS WHEN SATOSHI-KUN...
...BEAT HIS AUNT TO DEATH TO PROTECT SATOKO-CHAN FROM HER BULLYING.

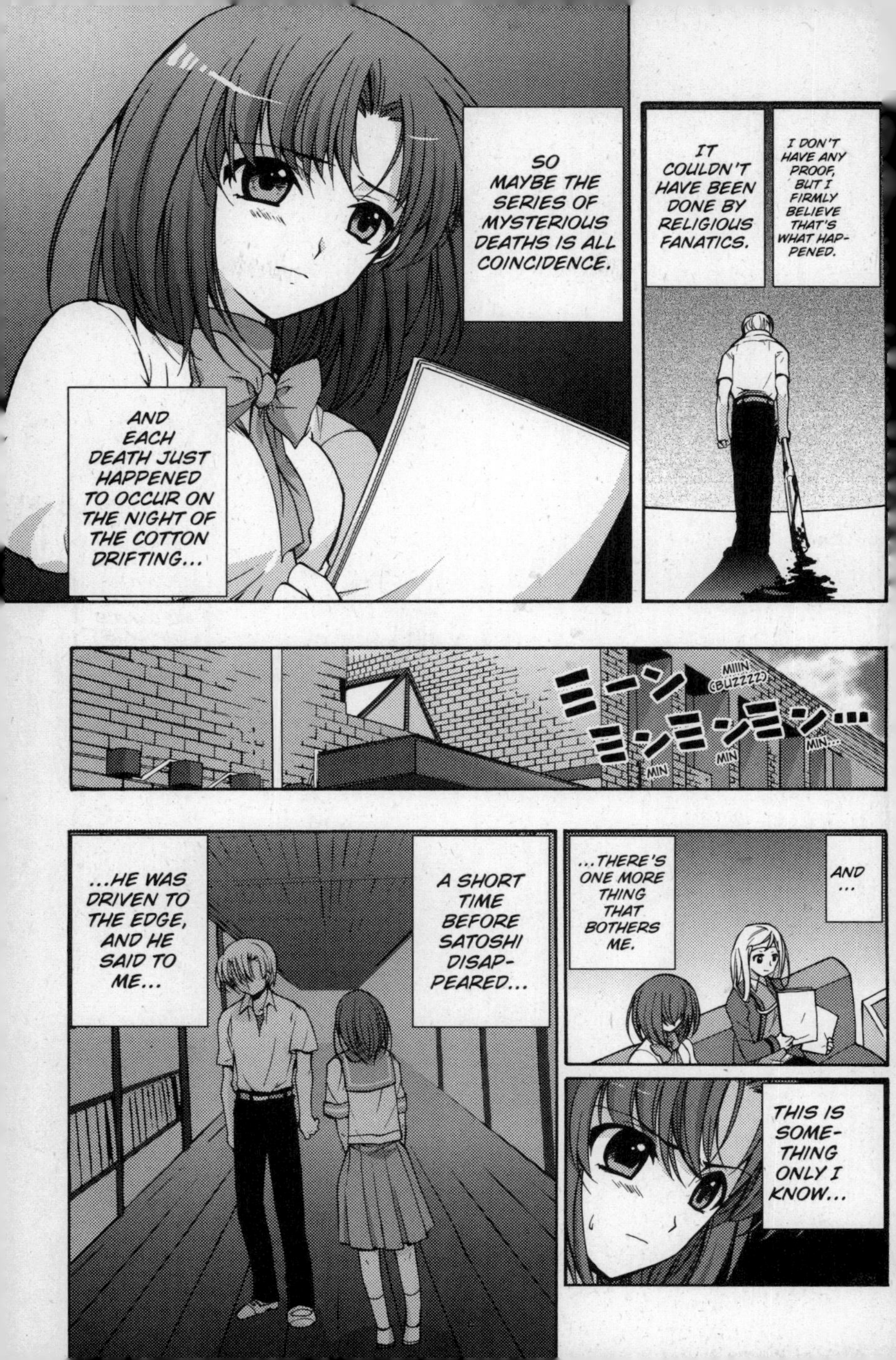
I DON'T HAVE ANY PROOF, BUT I FIRMLY BELIEVE THAT'S WHAT HAPPENED.
IT COULDN'T HAVE BEEN DONE BY RELIGIOUS FANATICS.
SO MAYBE THE SERIES OF MYSTERIOUS DEATHS IS ALL COINCIDENCE.
AND EACH DEATH JUST HAPPENED TO OCCUR ON THE NIGHT OF THE COTTON DRIFTING...
ミーン
MIIN (BUZZZZ)
ミンミンミン…
MIN MIN MIN...
AND...
...THERE'S ONE MORE THING THAT BOTHERS ME.
THIS IS SOMETHING ONLY I KNOW...
A SHORT TIME BEFORE SATOSHI DISAPPEARED...
...HE WAS DRIVEN TO THE EDGE, AND HE SAID TO ME...

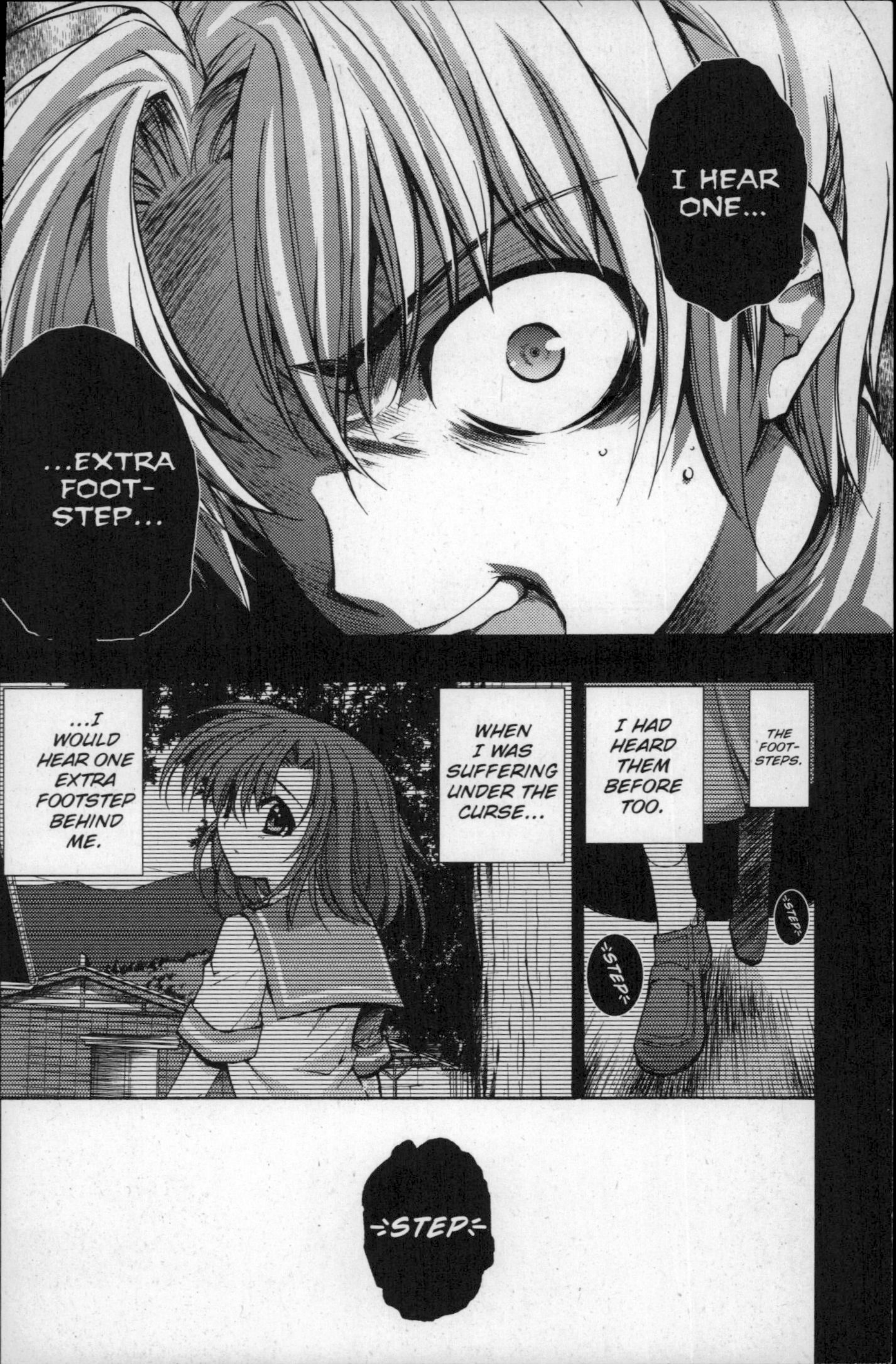
I HEAR ONE...
...EXTRA FOOT-STEP...
THE FOOT-STEPS.
I HAD HEARD THEM BEFORE TOO.
STEP
STEP
WHEN I WAS SUFFERING UNDER THE CURSE...
...I WOULD HEAR ONE EXTRA FOOTSTEP BEHIND ME.
STEP

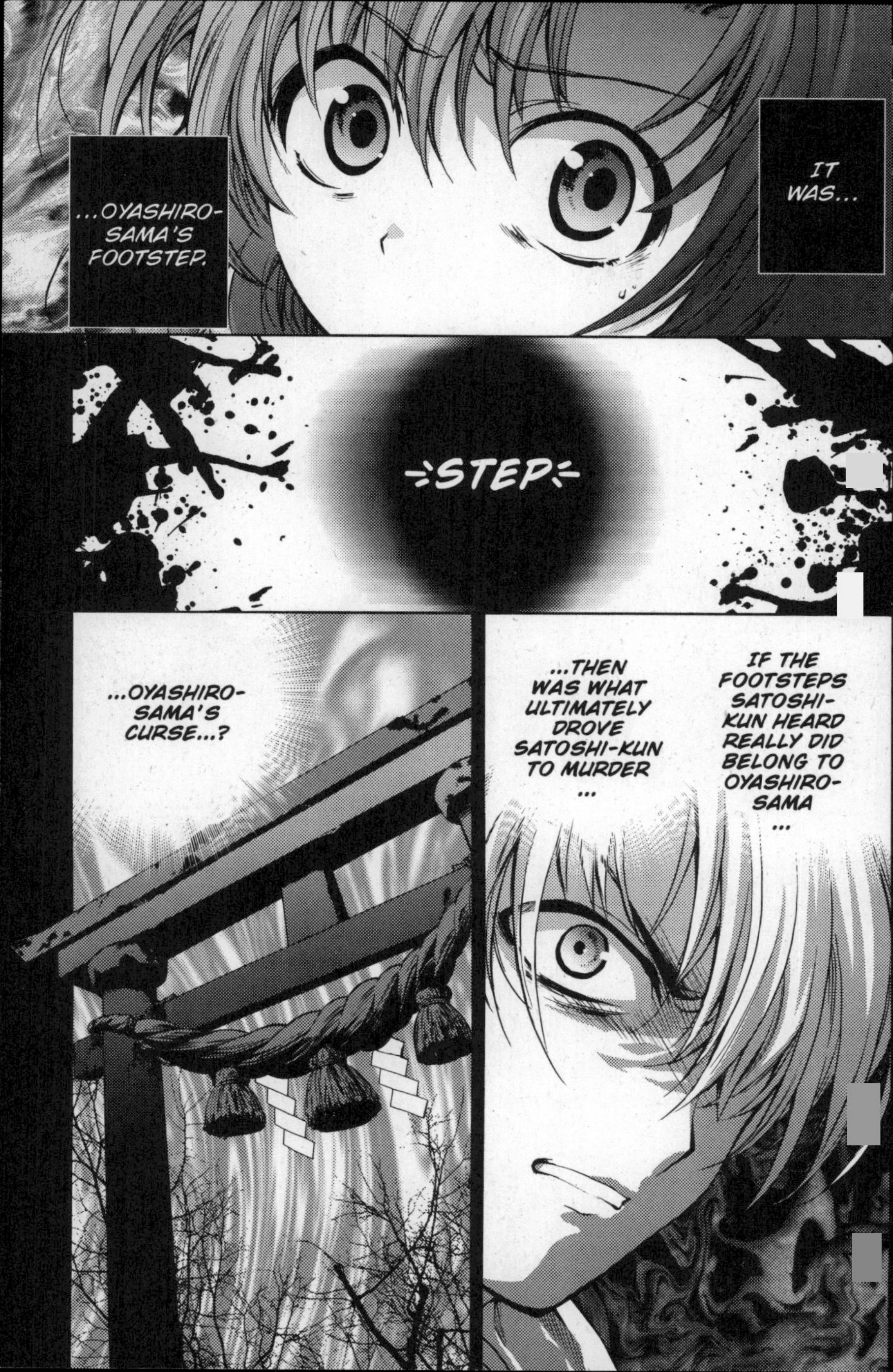
IT WAS...
...OYASHIRO-SAMA'S FOOTSTEP.
STEP
IF THE FOOTSTEPS SATOSHI-KUN HEARD REALLY DID BELONG TO OYASHIRO-SAMA ...
...THEN WAS WHAT ULTIMATELY DROVE SATOSHI-KUN TO MURDER ...
...OYASHIRO-SAMA'S CURSE...?

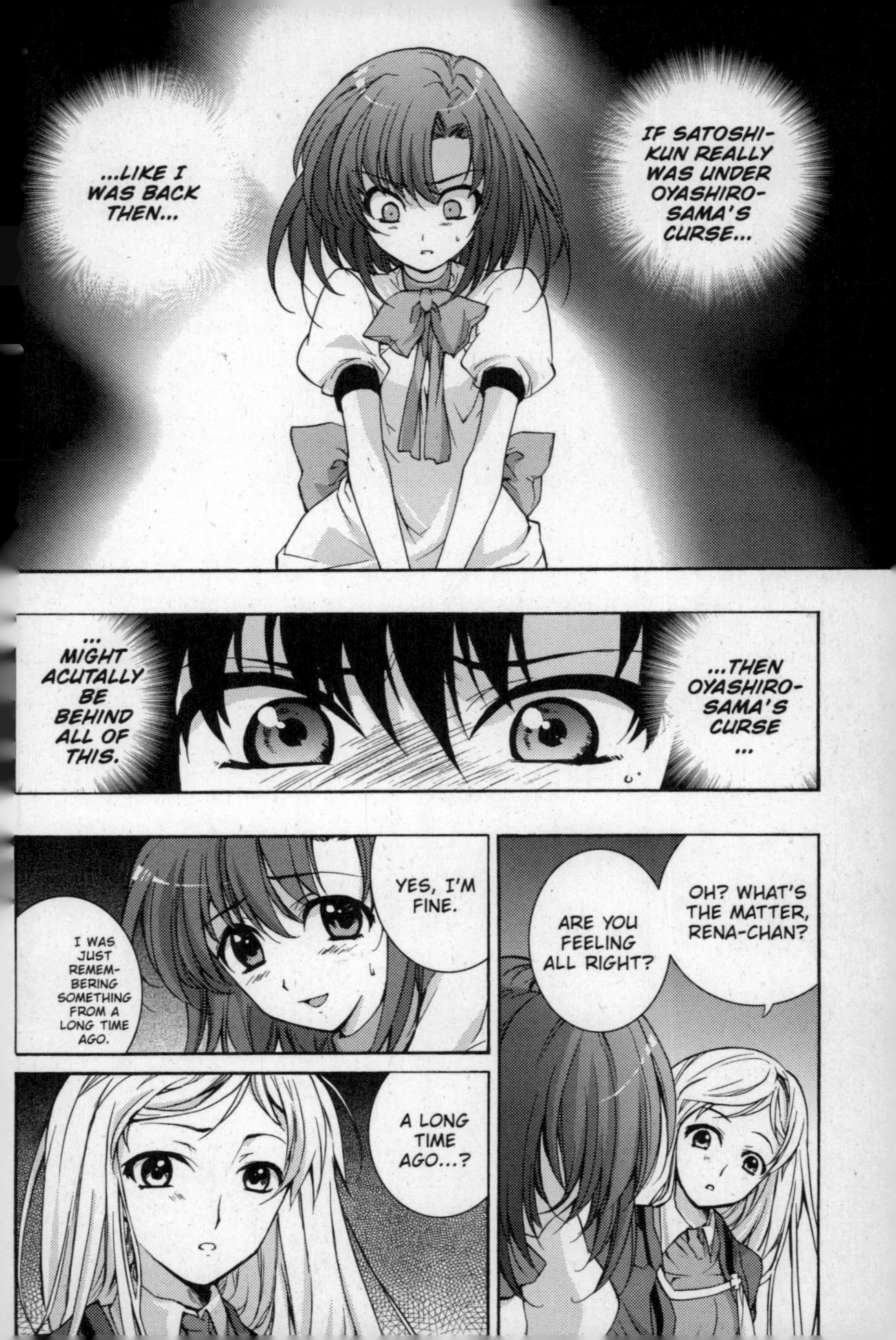
IF SATOSHI-KUN REALLY WAS UNDER OYASHIRO-SAMA'S CURSE...
...LIKE I WAS BACK THEN...
...THEN OYASHIRO-SAMA'S CURSE ...
... MIGHT ACUTALLY BE BEHIND ALL OF THIS.
OH? WHAT'S THE MATTER, RENA-CHAN?
ARE YOU FEELING ALL RIGHT?
YES, I'M FINE.
I WAS JUST REMEMBERING SOMETHING FROM A LONG TIME AGO.
A LONG TIME AGO...?

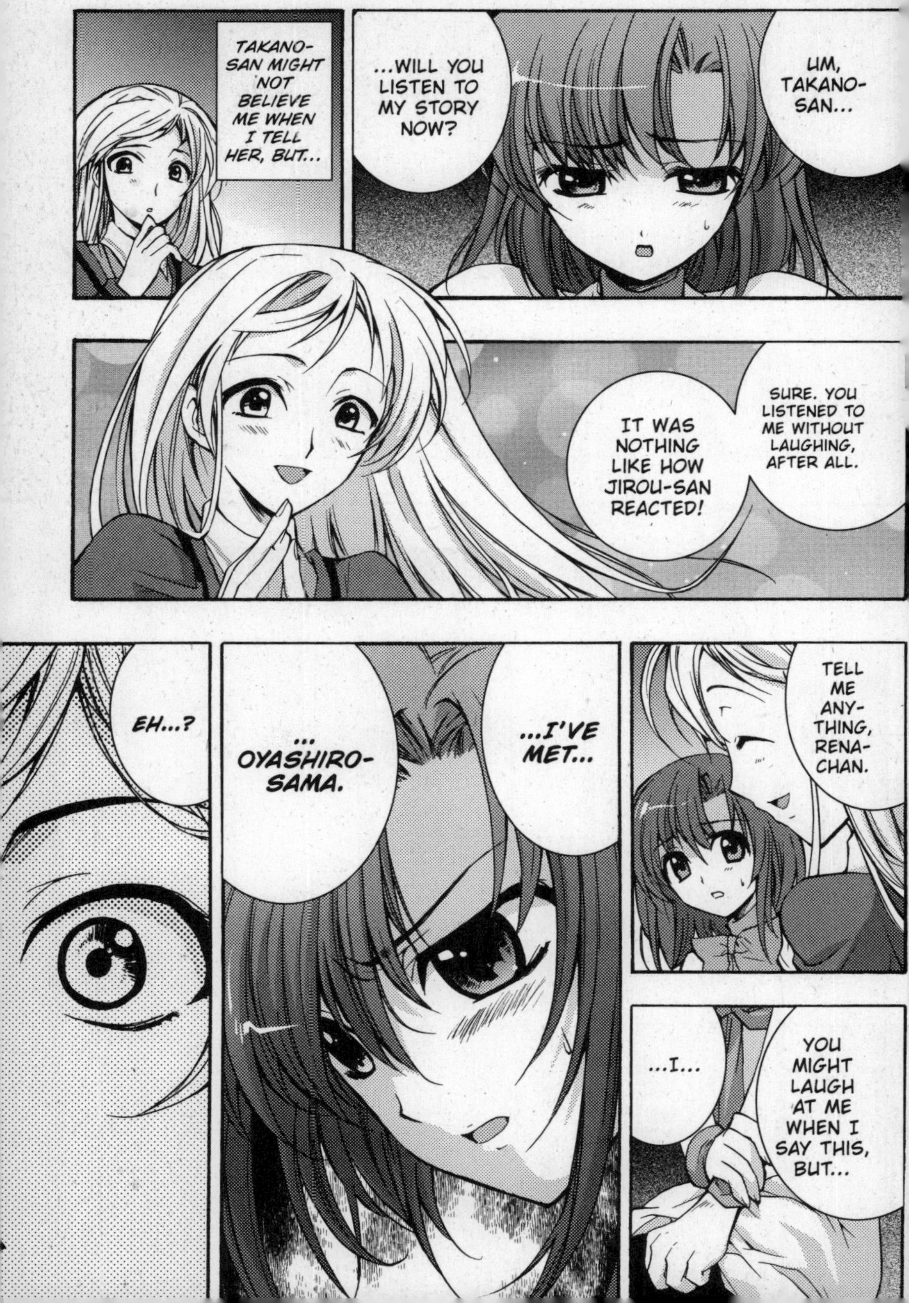
UM, TAKANO-SAN...
...WILL YOU LISTEN TO MY STORY NOW?
TAKANO-SAN MIGHT NOT BELIEVE ME WHEN I TELL HER, BUT...
SURE. YOU LISTENED TO ME WITHOUT LAUGHING, AFTER ALL.
IT WAS NOTHING LIKE HOW JIROU-SAN REACTED!
TELL ME ANYTHING, RENA-CHAN.
YOU MIGHT LAUGH AT ME WHEN I SAY THIS, BUT...
...I...
...I'VE MET...
... OYASHIRO-SAMA.
EH...?

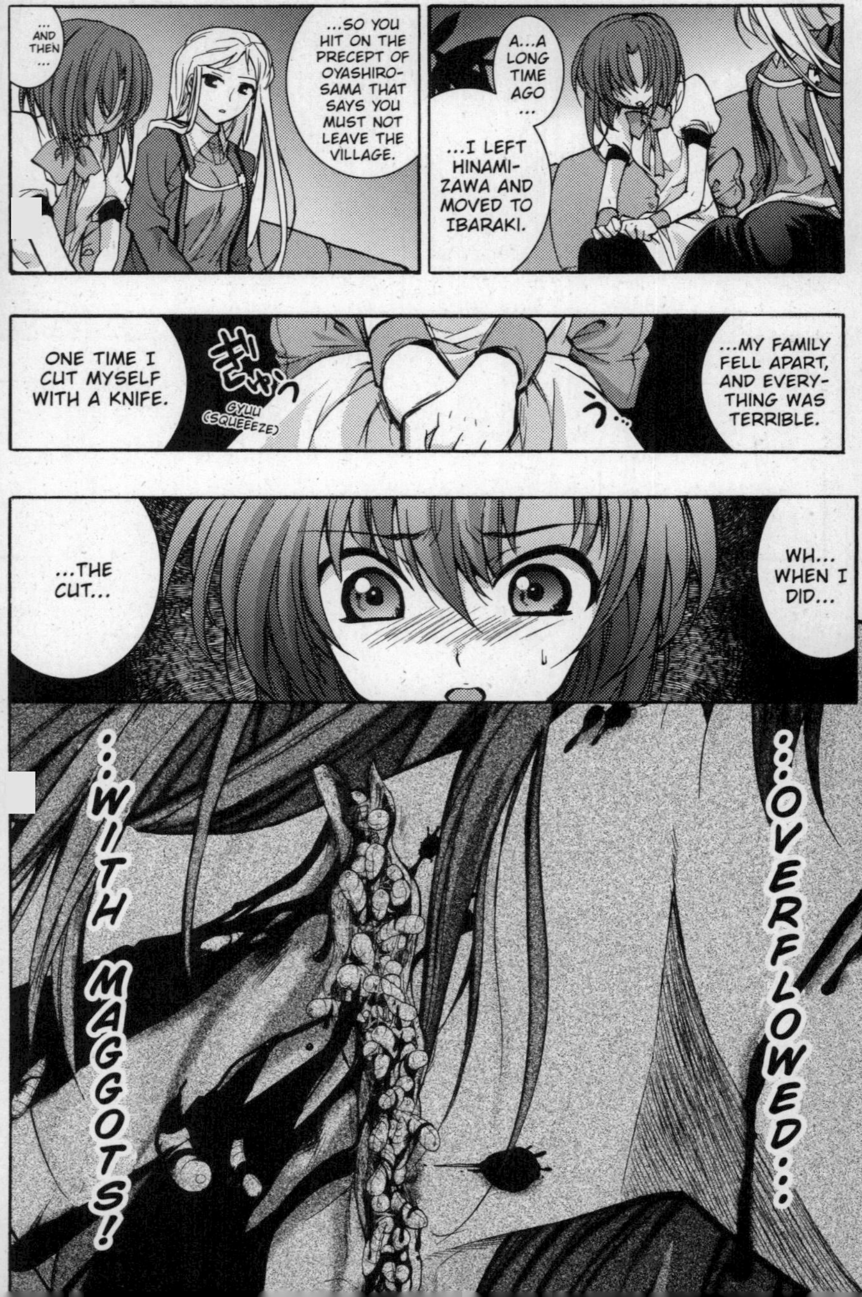
A...A LONG TIME AGO...
...I LEFT HINAMIZAWA AND MOVED TO IBARAKI.
...SO YOU HIT ON THE PRECEPT OF OYASHIRO-SAMA THAT SAYS YOU MUST NOT LEAVE THE VILLAGE.
...AND THEN...
...MY FAMILY FELL APART, AND EVERYTHING WAS TERRIBLE.
う…
ぎゅっ
GYUU (SQUEEEZE)
ONE TIME I CUT MYSELF WITH A KNIFE.
WH... WHEN I DID...
...THE CUT...
...OVERFLOWED...
...WITH MAGGOTS!

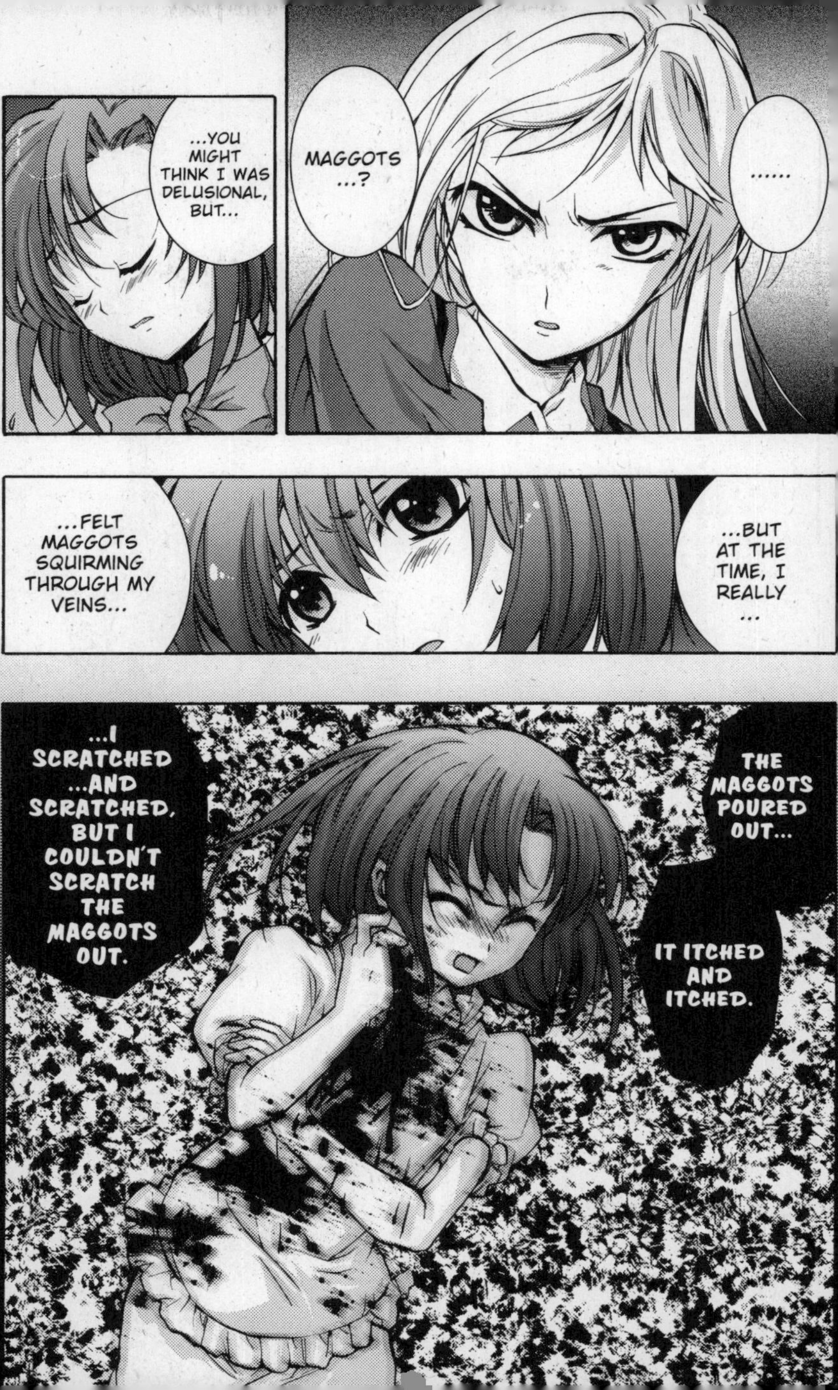

......
MAGGOTS ...?
...YOU MIGHT THINK I WAS DELUSIONAL, BUT...
...BUT AT THE TIME, I REALLY ...
...FELT MAGGOTS SQUIRMING THROUGH MY VEINS...
THE MAGGOTS POURED OUT...
IT ITCHED AND ITCHED.
...I SCRATCHED ...AND SCRATCHED, BUT I COULDN'T SCRATCH THE MAGGOTS OUT.

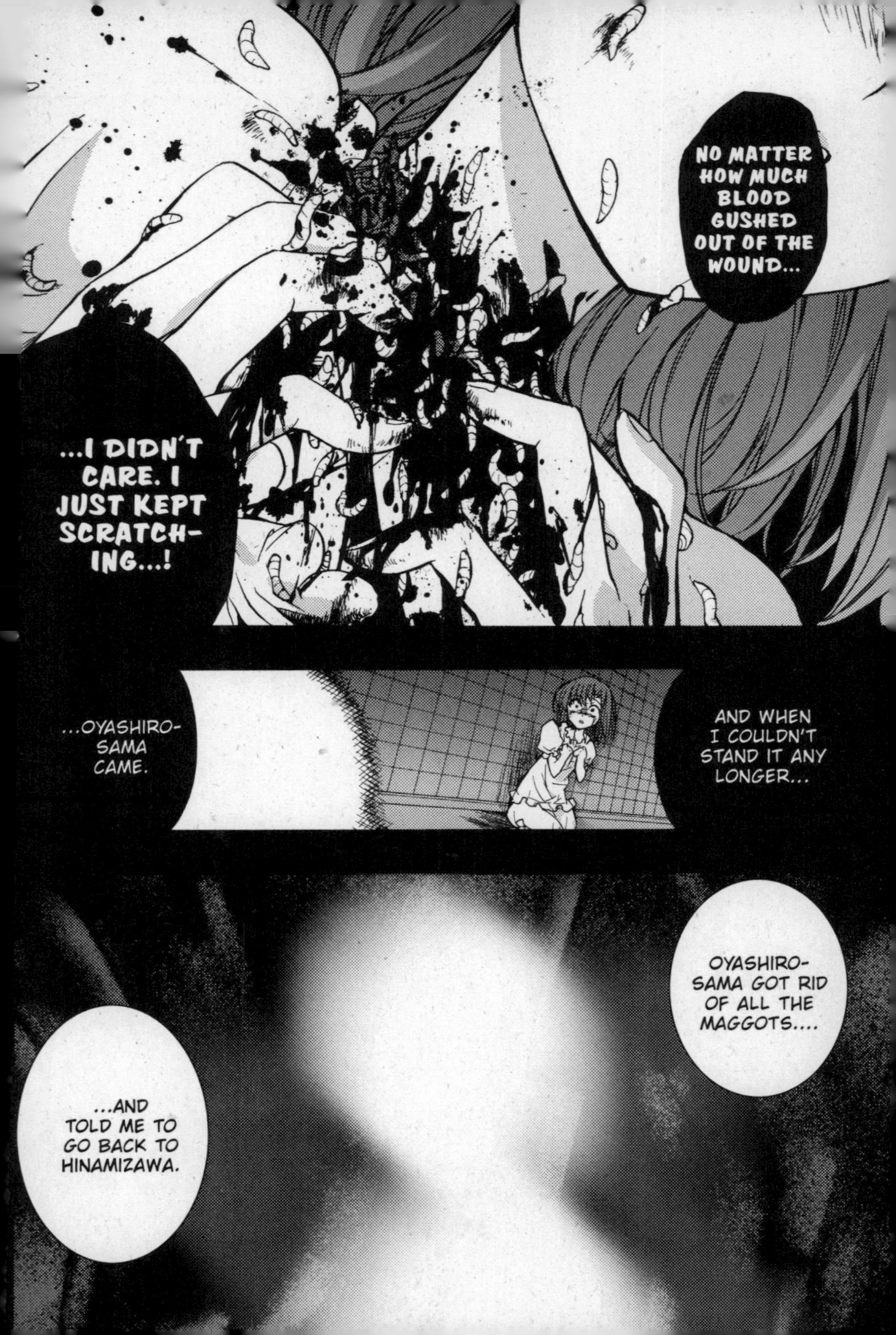
NO MATTER HOW MUCH BLOOD GUSHED OUT OF THE WOUND...
...I DIDN'T CARE. I JUST KEPT SCRATCH-ING...!
AND WHEN I COULDN'T STAND IT ANY LONGER...
...OYASHIRO-SAMA CAME.
OYASHIRO-SAMA GOT RID OF ALL THE MAGGOTS....
...AND TOLD ME TO GO BACK TO HINAMIZAWA.

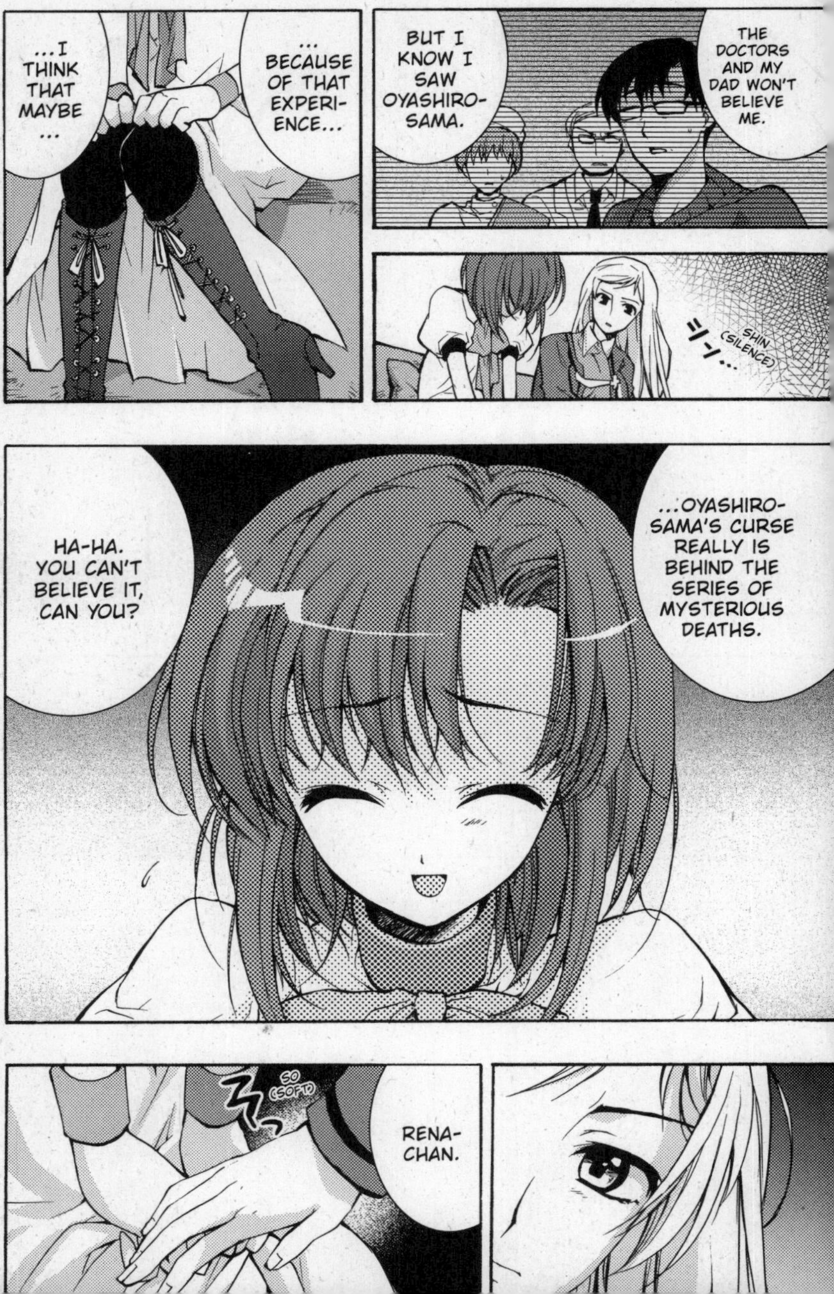
THE DOCTORS AND MY DAD WON'T BELIEVE ME.
BUT I KNOW I SAW OYASHIRO-SAMA.
...BECAUSE OF THAT EXPERIENCE...
...I THINK THAT MAYBE ...
SHIN- (SILENCE)
...OYASHIRO-SAMA'S CURSE REALLY IS BEHIND THE SERIES OF MYSTERIOUS DEATHS.
HA-HA. YOU CAN'T BELIEVE IT, CAN YOU?
RENA-CHAN.
SO (SOFT)

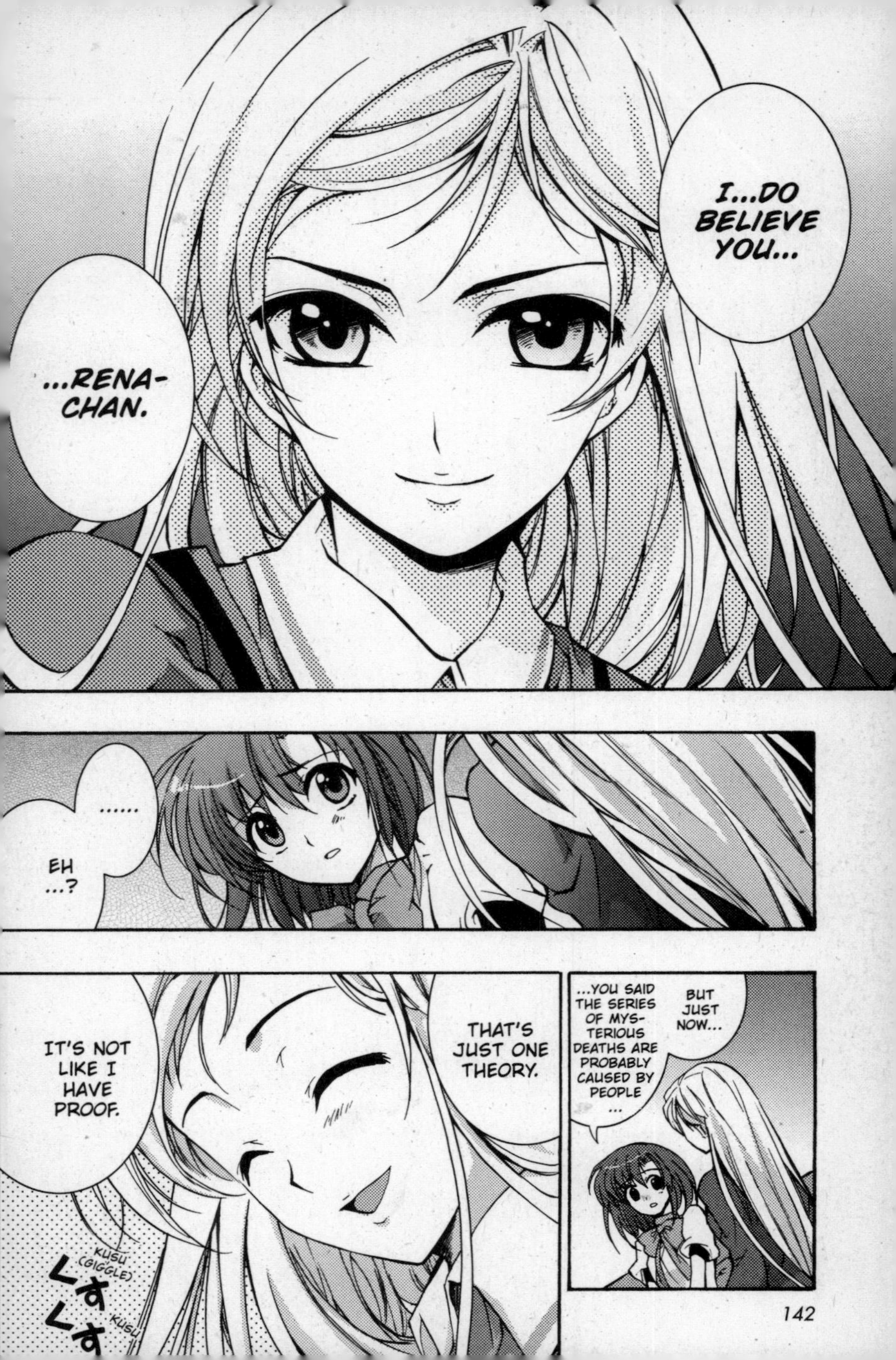
I...DO BELIEVE YOU...
...RENA-CHAN.
......
EH ...?
BUT JUST NOW...
...YOU SAID THE SERIES OF MYS-TERIOUS DEATHS ARE PROBABLY CAUSED BY PEOPLE ...
THAT'S JUST ONE THEORY.
IT'S NOT LIKE I HAVE PROOF.
KUSU (GIGGLE)
くすくす
KUSU

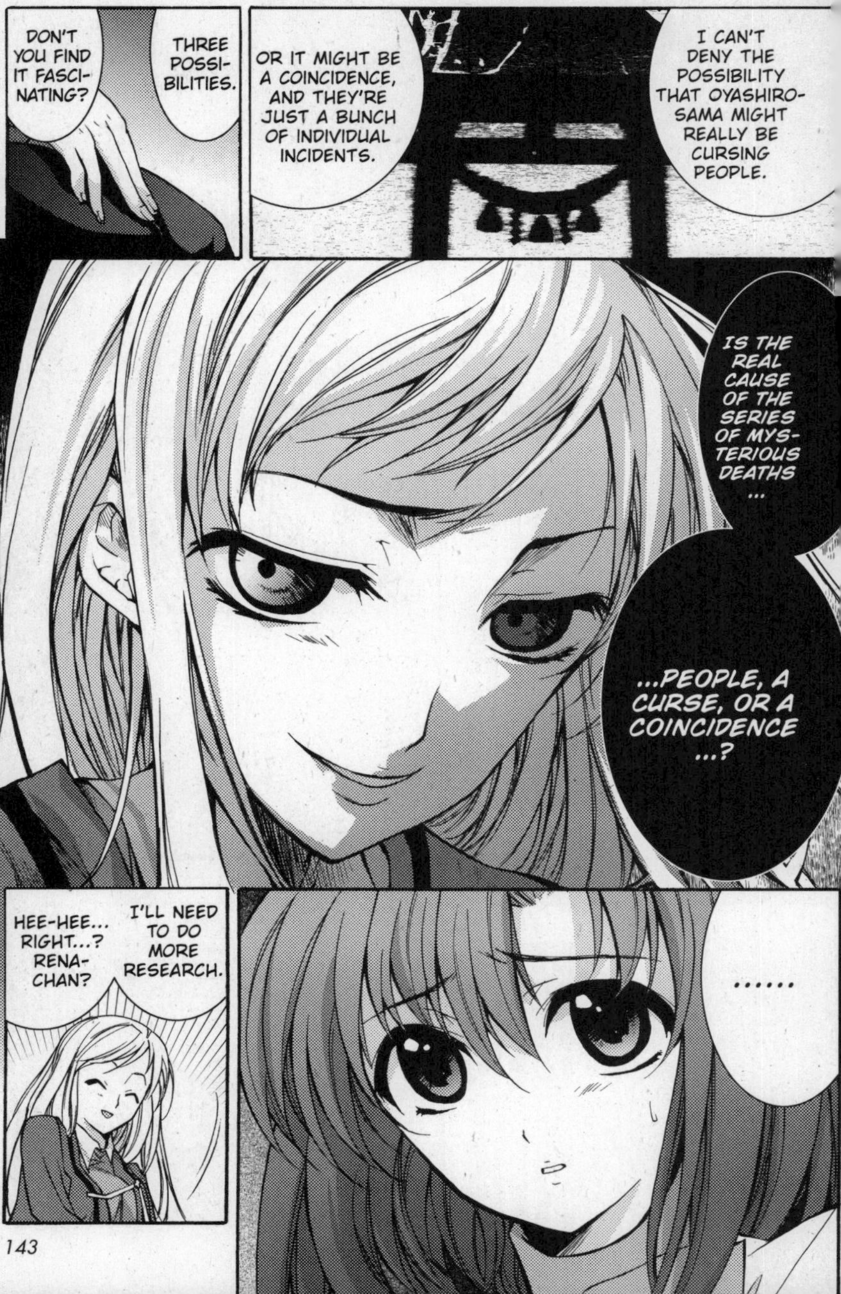
I CAN'T DENY THE POSSIBILITY THAT OYASHIRO-SAMA MIGHT REALLY BE CURSING PEOPLE.
OR IT MIGHT BE A COINCIDENCE, AND THEY'RE JUST A BUNCH OF INDIVIDUAL INCIDENTS.
THREE POSSI-BILITIES.
DON'T YOU FIND IT FASCI-NATING?
IS THE REAL CAUSE OF THE SERIES OF MYS-TERIOUS DEATHS ...
...PEOPLE, A CURSE, OR A COINCIDENCE ...?
......
I'LL NEED TO DO MORE RESEARCH.
HEE-HEE... RIGHT...? RENA-CHAN?

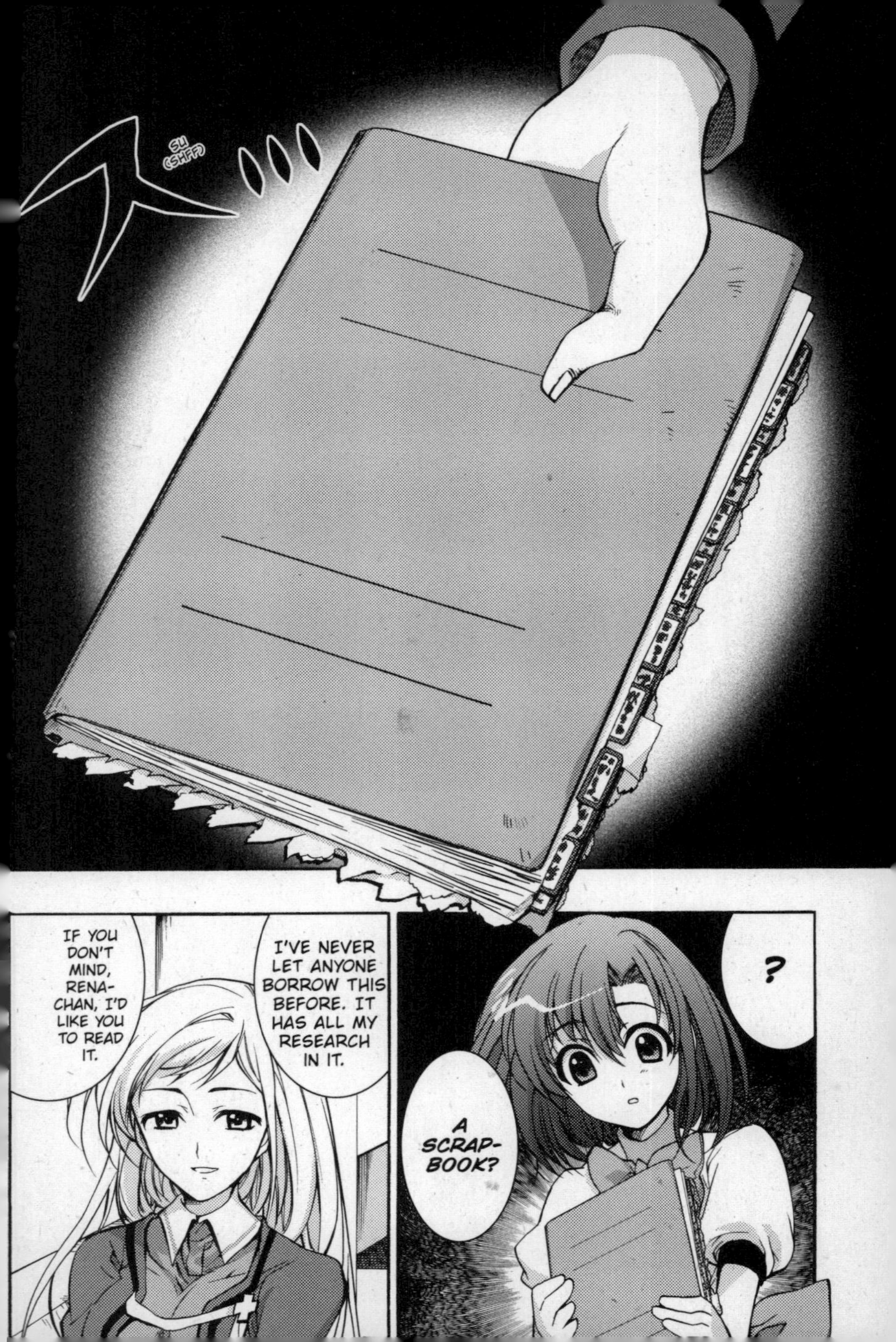
SU (SHFF)
?
A SCRAP-BOOK?
I'VE NEVER LET ANYONE BORROW THIS BEFORE. IT HAS ALL MY RESEARCH IN IT.
IF YOU DON'T MIND, RENA-CHAN, I'D LIKE YOU TO READ IT.

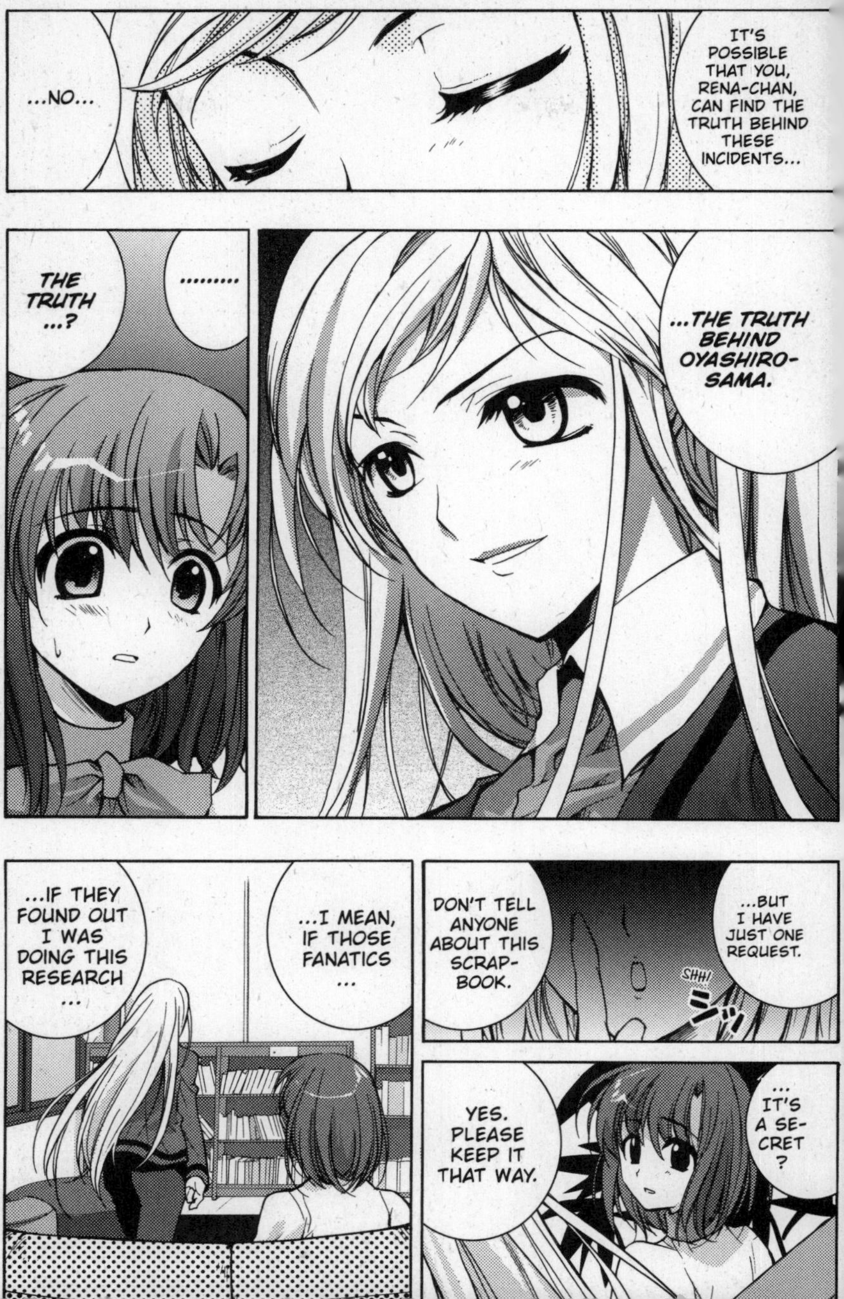
IT'S POSSIBLE THAT YOU, RENA-CHAN, CAN FIND THE TRUTH BEHIND THESE INCIDENTS...
...NO...
...THE TRUTH BEHIND OYASHIRO-SAMA.
....
THE TRUTH ...?
...BUT I HAVE JUST ONE REQUEST.
SHH!
DON'T TELL ANYONE ABOUT THIS SCRAP-BOOK.
...IT'S A SE-CRET?
YES. PLEASE KEEP IT THAT WAY.
...I MEAN, IF THOSE FANATICS...
...IF THEY FOUND OUT I WAS DOING THIS RESEARCH...

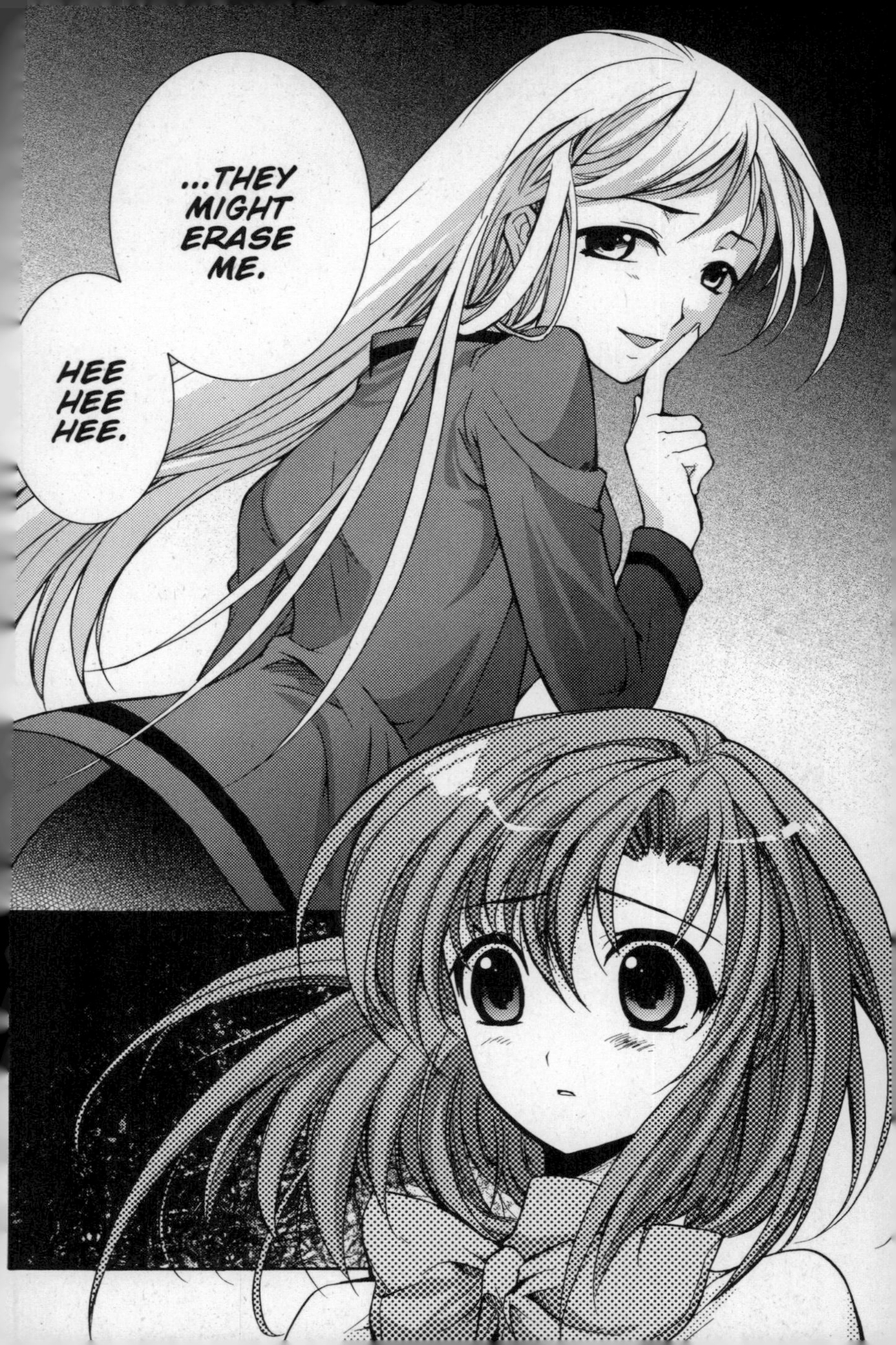
...THEY MIGHT ERASE ME.
HEE HEE HEE.

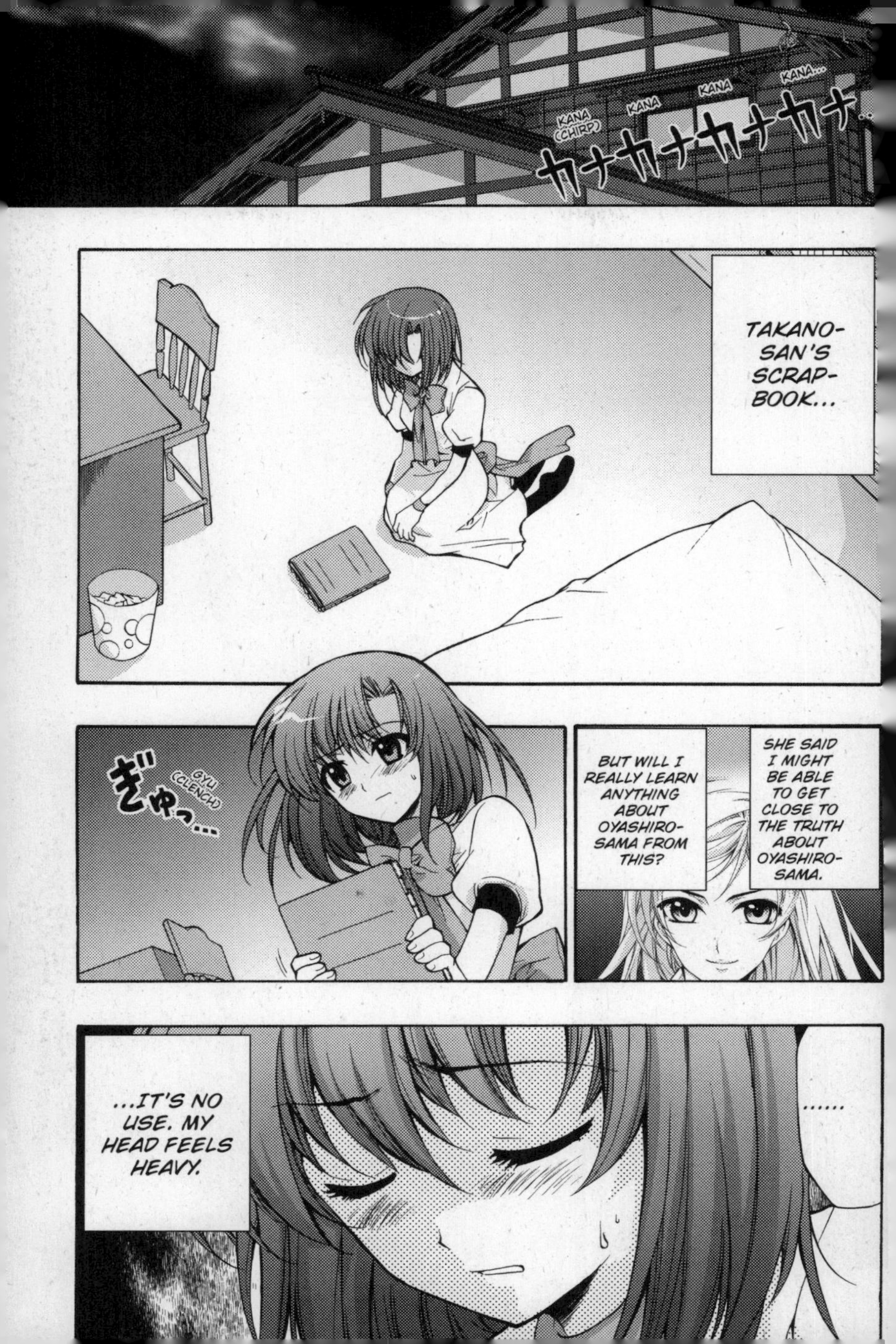

カナカナカナカナ…
KANA (CHIRP) KANA KANA KANA...
TAKANO-SAN'S SCRAPBOOK...
SHE SAID I MIGHT BE ABLE TO GET CLOSE TO THE TRUTH ABOUT OYASHIRO-SAMA.
BUT WILL I REALLY LEARN ANYTHING ABOUT OYASHIRO-SAMA FROM THIS?
ぎゅっ…
GYU (CLENCH)
......
...IT'S NO USE. MY HEAD FEELS HEAVY.

IS IT BECAUSE I TOLD TAKANO-SAN ABOUT WHAT HAPPENED IN IBARAKI?
I CAN'T CONCENTRATE. I FEEL LIKE I HAVE A BIT OF A FEVER.
...WHEN I REMEM-BER THE PAST...
...I ALWAYS FEEL A PRICK-LING PAIN IN MY HEAD.
パタン
PATAN (SHUT)
...I FEEL BAD DOING THIS TO TAKANO-SAN...
...BUT I DON'T THINK I CAN READ THIS NOW...
I'LL FORGET ABOUT OYASHIRO-SAMA'S CURSE.
I FINALLY GOT MY HAPPY LIFE BACK.

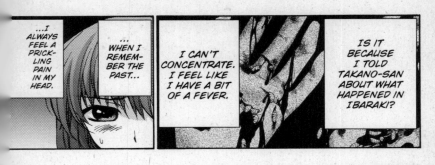

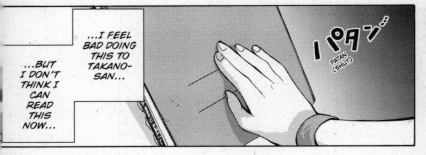

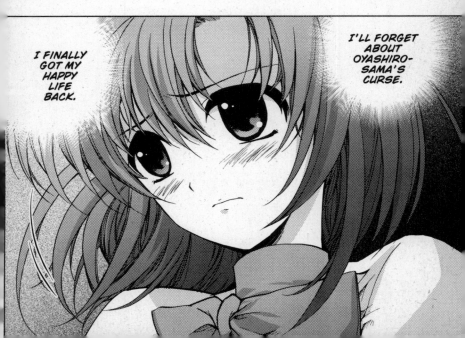

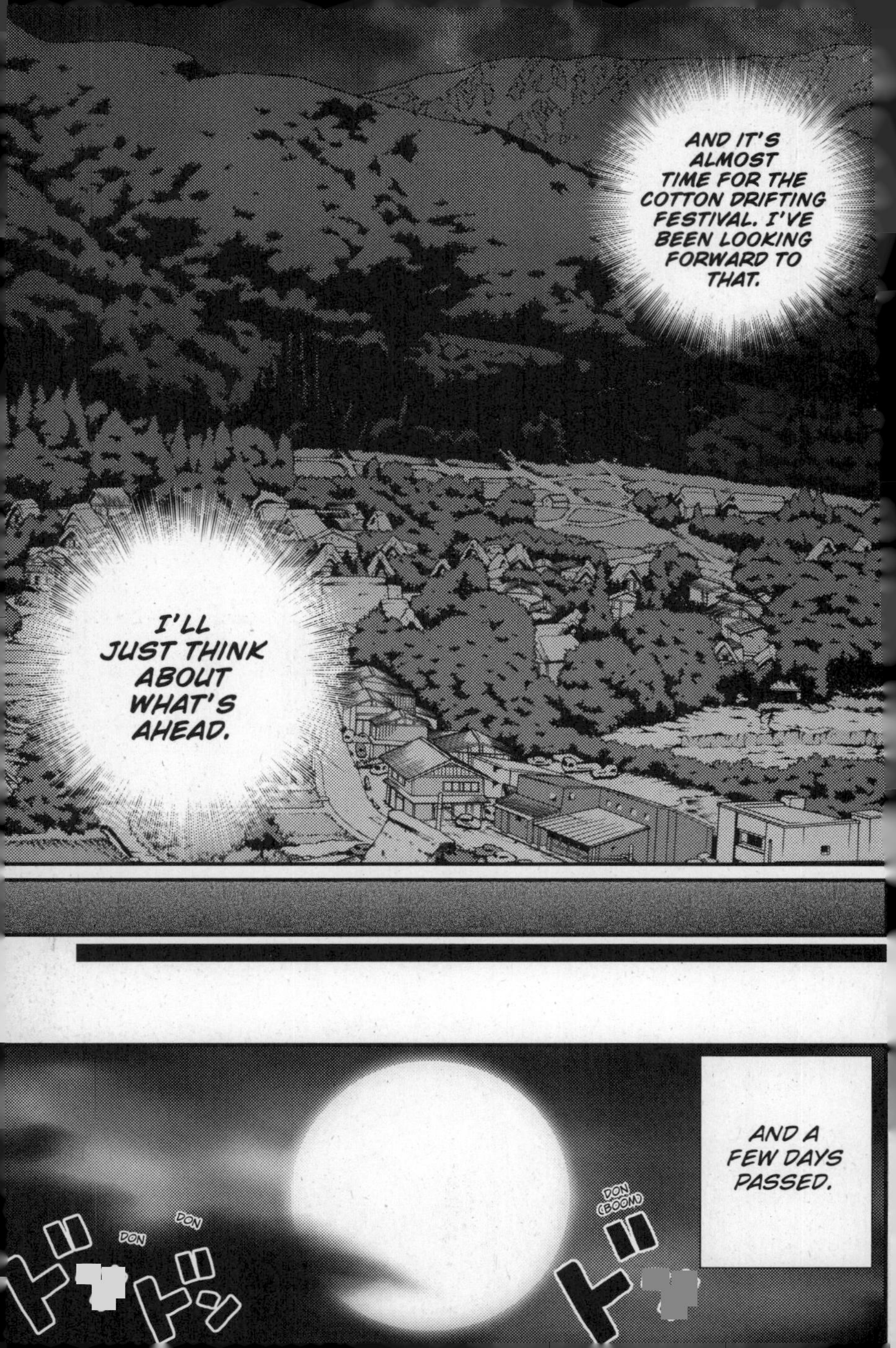
AND IT'S ALMOST TIME FOR THE COTTON DRIFTING FESTIVAL. I'VE BEEN LOOKING FORWARD TO THAT.
I'LL JUST THINK ABOUT WHAT'S AHEAD.
AND A FEW DAYS PASSED.
DON (BOOM)
DON
DON

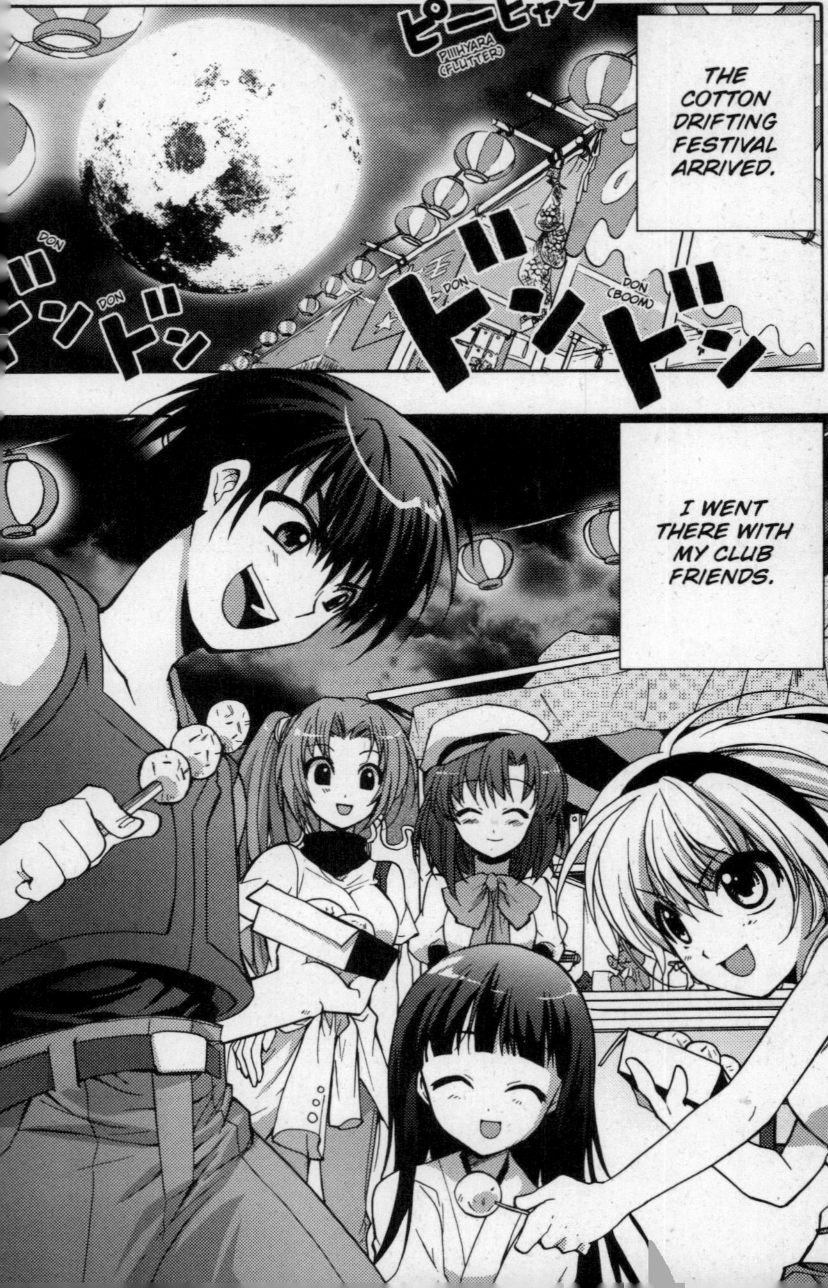
THE COTTON DRIFTING FESTIVAL ARRIVED.
ピーヒャラ
PIIIHYARA (FLUTTER)
ドンドン
DON (BOOM)
DON
ドンドン
DON
DON
I WENT THERE WITH MY CLUB FRIENDS.

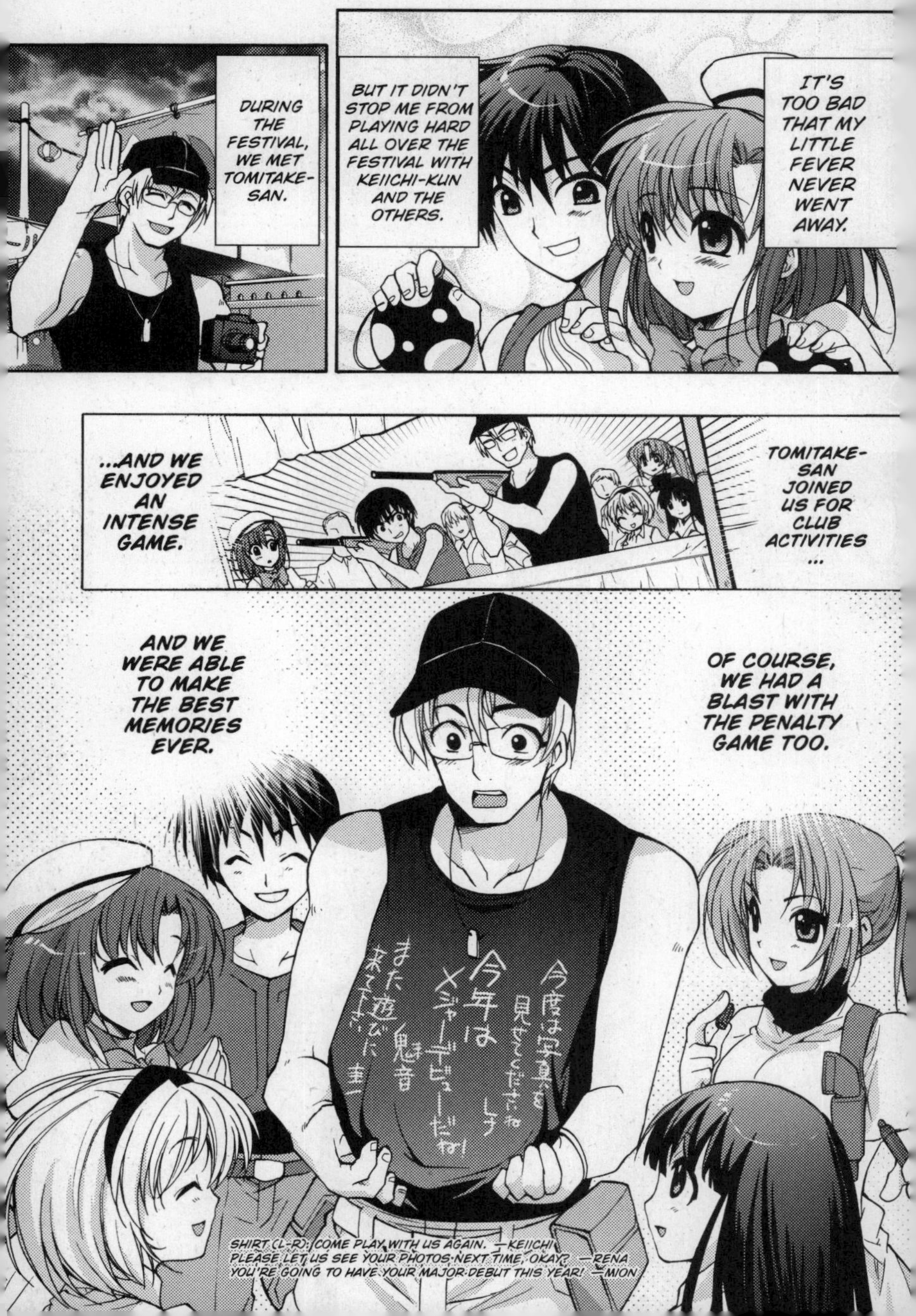
IT'S TOO BAD THAT MY LITTLE FEVER NEVER WENT AWAY.
BUT IT DIDN'T STOP ME FROM PLAYING HARD ALL OVER THE FESTIVAL WITH KEIICHI-KUN AND THE OTHERS.
DURING THE FESTIVAL, WE MET TOMITAKE-SAN.
TOMITAKE-SAN JOINED US FOR CLUB ACTIVITIES...
...AND WE ENJOYED AN INTENSE GAME.
OF COURSE, WE HAD A BLAST WITH THE PENALTY GAME TOO.
AND WE WERE ABLE TO MAKE THE BEST MEMORIES EVER.
今度は写真を見せてくださいね レナ
今年はメジャーデビューだね! 魅音
また遊びに来てよな!! 圭一
SHIRT (L-R): COME PLAY WITH US AGAIN. —KEIICHI
PLEASE LET US SEE YOUR PHOTOS NEXT TIME, OKAY? —RENA
YOU'RE GOING TO HAVE YOUR MAJOR DEBUT THIS YEAR! —MION

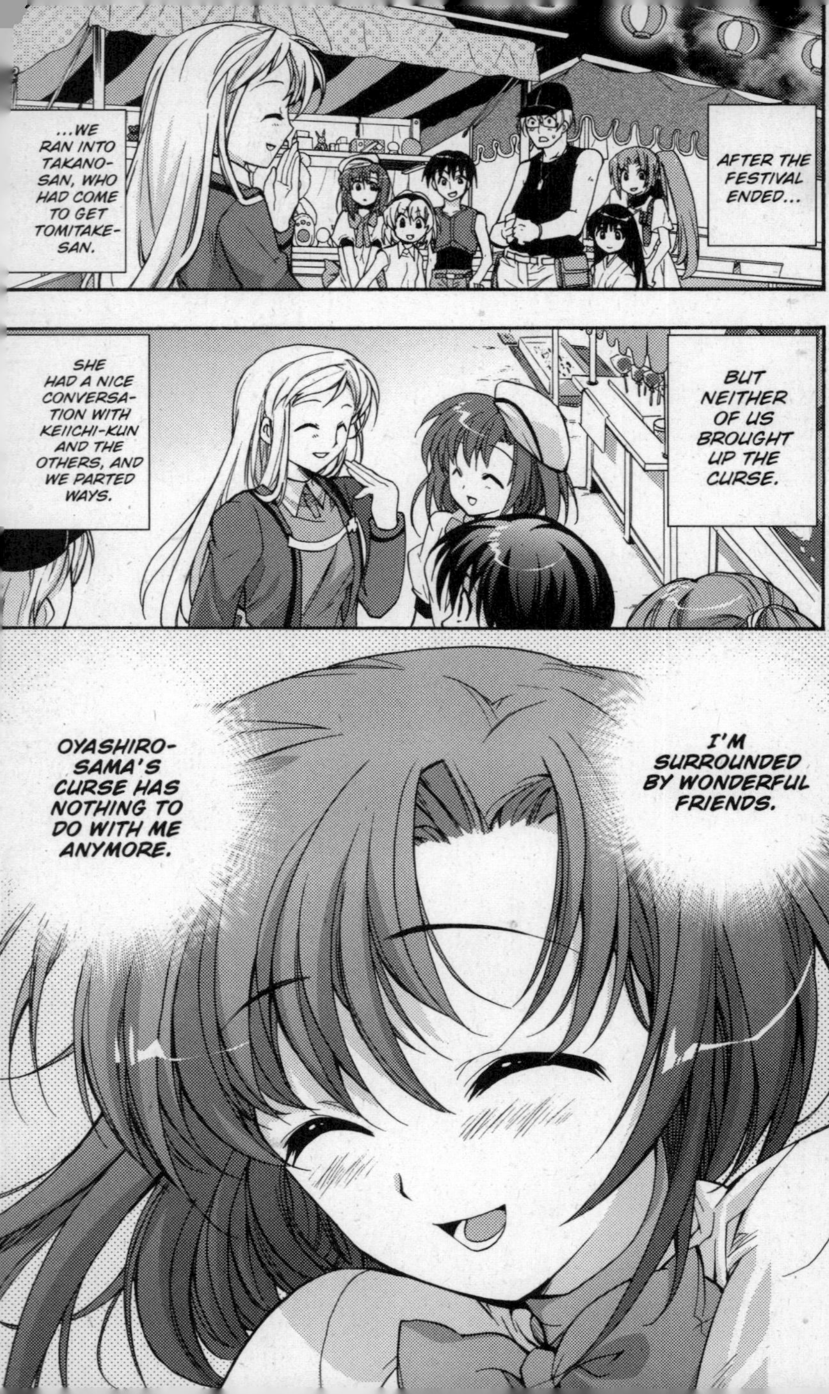
AFTER THE FESTIVAL ENDED...
...WE RAN INTO TAKANO-SAN, WHO HAD COME TO GET TOMITAKE-SAN.
BUT NEITHER OF US BROUGHT UP THE CURSE.
SHE HAD A NICE CONVERSATION WITH KEIICHI-KUN AND THE OTHERS, AND WE PARTED WAYS.
I'M SURROUNDED BY WONDERFUL FRIENDS.
OYASHIRO-SAMA'S CURSE HAS NOTHING TO DO WITH ME ANYMORE.

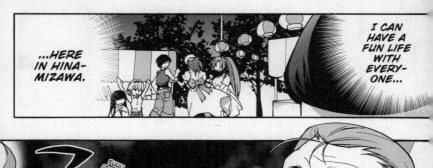

I CAN HAVE A FUN LIFE WITH EVERYONE...
...HERE IN HINAMIZAWA.

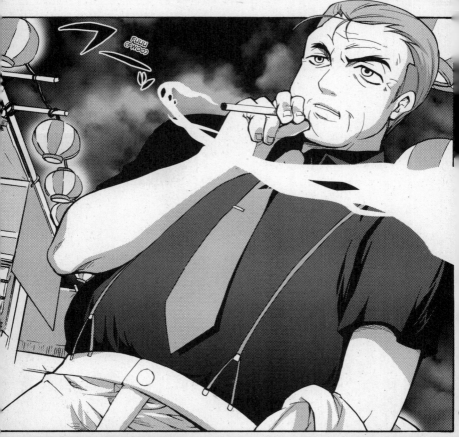

FUUU (FWOO)

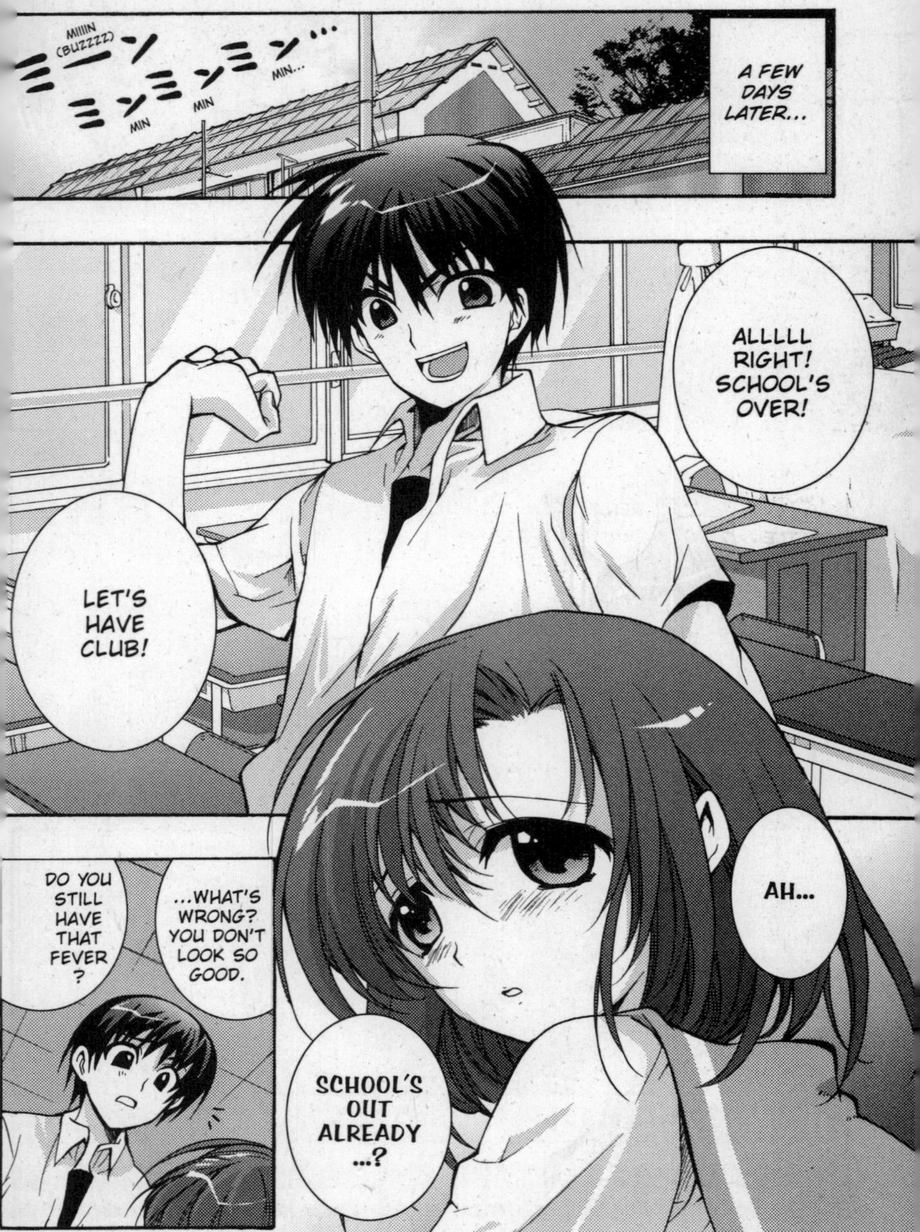
A FEW DAYS LATER...
ミーン
MIIIIN (BUZZZZ)
ミンミンミン…
MIN
MIN
MIN...
ALLLLL RIGHT! SCHOOL'S OVER!
LET'S HAVE CLUB!
AH...
SCHOOL'S OUT ALREADY ...?
...WHAT'S WRONG? YOU DON'T LOOK SO GOOD.
DO YOU STILL HAVE THAT FEVER ?

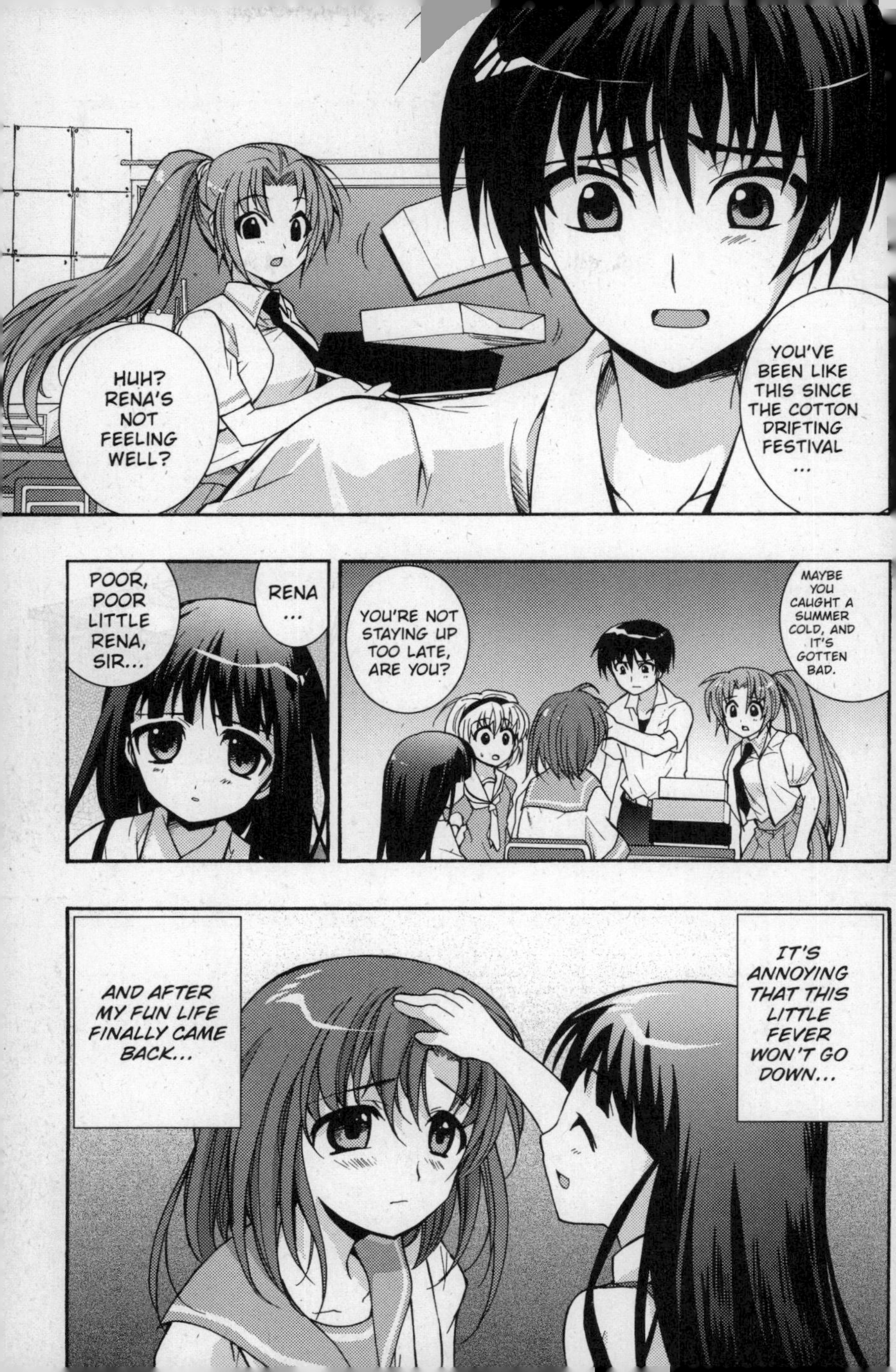

YOU'VE BEEN LIKE THIS SINCE THE COTTON DRIFTING FESTIVAL ...
HUH? RENA'S NOT FEELING WELL?
MAYBE YOU CAUGHT A SUMMER COLD, AND IT'S GOTTEN BAD.
YOU'RE NOT STAYING UP TOO LATE, ARE YOU?
RENA ...
POOR, POOR LITTLE RENA, SIR...
IT'S ANNOYING THAT THIS LITTLE FEVER WON'T GO DOWN...
AND AFTER MY FUN LIFE FINALLY CAME BACK...

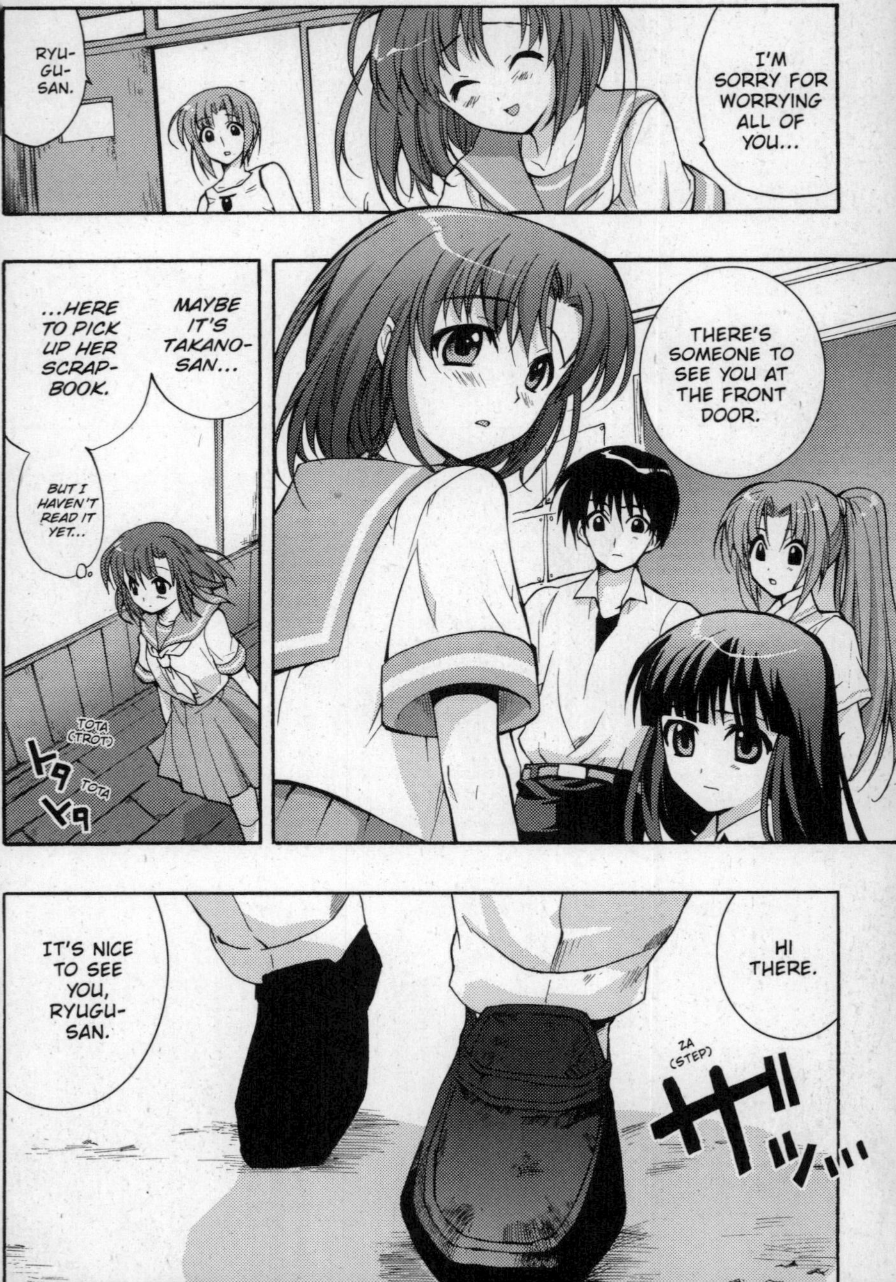
I'M SORRY FOR WORRYING ALL OF YOU...
RYU-GU-SAN.
THERE'S SOMEONE TO SEE YOU AT THE FRONT DOOR.
MAYBE IT'S TAKANO-SAN...
...HERE TO PICK UP HER SCRAP-BOOK.
BUT I HAVEN'T READ IT YET...
TOTA (TROT)
トタ
TOTA
トタ
HI THERE.
IT'S NICE TO SEE YOU, RYUGU-SAN.
ZA (STEP)
ザッ

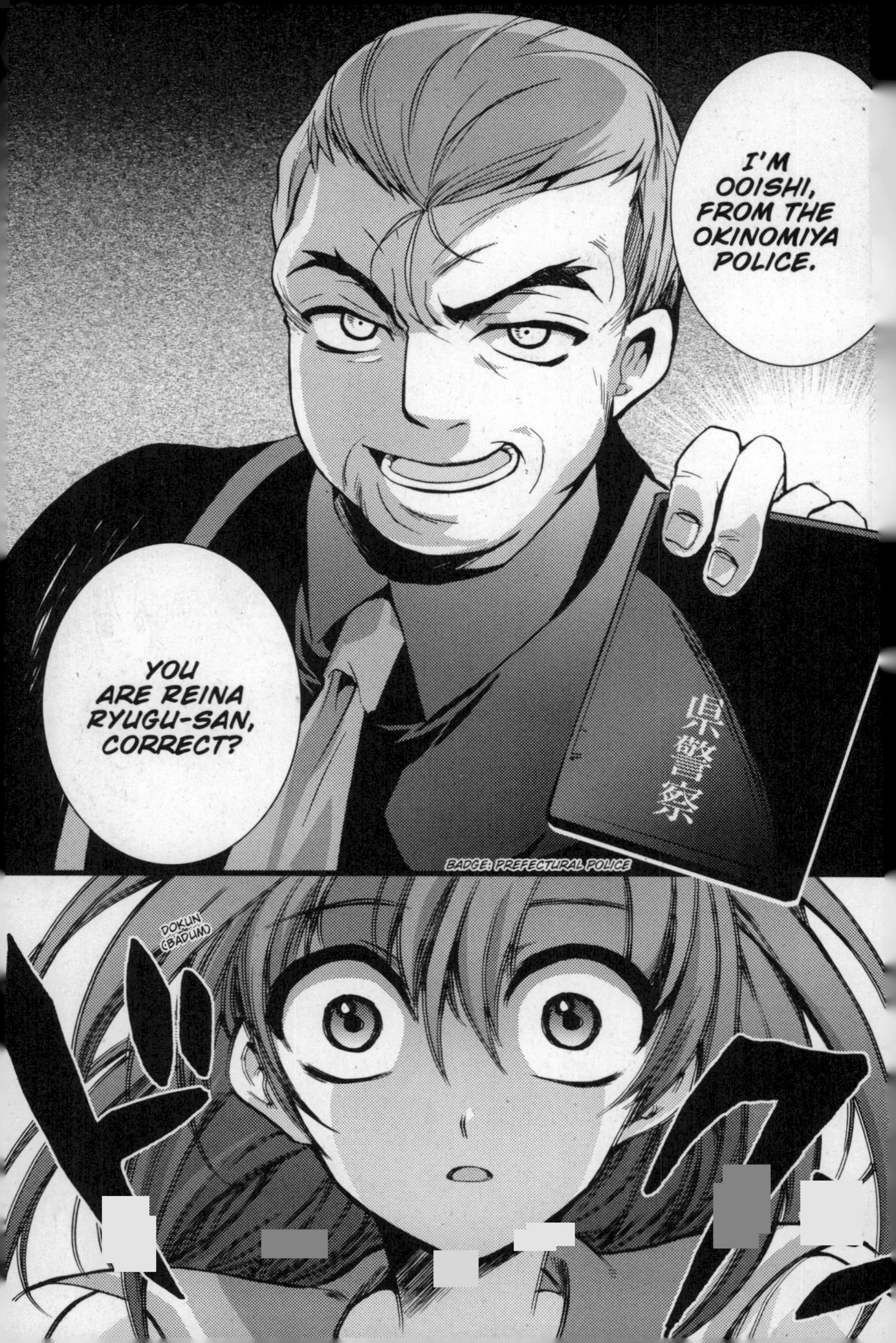
I'M OOISHI, FROM THE OKINOMIYA POLICE.
YOU ARE REINA RYUGU-SAN, CORRECT?
県警察
BADGE: PREFECTURAL POLICE
DOKUN (BADUM)

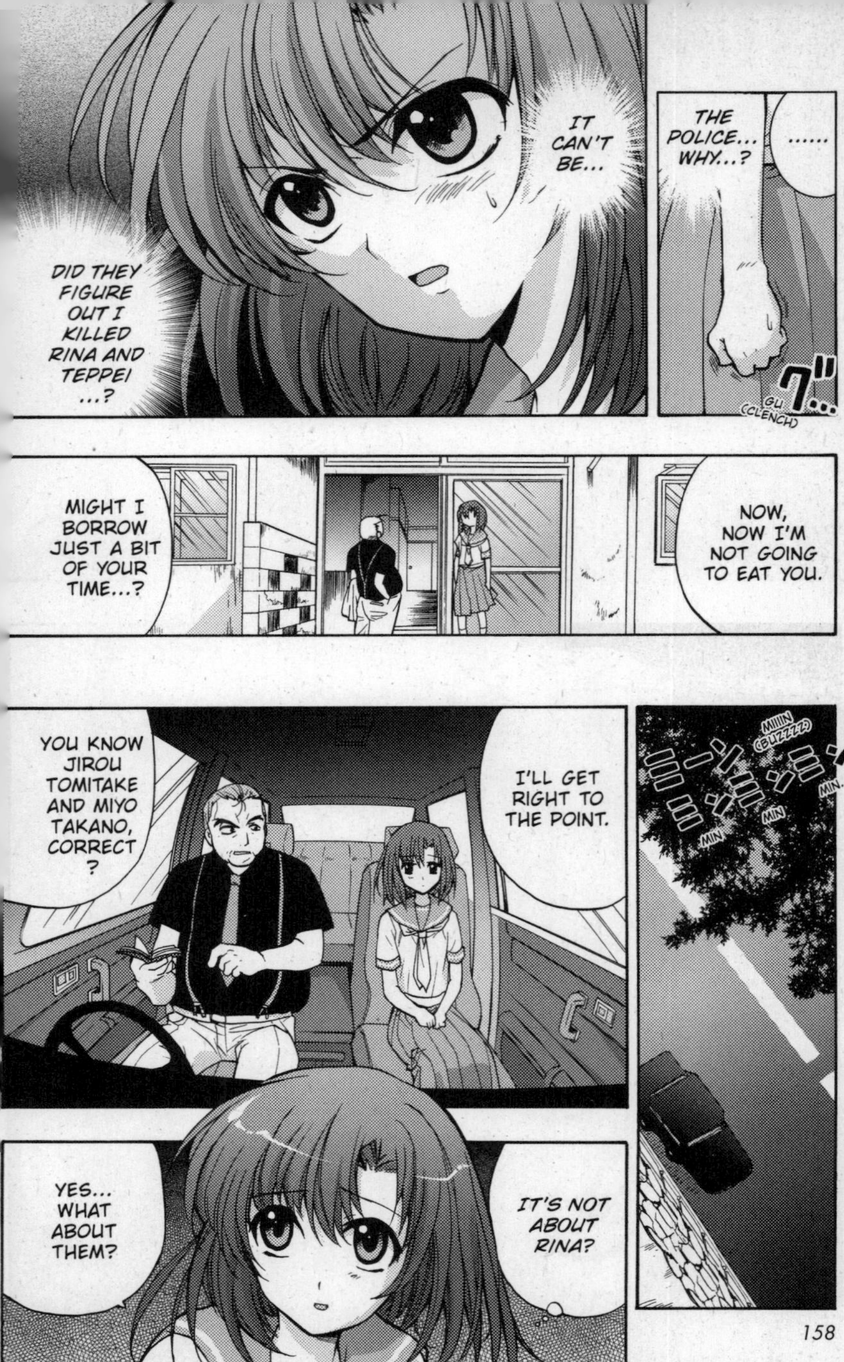
......
THE POLICE... WHY...?
GU (CLENCH)
IT CAN'T BE...
DID THEY FIGURE OUT I KILLED RINA AND TEPPEI ...?
NOW, NOW I'M NOT GOING TO EAT YOU.
MIGHT I BORROW JUST A BIT OF YOUR TIME...?
MIIIN (BUZZZZ)
MIN...
MIN
MIN
I'LL GET RIGHT TO THE POINT.
YOU KNOW JIROU TOMITAKE AND MIYO TAKANO, CORRECT ?
IT'S NOT ABOUT RINA?
YES... WHAT ABOUT THEM?

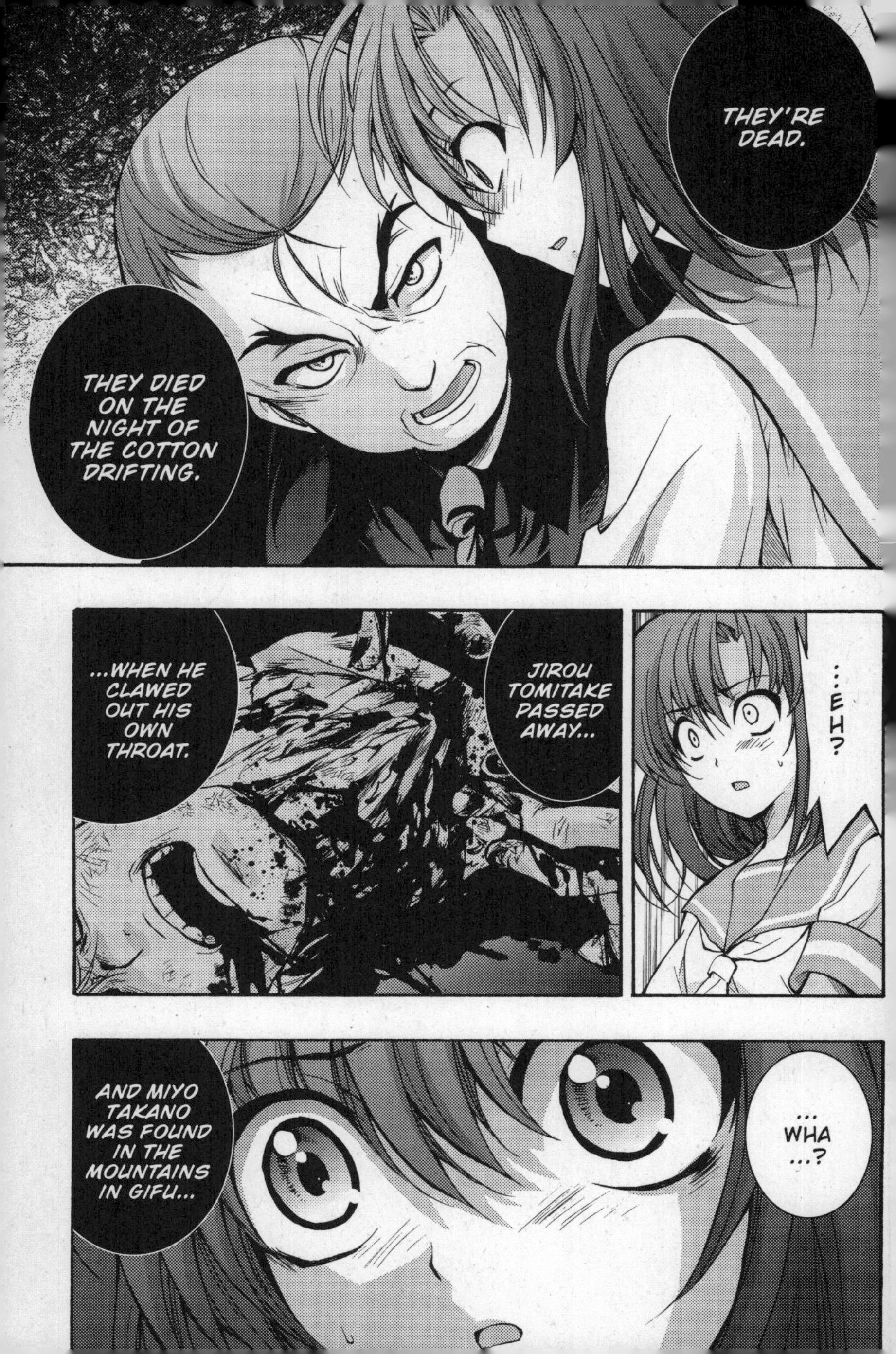
THEY'RE DEAD.
THEY DIED ON THE NIGHT OF THE COTTON DRIFTING.
...EH?
JIROU TOMITAKE PASSED AWAY...
...WHEN HE CLAWED OUT HIS OWN THROAT.
...WHA...?
AND MIYO TAKANO WAS FOUND IN THE MOUNTAINS IN GIFU...

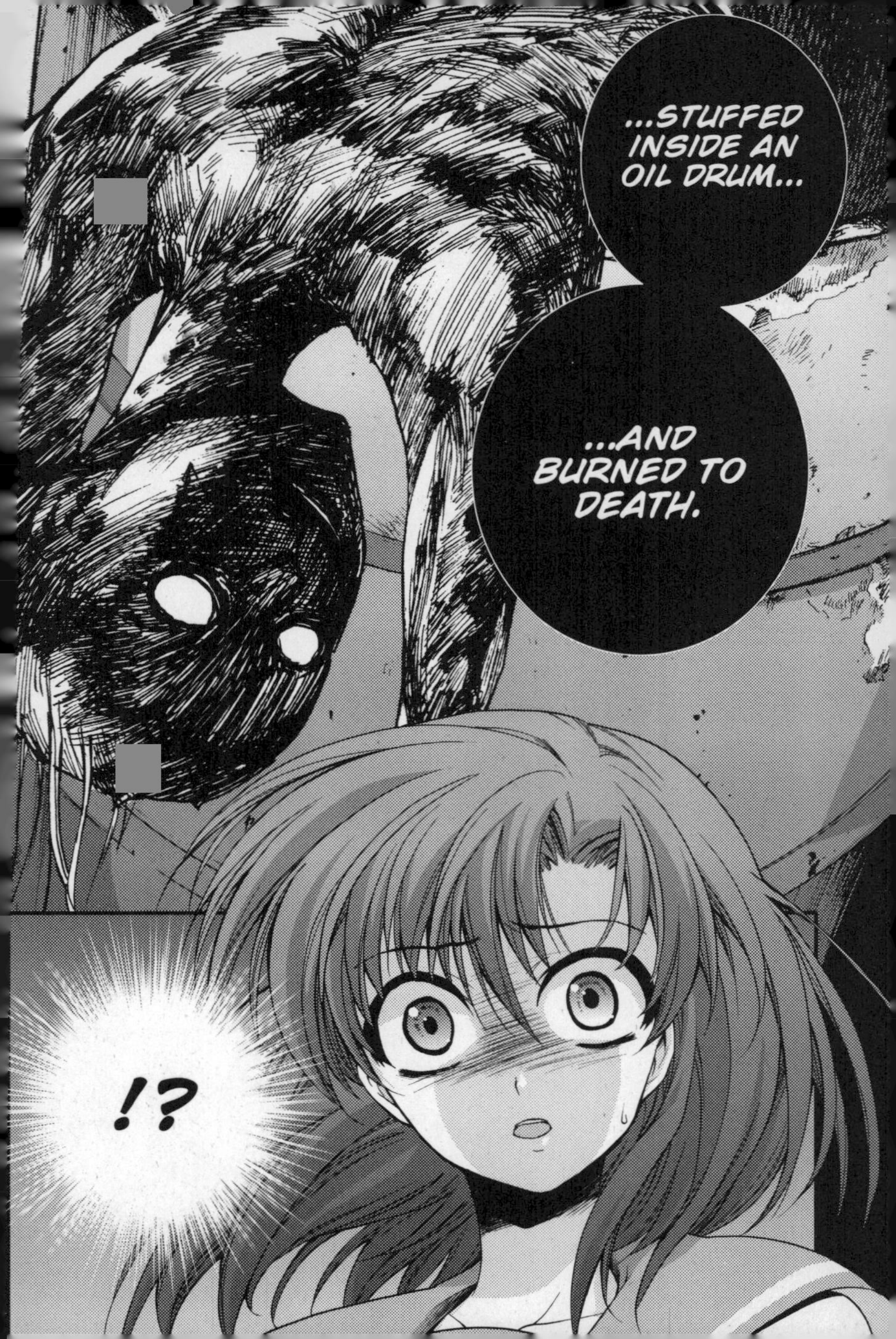
...STUFFED INSIDE AN OIL DRUM...
...AND BURNED TO DEATH.
!?

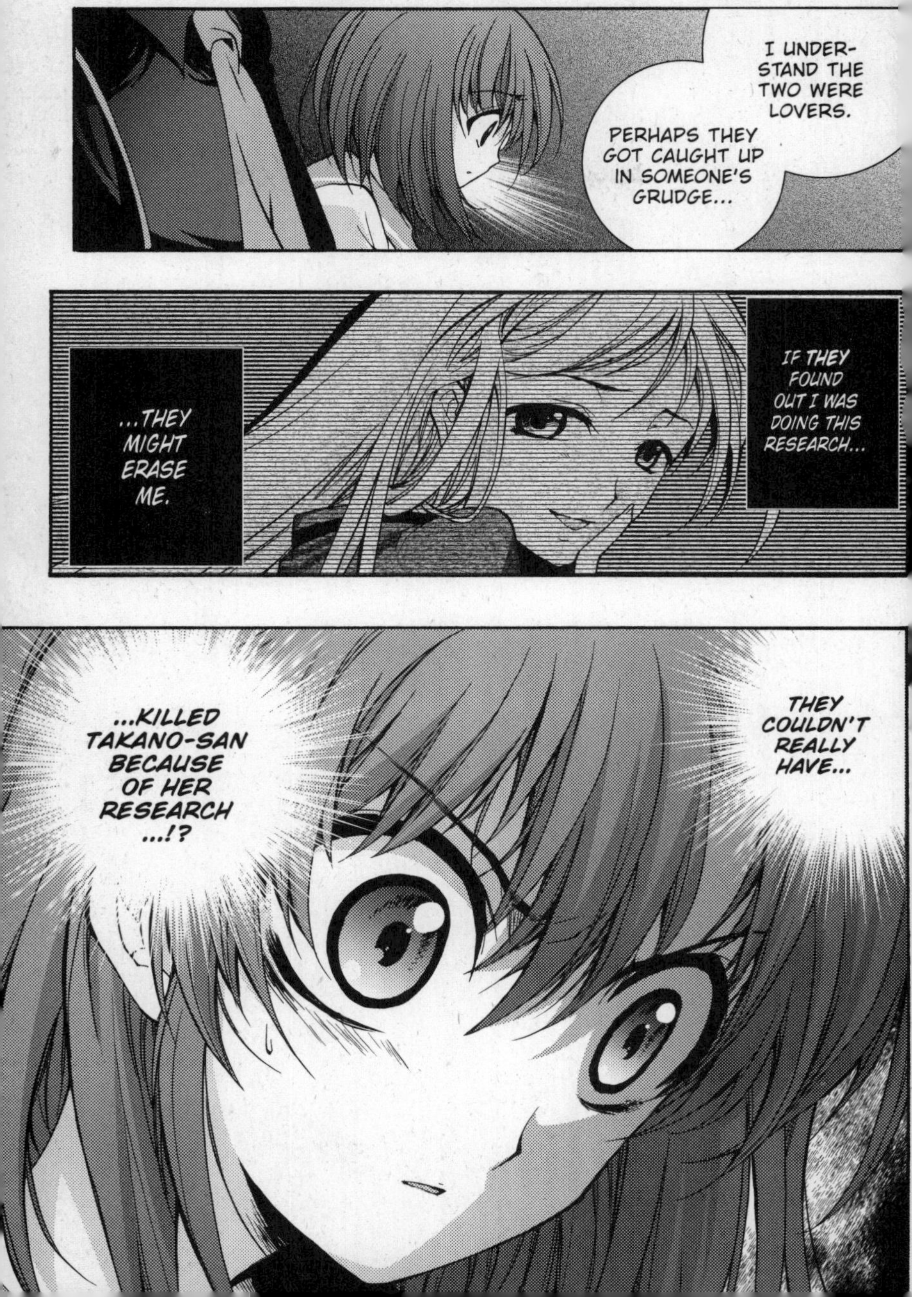
I UNDER-STAND THE TWO WERE LOVERS.
PERHAPS THEY GOT CAUGHT UP IN SOMEONE'S GRUDGE...
IF THEY FOUND OUT I WAS DOING THIS RESEARCH...
...THEY MIGHT ERASE ME.
THEY COULDN'T REALLY HAVE...
...KILLED TAKANO-SAN BECAUSE OF HER RESEARCH ...!?

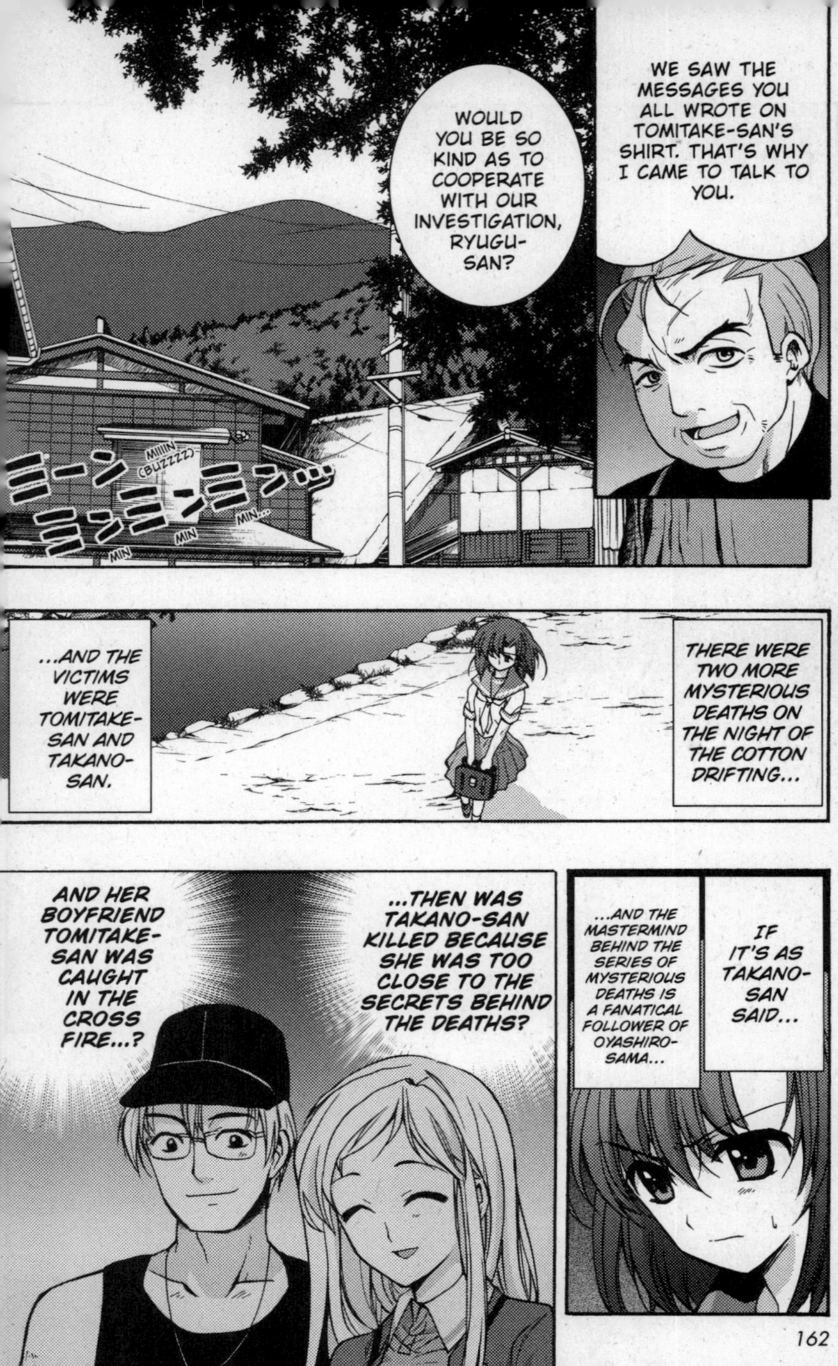
WE SAW THE MESSAGES YOU ALL WROTE ON TOMITAKE-SAN'S SHIRT. THAT'S WHY I CAME TO TALK TO YOU.
WOULD YOU BE SO KIND AS TO COOPERATE WITH OUR INVESTIGATION, RYUGU-SAN?
MIIIIN (BUZZZZ)
MIN
MIN
MIN...
THERE WERE TWO MORE MYSTERIOUS DEATHS ON THE NIGHT OF THE COTTON DRIFTING...
...AND THE VICTIMS WERE TOMITAKE-SAN AND TAKANO-SAN.
IF IT'S AS TAKANO-SAN SAID...
...AND THE MASTERMIND BEHIND THE SERIES OF MYSTERIOUS DEATHS IS A FANATICAL FOLLOWER OF OYASHIRO-SAMA...
...THEN WAS TAKANO-SAN KILLED BECAUSE SHE WAS TOO CLOSE TO THE SECRETS BEHIND THE DEATHS?
AND HER BOYFRIEND TOMITAKE-SAN WAS CAUGHT IN THE CROSS FIRE...?

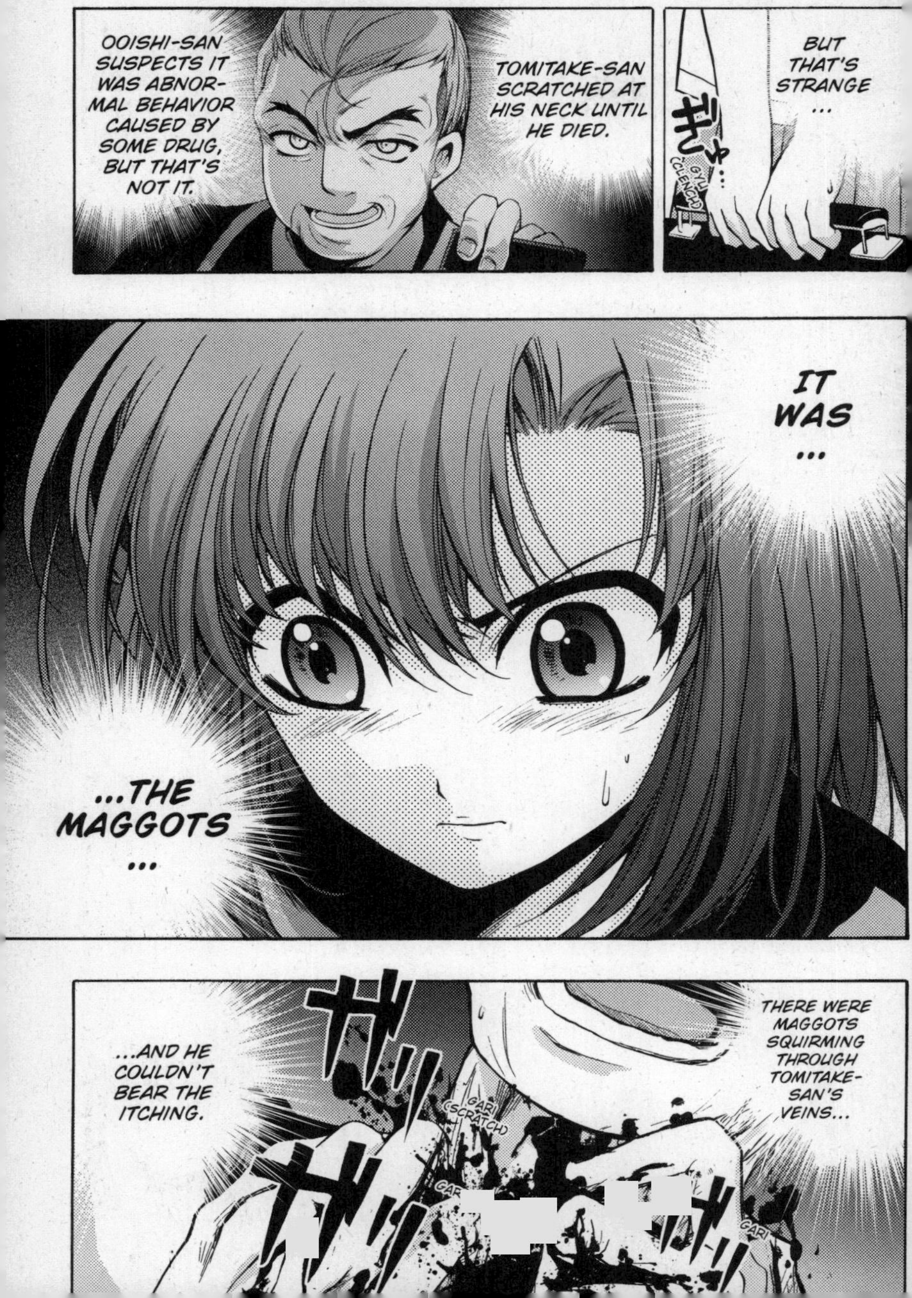
BUT THAT'S STRANGE ...
ぎゅ…
GYU (CLENCH)
TOMITAKE-SAN SCRATCHED AT HIS NECK UNTIL HE DIED.
OOISHI-SAN SUSPECTS IT WAS ABNORMAL BEHAVIOR CAUSED BY SOME DRUG, BUT THAT'S NOT IT.
IT WAS ...
...THE MAGGOTS ...
THERE WERE MAGGOTS SQUIRMING THROUGH TOMITAKE-SAN'S VEINS...
...AND HE COULDN'T BEAR THE ITCHING.
GARI (SCRATCH)
GARI
GARI

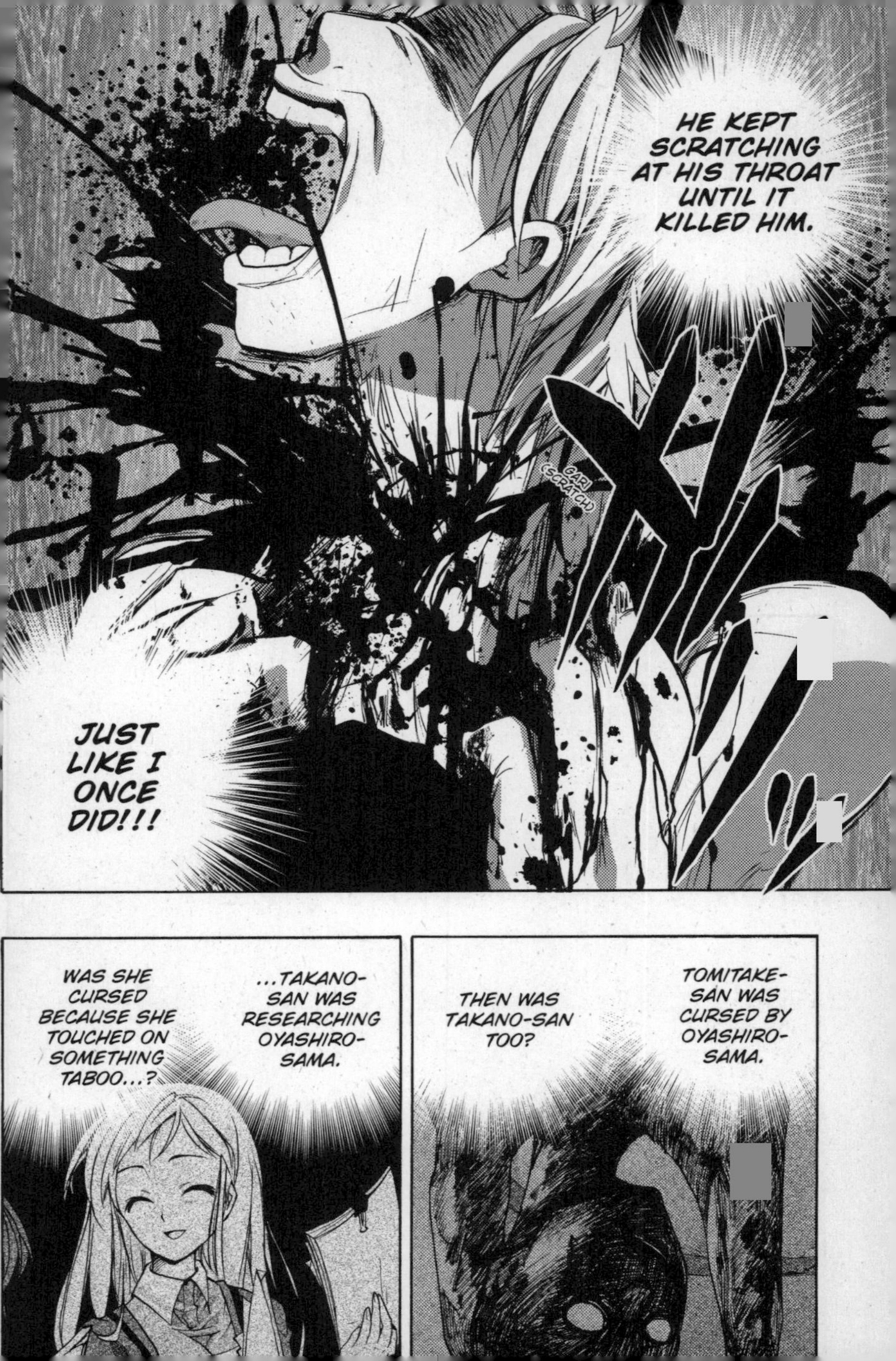
HE KEPT SCRATCHING AT HIS THROAT UNTIL IT KILLED HIM.
GARI (SCRATCH)
JUST LIKE I ONCE DID!!!
TOMITAKE-SAN WAS CURSED BY OYASHIRO-SAMA.
THEN WAS TAKANO-SAN TOO?
...TAKANO-SAN WAS RESEARCHING OYASHIRO-SAMA.
WAS SHE CURSED BECAUSE SHE TOUCHED ON SOMETHING TABOO...?

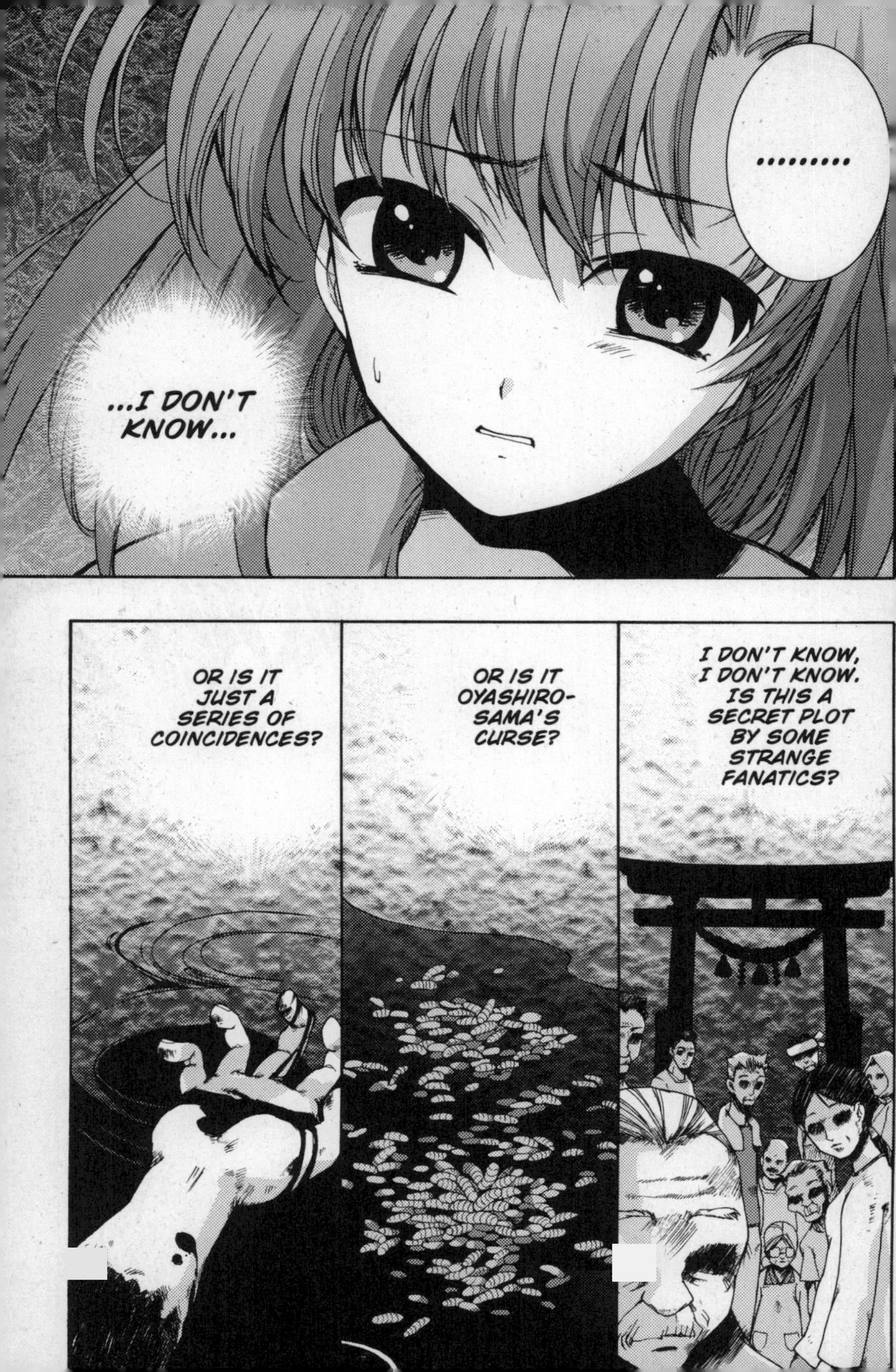
....
...I DON'T KNOW...
I DON'T KNOW, I DON'T KNOW. IS THIS A SECRET PLOT BY SOME STRANGE FANATICS?
OR IS IT OYASHIRO-SAMA'S CURSE?
OR IS IT JUST A SERIES OF COINCIDENCES?

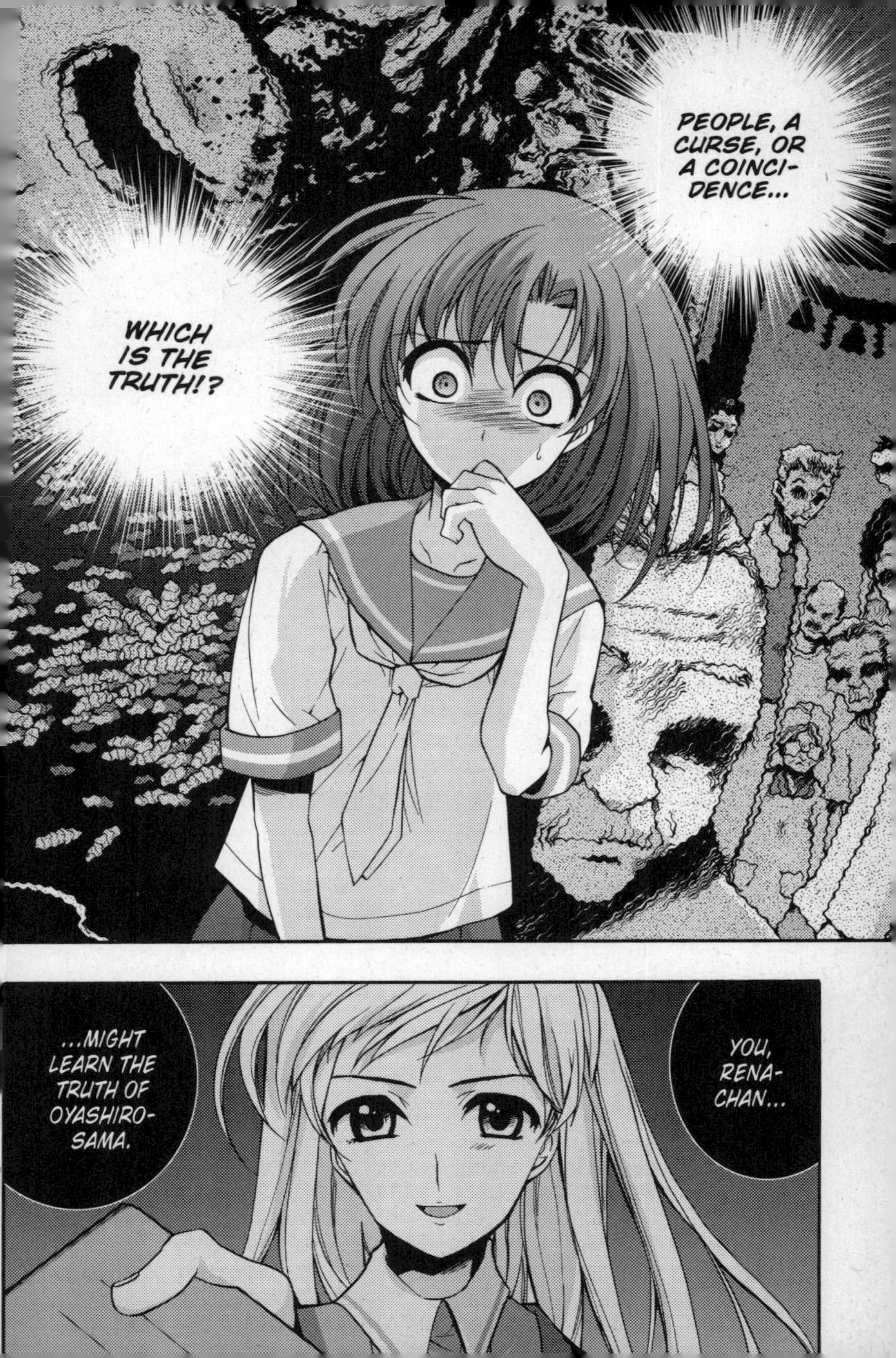
PEOPLE, A CURSE, OR A COINCIDENCE...
WHICH IS THE TRUTH!?
YOU, RENA-CHAN...
...MIGHT LEARN THE TRUTH OF OYASHIRO-SAMA.

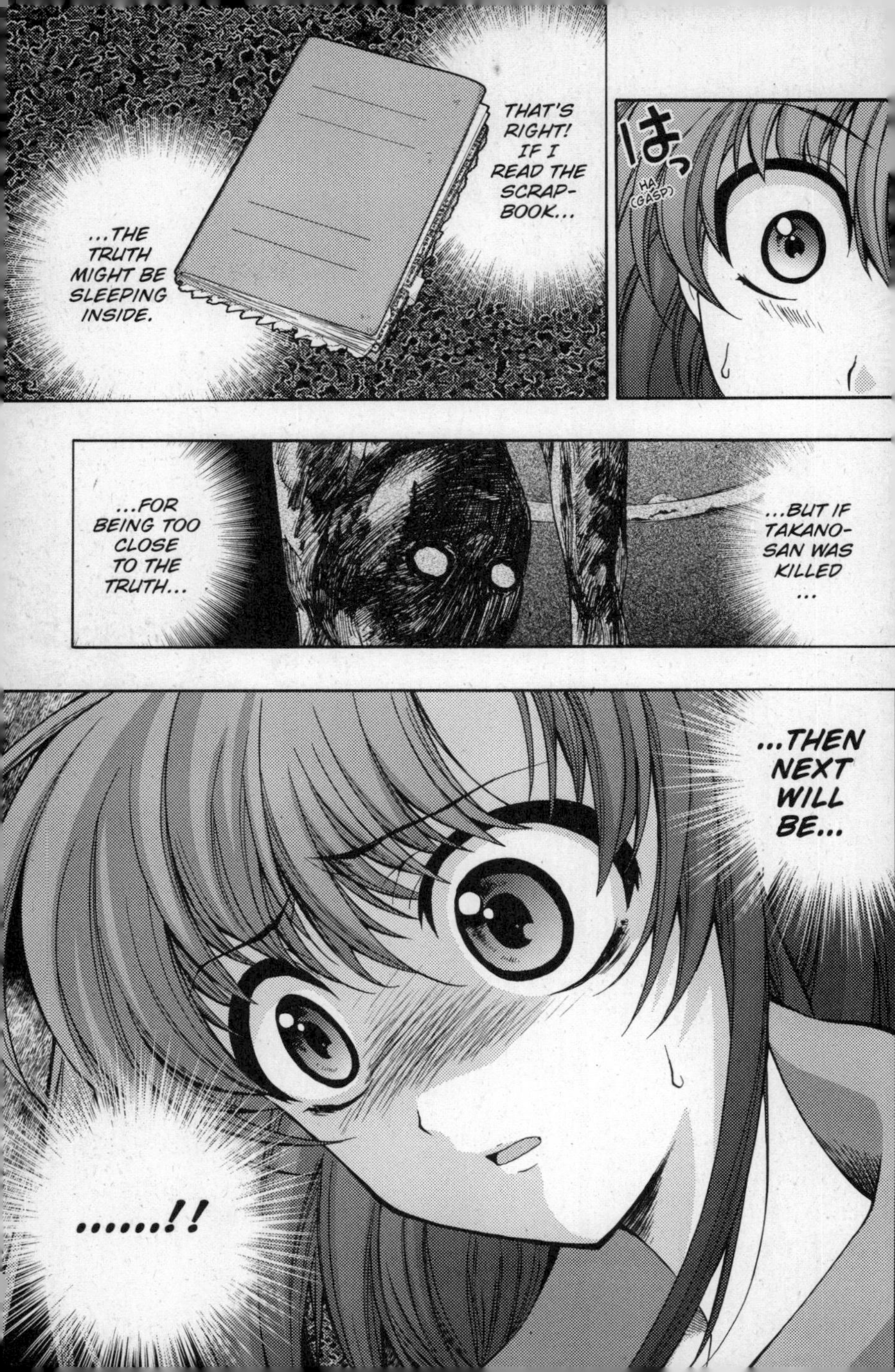
はっ
HA (GASP)
THAT'S RIGHT! IF I READ THE SCRAP-BOOK...
...THE TRUTH MIGHT BE SLEEPING INSIDE.
...BUT IF TAKANO-SAN WAS KILLED ...
...FOR BEING TOO CLOSE TO THE TRUTH...
...THEN NEXT WILL BE...
......!!

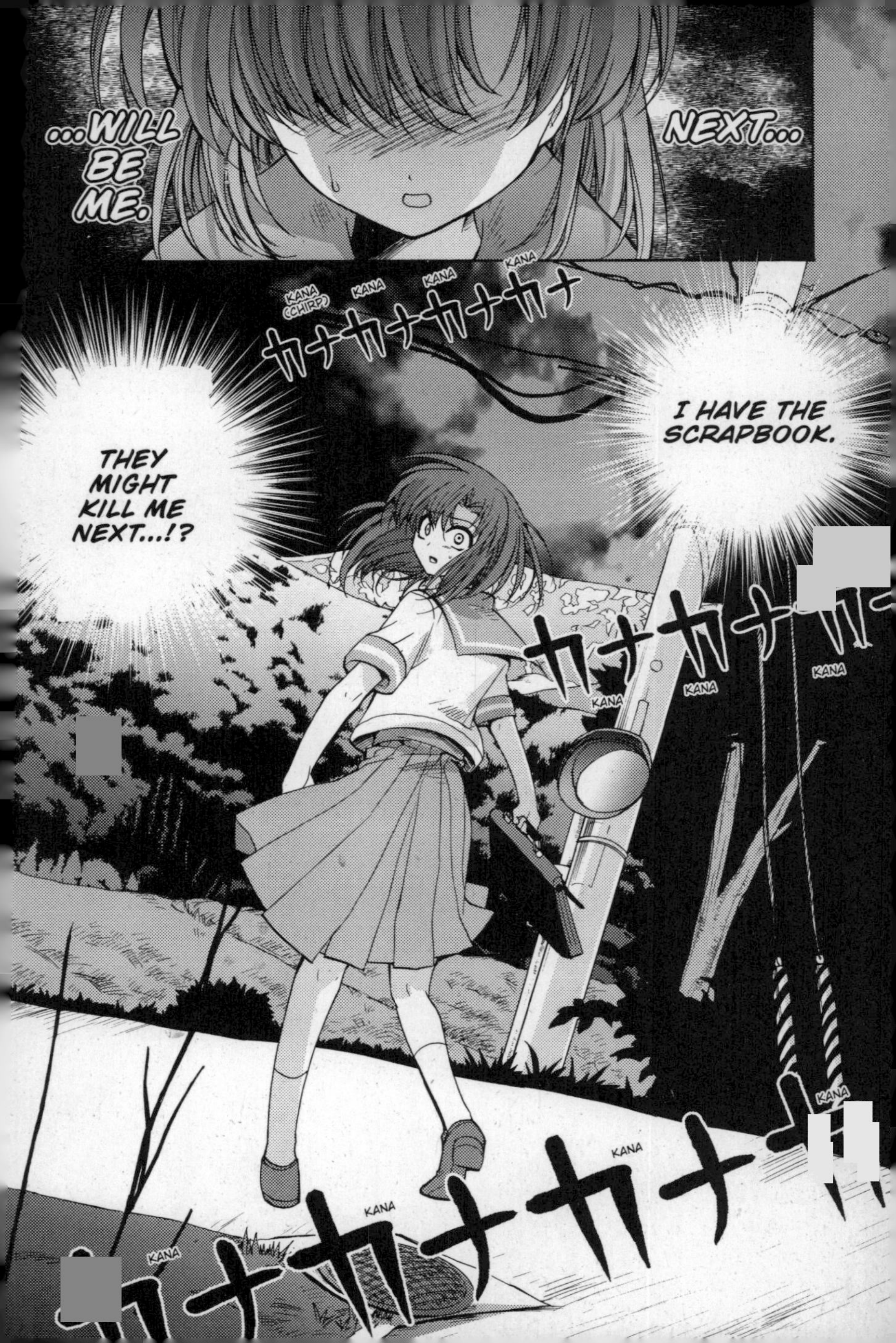
NEXT...
...WILL BE ME.
KANA KANA KANA KANA (CHIRP)
カナカナカナカナ
I HAVE THE SCRAPBOOK.
THEY MIGHT KILL ME NEXT...!?
KANA KANA KANA
カナカナ
KANA KANA KANA KANA
カナカナカナカナ

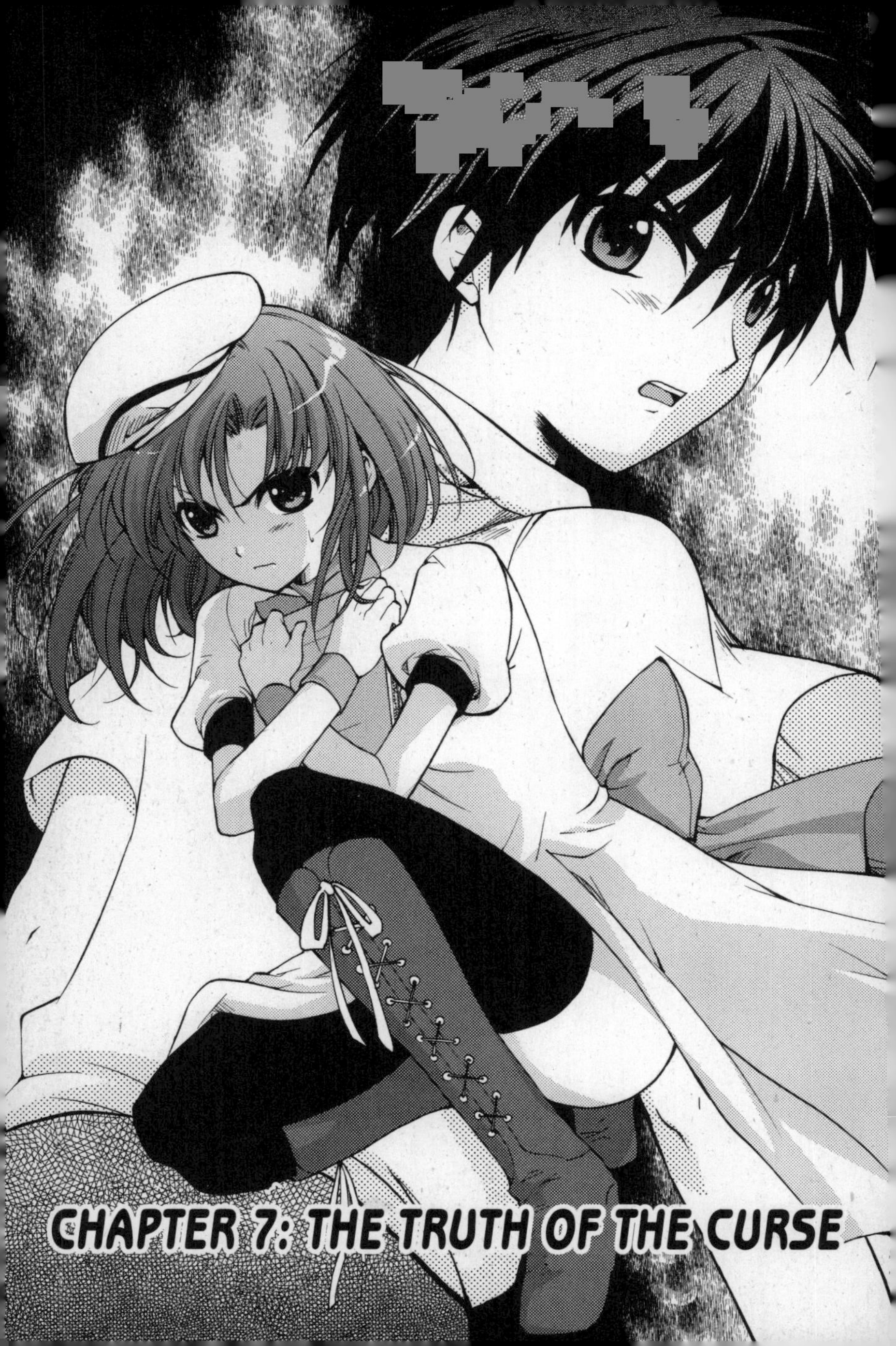
CHAPTER 7: THE TRUTH OF THE CURSE

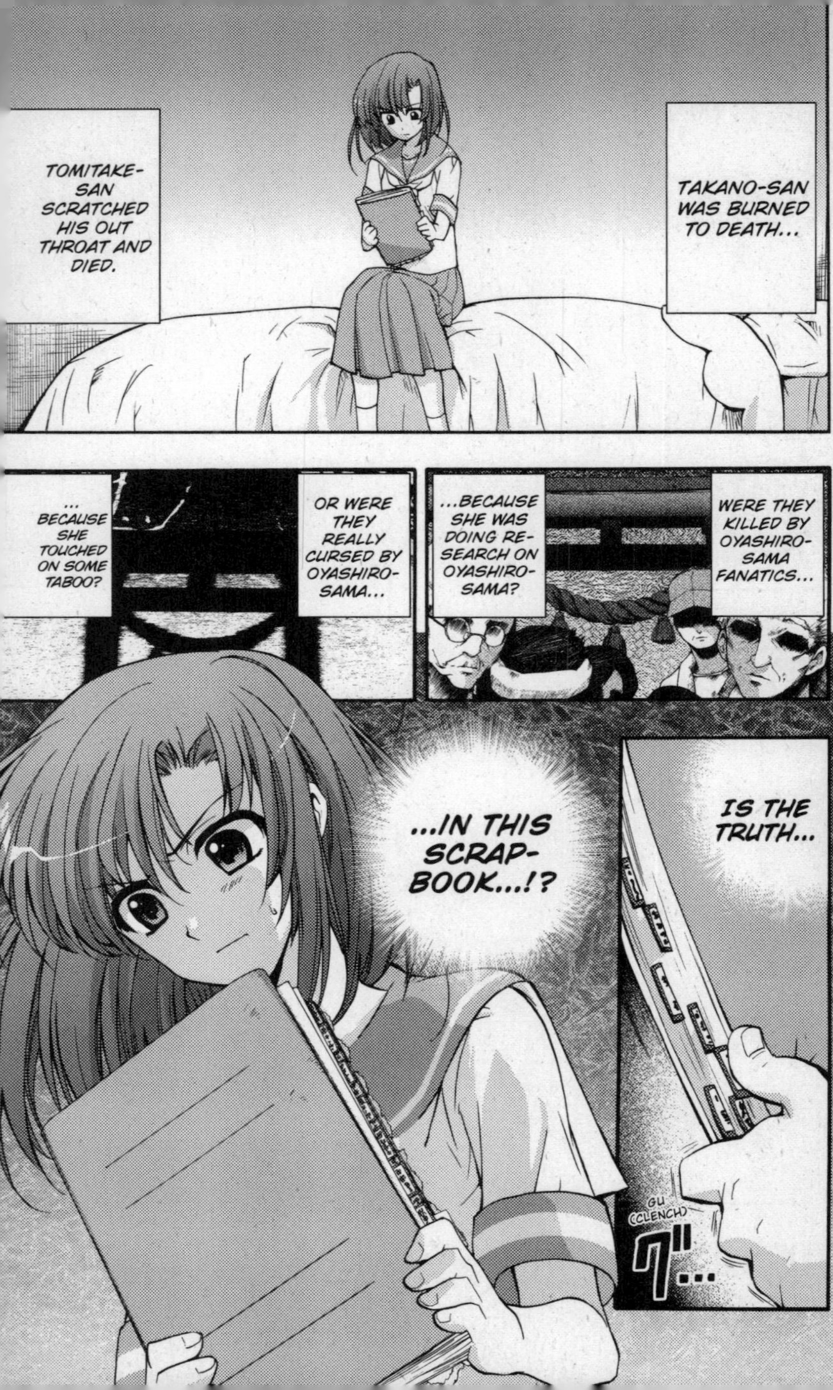
TAKANO-SAN WAS BURNED TO DEATH...
TOMITAKE-SAN SCRATCHED HIS OUT THROAT AND DIED.
WERE THEY KILLED BY OYASHIRO-SAMA FANATICS...
...BECAUSE SHE WAS DOING RE-SEARCH ON OYASHIRO-SAMA?
OR WERE THEY REALLY CURSED BY OYASHIRO-SAMA...
...BECAUSE SHE TOUCHED ON SOME TABOO?
IS THE TRUTH...
GU (CLENCH)
...IN THIS SCRAP-BOOK...!?

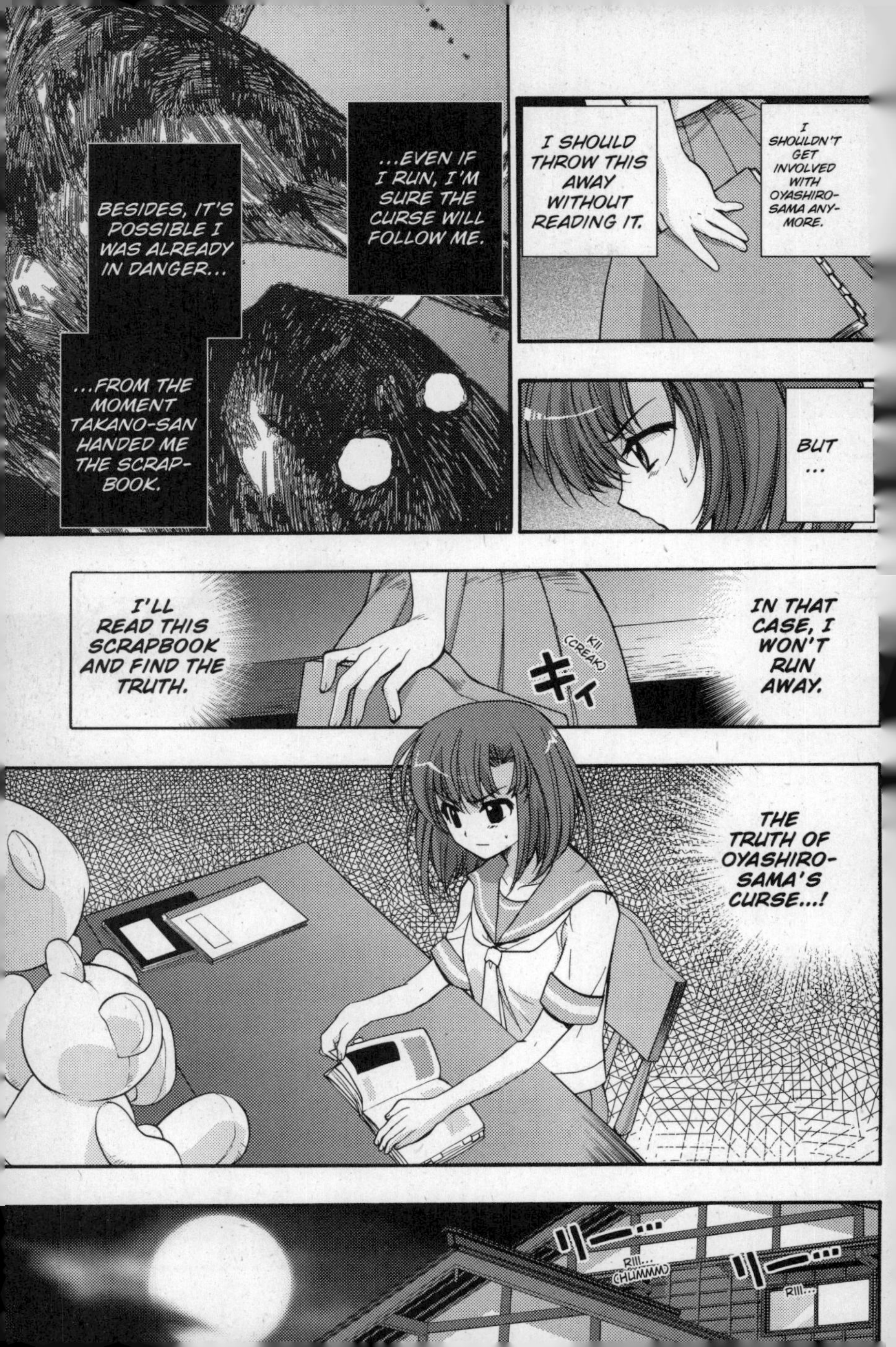
I SHOULDN'T GET INVOLVED WITH OYASHIRO-SAMA ANYMORE.
I SHOULD THROW THIS AWAY WITHOUT READING IT.
BUT...
...EVEN IF I RUN, I'M SURE THE CURSE WILL FOLLOW ME.
BESIDES, IT'S POSSIBLE I WAS ALREADY IN DANGER...
...FROM THE MOMENT TAKANO-SAN HANDED ME THE SCRAPBOOK.
IN THAT CASE, I WON'T RUN AWAY.
キィ
KII (CREAK)
I'LL READ THIS SCRAPBOOK AND FIND THE TRUTH.
THE TRUTH OF OYASHIRO-SAMA'S CURSE...!
リー…
RIII... (HUMMM)
リー…
RIII...

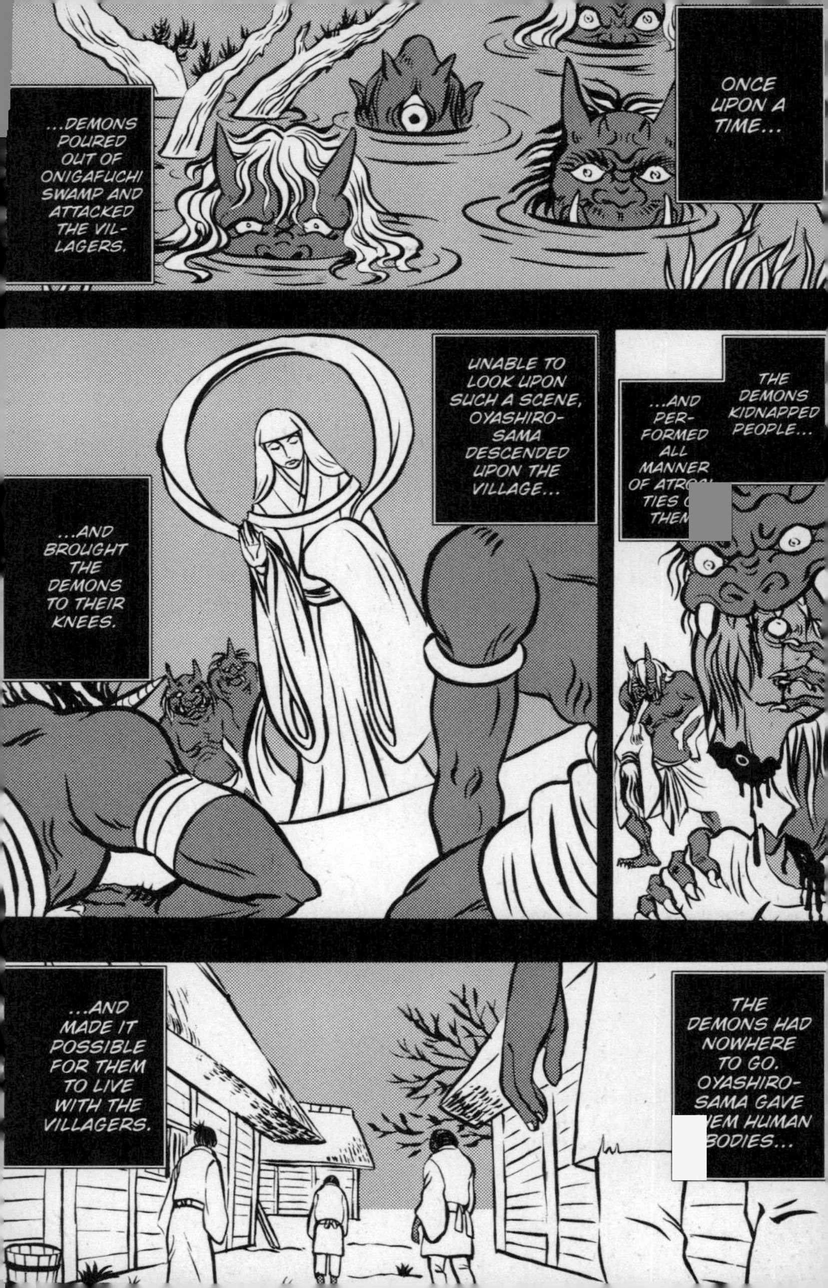
ONCE UPON A TIME...
...DEMONS POURED OUT OF ONIGAFUCHI SWAMP AND ATTACKED THE VILLAGERS.
THE DEMONS KIDNAPPED PEOPLE...
...AND PERFORMED ALL MANNER OF ATRO TIES O THEM
UNABLE TO LOOK UPON SUCH A SCENE, OYASHIRO-SAMA DESCENDED UPON THE VILLAGE...
...AND BROUGHT THE DEMONS TO THEIR KNEES.
THE DEMONS HAD NOWHERE TO GO. OYASHIRO-SAMA GAVE EM HUMAN BODIES...
...AND MADE IT POSSIBLE FOR THEM TO LIVE WITH THE VILLAGERS.

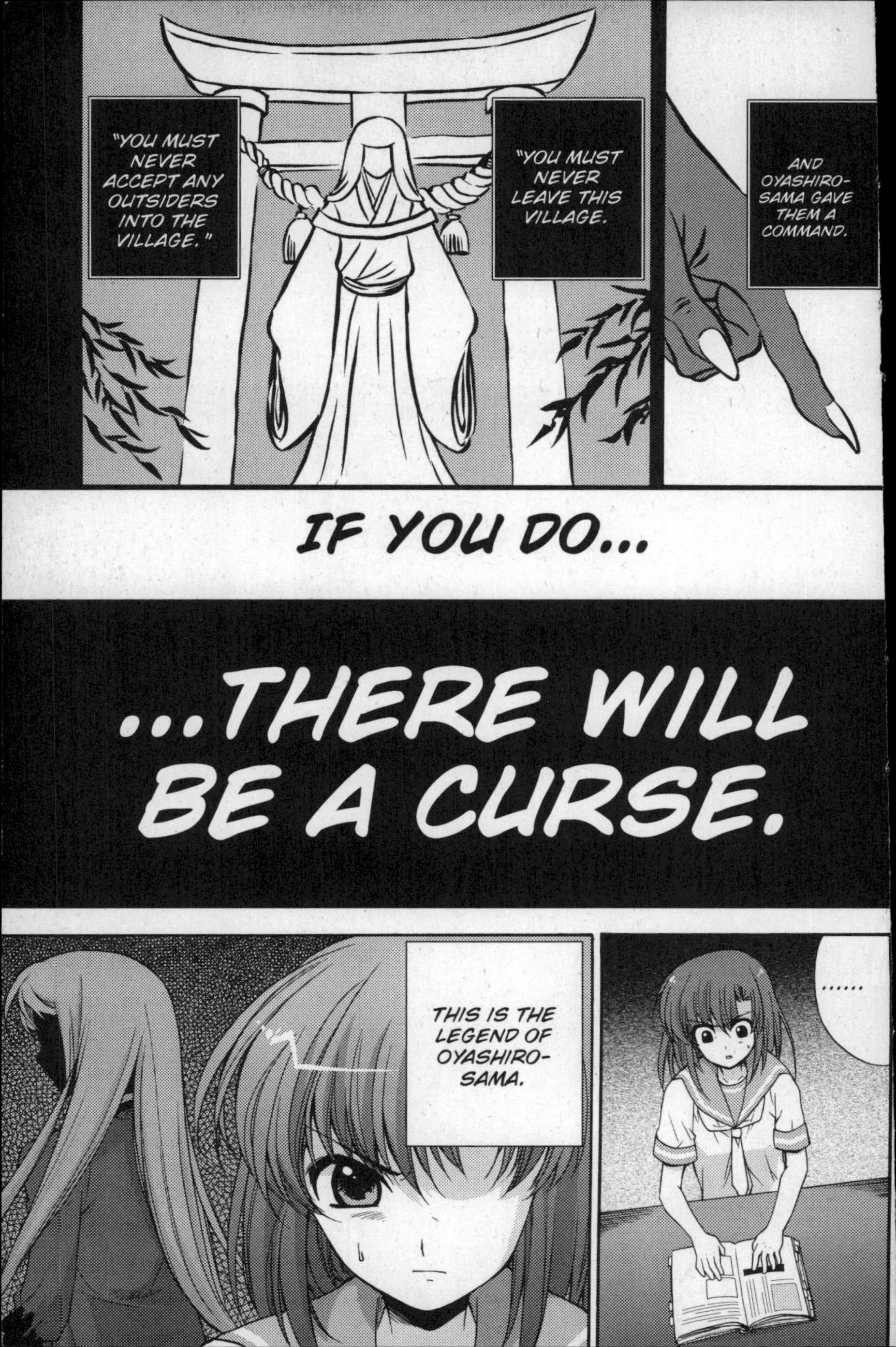
AND OYASHIRO-SAMA GAVE THEM A COMMAND.
"YOU MUST NEVER LEAVE THIS VILLAGE.
"YOU MUST NEVER ACCEPT ANY OUTSIDERS INTO THE VILLAGE."
IF YOU DO...
...THERE WILL BE A CURSE.
......
THIS IS THE LEGEND OF OYASHIRO-SAMA.

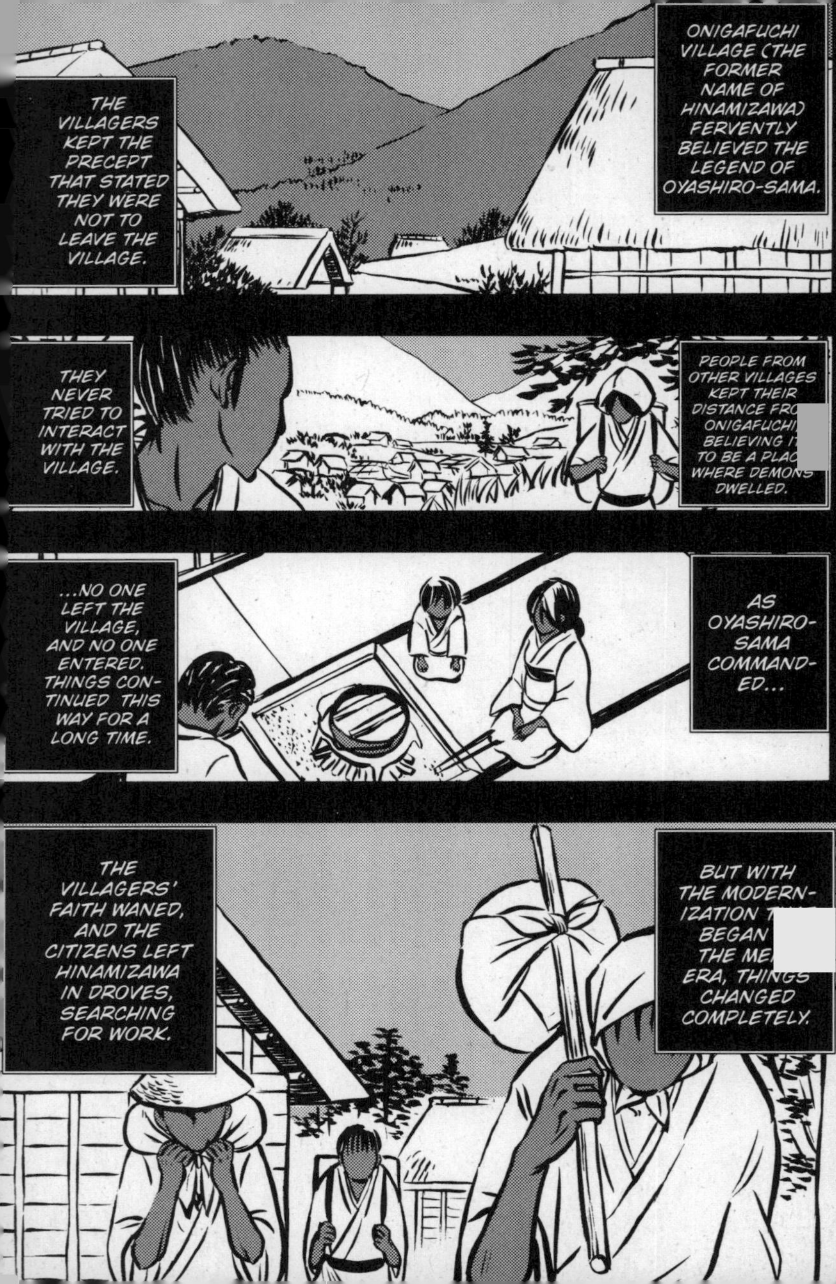
ONIGAFUCHI VILLAGE (THE FORMER NAME OF HINAMIZAWA) FERVENTLY BELIEVED THE LEGEND OF OYASHIRO-SAMA.
THE VILLAGERS KEPT THE PRECEPT THAT STATED THEY WERE NOT TO LEAVE THE VILLAGE.
PEOPLE FROM OTHER VILLAGES KEPT THEIR DISTANCE FRO ONIGAFUCHI BELIEVING I TO BE A PLA WHERE DEMON DWELLED.
THEY NEVER TRIED TO INTERACT WITH THE VILLAGE.
AS OYASHIRO-SAMA COMMAND-ED...
...NO ONE LEFT THE VILLAGE, AND NO ONE ENTERED. THINGS CON-TINUED THIS WAY FOR A LONG TIME.
BUT WITH THE MODERN-IZATION T BEGAN THE ME ERA, THINGS CHANGED COMPLETELY.
THE VILLAGERS' FAITH WANED, AND THE CITIZENS LEFT HINAMIZAWA IN DROVES, SEARCHING FOR WORK.

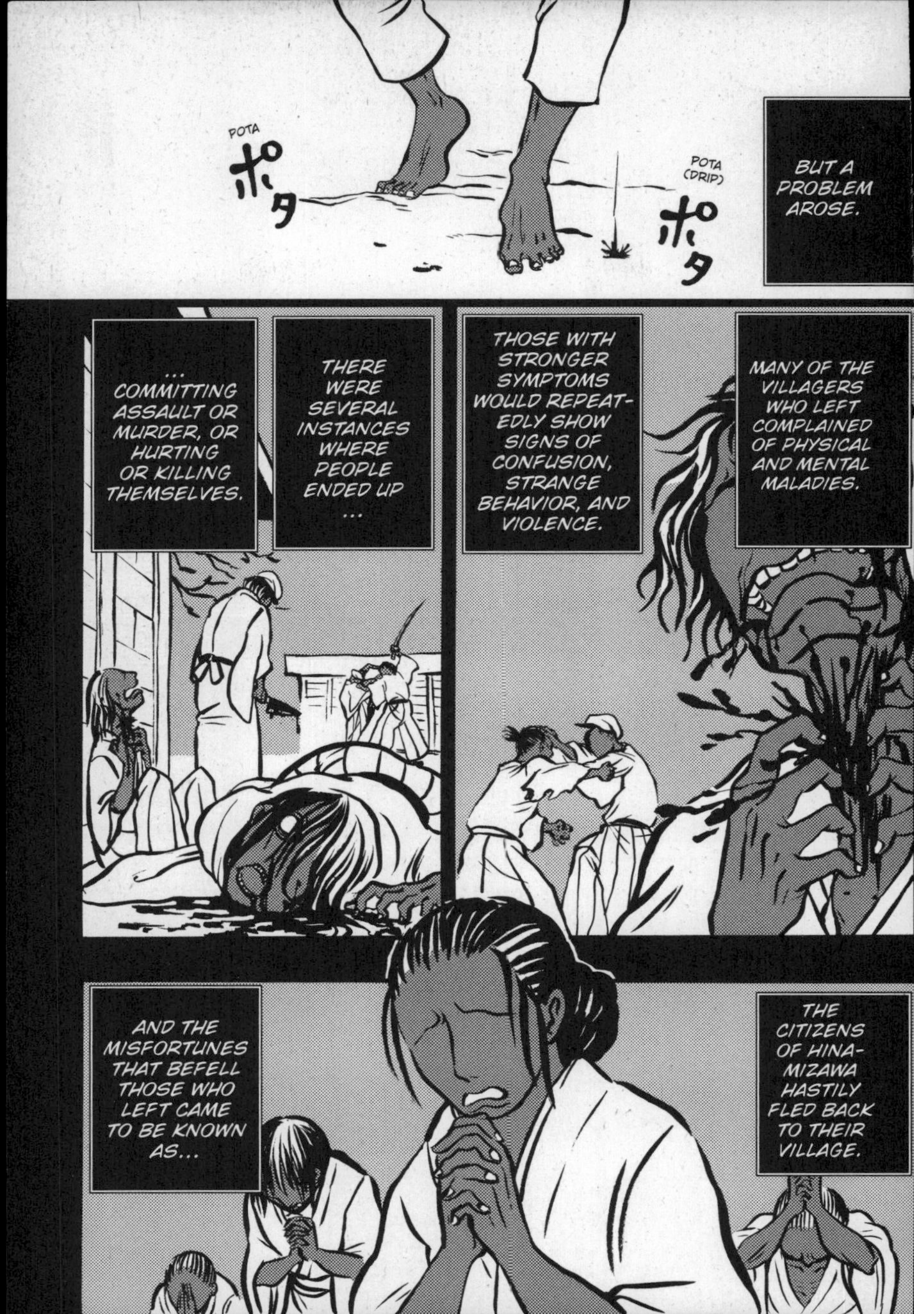
BUT A PROBLEM AROSE.
POTA (DRIP) ポタ
POTA ポタ
MANY OF THE VILLAGERS WHO LEFT COMPLAINED OF PHYSICAL AND MENTAL MALADIES.
THOSE WITH STRONGER SYMPTOMS WOULD REPEAT-EDLY SHOW SIGNS OF CONFUSION, STRANGE BEHAVIOR, AND VIOLENCE.
THERE WERE SEVERAL INSTANCES WHERE PEOPLE ENDED UP ...
... COMMITTING ASSAULT OR MURDER, OR HURTING OR KILLING THEMSELVES.
THE CITIZENS OF HINA-MIZAWA HASTILY FLED BACK TO THEIR VILLAGE.
AND THE MISFORTUNES THAT BEFELL THOSE WHO LEFT CAME TO BE KNOWN AS...

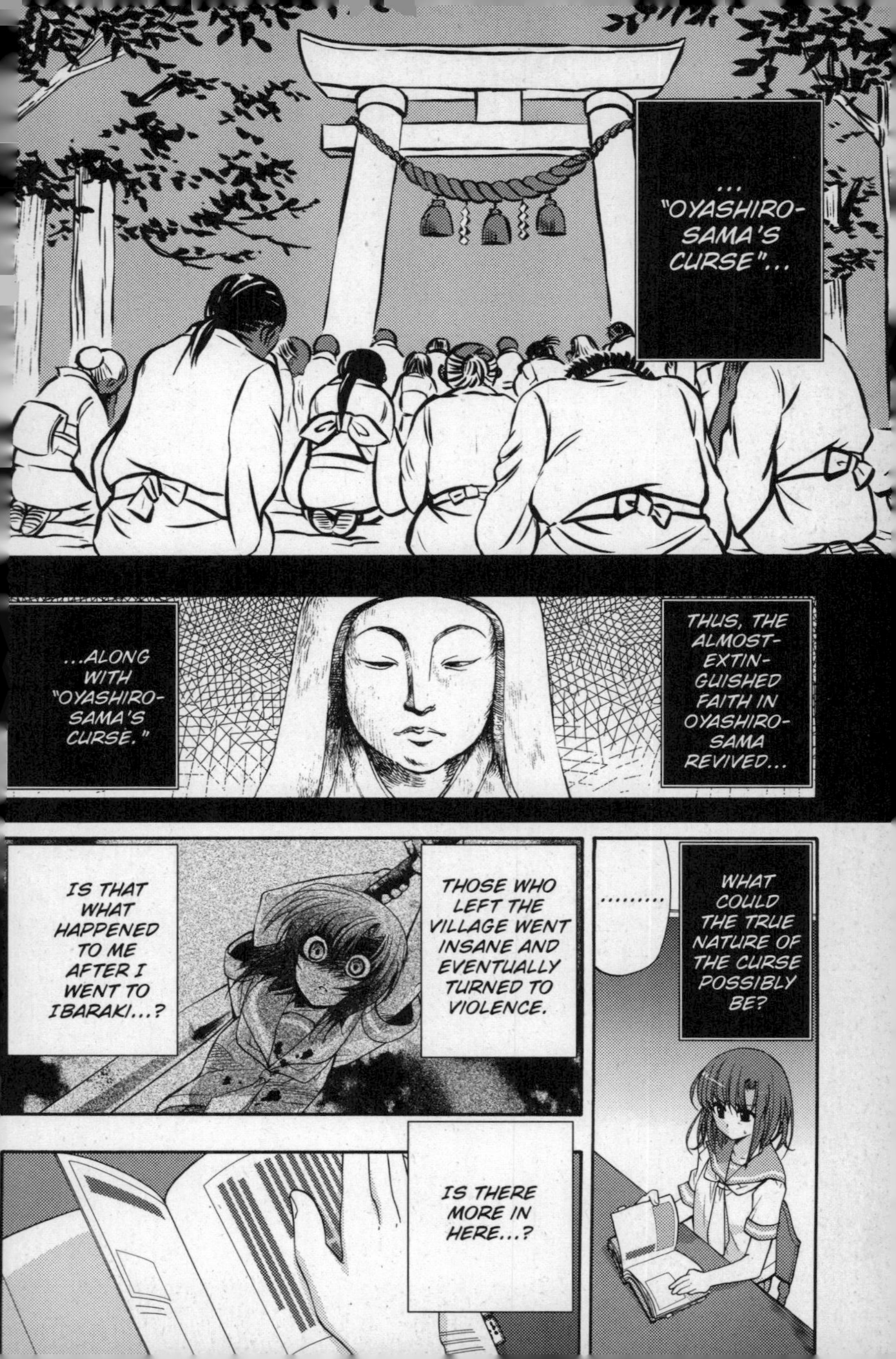
... "OYASHIRO-SAMA'S CURSE"...
THUS, THE ALMOST-EXTIN-GUISHED FAITH IN OYASHIRO-SAMA REVIVED...
...ALONG WITH "OYASHIRO-SAMA'S CURSE."
WHAT COULD THE TRUE NATURE OF THE CURSE POSSIBLY BE?
....
THOSE WHO LEFT THE VILLAGE WENT INSANE AND EVENTUALLY TURNED TO VIOLENCE.
IS THAT WHAT HAPPENED TO ME AFTER I WENT TO IBARAKI...?
IS THERE MORE IN HERE...?

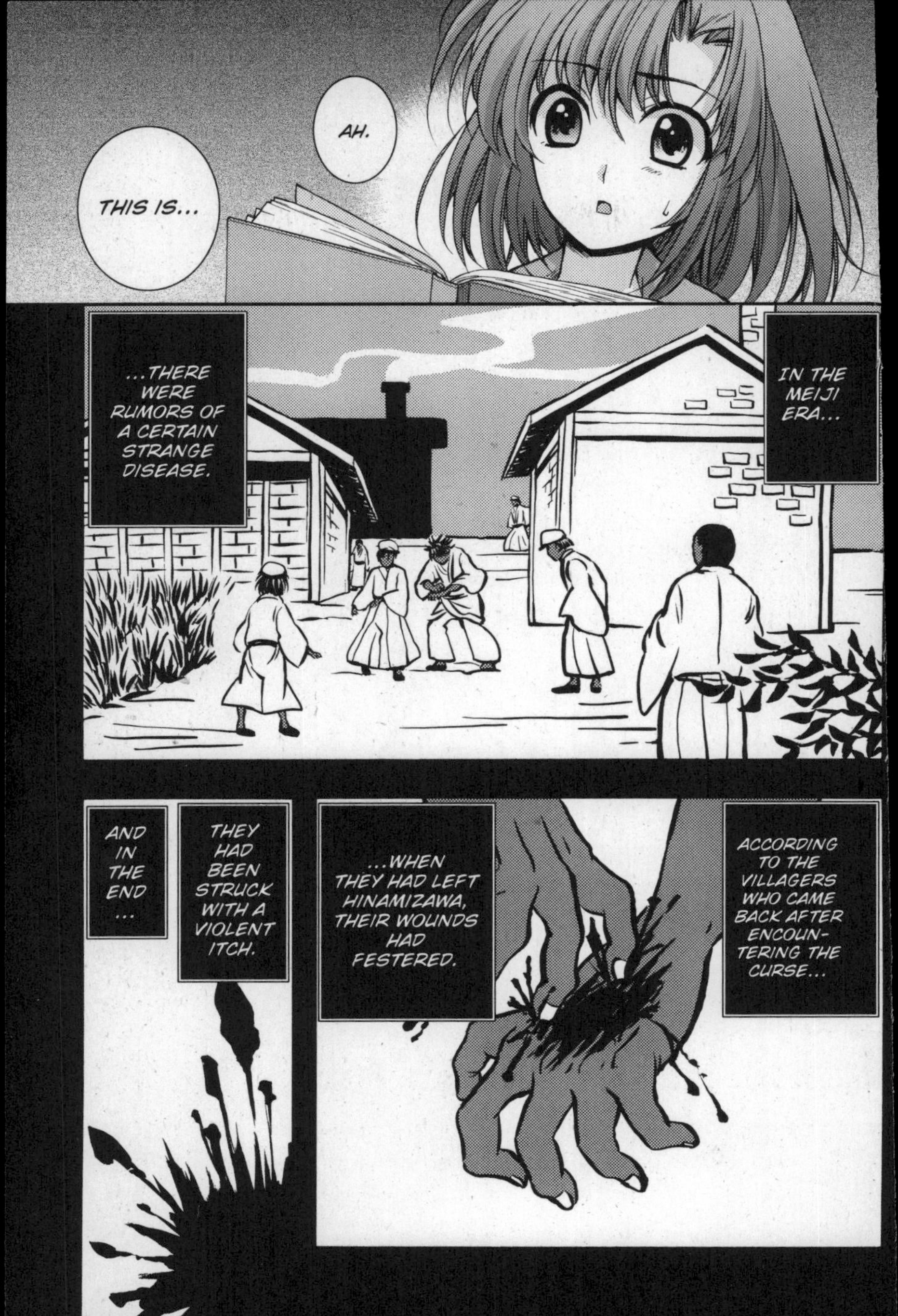
AH.
THIS IS...
IN THE MEIJI ERA...
...THERE WERE RUMORS OF A CERTAIN STRANGE DISEASE.
ACCORDING TO THE VILLAGERS WHO CAME BACK AFTER ENCOUN-TERING THE CURSE...
...WHEN THEY HAD LEFT HINAMIZAWA, THEIR WOUNDS HAD FESTERED.
THEY HAD BEEN STRUCK WITH A VIOLENT ITCH.
AND IN THE END...

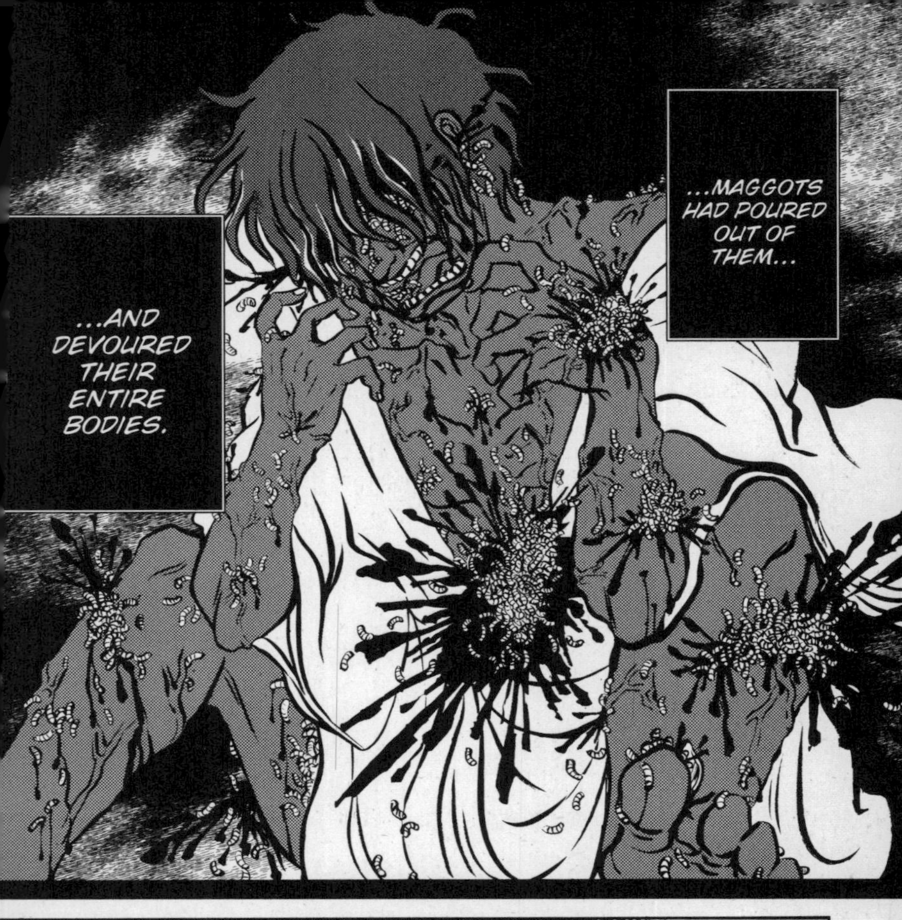
...MAGGOTS HAD POURED OUT OF THEM...
...AND DEVOURED THEIR ENTIRE BODIES.
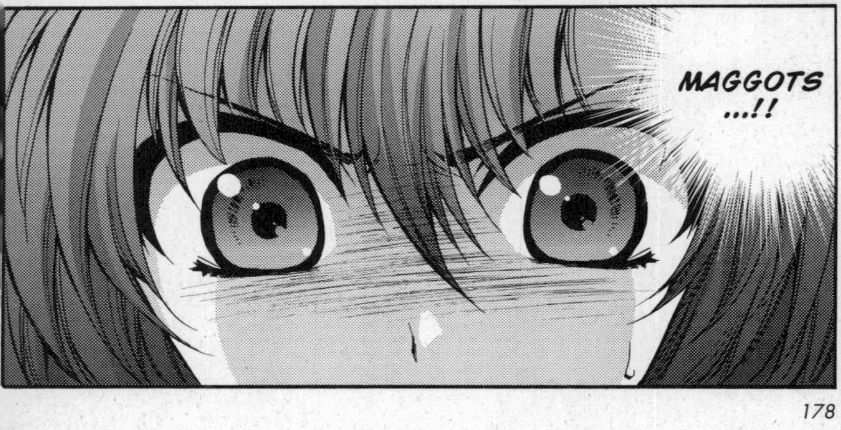
MAGGOTS ...!!

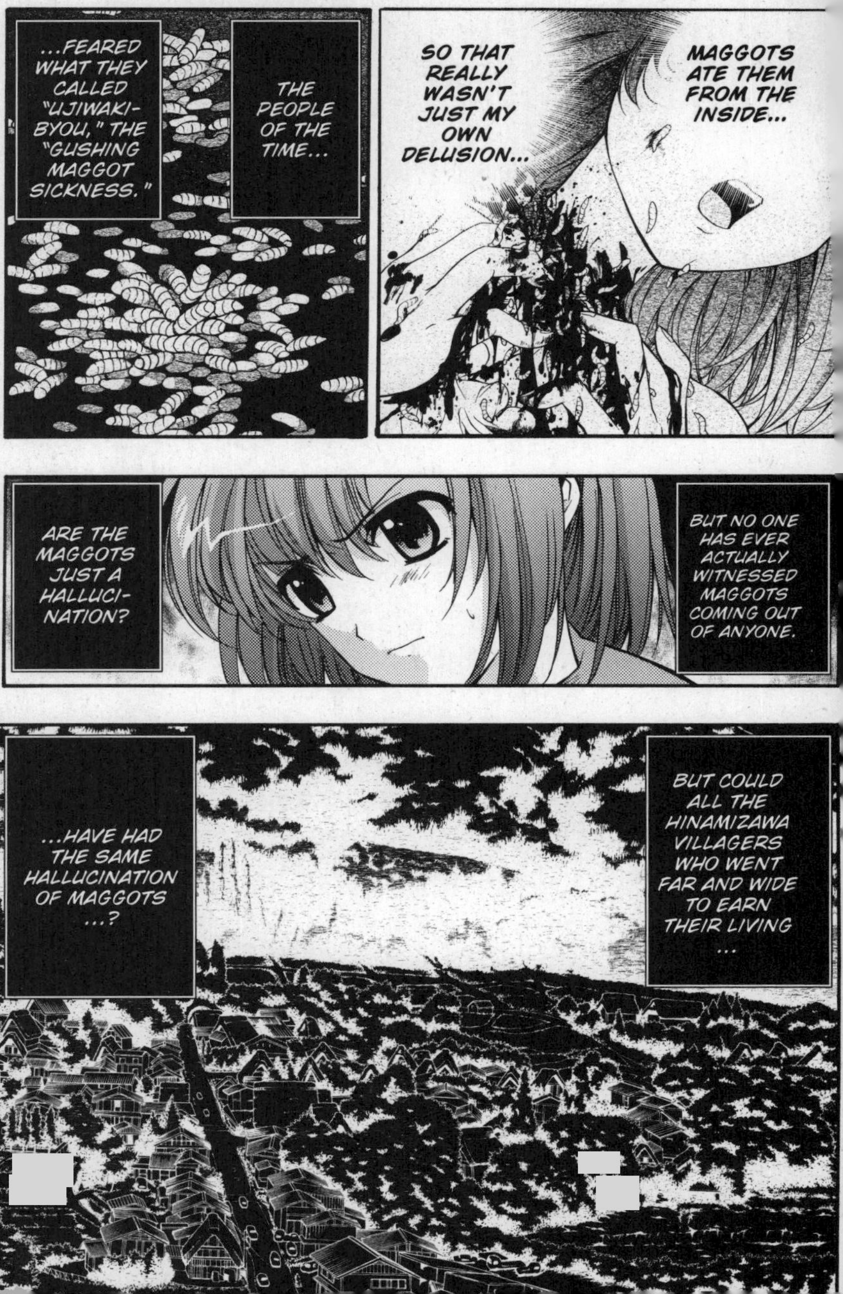
MAGGOTS ATE THEM FROM THE INSIDE...
SO THAT REALLY WASN'T JUST MY OWN DELUSION...
THE PEOPLE OF THE TIME...
...FEARED WHAT THEY CALLED "UJIWAKI-BYOU," THE "GUSHING MAGGOT SICKNESS."
BUT NO ONE HAS EVER ACTUALLY WITNESSED MAGGOTS COMING OUT OF ANYONE.
ARE THE MAGGOTS JUST A HALLUCI-NATION?
BUT COULD ALL THE HINAMIZAWA VILLAGERS WHO WENT FAR AND WIDE TO EARN THEIR LIVING...
...HAVE HAD THE SAME HALLUCINATION OF MAGGOTS...?

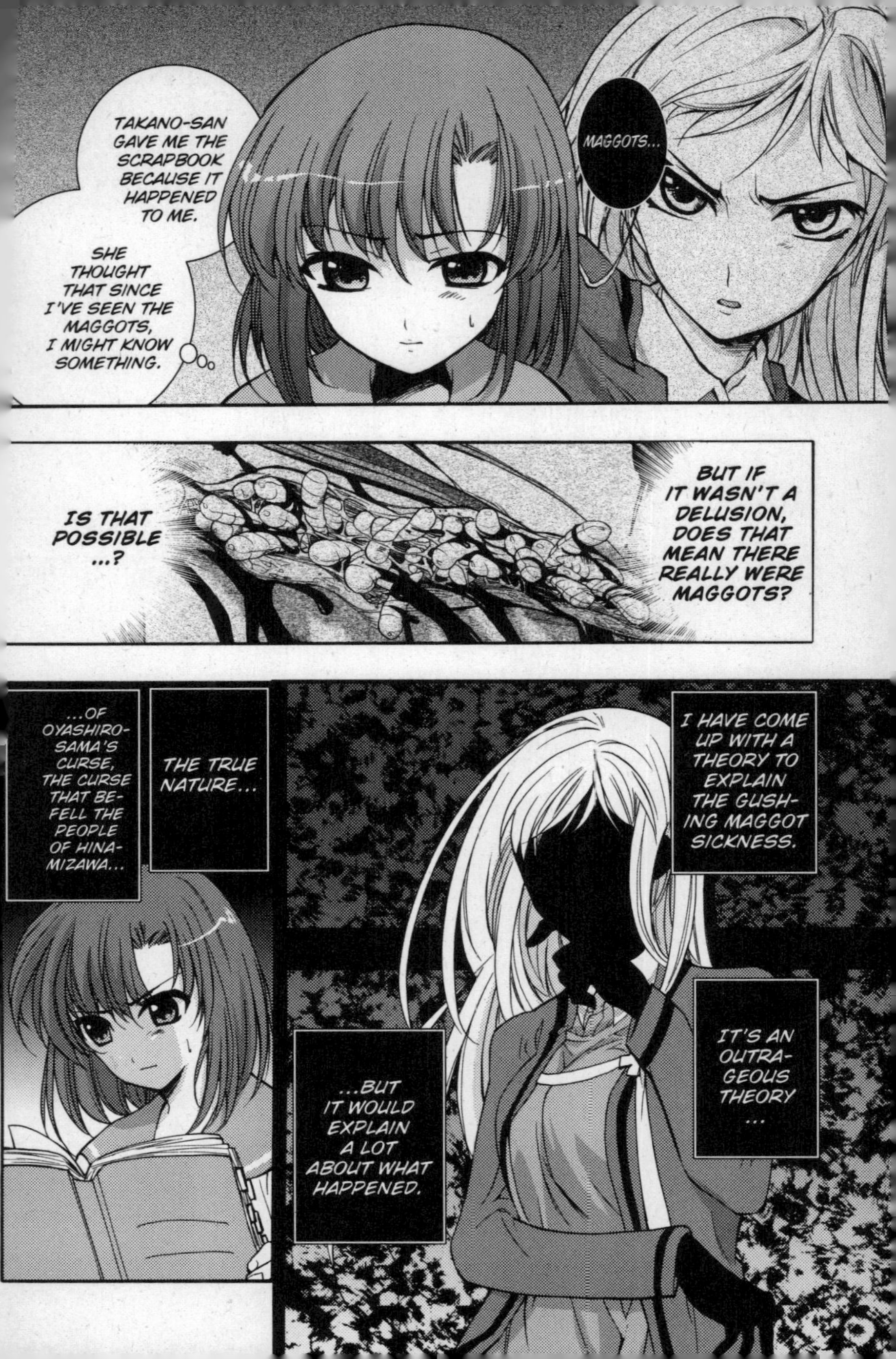
MAGGOTS...
TAKANO-SAN GAVE ME THE SCRAPBOOK BECAUSE IT HAPPENED TO ME.
SHE THOUGHT THAT SINCE I'VE SEEN THE MAGGOTS, I MIGHT KNOW SOMETHING.
BUT IF IT WASN'T A DELUSION, DOES THAT MEAN THERE REALLY WERE MAGGOTS?
IS THAT POSSIBLE ...?
I HAVE COME UP WITH A THEORY TO EXPLAIN THE GUSHING MAGGOT SICKNESS.
IT'S AN OUTRAGEOUS THEORY ...
...BUT IT WOULD EXPLAIN A LOT ABOUT WHAT HAPPENED.
THE TRUE NATURE...
...OF OYASHIRO-SAMA'S CURSE, THE CURSE THAT BEFELL THE PEOPLE OF HINAMIZAWA...

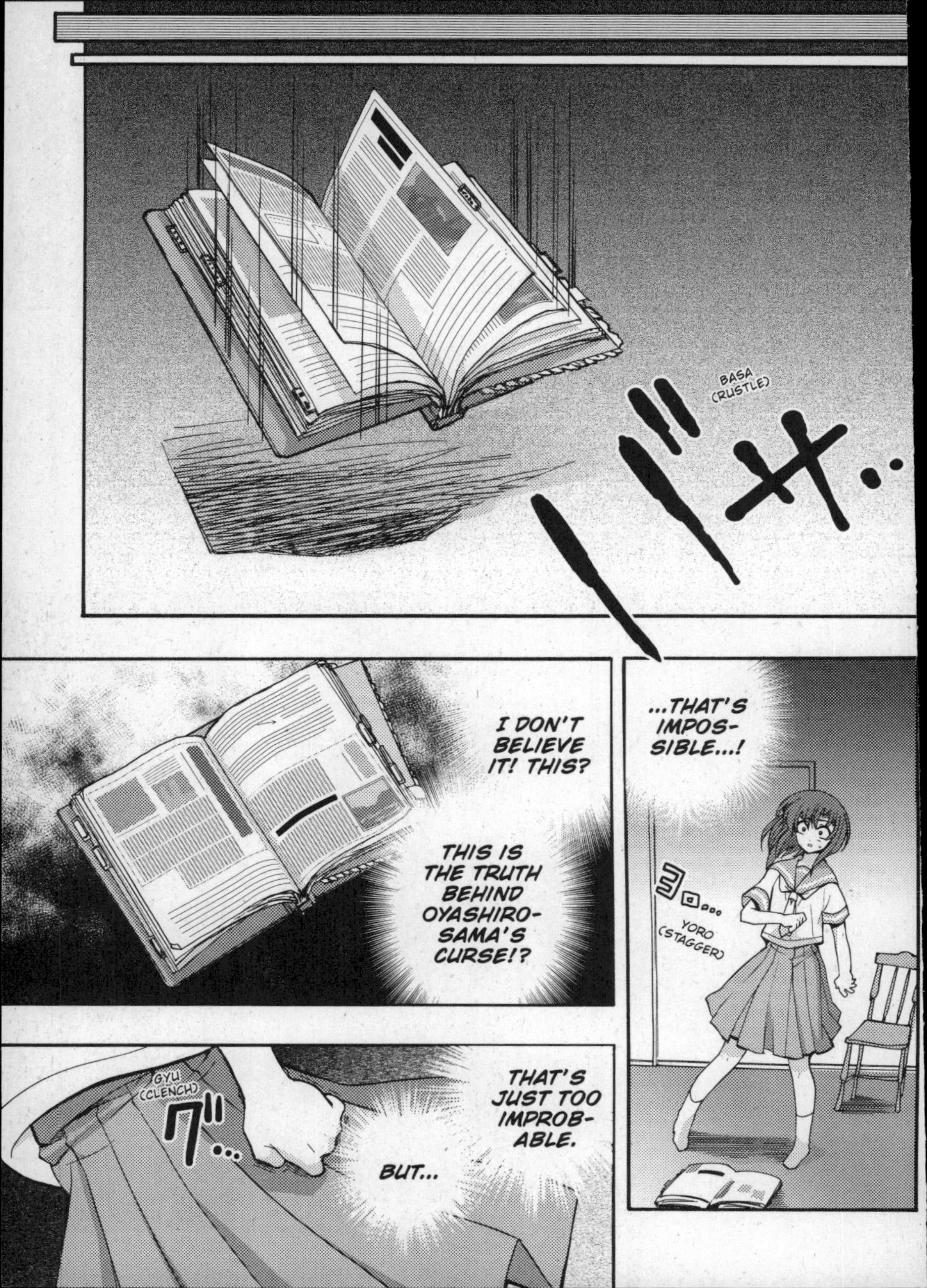
BASA
(RUSTLE)
...THAT'S IMPOS-SIBLE...!
YORO
(STAGGER)
I DON'T BELIEVE IT! THIS?
THIS IS THE TRUTH BEHIND OYASHIRO-SAMA'S CURSE!?
THAT'S JUST TOO IMPROB-ABLE.
BUT...
GYU
(CLENCH)

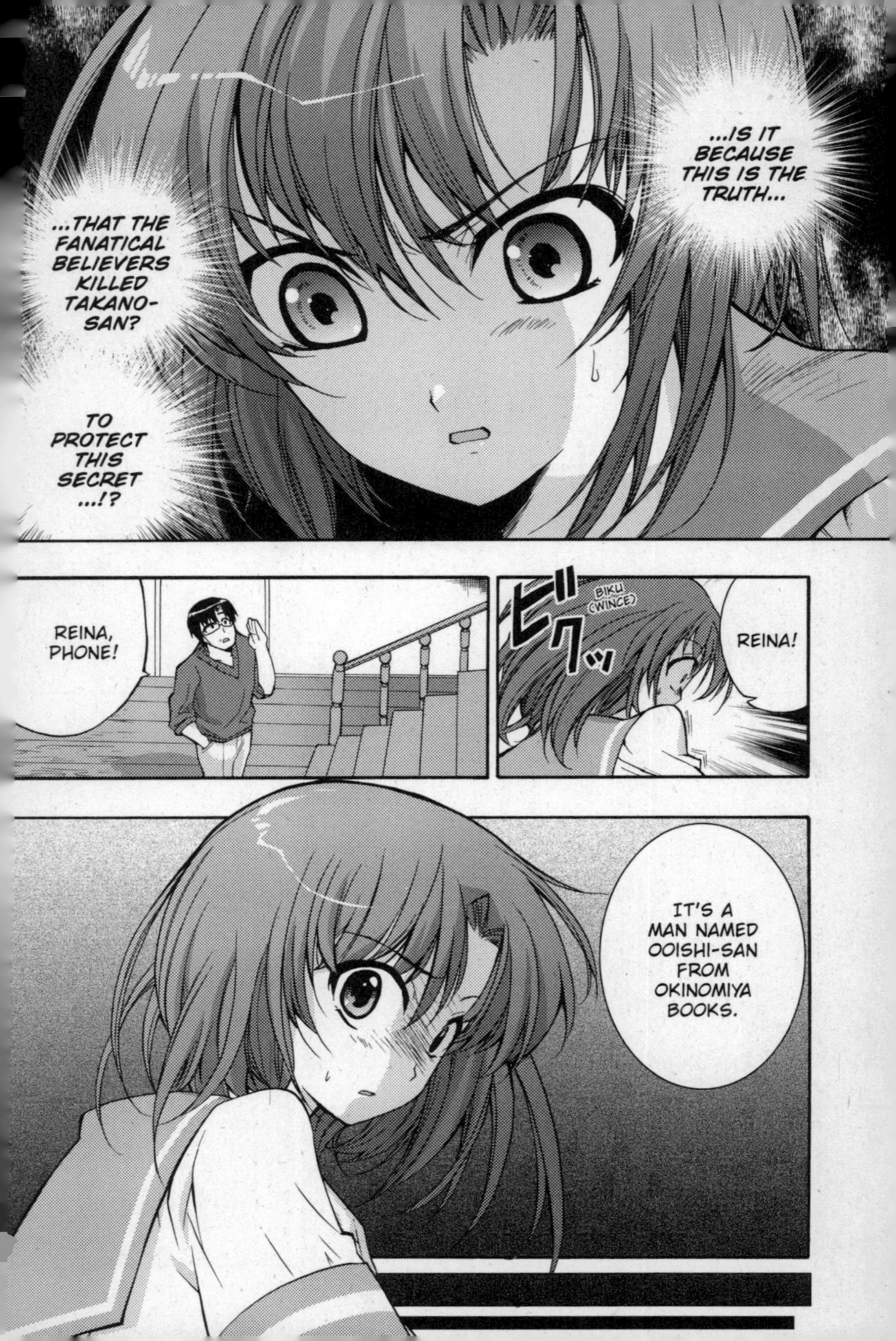
...IS IT BECAUSE THIS IS THE TRUTH...
...THAT THE FANATICAL BELIEVERS KILLED TAKANO-SAN?
TO PROTECT THIS SECRET ...!?
REINA!
ビクッ
BIKU (WINCE)
REINA, PHONE!
IT'S A MAN NAMED OOISHI-SAN FROM OKINOMIYA BOOKS.

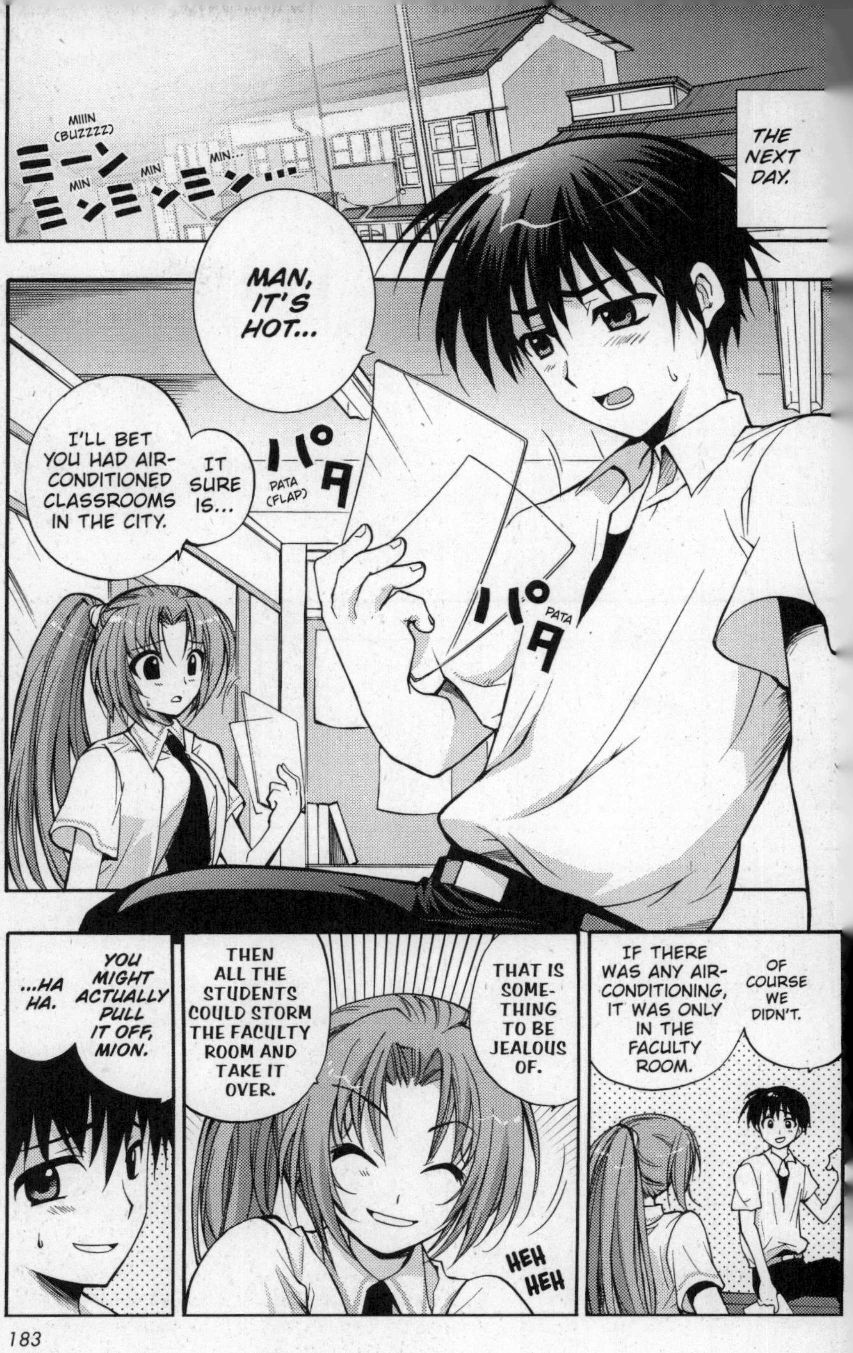
THE NEXT DAY.
ミーン MIIN (BUZZZZ)
ミンミンミン… MIN MIN MIN...
MAN, IT'S HOT...
IT SURE IS...
I'LL BET YOU HAD AIR-CONDITIONED CLASSROOMS IN THE CITY.
パタ PATA (FLAP)
パタ PATA
OF COURSE WE DIDN'T.
IF THERE WAS ANY AIR-CONDITIONING, IT WAS ONLY IN THE FACULTY ROOM.
THAT IS SOME-THING TO BE JEALOUS OF.
THEN ALL THE STUDENTS COULD STORM THE FACULTY ROOM AND TAKE IT OVER.
HEH HEH
YOU MIGHT ACTUALLY PULL IT OFF, MION.
...HA HA.

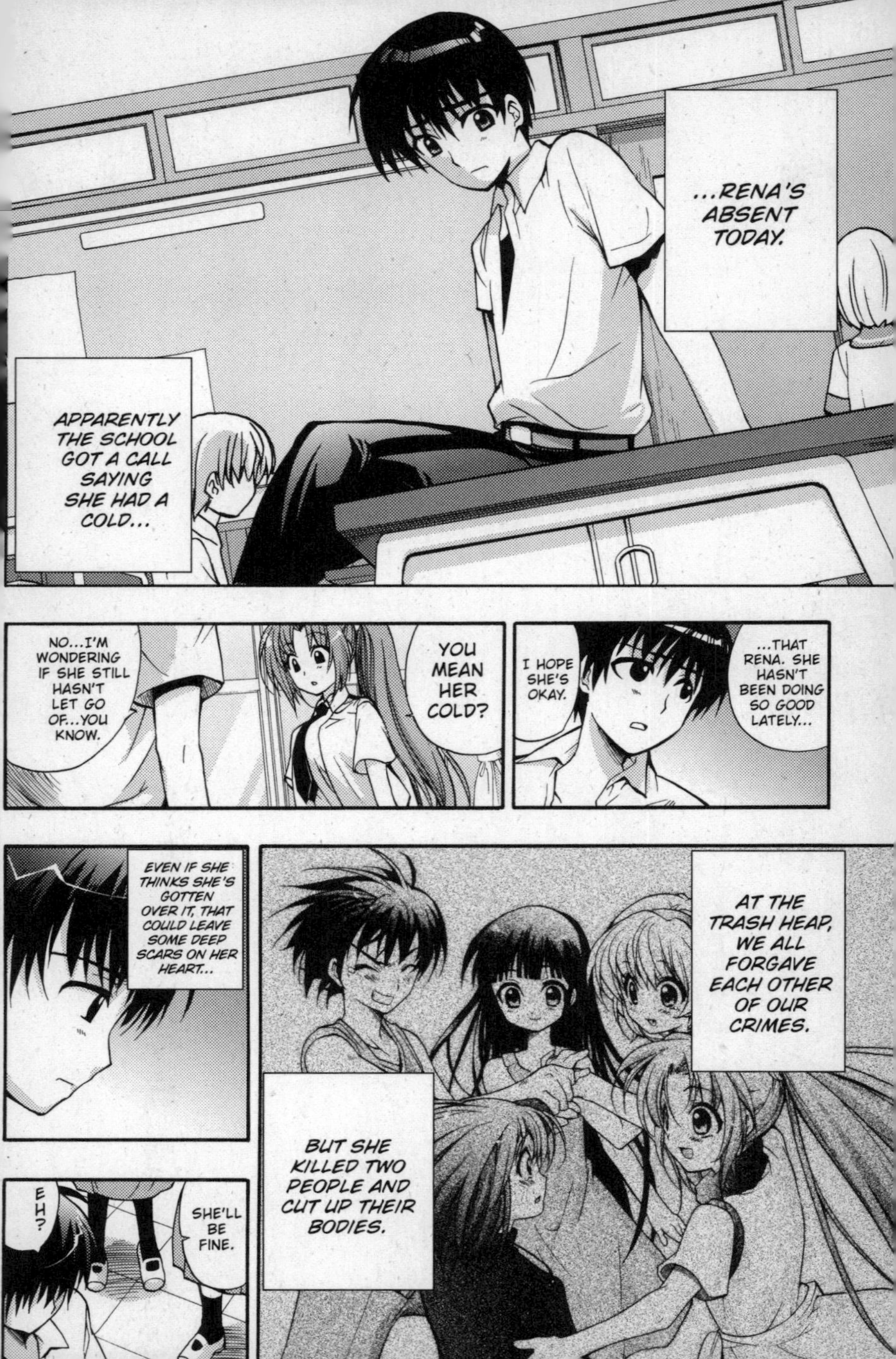
...RENA'S ABSENT TODAY.
APPARENTLY THE SCHOOL GOT A CALL SAYING SHE HAD A COLD...
...THAT RENA. SHE HASN'T BEEN DOING SO GOOD LATELY...
I HOPE SHE'S OKAY.
YOU MEAN HER COLD?
NO...I'M WONDERING IF SHE STILL HASN'T LET GO OF...YOU KNOW.
AT THE TRASH HEAP, WE ALL FORGAVE EACH OTHER OF OUR CRIMES.
BUT SHE KILLED TWO PEOPLE AND CUT UP THEIR BODIES.
EVEN IF SHE THINKS SHE'S GOTTEN OVER IT, THAT COULD LEAVE SOME DEEP SCARS ON HER HEART...
SHE'LL BE FINE.
EH?

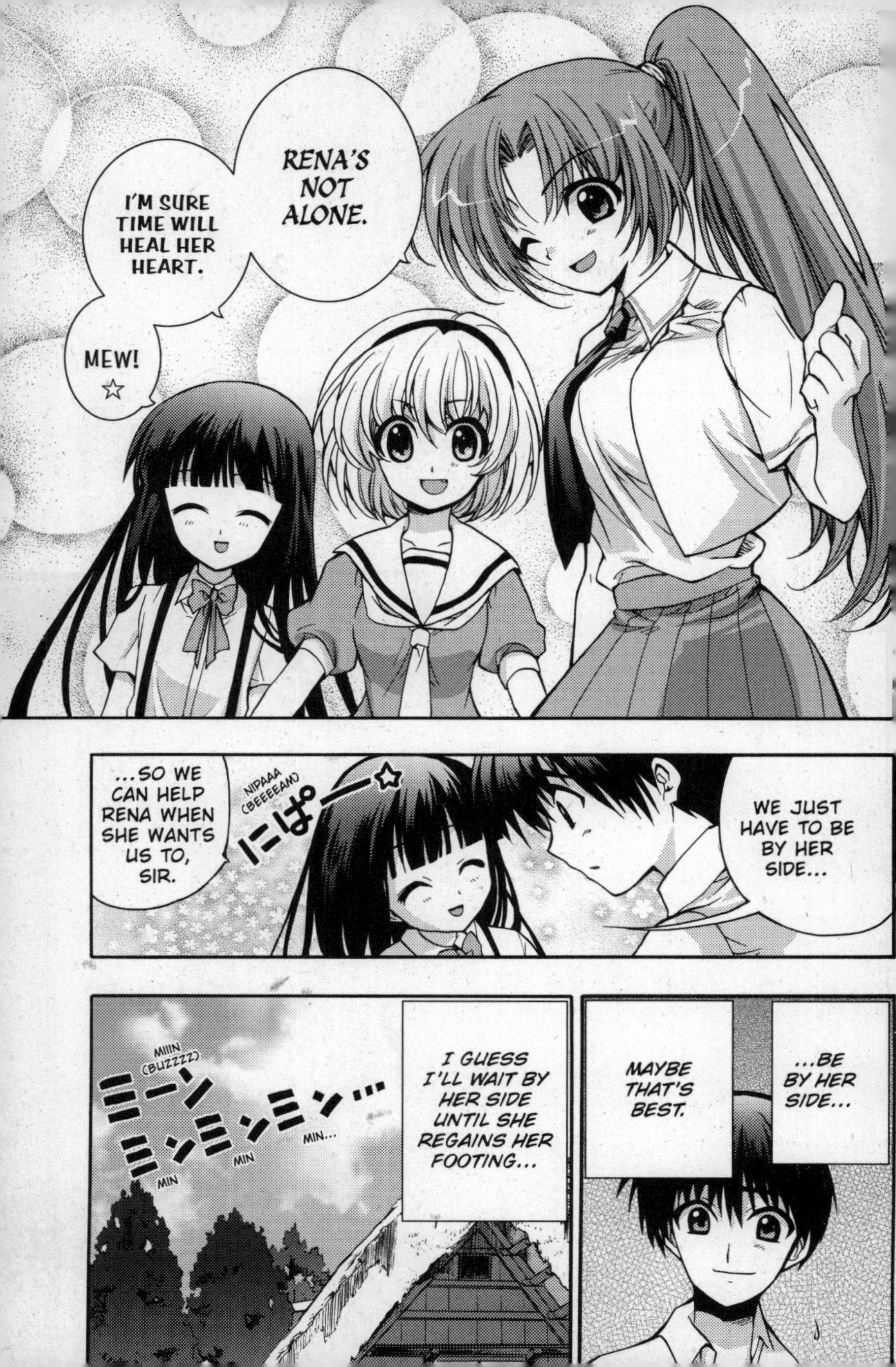
RENA'S NOT ALONE.
I'M SURE TIME WILL HEAL HER HEART.
MEW! ☆
WE JUST HAVE TO BE BY HER SIDE...
NIPAAA (BEEEEAM)
にぱー☆
...SO WE CAN HELP RENA WHEN SHE WANTS US TO, SIR.
...BE BY HER SIDE...
MAYBE THAT'S BEST.
I GUESS I'LL WAIT BY HER SIDE UNTIL SHE REGAINS HER FOOTING...
MIIN (BUZZZZ)
ミーンミンミンミン…
MIN
MIN
MIN...

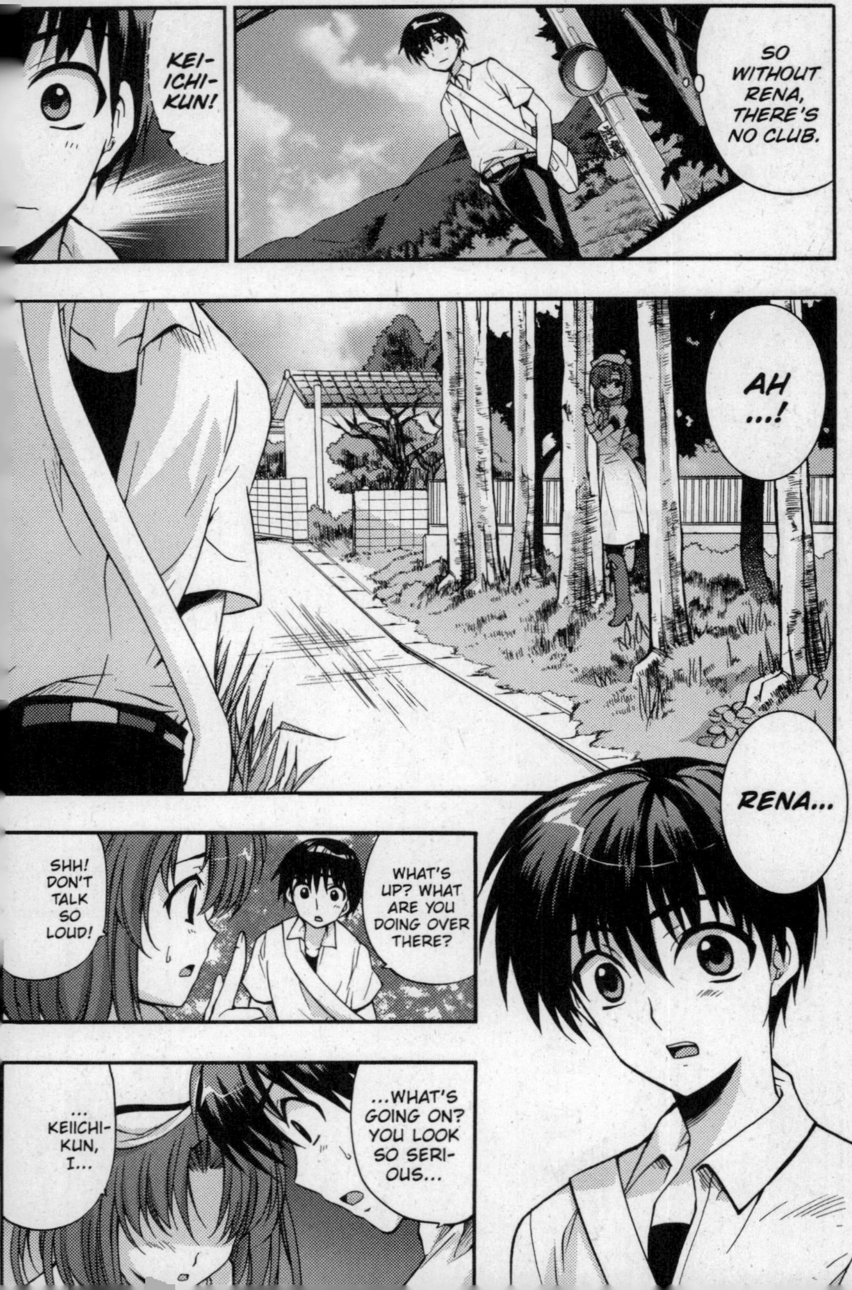
SO WITHOUT RENA, THERE'S NO CLUB.
KEI-ICHI-KUN!
AH ...!
RENA...
WHAT'S UP? WHAT ARE YOU DOING OVER THERE?
SHH! DON'T TALK SO LOUD!
...WHAT'S GOING ON? YOU LOOK SO SERI-OUS...
... KEIICHI-KUN, I...

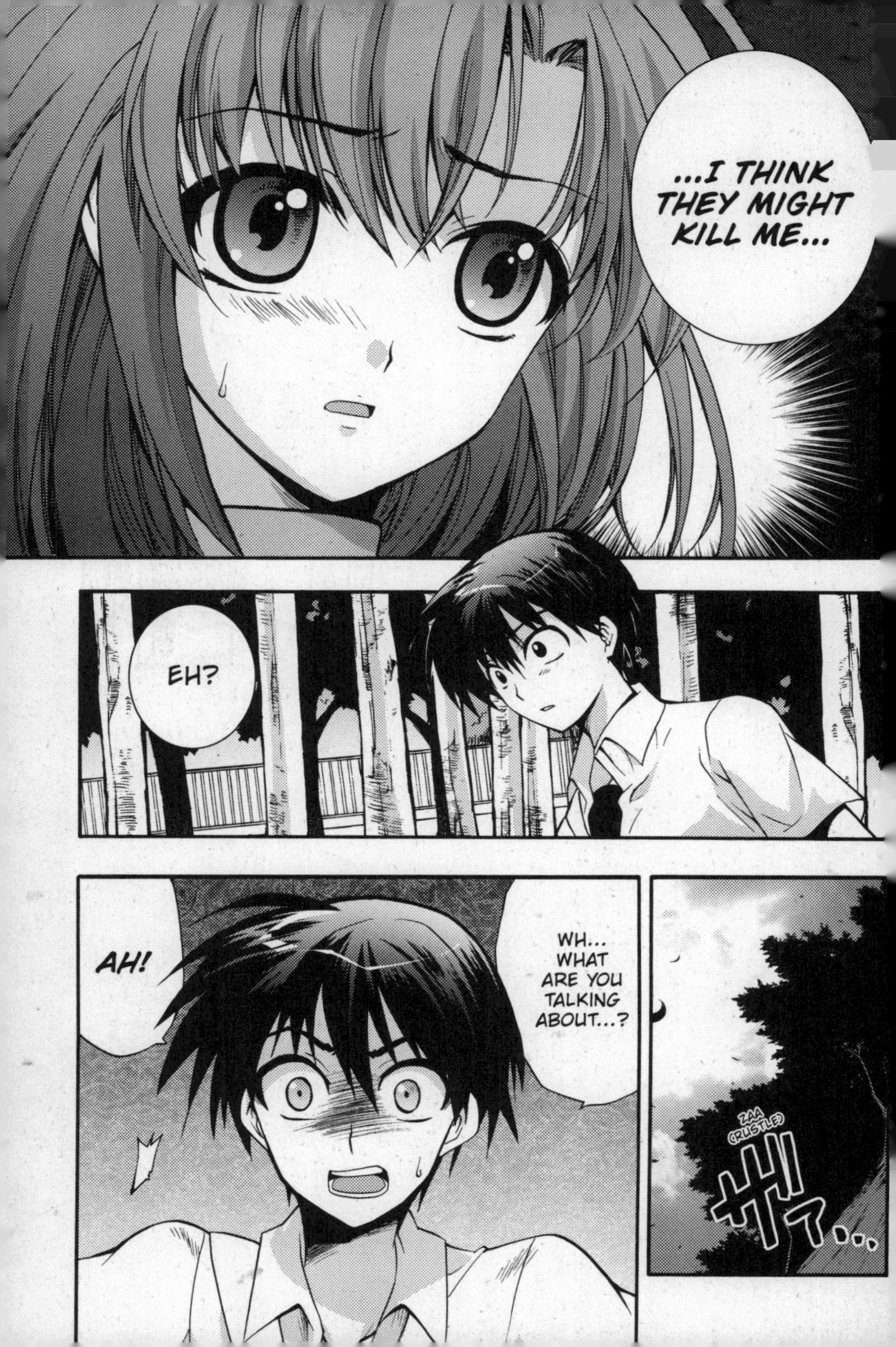

...I THINK THEY MIGHT KILL ME...
EH?
ZAA (RUSTLE)
ザァ...
WH... WHAT ARE YOU TALKING ABOUT...?
AH!

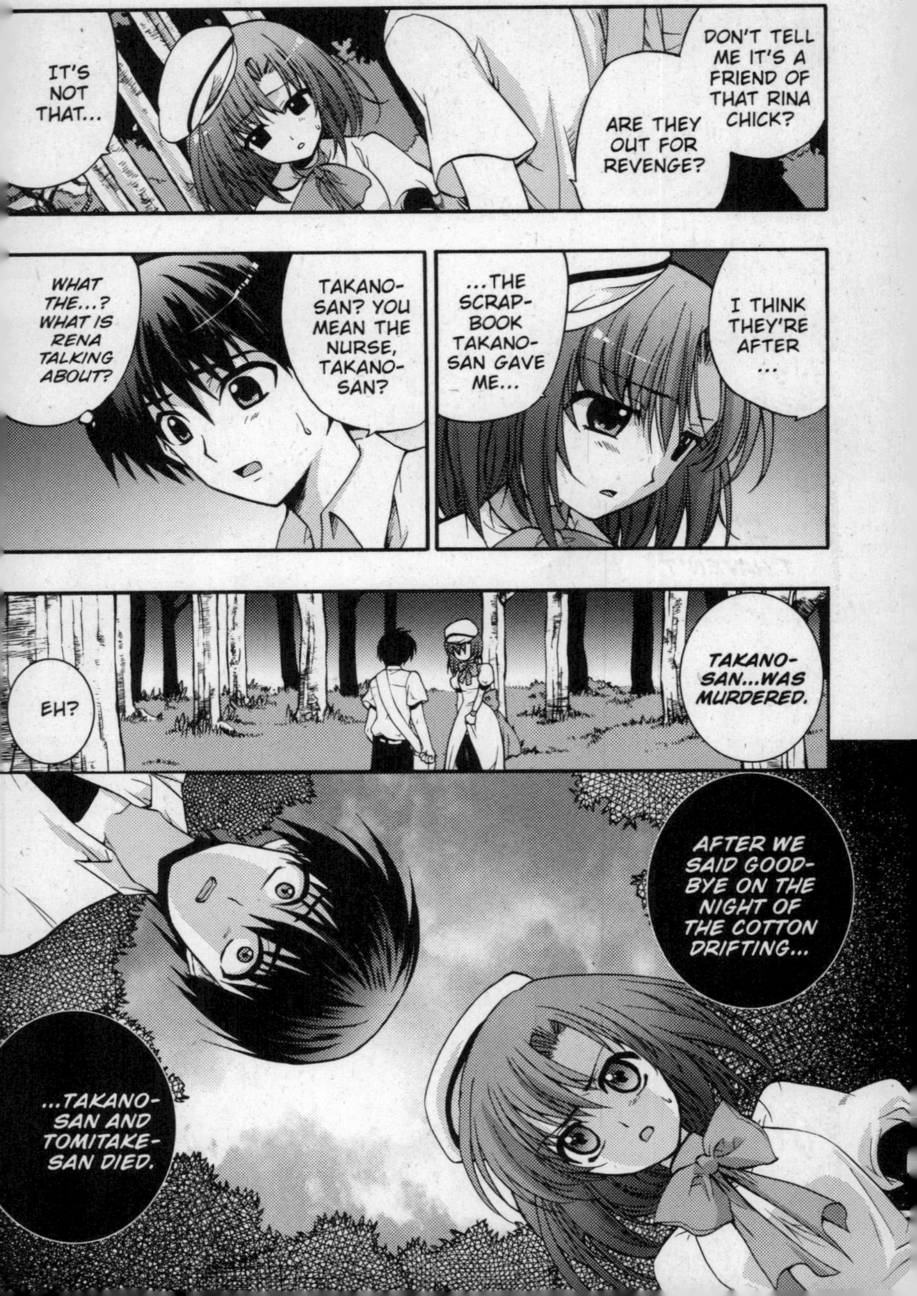
DON'T TELL ME IT'S A FRIEND OF THAT RINA CHICK?
ARE THEY OUT FOR REVENGE?
IT'S NOT THAT...
I THINK THEY'RE AFTER ...
...THE SCRAPBOOK TAKANO-SAN GAVE ME...
TAKANO-SAN? YOU MEAN THE NURSE, TAKANO-SAN?
WHAT THE...? WHAT IS RENA TALKING ABOUT?
TAKANO-SAN...WAS MURDERED.
EH?
AFTER WE SAID GOOD-BYE ON THE NIGHT OF THE COTTON DRIFTING...
...TAKANO-SAN AND TOMITAKE-SAN DIED.

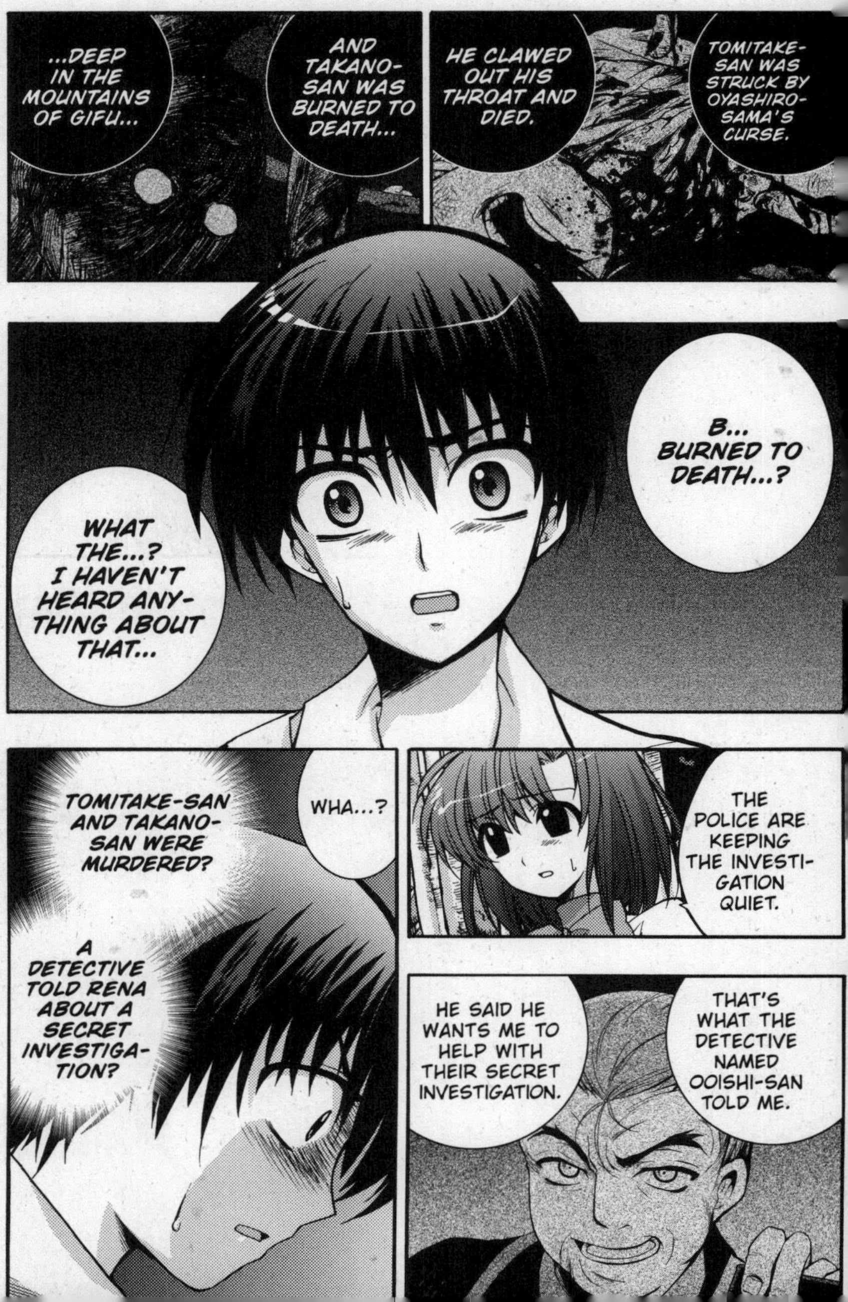

TOMITAKE-SAN WAS STRUCK BY OYASHIRO-SAMA'S CURSE.
HE CLAWED OUT HIS THROAT AND DIED.
AND TAKANO-SAN WAS BURNED TO DEATH...
...DEEP IN THE MOUNTAINS OF GIFU...
B... BURNED TO DEATH...?
WHAT THE...? I HAVEN'T HEARD ANYTHING ABOUT THAT...
THE POLICE ARE KEEPING THE INVESTIGATION QUIET.
THAT'S WHAT THE DETECTIVE NAMED OOISHI-SAN TOLD ME.
HE SAID HE WANTS ME TO HELP WITH THEIR SECRET INVESTIGATION.
WHA...?
TOMITAKE-SAN AND TAKANO-SAN WERE MURDERED?
A DETECTIVE TOLD RENA ABOUT A SECRET INVESTIGATION?

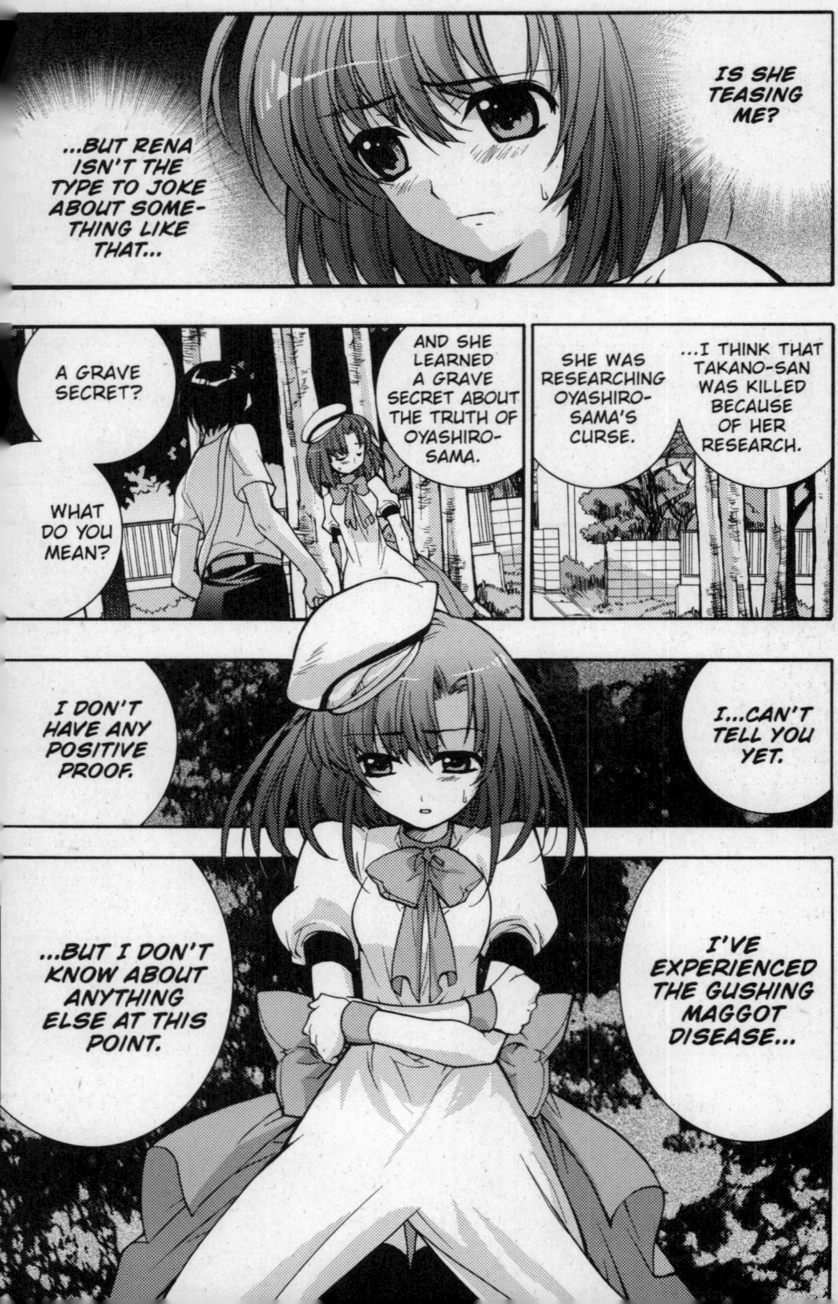
IS SHE TEASING ME?
...BUT RENA ISN'T THE TYPE TO JOKE ABOUT SOME-THING LIKE THAT...
...I THINK THAT TAKANO-SAN WAS KILLED BECAUSE OF HER RESEARCH.
SHE WAS RESEARCHING OYASHIRO-SAMA'S CURSE.
AND SHE LEARNED A GRAVE SECRET ABOUT THE TRUTH OF OYASHIRO-SAMA.
A GRAVE SECRET?
WHAT DO YOU MEAN?
I...CAN'T TELL YOU YET.
I DON'T HAVE ANY POSITIVE PROOF.
I'VE EXPERIENCED THE GUSHING MAGGOT DISEASE...
...BUT I DON'T KNOW ABOUT ANYTHING ELSE AT THIS POINT.

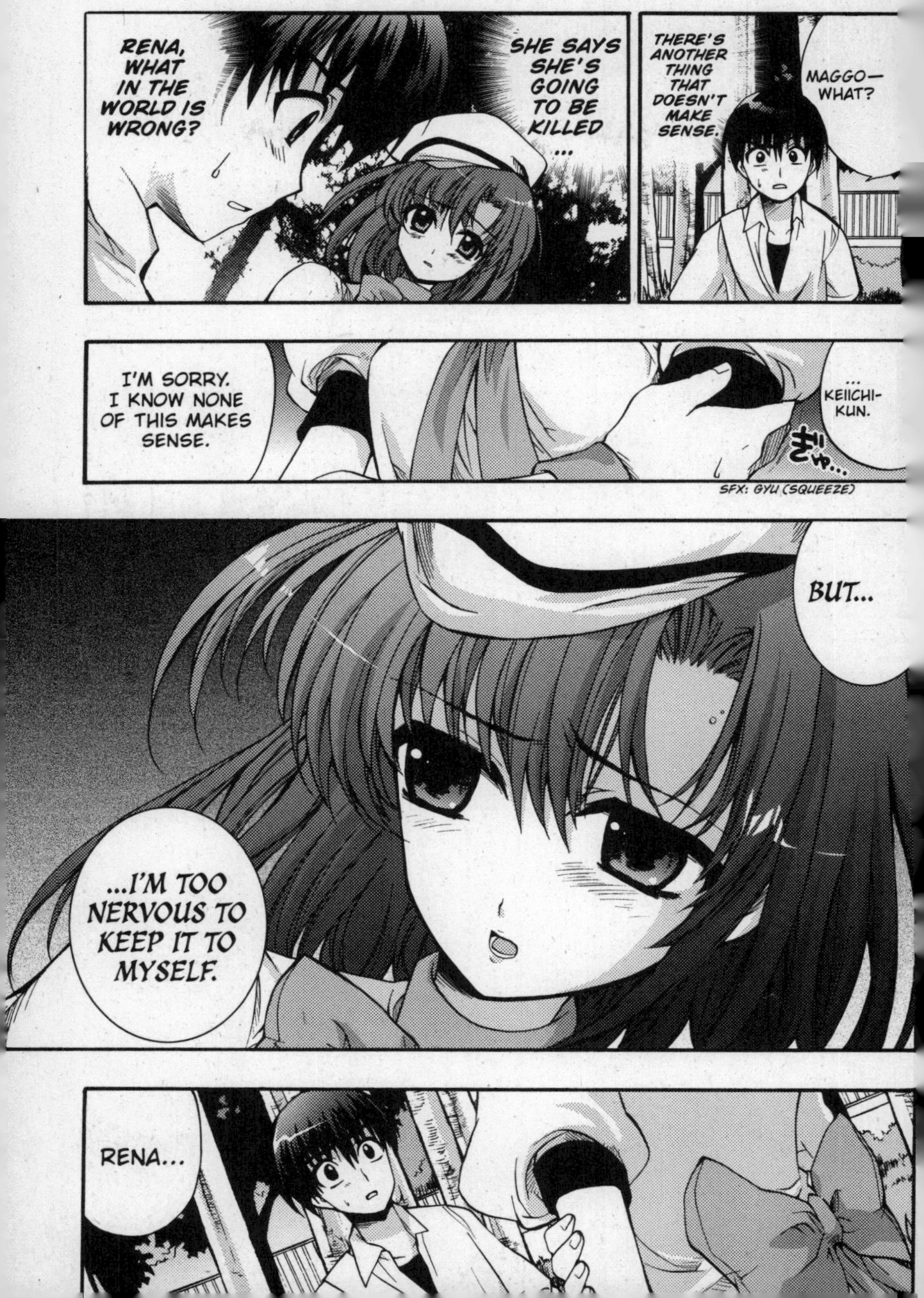
MAGGO—WHAT?
THERE'S ANOTHER THING THAT DOESN'T MAKE SENSE.
SHE SAYS SHE'S GOING TO BE KILLED ...
RENA, WHAT IN THE WORLD IS WRONG?
... KEIICHI-KUN.
ぎゅ...
I'M SORRY. I KNOW NONE OF THIS MAKES SENSE.
SFX: GYU (SQUEEZE)
BUT...
...I'M TOO NERVOUS TO KEEP IT TO MYSELF.
RENA...

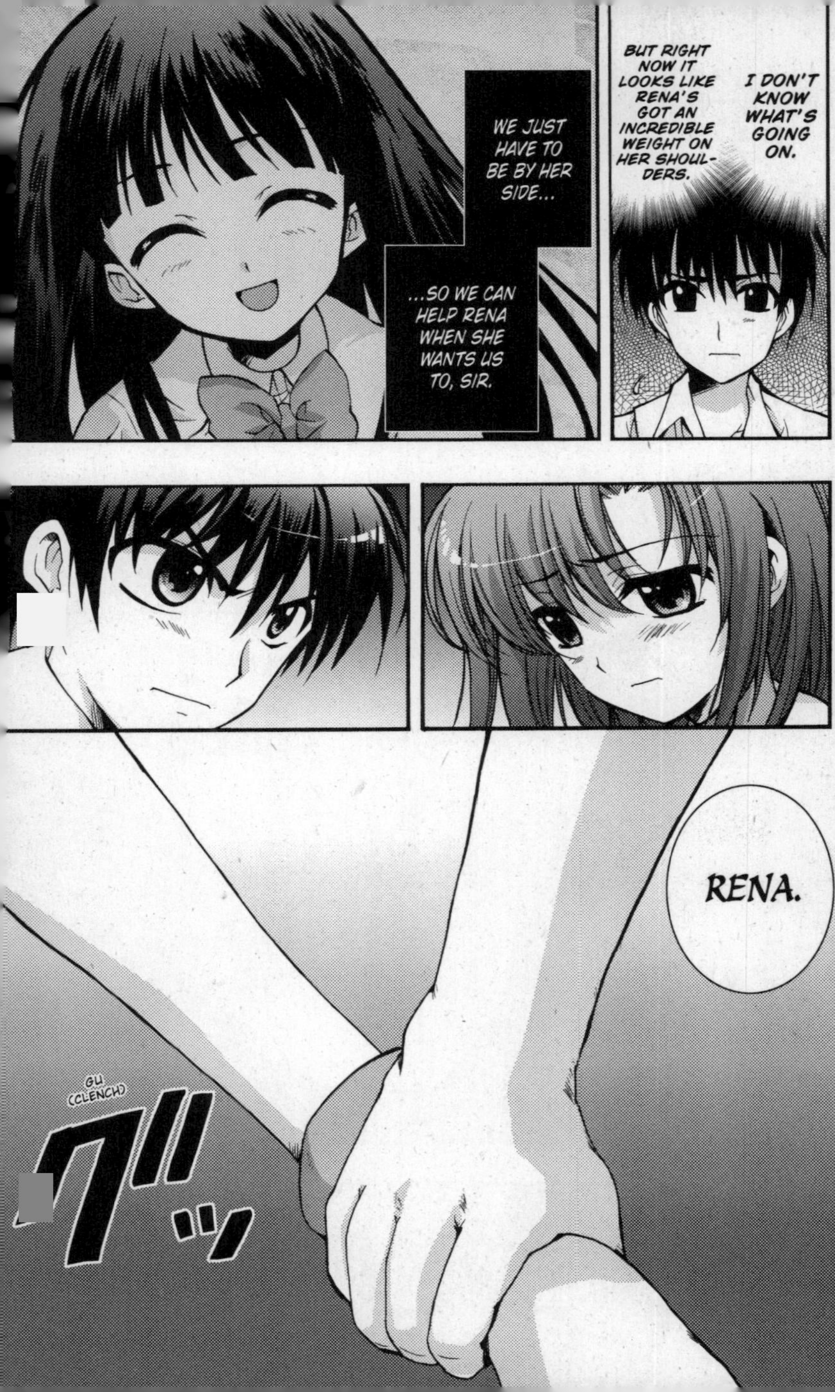
I DON'T KNOW WHAT'S GOING ON.
BUT RIGHT NOW IT LOOKS LIKE RENA'S GOT AN INCREDIBLE WEIGHT ON HER SHOUL-DERS.
WE JUST HAVE TO BE BY HER SIDE...
...SO WE CAN HELP RENA WHEN SHE WANTS US TO, SIR.
RENA.
GU (CLENCH)
グッ

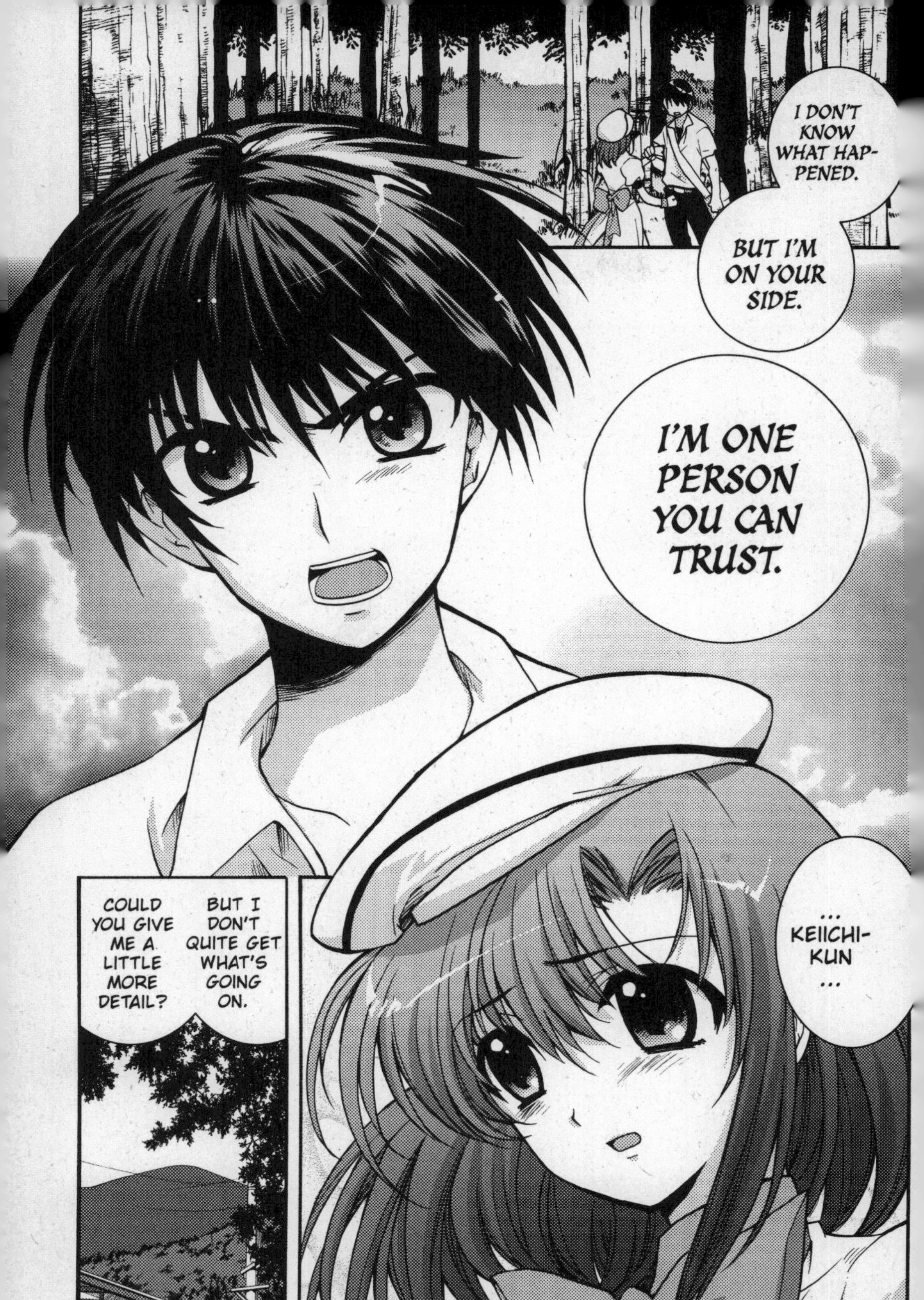
I DON'T KNOW WHAT HAP-PENED.
BUT I'M ON YOUR SIDE.
I'M ONE PERSON YOU CAN TRUST.
... KEIICHI-KUN ...
BUT I DON'T QUITE GET WHAT'S GOING ON.
COULD YOU GIVE ME A LITTLE MORE DETAIL?

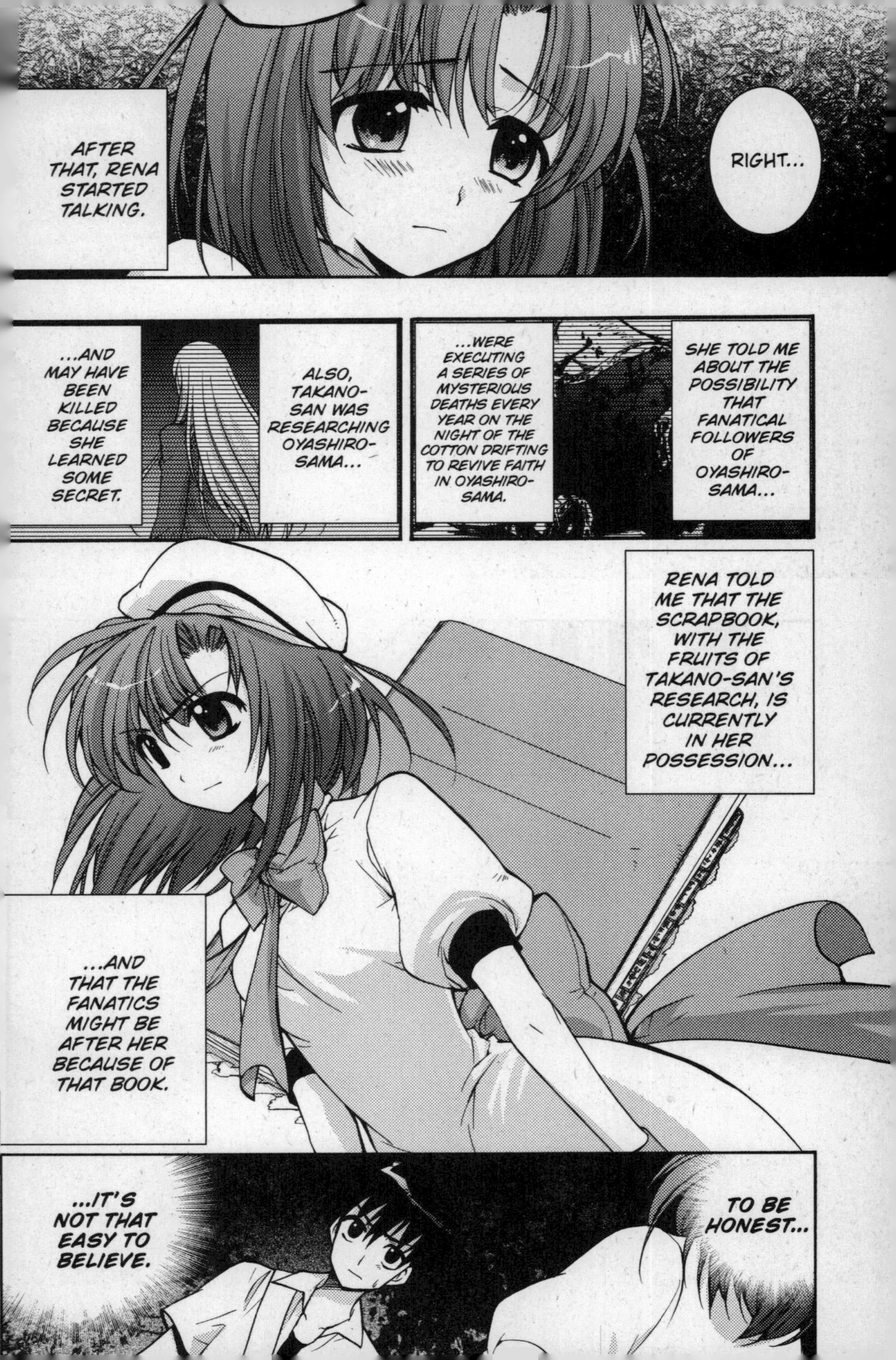
RIGHT...
AFTER THAT, RENA STARTED TALKING.
SHE TOLD ME ABOUT THE POSSIBILITY THAT FANATICAL FOLLOWERS OF OYASHIRO-SAMA...
...WERE EXECUTING A SERIES OF MYSTERIOUS DEATHS EVERY YEAR ON THE NIGHT OF THE COTTON DRIFTING TO REVIVE FAITH IN OYASHIRO-SAMA.
ALSO, TAKANO-SAN WAS RESEARCHING OYASHIRO-SAMA...
...AND MAY HAVE BEEN KILLED BECAUSE SHE LEARNED SOME SECRET.
RENA TOLD ME THAT THE SCRAPBOOK, WITH THE FRUITS OF TAKANO-SAN'S RESEARCH, IS CURRENTLY IN HER POSSESSION...
...AND THAT THE FANATICS MIGHT BE AFTER HER BECAUSE OF THAT BOOK.
TO BE HONEST...
...IT'S NOT THAT EASY TO BELIEVE.

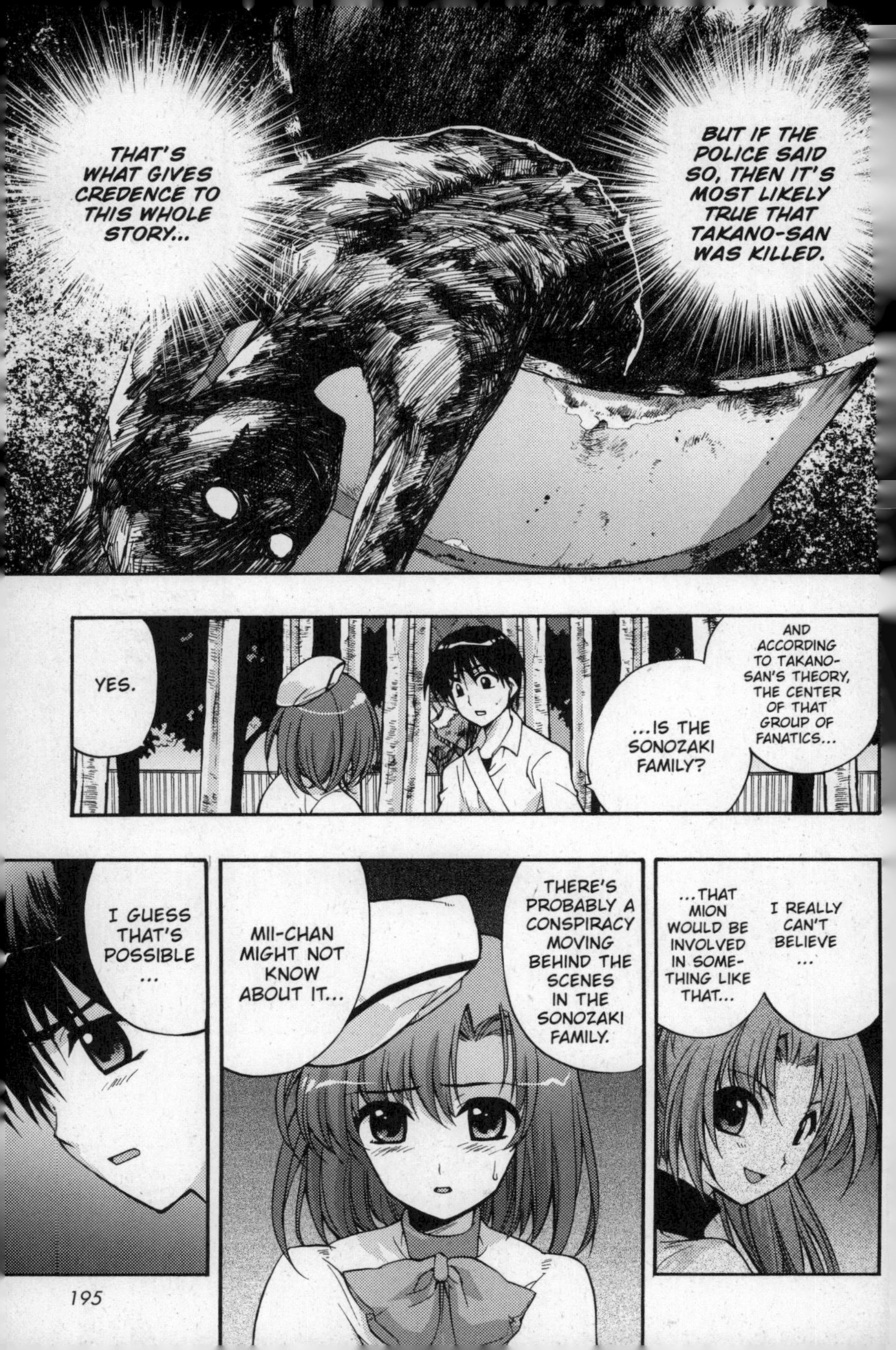
BUT IF THE POLICE SAID SO, THEN IT'S MOST LIKELY TRUE THAT TAKANO-SAN WAS KILLED.
THAT'S WHAT GIVES CREDENCE TO THIS WHOLE STORY...
AND ACCORDING TO TAKANO-SAN'S THEORY, THE CENTER OF THAT GROUP OF FANATICS...
...IS THE SONOZAKI FAMILY?
YES.
I REALLY CAN'T BELIEVE ...
...THAT MION WOULD BE INVOLVED IN SOME-THING LIKE THAT...
THERE'S PROBABLY A CONSPIRACY MOVING BEHIND THE SCENES IN THE SONOZAKI FAMILY.
MII-CHAN MIGHT NOT KNOW ABOUT IT...
I GUESS THAT'S POSSIBLE ...

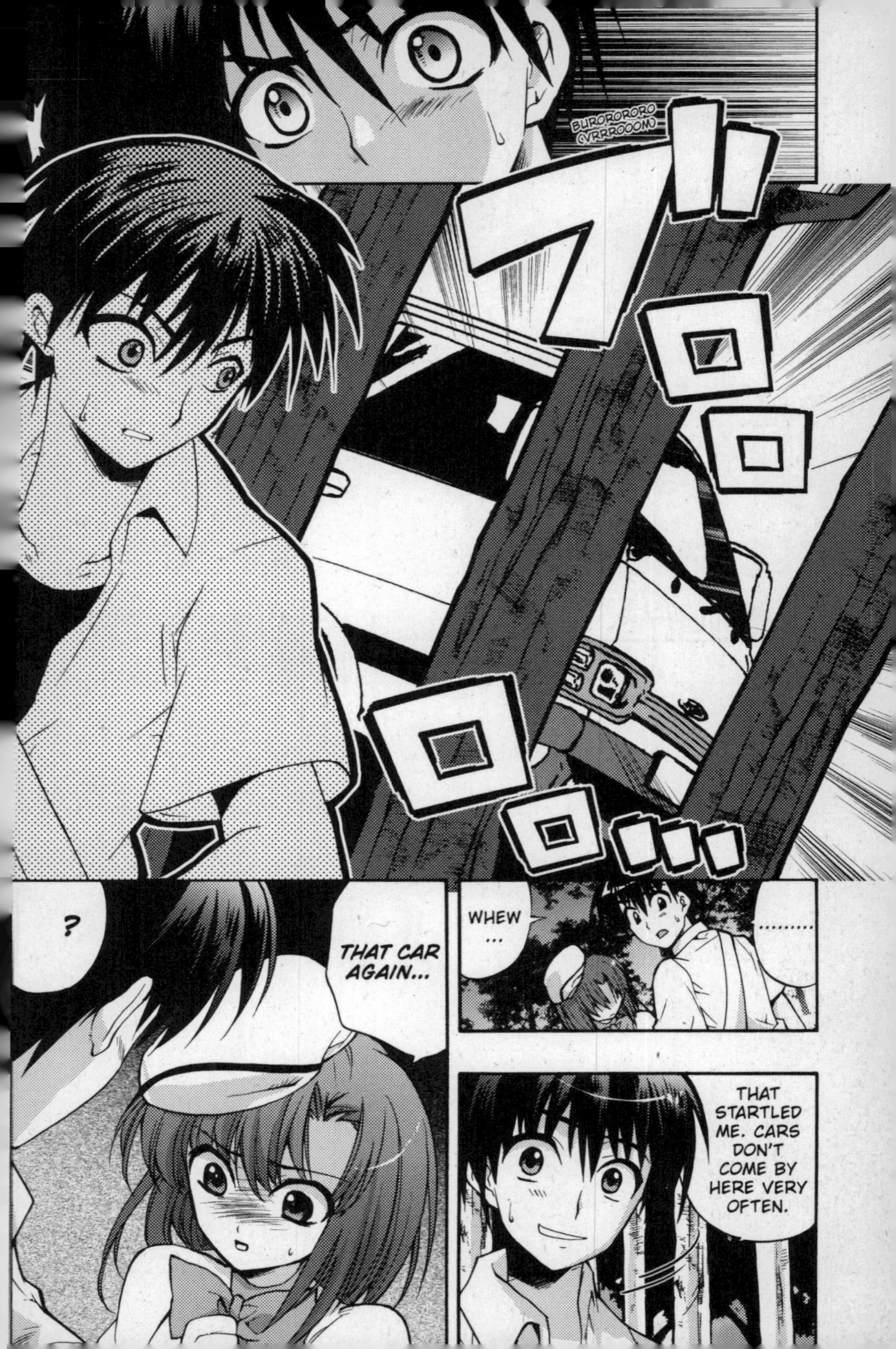
BURORORORO (VRRROOOM)
....
WHEW ...
THAT STARTLED ME. CARS DON'T COME BY HERE VERY OFTEN.
THAT CAR AGAIN...
?

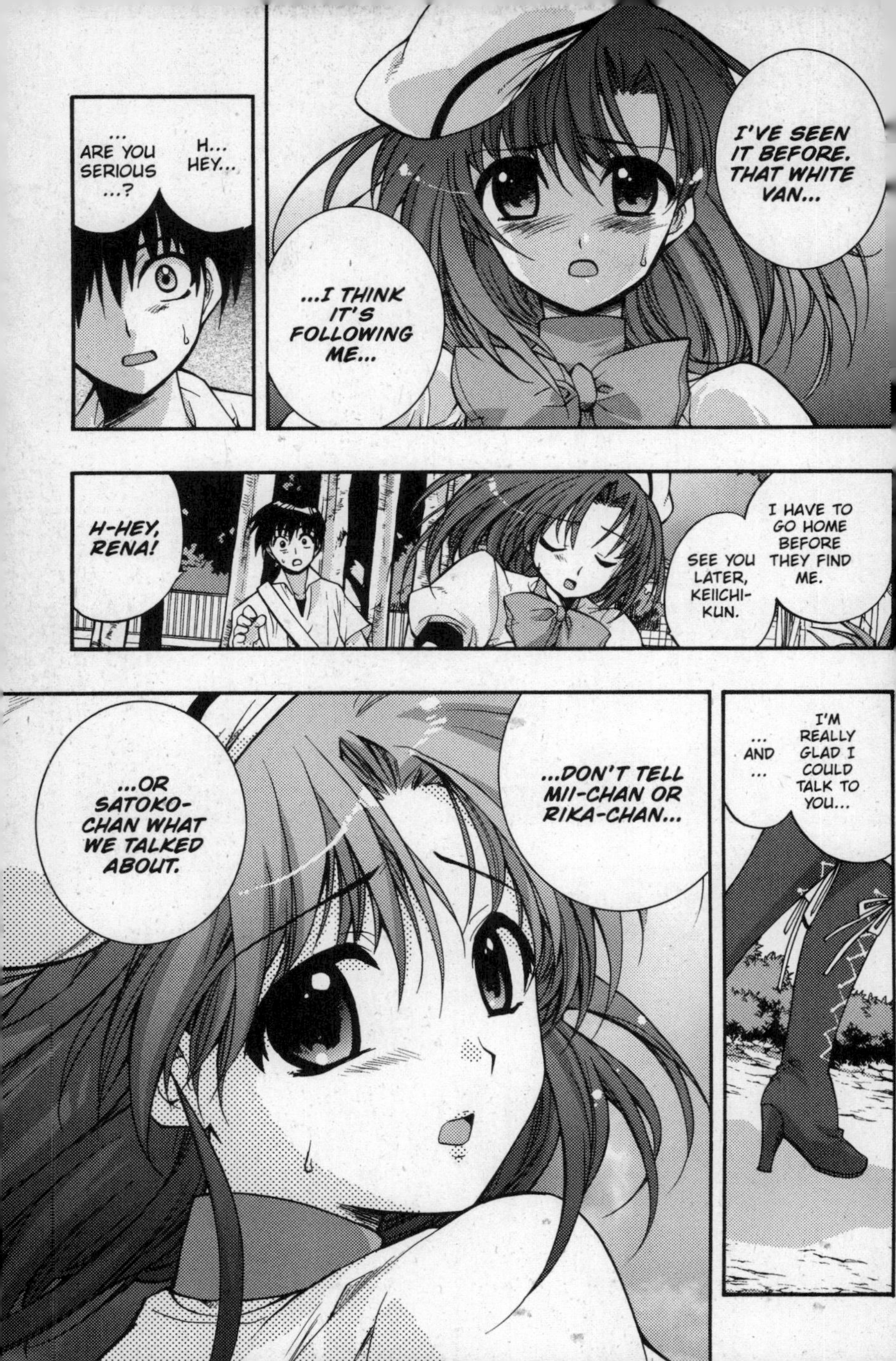
I'VE SEEN IT BEFORE. THAT WHITE VAN...
...I THINK IT'S FOLLOWING ME...
H... HEY...
...ARE YOU SERIOUS...?
I HAVE TO GO HOME BEFORE THEY FIND ME.
SEE YOU LATER, KEIICHI-KUN.
H-HEY, RENA!
I'M REALLY GLAD I COULD TALK TO YOU...
...AND...
...DON'T TELL MII-CHAN OR RIKA-CHAN...
...OR SATOKO-CHAN WHAT WE TALKED ABOUT.

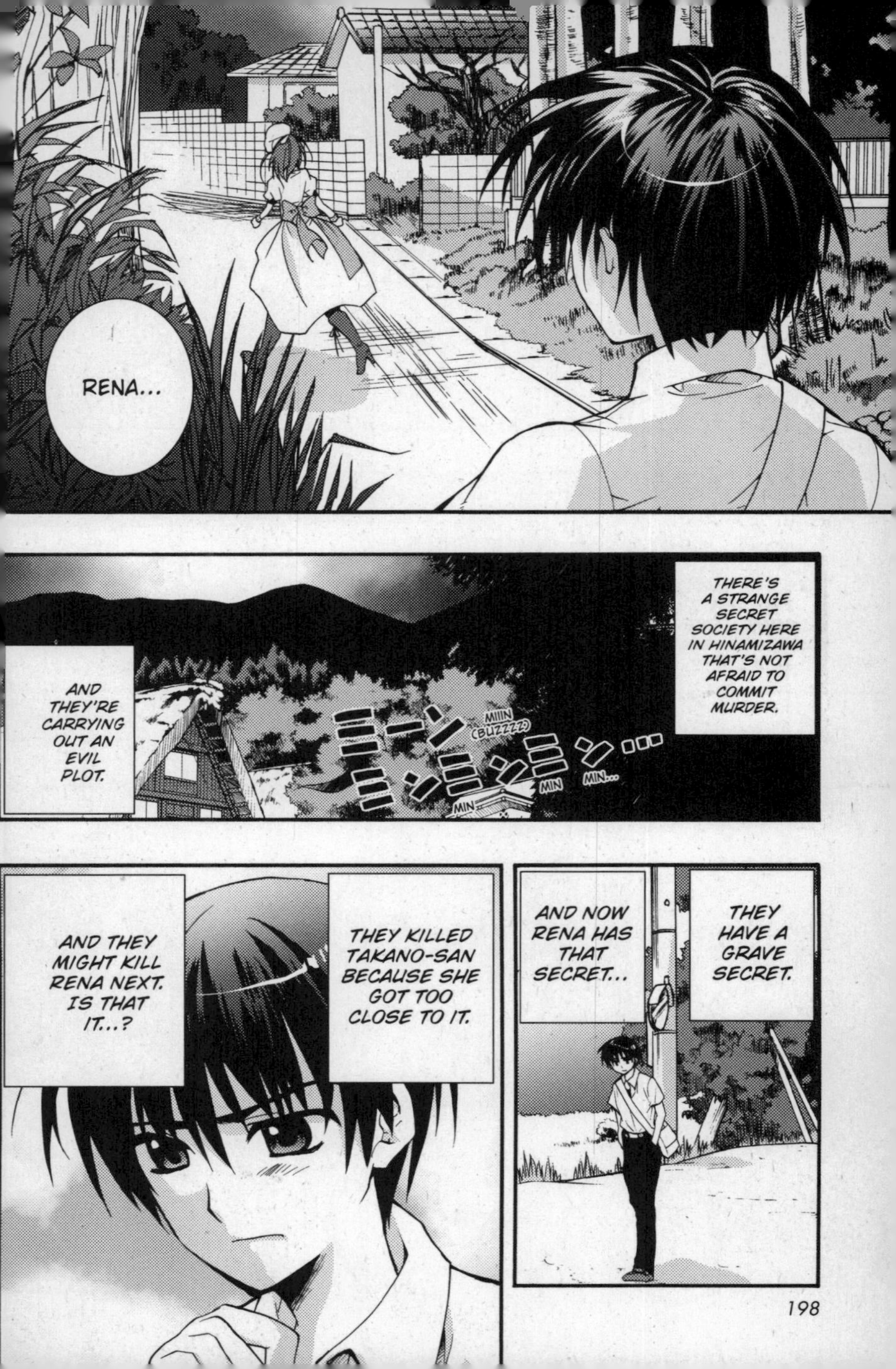
RENA...
THERE'S A STRANGE SECRET SOCIETY HERE IN HINAMIZAWA THAT'S NOT AFRAID TO COMMIT MURDER.
MIIN (BUZZZZ)
MIN
MIN
MIN...
AND THEY'RE CARRYING OUT AN EVIL PLOT.
THEY HAVE A GRAVE SECRET.
AND NOW RENA HAS THAT SECRET...
THEY KILLED TAKANO-SAN BECAUSE SHE GOT TOO CLOSE TO IT.
AND THEY MIGHT KILL RENA NEXT. IS THAT IT...?

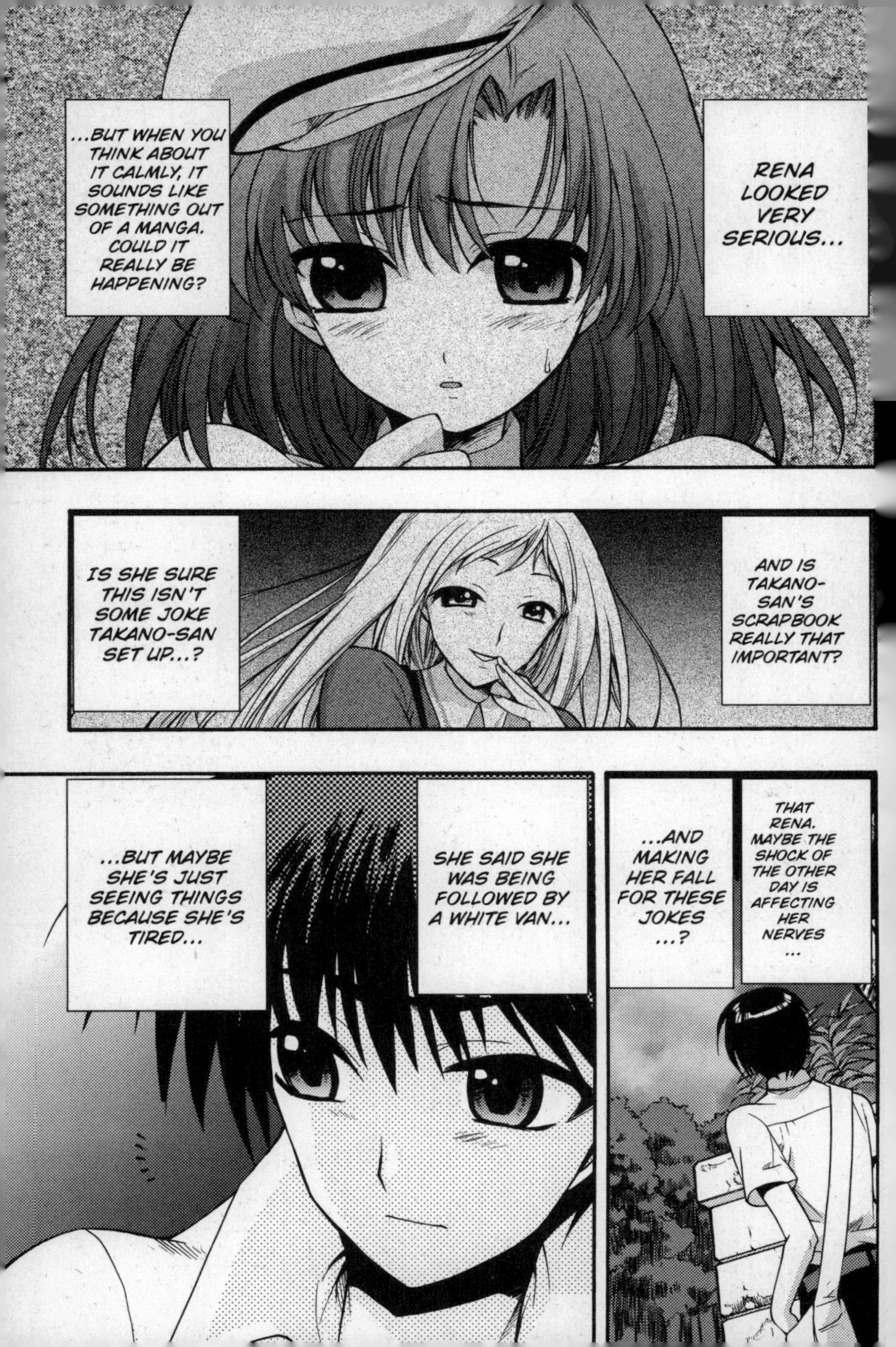
RENA LOOKED VERY SERIOUS...
...BUT WHEN YOU THINK ABOUT IT CALMLY, IT SOUNDS LIKE SOMETHING OUT OF A MANGA. COULD IT REALLY BE HAPPENING?
AND IS TAKANO-SAN'S SCRAPBOOK REALLY THAT IMPORTANT?
IS SHE SURE THIS ISN'T SOME JOKE TAKANO-SAN SET UP...?
THAT RENA. MAYBE THE SHOCK OF THE OTHER DAY IS AFFECTING HER NERVES ...
...AND MAKING HER FALL FOR THESE JOKES ...?
SHE SAID SHE WAS BEING FOLLOWED BY A WHITE VAN...
...BUT MAYBE SHE'S JUST SEEING THINGS BECAUSE SHE'S TIRED...

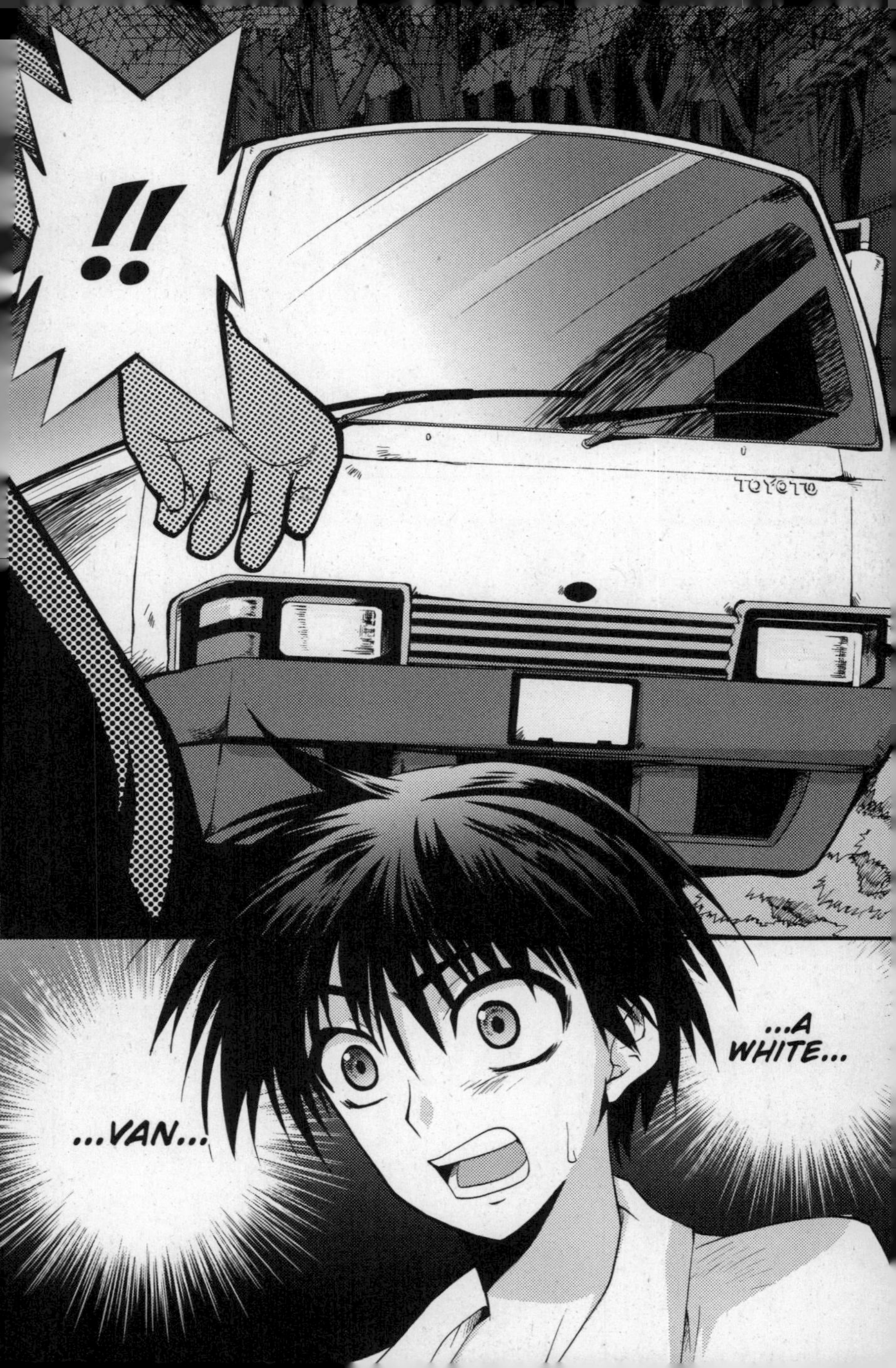
!!
...A WHITE...
...VAN...

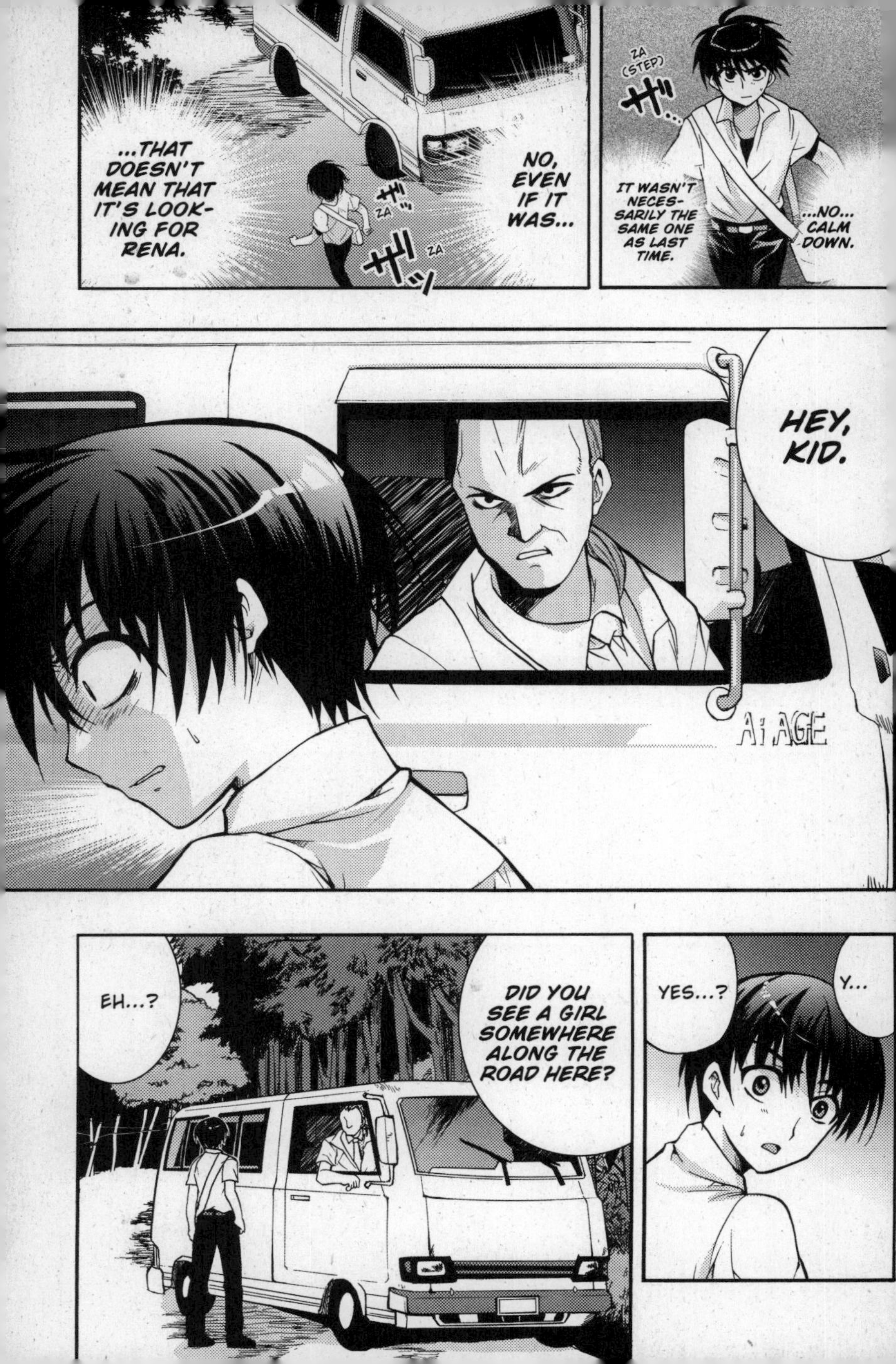
ZA (STEP)
ザ...
...NO... CALM DOWN.
IT WASN'T NECES-SARILY THE SAME ONE AS LAST TIME.
NO, EVEN IF IT WAS...
...THAT DOESN'T MEAN THAT IT'S LOOKING FOR RENA.
ZA
ZA
HEY, KID.
Ai AGE
Y...
YES...?
DID YOU SEE A GIRL SOMEWHERE ALONG THE ROAD HERE?
EH...?

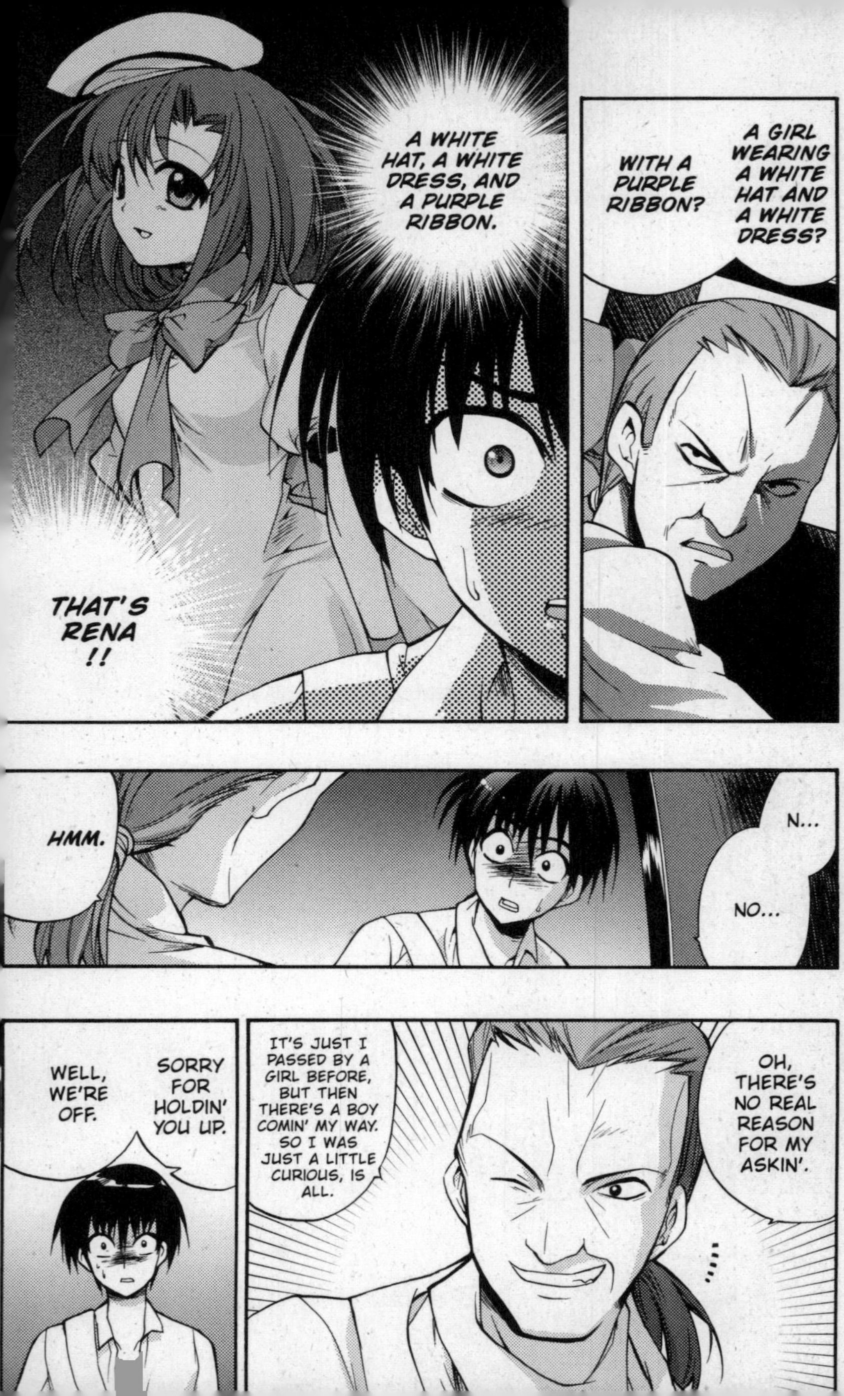
A GIRL WEARING A WHITE HAT AND A WHITE DRESS?
WITH A PURPLE RIBBON?
A WHITE HAT, A WHITE DRESS, AND A PURPLE RIBBON.
THAT'S RENA!!
N...
NO...
HMM.
OH, THERE'S NO REAL REASON FOR MY ASKIN'.
IT'S JUST I PASSED BY A GIRL BEFORE, BUT THEN THERE'S A BOY COMIN' MY WAY. SO I WAS JUST A LITTLE CURIOUS, IS ALL.
......
SORRY FOR HOLDIN' YOU UP.
WELL, WE'RE OFF.

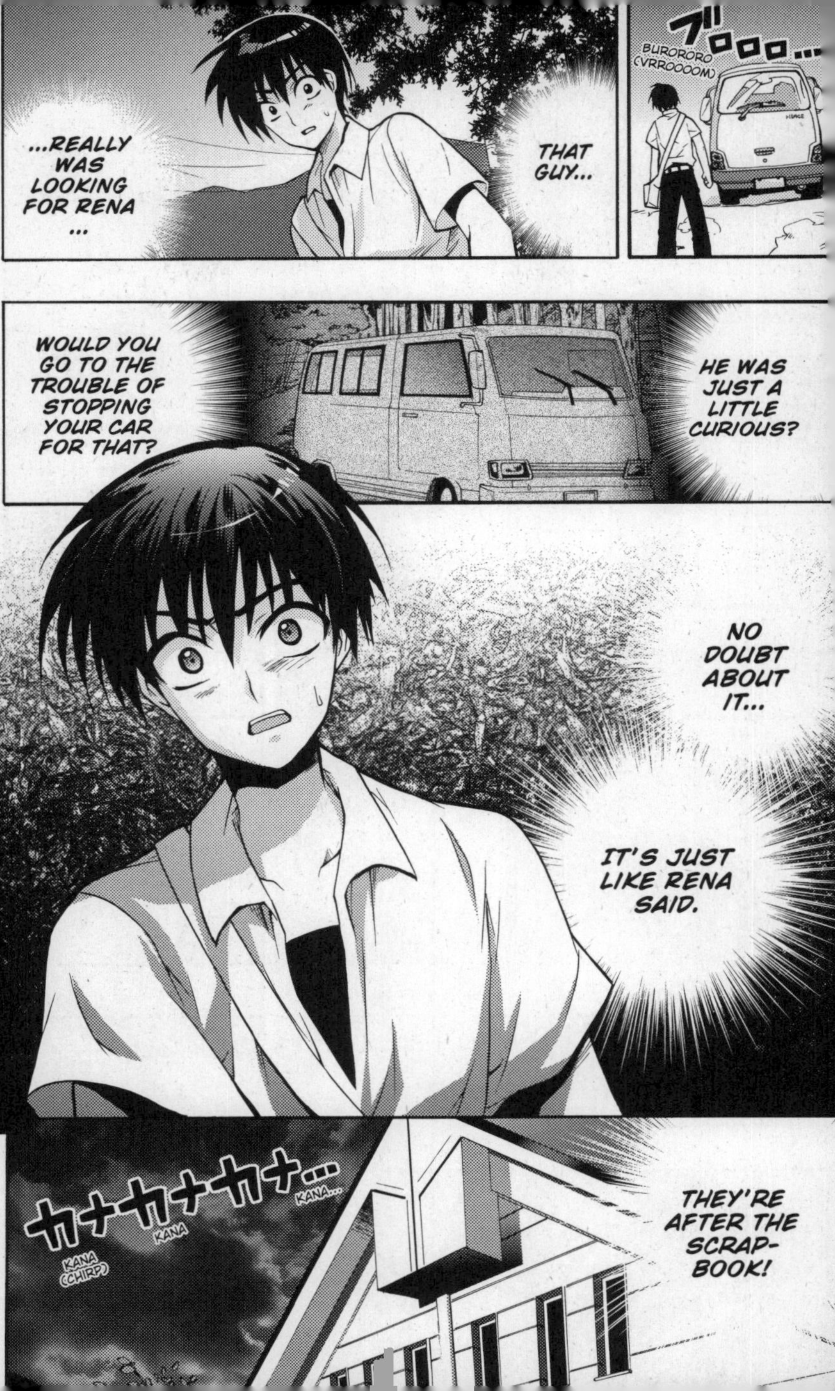
ブロロロ...
BURORORO (VRROOOM)
THAT GUY...
...REALLY WAS LOOKING FOR RENA ...
HE WAS JUST A LITTLE CURIOUS?
WOULD YOU GO TO THE TROUBLE OF STOPPING YOUR CAR FOR THAT?
NO DOUBT ABOUT IT...
IT'S JUST LIKE RENA SAID.
THEY'RE AFTER THE SCRAP-BOOK!
カナカナカナ...
KANA...
KANA
KANA (CHIRP)

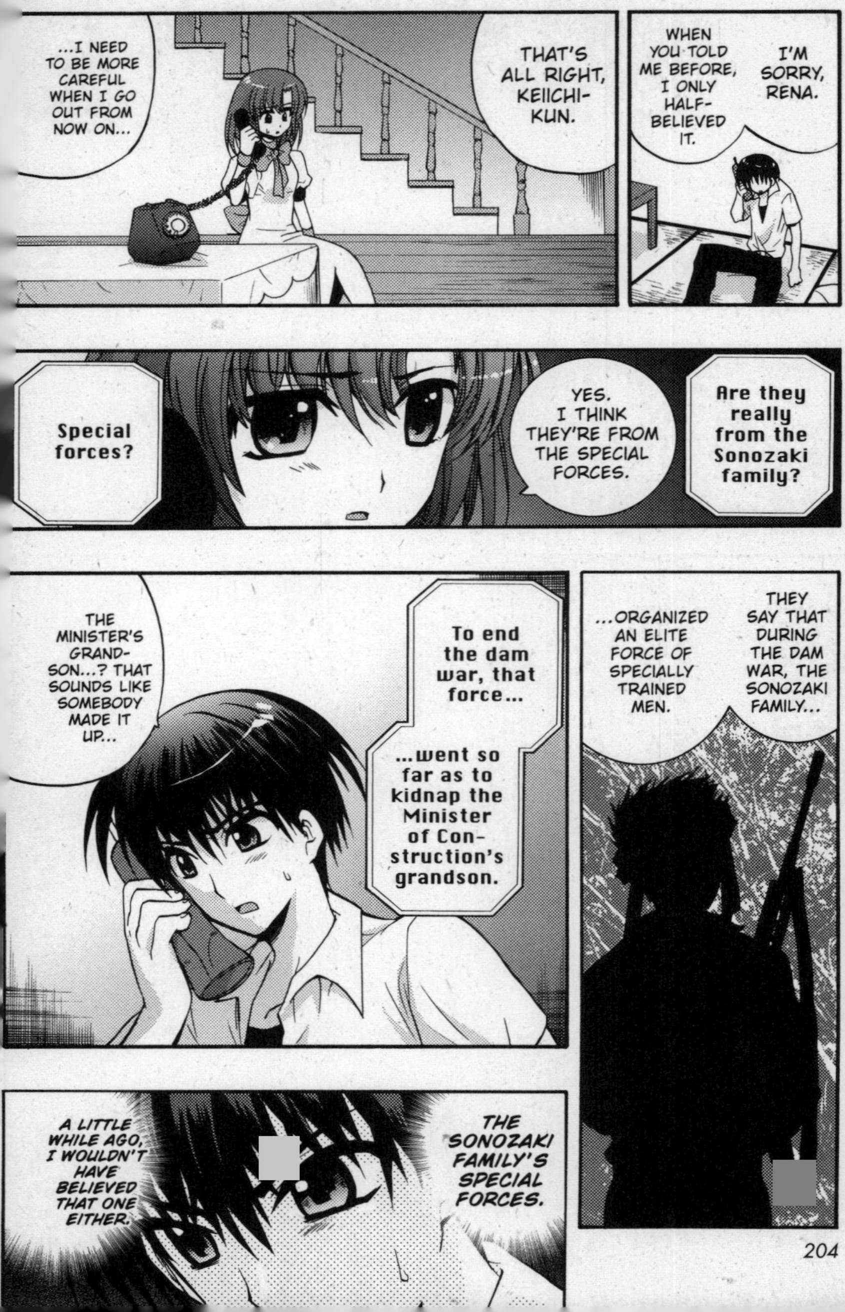
I'M SORRY, RENA.
WHEN YOU TOLD ME BEFORE, I ONLY HALF-BELIEVED IT.
THAT'S ALL RIGHT, KEIICHI-KUN.
...I NEED TO BE MORE CAREFUL WHEN I GO OUT FROM NOW ON...
Are they really from the Sonozaki family?
YES. I THINK THEY'RE FROM THE SPECIAL FORCES.
Special forces?
THEY SAY THAT DURING THE DAM WAR, THE SONOZAKI FAMILY...
...ORGANIZED AN ELITE FORCE OF SPECIALLY TRAINED MEN.
To end the dam war, that force...
...went so far as to kidnap the Minister of Construction's grandson.
THE MINISTER'S GRANDSON...? THAT SOUNDS LIKE SOMEBODY MADE IT UP...
THE SONOZAKI FAMILY'S SPECIAL FORCES.
A LITTLE WHILE AGO, I WOULDN'T HAVE BELIEVED THAT ONE EITHER.

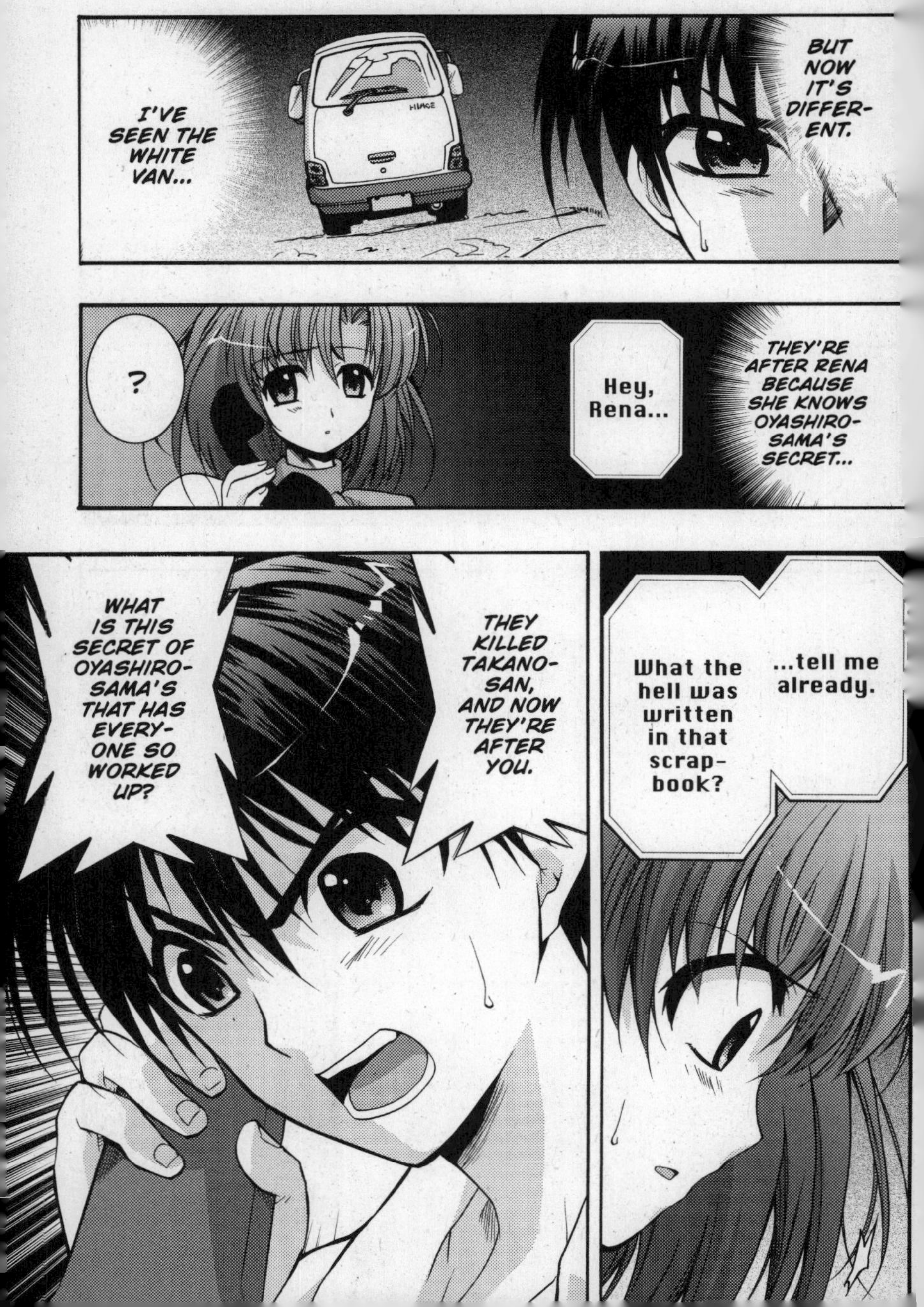
BUT NOW IT'S DIFFERENT.
I'VE SEEN THE WHITE VAN...
THEY'RE AFTER RENA BECAUSE SHE KNOWS OYASHIRO-SAMA'S SECRET...
Hey, Rena...
?
...tell me already.
What the hell was written in that scrapbook?
THEY KILLED TAKANO-SAN, AND NOW THEY'RE AFTER YOU.
WHAT IS THIS SECRET OF OYASHIRO-SAMA'S THAT HAS EVERYONE SO WORKED UP?

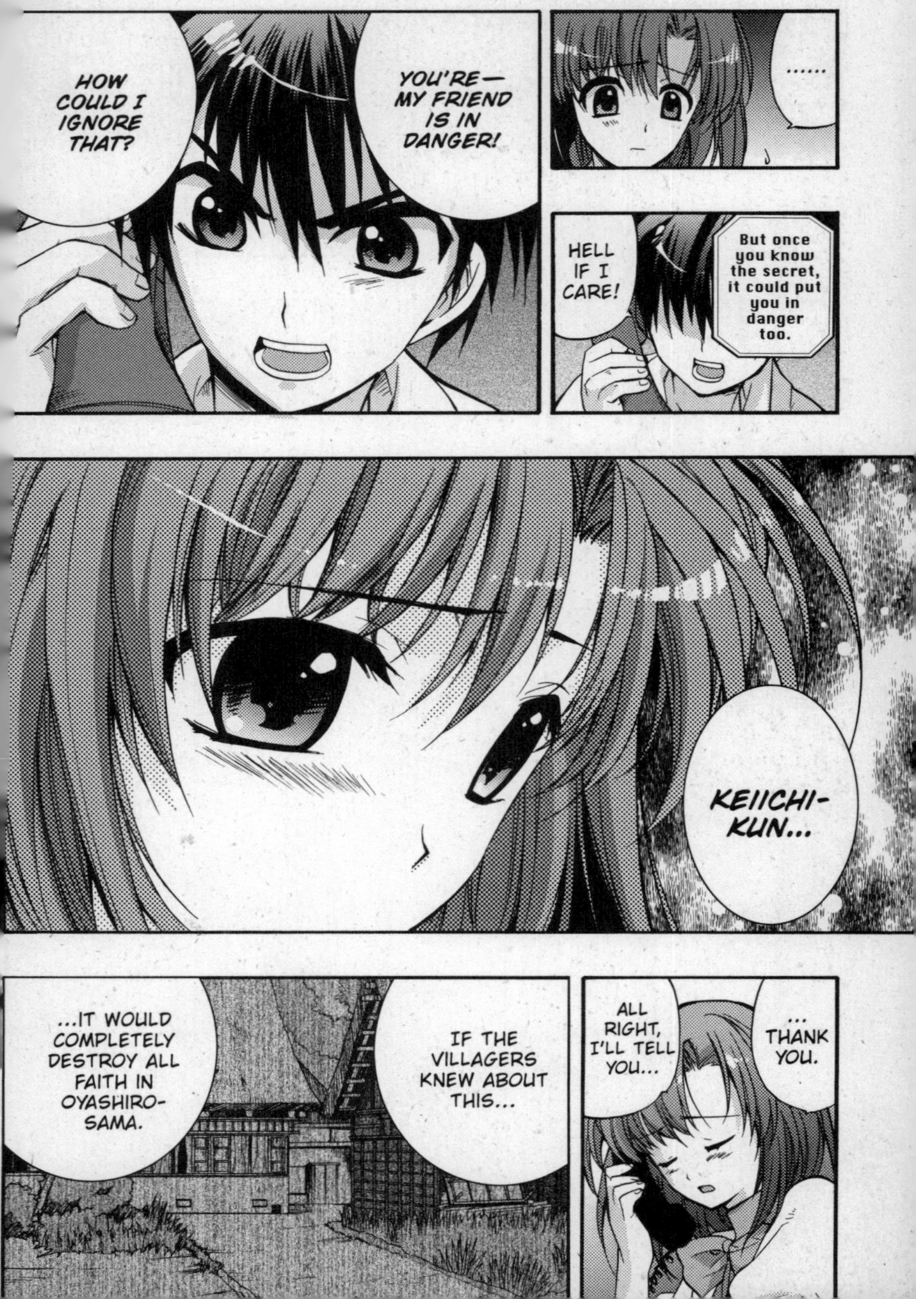
......
But once you know the secret, it could put you in danger too.
HELL IF I CARE!
YOU'RE— MY FRIEND IS IN DANGER!
HOW COULD I IGNORE THAT?
KEIICHI-KUN...
... THANK YOU.
ALL RIGHT, I'LL TELL YOU...
IF THE VILLAGERS KNEW ABOUT THIS...
...IT WOULD COMPLETELY DESTROY ALL FAITH IN OYASHIRO-SAMA.

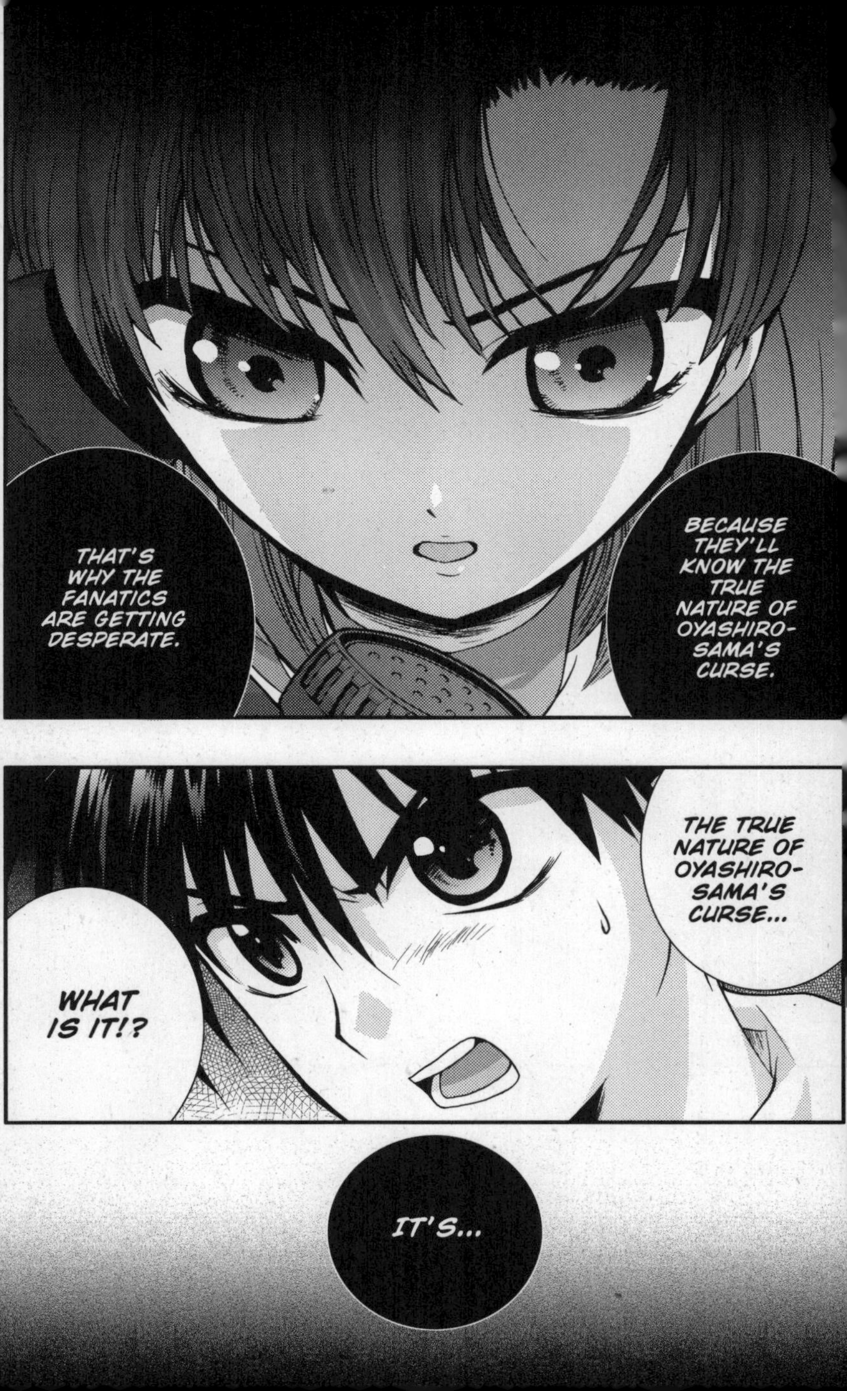
BECAUSE THEY'LL KNOW THE TRUE NATURE OF OYASHIRO-SAMA'S CURSE.
THAT'S WHY THE FANATICS ARE GETTING DESPERATE.
THE TRUE NATURE OF OYASHIRO-SAMA'S CURSE...
WHAT IS IT!?
IT'S...

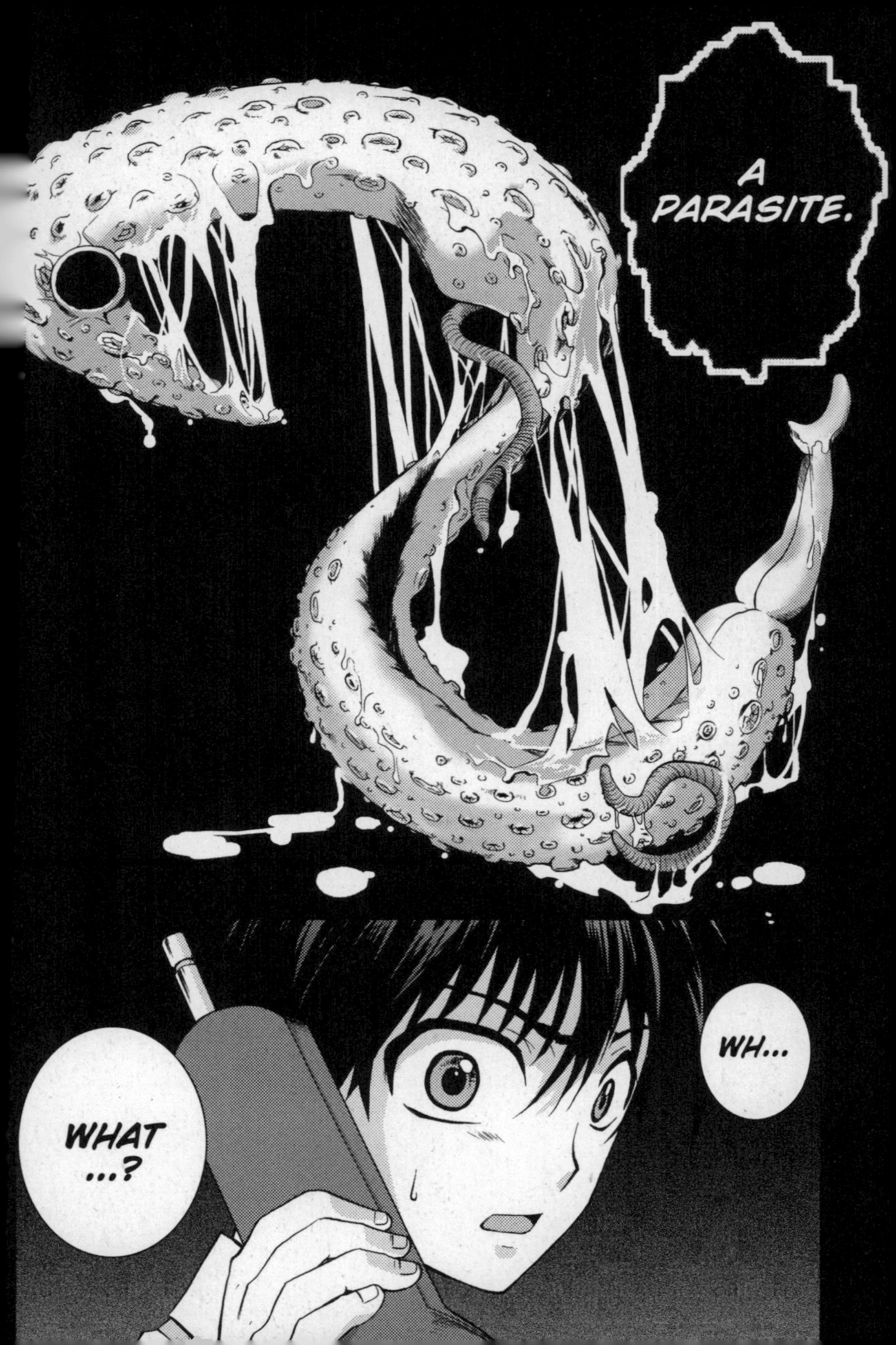
A PARASITE.
WH...
WHAT ...?

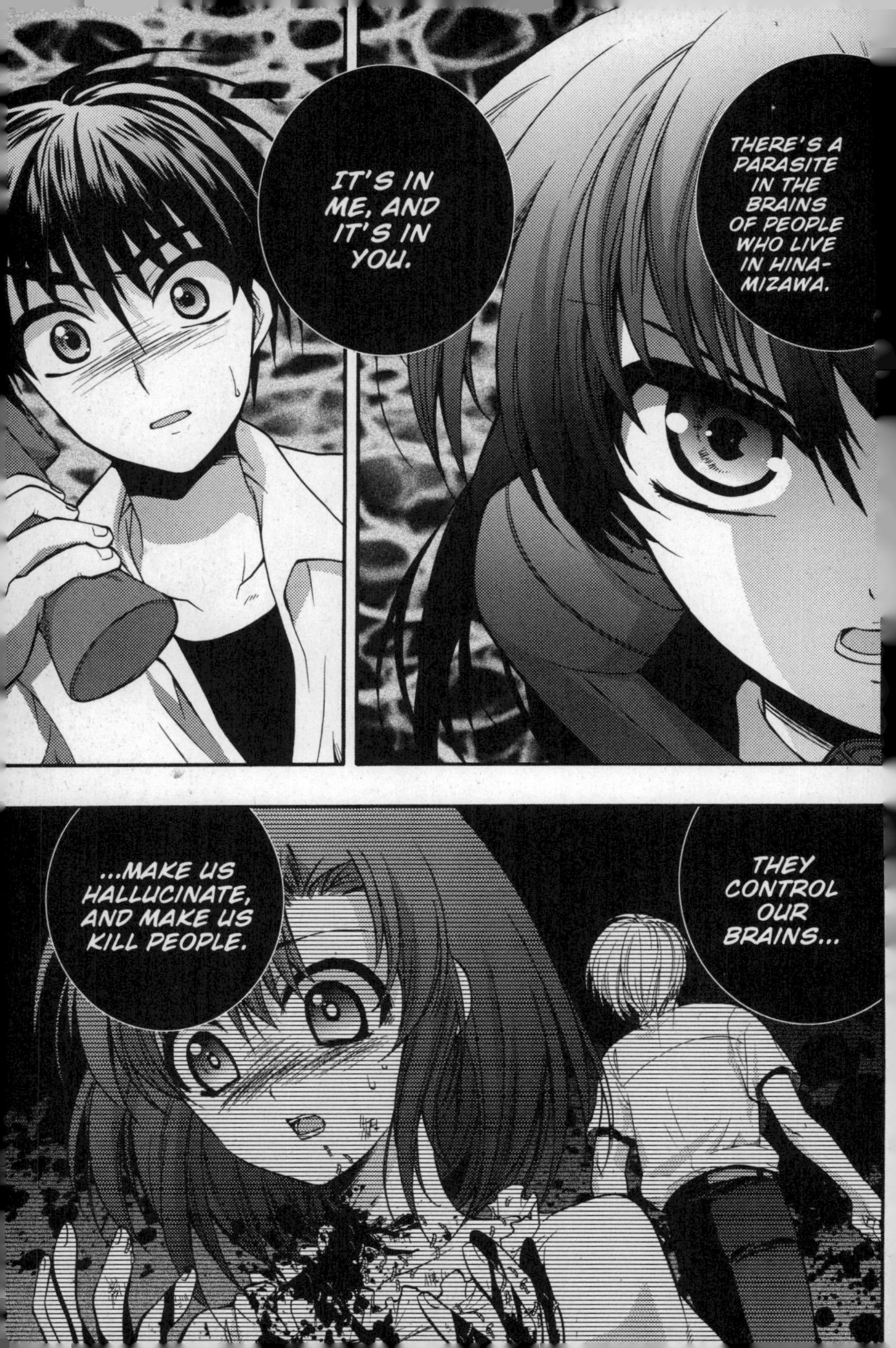
THERE'S A PARASITE IN THE BRAINS OF PEOPLE WHO LIVE IN HINA-MIZAWA.
IT'S IN ME, AND IT'S IN YOU.
THEY CONTROL OUR BRAINS...
...MAKE US HALLUCINATE, AND MAKE US KILL PEOPLE.

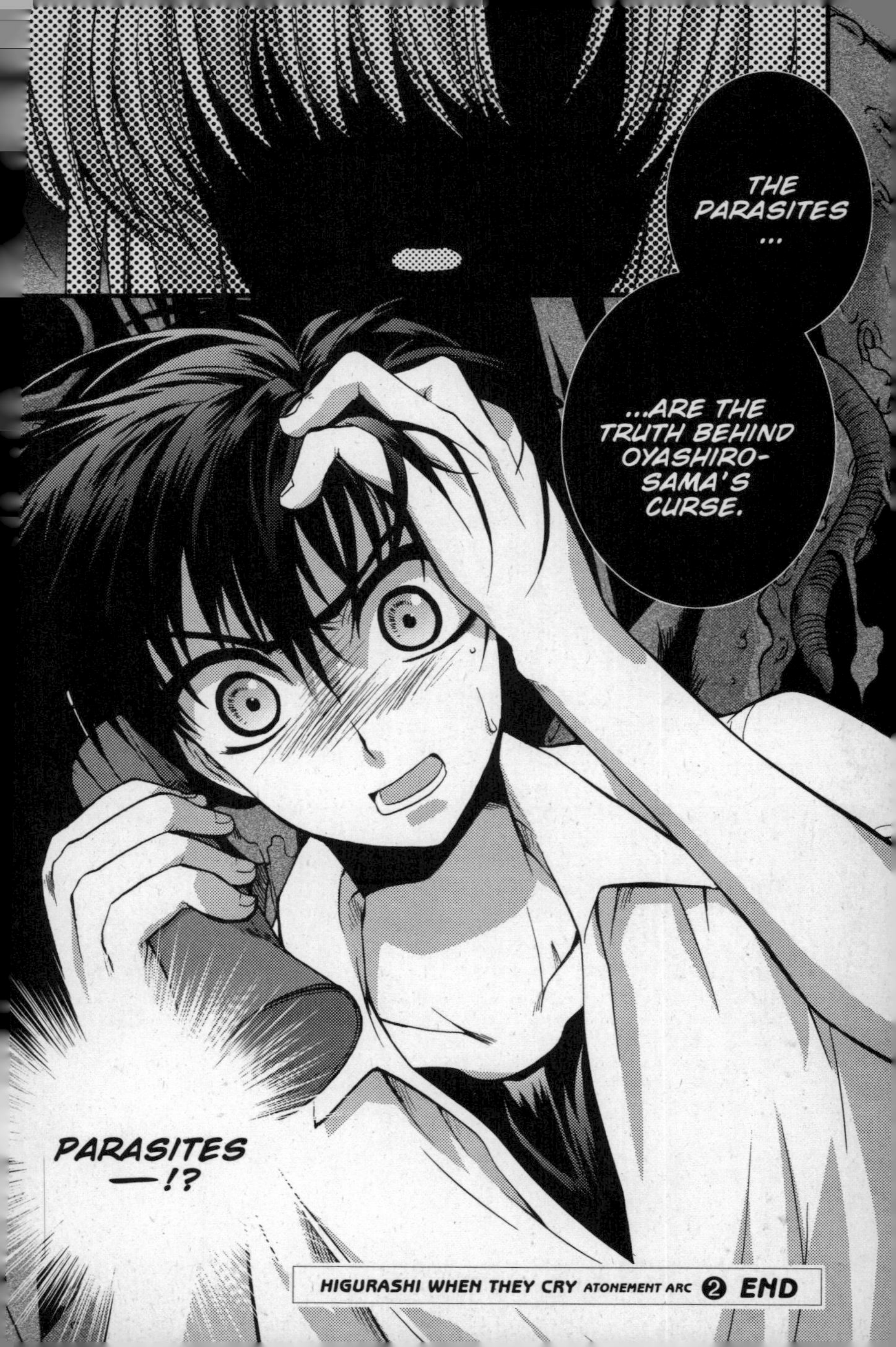
THE PARASITES ...
...ARE THE TRUTH BEHIND OYASHIRO-SAMA'S CURSE.
PARASITES —!?
HIGURASHI WHEN THEY CRY ATONEMENT ARC 2 END

ABOUT THE "ATONEMENT ARC" WHEN IT WAS BEING WRITTEN

ORIGINAL STORY, SUPERVISOR: RYUKISHI07

VOLUME TWO OF THE "ATONEMENT ARC" IS OVER, AND OUR STORY IS FINALLY RUSHING TO ITS CLIMAX.

OF ALL THE ARCS IN *HIGURASHI WHEN THEY CRY*, THE "ATONEMENT ARC" HAS GREAT SIGNIFICANCE AND IS A MAJOR TURNING POINT IN THE SERIES. IN THAT SENSE, THE NEXT VOLUME, VOLUME THREE OF THE "ATONEMENT ARC," MAY BE THE ONE VOLUME OF ALL THE VOLUMES OF *HIGURASHI* THAT YOU REALLY WON'T BE ABLE TO TAKE YOUR EYES AWAY FROM. I HOPE YOU WILL CONTINUE TO HAVE HIGH EXPECTATIONS OF THE "ATONEMENT ARC" AS WOVEN BY SUZURAGI-SENSEI'S PEN!

NOW, WHEN I STARTED WRITING *HIGURASHI* IT WASN'T VERY WELL KNOWN. BUT WITH THE RELEASE OF THE "EYE OPEN-ING ARC," THE ARC RIGHT BEFORE THIS ARC, IT BECAME VERY POPULAR, AND MY PARENTS FOUND OUT ABOUT IT. SO, FOR THE "ATONEMENT ARC," THERE WERE SOME HEARTWARMING AND EMBARRASSING EPISODES DURING WHICH I GOT ADVICE FROM MY PARENTS ABOUT THE STORY'S SETTING AND THE LIKE. FOR MY UNLEARNED SELF, THE EXPERIENCE AND KNOWLEDGE OF MY PARENTS, WHO HAD LIVED MORE THAN TWICE AS LONG AS I HAD, WAS A POWERFUL WEAPON.

...THINKING ABOUT IT, GOING TO OTHER PEOPLE FOR ADVICE INSTEAD OF WORRYING ABOUT THINGS ON YOUR OWN IS ONE OF THE THINGS KEIICHI IMPLORED RENA TO DO IN THE "ATONEMENT ARC." MAYBE I SHOULD HAVE STOPPED BEING EMBARRASSED AND ASKED THEM FOR MORE HELP. I'M GRATEFUL TO MY SCIENTIFIC FATHER, WHO LOOKED IT RIGHT UP WHEN I ASKED "HOW MANY LITERS OF XXXX WOULD YOU NEED TO XXX A CLASSROOM?" (WRY LAUGH)

EVERYONE, IF THERE'S ANYTHING BOTHERING YOU, PLEASE GO TO YOUR FATHER OR MOTHER FIRST.

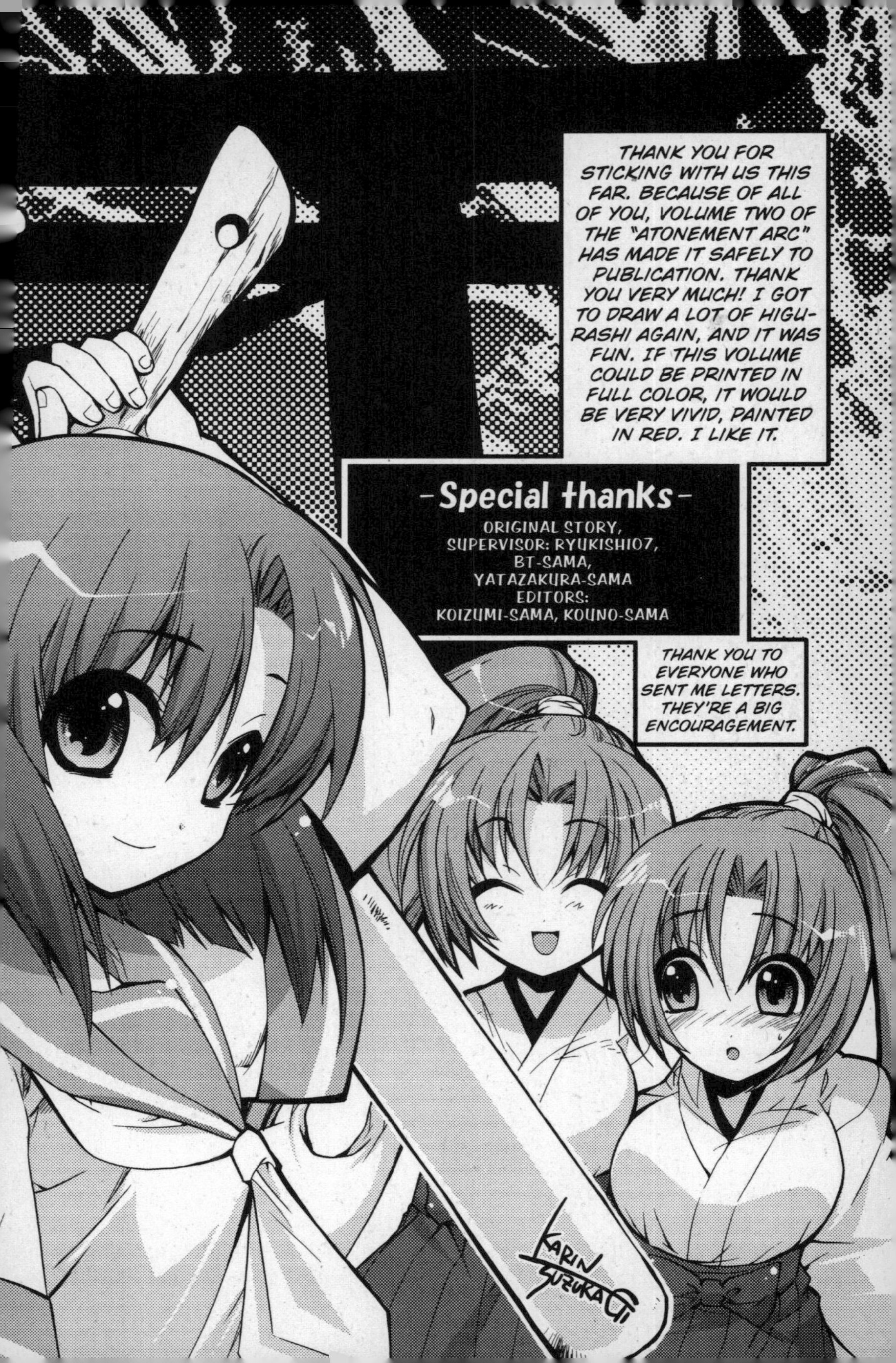

THANK YOU FOR STICKING WITH US THIS FAR. BECAUSE OF ALL OF YOU, VOLUME TWO OF THE "ATONEMENT ARC" HAS MADE IT SAFELY TO PUBLICATION. THANK YOU VERY MUCH! I GOT TO DRAW A LOT OF HIGU-RASHI AGAIN, AND IT WAS FUN. IF THIS VOLUME COULD BE PRINTED IN FULL COLOR, IT WOULD BE VERY VIVID, PAINTED IN RED. I LIKE IT.
-Special thanks-
ORIGINAL STORY, SUPERVISOR: RYUKISHI07, BT-SAMA, YATAZAKURA-SAMA
EDITORS: KOIZUMI-SAMA, KOUNO-SAMA
THANK YOU TO EVERYONE WHO SENT ME LETTERS. THEY'RE A BIG ENCOURAGEMENT.
KARIN SUZUKAGI

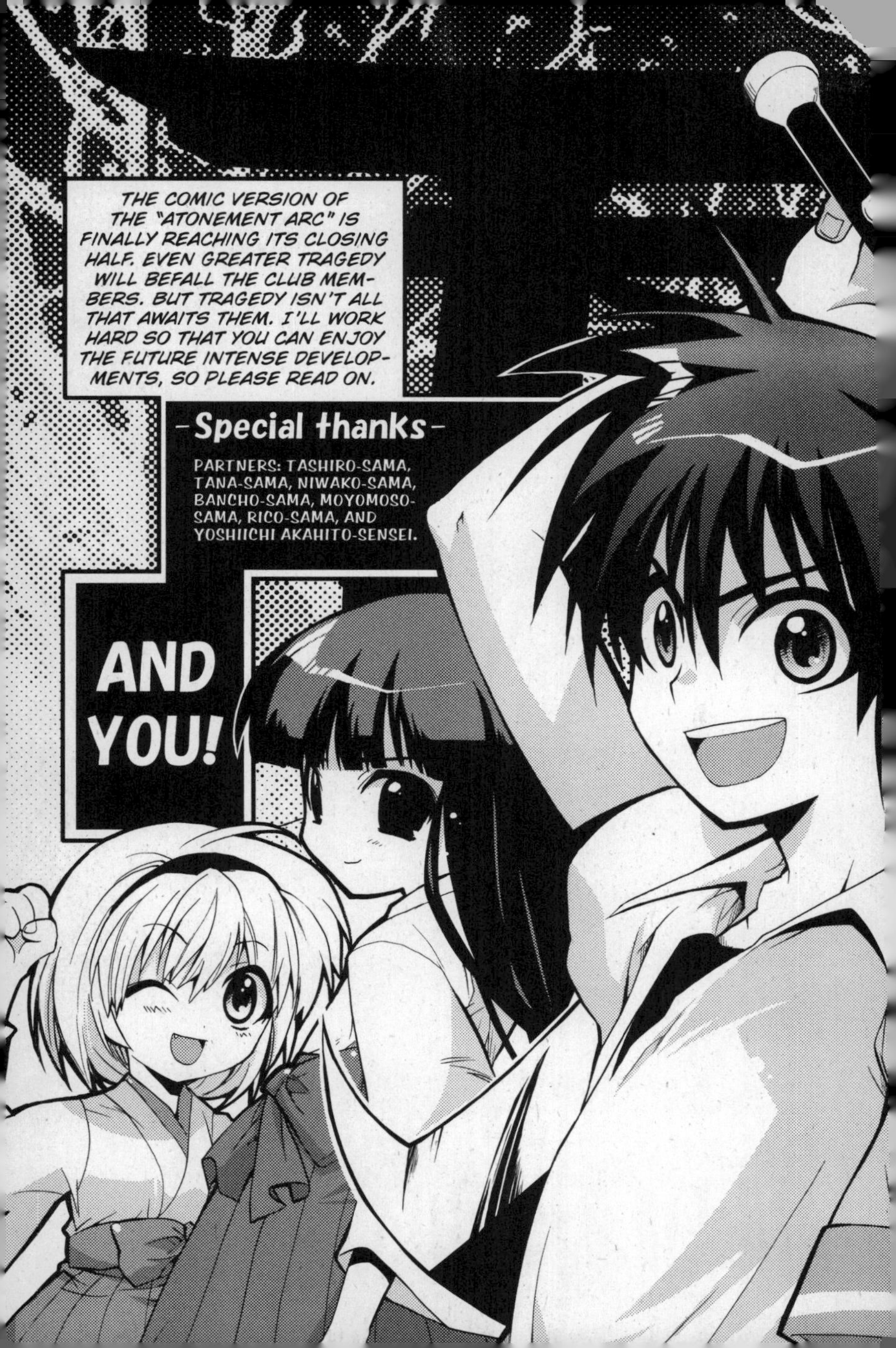
THE COMIC VERSION OF THE "ATONEMENT ARC" IS FINALLY REACHING ITS CLOSING HALF. EVEN GREATER TRAGEDY WILL BEFALL THE CLUB MEMBERS. BUT TRAGEDY ISN'T ALL THAT AWAITS THEM. I'LL WORK HARD SO THAT YOU CAN ENJOY THE FUTURE INTENSE DEVELOPMENTS, SO PLEASE READ ON.
-Special thanks-
PARTNERS: TASHIRO-SAMA, TANA-SAMA, NIWAKO-SAMA, BANCHO-SAMA, MOYOMOSO-SAMA, RICO-SAMA, AND YOSHIICHI AKAHITO-SENSEI.
AND YOU!

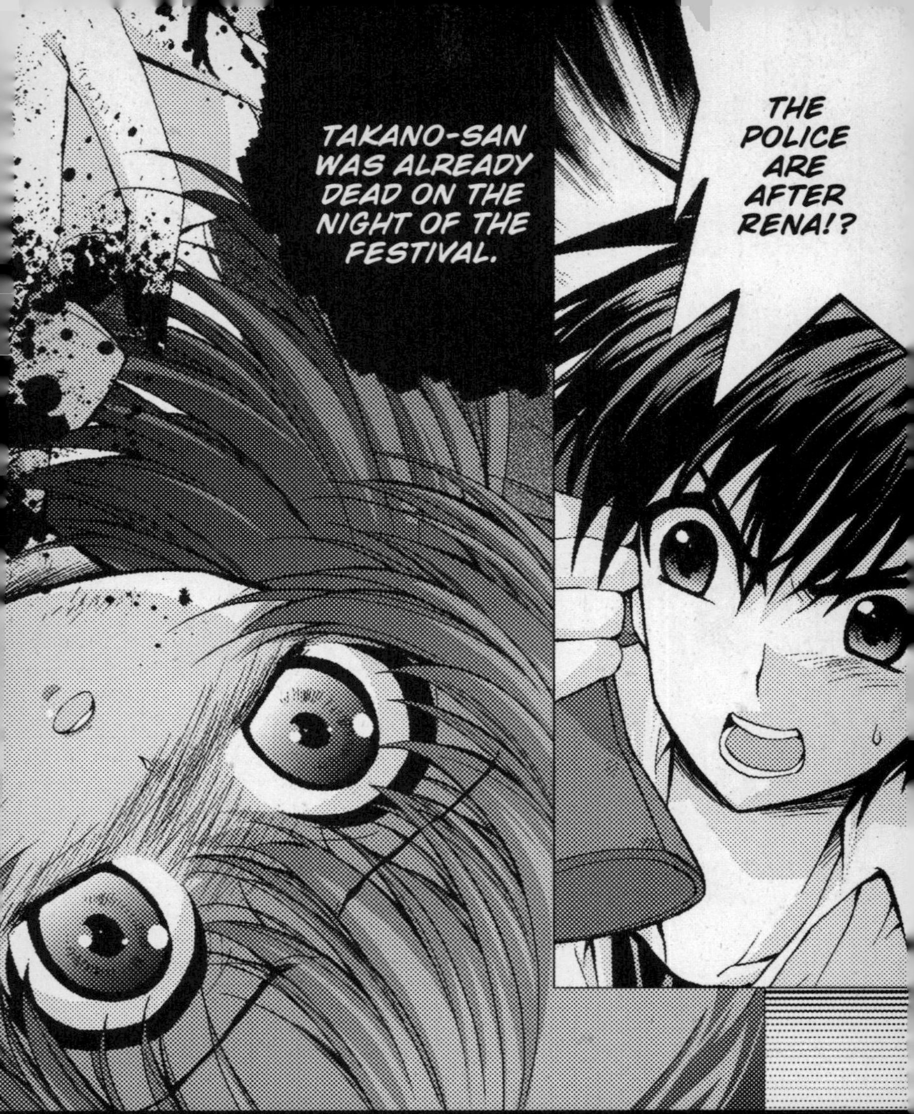
THE POLICE ARE AFTER RENA!?
TAKANO-SAN WAS ALREADY DEAD ON THE NIGHT OF THE FESTIVAL.

ITS GREATEST TURNING POINT.

ON SALE FEBRUARY 2012!!!

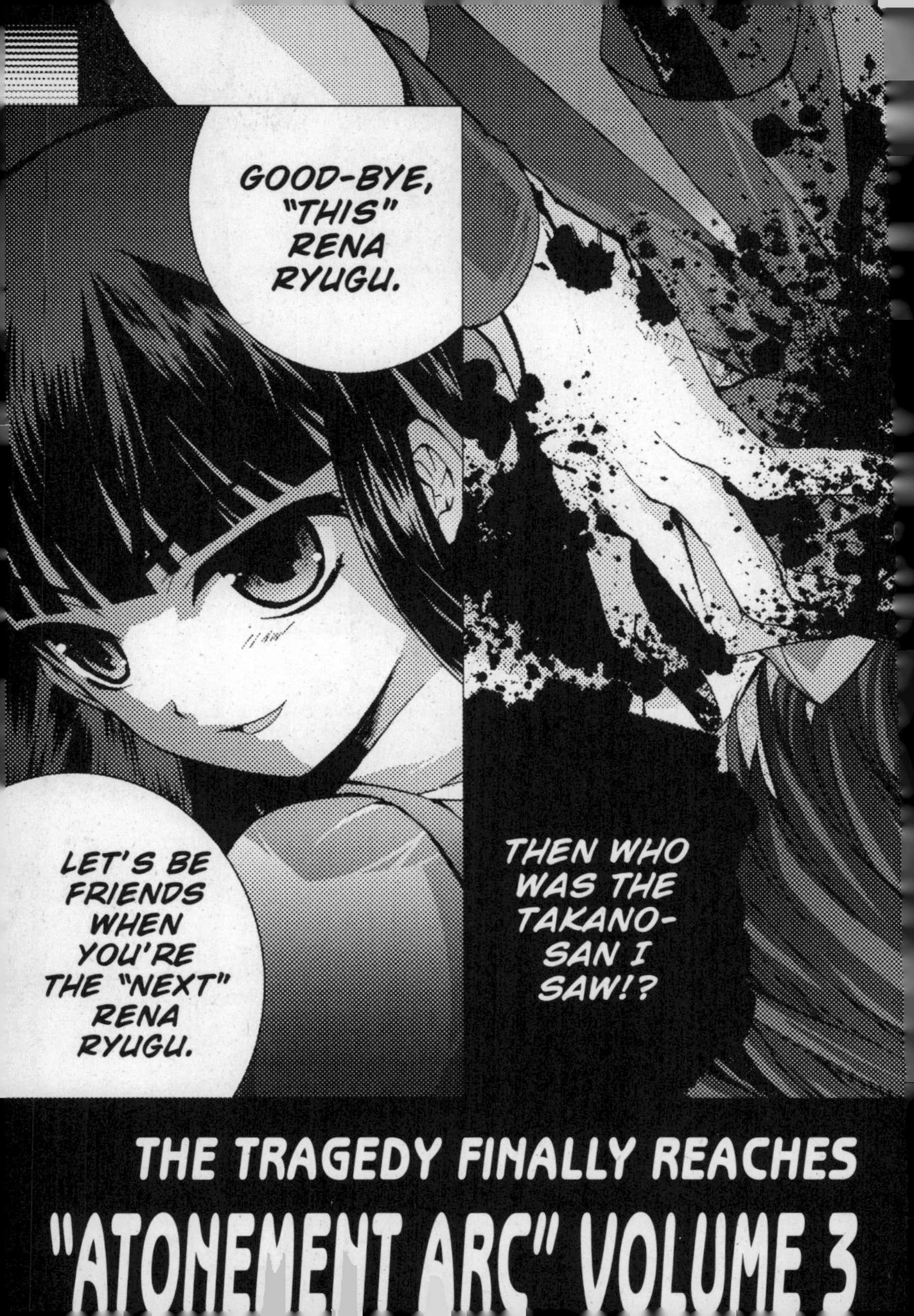
THEN WHO WAS THE TAKANO-SAN I SAW!?
GOOD-BYE, "THIS" RENA RYUGU.
LET'S BE FRIENDS WHEN YOU'RE THE "NEXT" RENA RYUGU.

THE TRAGEDY FINALLY REACHES

"ATONEMENT ARC" VOLUME 3

HIGURASHI
WHEN THEY CRY
ATONEMENT ARC ②

RYUKISHI07
KARIN SUZURAGI

Translation: Alethea Nibley and Athena Nibley

Lettering: AndWorld Design

Higurashi WHEN THEY CRY Atonement Arc, Vol. 2 © RYUKISHI07 / 07th Expansion © 2007 Karin Suzuragi / SQUARE ENIX CO., LTD. All rights reserved. First published in Japan in 2007 by SQUARE ENIX CO., LTD. English translation rights arranged with SQUARE ENIX CO., LTD. and Hachette Book Group through Tuttle-Mori Agency, Inc. Translation © 2011 by SQUARE ENIX CO., LTD.

Yen Press
Hachette Book Group
237 Park Avenue, New York, NY 10017

www.HachetteBookGroup.com
www.YenPress.com

Yen Press is an imprint of Hachette Book Group, Inc. The Yen Press name and logo are trademarks of Hachette Book Group, Inc.

First Yen Press Edition: December 2011

ISBN: 978-0-316-12385-3

10 9 8 7 6 5 4 3 2 1

BVG

Printed in the United States of America